UNDERSTANDING READING PROBLEMS

Assessment and Instruction

FOURTH EDITION

JEAN WALLACE GILLET
Charlottesville (VA) Public Schools

CHARLES TEMPLE
Hobart and William Smith Colleges

WITH

SAMUEL R. MATHEWS II
The University of West Florida

AND

JOSEPHINE PEYTON YOUNG
University of Georgia

HarperCollins*CollegePublishers*

In memory of
EDMUND H. HENDERSON,
1926–1989

Acquisitions Editor: Christopher Jennison
Project Coordination, Text and Cover Design: Proof Positive/Farrowlyne
    Associates, Inc.
Production Manager: Kewal Sharma
Compositor: Proof Positive/Farrowlyne Associates, Inc.
Printer and Binder: R. R. Donnelley & Sons Company
Cover Printer: Phoenix Color Corporation

Understanding Reading Problems: Assessment and Instruction, Fourth Edition
Copyright © 1994 by Jean Wallace Gillet and Charles Temple

Library of Congress Cataloging-in-Publication Data
Gillet, Jean Wallace.
    Understanding reading problems : assessment and instruction / Jean Wallace
Gillet, Charles Temple : with Samuel R. Mathews and Josephine Peyton Young. —
4th ed.
        p.   cm.
    Includes bibliographical references and index.
    ISBN 0-673-52327-6
    1. Reading—Ability testing. 2. Reading—Remedial teaching.
I. Temple, Charles A.   II. Title.
LB1050.46.G55   1994
428.4—dc20
                                                                93-39603
                                                                    CIP

93 94 95 96 9 8 7 6 5 4 3 2 1

Contents

3

Emergent Literacy: Assessment and Instruction   57

Informal Reading Assessment   101

Portfolio Assessment

Corrective Teaching Strategies

161

183

7

Adolescent Students with Reading Problems 247

8

Reading to Learn in the Content Areas 295

9

Formal Measures of Reading Ability 341

10

Assessing Factors Related to Reading Problems   377

Index

Preface

Helping all students to become effective, strategic readers who read and write enthusiastically and purposefully is one of the greatest challenges facing teachers today. Teachers need to know how to use a wide variety of teaching methods, materials, and strategies to help children lean to read; must be able to monitor students' progress in order to prevent literacy problems; and must be able to deal with existing problems using corrective instruction. To do so, they need well-informed diagnostic judgment and the tools and strategies to monitor students' development effectively. Such strategies and tools must be flexible and practical, tapping the kinds of everyday reading and writing that students use in and out of the classroom. Teachers also need a wealth of corrective procedures that allow them to effectively teach children in the context of regular ongoing instruction, without setting problem readers apart from others. Such diagnostic and instructional strategies are the heart of this book.

The field of reading education is undergoing exciting changes. Basal reading programs, management systems for teaching reading skills, and group standardized tests are being challenged on all sides. In their place, teachers are being expected to use continuous developmental-assessment devices; to use portfolios of students' work samples to evaluate students' progress; to teach reading using authentic literature; to integrate reading and writing across all facets of the curriculum; and to help all students, regardless of their level of literacy, to become effective, strategic readers. This book provides the kind of clear, detailed, and realistic help they need.

The concepts and principles that guided the development of the first three editions, and which made this book a leader in its field, have been strengthened and expanded in the fourth edition. In this edition we have

- Updated and expanded our treatment of important trends in research and practice, including emergent literacy, portfolio assessment, whole language and literature-based instruction, and developmentally appropriate assessment and instruction;

• Expanded and elaborated upon our extensive coverage of instruction-al approaches and methods, including new material on emergent literacy, developing sight vocabulary, shared reading, effective teaching of phonics, developing predictive thinking, teaching adolescent poor readers, increasing students' time spent reading, and developing students' content-area reading strategies; and

• Added new emphasis on authentic assessment, with detailed discus-sions of portfolio assessment, an emphasis on promoting "literacy for life," and detailed treatment of adolescent readers' problems and remediation.

Convincing case studies of real readers are used throughout the book to illustrate points and help users develop diagnostic judgment.

This edition examines both traditional and innovative means of assessing reading strengths and needs as well as developmental and corrective instruc-tion. Emphasis is placed on the prevention of reading problems by providing necessary experiences for children to develop and progress as readers, as well as on correction and remediation. Chapter 1 describes the various roles read-ing plays in people's lives and the fundamental principles of diagnosis and instruction, which provide the philosophical bases for working with all stu-dents. Chapters 2 and 3 explain how children become literate; what experi-ences and competencies are necessary for children to learn to read, write, and spell easily and successfully; how early literacy problems my be prevented and treated; and how children's progress toward literacy may be assessed and nurtured.

Chapter 4, which deals with the assessment of reading skills and strate-gies by informal diagnostic means, demonstrates how to use scores, reading behaviors, and observations to determine students' reading strengths, needs, and present levels of performance and potential.

Also included is a discussion of the assessment of text readability.

Chapter 5 details how to assess and monitor students' progress using portfolios and work samples. This chapter is new to this edition.

Chapter 6 explains how to use diagnostic findings to plan corrective instruction and achieve balance in prescriptive teaching. It describes, in detail, methods of group and individual instruction in reading comprehension, lis-tening comprehension, sight word recognition, word analysis and reading fluency. The chapter also includes new material on the use of predictable books and shared reading, the effective teaching of phonics in a balanced word-recognition effort, and specific techniques for developing students' pre-dictive thinking, prior knowledge, and awareness of story structures.

Chapter 7, also new to this edition, deals with the special challenges of assessing and teaching adolescents with reading problems. Using actual case studies as illustrations, the chapter describes the diagnostic procedures and instructional strategies that are useful in dealing with adolescent nonreaders, remedial readers, and reluctant, or disenchanted, readers. Emphasis is placed on the importance of increasing the amount of time older poor readers spend reading and on maximizing the effectiveness of the reading strategies they may already have. Chapter 8 continues the corrective teaching strand with discussions of effective strategies for dealing with nonfiction and subject-area texts. Comprehension strategies, patterns of text organization, and building vocabulary are stressed.

Chapter 9 describes formal assessment measures, including tests and measurement concepts and vocabulary necessary to any informed test-user, and types and uses of norm-referenced and criterion-referenced tests. Chapter 10 includes much new or updated material on intellectual, physical, and affective factors related to reading including intelligence and its assessment, vision and hearing problems and assessment, self-concept, and reading attitudes. Special attention is paid to the topics of learning disabilities and dyslexia, and to the growing need for regular education teachers to be informed about and involved in the identification and everyday instruction of students with special learning needs.

Features of the text include case studies and narrative descriptions of the problems and successes of many pupils with whom we have worked, chapter summaries, and illustrations. The accompanying Instructor's Resource Book contains a wide variety of demonstrations and activities designed to involve students and help them gain experience and diagnostic judgment, as well as discussion questions, suggestions for projects, and test items.

As in the previous three editions, we are indebted to a growing list of people for their involvement, advice, encouragement, and support. We are grateful to our colleagues Josephine Young and Sam Mathews for their outstanding contributions to this edition, and for their expertise and their friendship. We owe more than our thanks to our families for their support, patience, and pride in our endeavors. We owe a debt to our fourth-edition reviewers for their careful reading and insightful criticism of our manuscript:

Michael McKenna, Wichita State University
William A. Henk, Pennsylvania State University at Harrisburg
Sheila Cohen, State University of New York at Cortland
M. Jean Dreher, University of Maryland

We continue to be grateful to our third-edition reviewers: Bill Henk, Pennsylvania State University; Michael McKenna, Wichita State University; and Eva Jane Noe, Northeast Missouri State University; our second-edition reviewers: Camille Blachowitz, National Louis University; Bill Teale, University of Texas at San Antonio; Page Bristow, University of Delaware; Larry Miller, Queen's College, Kingston, Ontario, Canada; Donald O'Brien, State University College at Buffalo; and our first-edition reviewers: Leo Geoffrion, State University of New York at Albany; Zelda Maggart,

University of New Mexico; Janell Klesius, University of South Florida; and David W. Moore, University of Connecticut.

We also extend our thanks to our editor, Chris Jennison, and his staff at HarperCollins, and to the production staffs at HarperCollins and Proof Positive/Farrowlyne Associates, Inc. Finally, we are grateful to our students and colleagues at Hobart and William Smith Colleges and the University of North Florida, and our students and colleagues in the public schools of Charlottesville, Virginia, and Pensacola, Florida. Many, many people helped make this book what it is; we acknowledge their influences with gratitude and offer our work to you with pride.

Jean Wallace Gillet
Charles Temple

An Introduction to Reading Assessment and Corrective Instruction

Chapter Outline

T o 60 million Americans, reading is a chore, an embarrassment, even the reason they cannot get or keep a fulfilling job. The term used to describe these people is *functionally illiterate*. It's a deceptive term, because the condition it describes is constantly changing. A factory closes, and workers whose modest reading and writing skills were never at issue suddenly find that their next jobs will require the consumption and production of written information. Overnight they find themselves functionally illiterate.

Such plants are closing all over America. Our economy, it would seem, is changing faster than our school systems. We may be doing a better job teaching people to read than teachers did a generation ago, but according to Jonathan Kozol (1985), in 60 million cases the job falls painfully short of what is needed.

Teaching reading is still the most important task of the schools. Finding and helping the students who are at risk of failing to learn to read used to be the single most important part of that task. Now it shares top billing with an equally urgent priority: to cultivate in students a love of books so that students will want to read, so that they will read.

These two priorities reflect two themes that run throughout this book. The first theme is that while children can experience many kinds of difficulty in learning to read, there is a handful of causes of reading failure that turn up over and over again. We need to be able to identify children having these difficulties and help them. The second theme is that *not reading* also causes reading failure, and worse—it also leads to difficulties that spread across the curriculum and throughout the personality. These two themes suggest a third: that it is necessary for teachers to understand how children learn to read in order to help them through their problems.

When we seriously consider how children learn to read, the issues are not as obvious as we might have thought. There is a core of mystery to the process that has resisted a clear explanation in spite of the hundreds of books and thousands of investigations reading has inspired over the years—far more work than any other topic in education. This in not to discourage future teachers and reading specialists: In the past decade there have been dramatic breakthroughs in our understanding of the way children learn to read, and we are in a position to help children far more effectively now than we have ever been before.

THE MANY SIDES OF READING

Why has the process of learning to read been so hard to understand? Probably because the act of reading calls upon so many important abilities and affects people's lives in so many important ways. That is a cliché, but it has a consequence. Much of our knowledge of the world comes to us through academic research, and academic research is compartmentalized into the disciplines of linguistics, psychology, literary studies, sociology, and others (not to mention the many subfields of each of these, subfields that often function as if they were separate disciplines). A topic as complex as reading will require us to use the insights and techniques of many different disciplines. Relying on many perspectives gains us plenty of information, but it has a price, summed up nicely by the parable of the five blind citizens examining the elephant: They had such different individual experiences of the beast they didn't realize they were all studying an elephant! Our task, as we consider the insights provided by many different specialties, will be to pull these insights together to further our understanding of reading and reading problems. Here are some examples of the insights we are talking about.

Reading Is a Language Ability

Reading is first of all a language ability. The raw material of reading—sounds, words, sentences, and communicative intentions—is much the same as that of language in general. Thus over the years we have seen "linguistic readers," and heard reading described as a "psycholinguistic guessing game." The processes of learning to talk and learning to read do have many parallels. People who currently use the term *whole language* acknowledge that reading is a language ability and should be taught in close and meaningful connection with the whole spectrum of language abilities, including talking, listening, writing, and thinking.

Reading Poses Special Cognitive Challenges

Nearly everyone learns to talk, but far fewer people, even given the opportunity, learn to read. There is more to reading than using language. To illustrate, let us think of language as a symbolizing system that is a step removed from the concrete things in the world it names—the word *ball* is not really a ball; it just names the class of things we call "ball." To write the word *ball* is to remove ourselves a further step to a written form of the spoken word that names the class of things made up of the separate items we call by the name "ball." Thus it has been noted that reading, as a symbolization of a symbolization, bears the same relation to speech that algebra bears to numbers.

Reading Is a Set of Perceptual Abilities

Compared to spoken language, reading makes greater, or at least different demands on a person's perceptual abilities. Where is the difficulty? The obvious challenge posed by reading, but not by speech, is to recognize the visual symbols. This is where special educators have traditionally staked their claims. But there is another, more subtle difficulty. To read an alphabetic writing system such as the English one—but not an ideographic one such as that of Chinese—requires that you be able mentally to divide the words you speak into their individual sound parts, or *phonemes* (*cat*, for instance has three phonemes: /k/ /æ/ /t/). That is so you will have sound units available in your mind to match with the written units on the page. And this, as we shall see in the next chapter, turns out to be a far more serious source of difficulty than visual perception.

Reading Is a Literary Act

Readers read texts, and texts have particular structures, quite different from talk, that make special demands on readers' understanding. Ask an English teacher, and you'll be told, like as not, that the whole challenge and whole point of reading is to come to know these structures and the great works of literature that employ them, because only by being familiar with many written texts can a reader pick up a new text and read it with real comprehension, not to mention appreciation.

Reading Ability Is a Measure of One's General Knowledge

Texts tell about the world. A general rule about learning is that you relate the unknown to the known; that is, you have to know a little something about a topic in order to understand something new that you are reading about it. At the same time, from the middle elementary grades on, we pick up a great deal of knowledge of the world through reading. So here's a Catch–22: More knowledgeable people read with greater understanding, and hence, probably read with more satisfaction, and thus read more often. People who read more often become more knowledgeable, so they read with more satisfaction, and hence read more often. . . . Sadly, the cycle also appears to work in reverse.

Reading Is an Automatized Perceptual-Motor Act

We occasionally come across reports of severely retarded people who are able to pick up a difficult text and rapidly pronounce the words aloud, although without intelligent inflection. They can't be thinking their way through the text. They must have learned some more or less mechanical set of processes that enables them to render the words aloud.

Reading is sometimes compared to playing tennis, or even walking. On some level, you do it automatically, without thinking about it, so that your thoughts are free to consider your overall strategy: where your opponent's weak points are, where you are going, or what you mean to find out from this text. In other words, on one level, reading is a skill, and like any skill reading improves with practice—lots of practice.

Reading Has a Social Dimension

People learn to read from each other. Whether you consider society in units of families or social classes, in some social groups children will receive a great deal of encouragement to learn to read, and they will so regularly see people they admire reading and writing that they will naturally aspire to do these things themselves. Or to be more precise, as Shirley Brice Heath (1983) has taught us, reading, writing, and even language itself have values and uses that differ among social groups. It may not simply be the case that different social groups have more or less language or more or less literacy, but that the uses of language and literacy within some groups fit much better what is expected in school.

Reading Is a Political Issue

As a reading teacher once said to us, we don't read sawdust: All reading materials are about something. They are usually about people and their problems, hopes, and values; but *what* people? Whose stories (and whose culture) will we tell? Whites? African Americans? Hispanics? Asian Americans? Native Americans? Women? Men? The aged? Atheists? Christians? Jews? Hindus?

What should our reading materials say about what is worthwhile and heroic, about what is to be condemned or even ignored? What account will these materials give of how society was built—will they focus on the exploits of famous leaders, or will they tell of the solidarity and sacrifice of common people?

In a nation made up of many peoples, such as the United States or Canada, the content of books—whether they are basal textbooks or individual trade books—is often a political issue.

Reading Is a Matter of Personality Formation, of Self-Worth

Learning to read is perhaps the single most important academic achievement children ever attain. Success or failure in reading can be integral to a young person's sense of personal competence and can lend or withhold confidence to any number of tasks unrelated to reading that a student will undertake. A person who doesn't read well may consider him- or herself a "dummy," even if he or she is perfectly intelligent and competent in every other respect. It is rare to meet an older troubled reader whose reading difficulties are not thickly intertwined with self-doubts.

Reading Is a Pressing Economic Issue

We often hear of *functional literacy*, the ability to use reading and writing adequately to the degree of sophistication required by one's circumstances— usually vocational circumstances. We also know that the average level of literacy required to function successfully in the American workplace is rising rapidly. Such things are hard to quantify, but it is said that the average level of functional literacy required in current American life has surpassed the twelfth-grade level. According to Jonathan Kozol's (1985) estimates, however, as many as one-fourth of American adults are functionally illiterate at the eighth-grade level. In this age of information processing, their deficiencies in reading translate into a problem of economic competitiveness for society.

Reading Is a Passionate Avocation

Ask any librarian. Not all of the people in most towns own library cards, and a small number of those who do account for the lion's share of any library's circulation. It seems that many people who *can* read rarely read for pleasure. For others, however, reading is a way of life, a lifetime habit, a passionate avocation. These readers claim that they don't simply escape while reading; they transform themselves. The project themselves into texts, and they have new versions of themselves reflected back by the texts.

Reading Is a Critical Instructional Concern

As the most important subject in the elementary school curriculum, reading instruction has inspired a huge outpouring of methods and materials. Reading lessons are given the largest block of time and generate the most testing and remedial instruction.

Reading Is an Outcome of Self-Directed Discovery Learning

In an important sense, learning to read is not the sum total of all the instruction a child receives. Children learn to read through their own discovery processes, too. It can be demonstrated that children must know more about reading than they are ever taught directly.

Reading Is Strategic

People learn to read, and continue to read, by executing a set of complex strategies. As teachers, we should encourage the students' initiative and purposefulness as early and as often as possible.

Each of the preceding statements says something true and important about reading. Indeed, for each one, these is a cluster of experts who argue that it identifies *the most important* truth about reading. No wonder there has been so much disagreement about the way children learn to read and what causes reading problems.

Any comprehensive understanding of reading will take all or most of these aspects into account and will consider also the individual learners, their strengths, strategies and goals, and the contexts in which we find them.

How do we come to know learners and the dynamics of their reading? This is the topic of the next section.

INSIGHTS ABOUT DIAGNOSIS AND REMEDIATION

Diagnosis is derived from the Greek stems *dia-*, meaning "across or between," and *gnosis*, meaning "to know." *Diagnosis* means to "know across" learners, knowing how they are similar and different, and how what they do is like (or unlike) what mature or fluent readers do (Johnston & Allington, 1991). *Remediation* comes from the Latin *medere*, "to heal." Something that heals or cures is a remedy; remediation is the act or process of remedying.

Our philosophies and methods of diagnosing and remediating reading and learning problems have been derived from medicine and psychology. So, we often view diagnosis as a process of identifying a learner's deficits, and remediation as a process of applying instructional remedies. Most often, the focus is on identifying deficits in the learner rather than in the classroom, school, home, or community. Being "remedial" has become a characteristic of a learner rather than of instruction. Somehow it has become the reader, rather than the instructional model, that is considered remedial; and practice has shown us that once we begin to label children rather than their instruction, the labels tend to stick and become permanent. Labels promote stereotypical thinking; they dehumanize by encouraging us to think of all children wearing a particular label as essentially the same. Yet there is no typical "remedial reader," or reader in need of remedial instruction.

Principles of Diagnostic Assessment

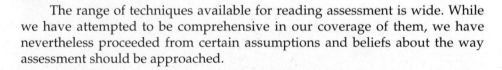

The range of techniques available for reading assessment is wide. While we have attempted to be comprehensive in our coverage of them, we have nevertheless proceeded from certain assumptions and beliefs about the way assessment should be approached.

1. *Diagnosis is more than testing.* Testing is a contrived activity. Children respond differently in testing from the way they respond in their everyday work. Tests give us arbitrary standards by which we measure children's performance. Placing a child in an artificial situation and applying arbitrary standards to the performance give us a restricted view of what a child can do. Diagnosis is a process of becoming informed about what a child does; it requires gathering many types of information about the child's reading, synthesizing this information, and creating informed hypotheses. These hypotheses remain tentative until they are tested by actually teaching the child.

2. *There is no formula for diagnosis.* No single set of procedures, tests, or formulae are sufficient to diagnose all students. Children do not all learn in the same ways; they do not all read for the same purposes or under the same conditions; they do not all use the same strategies as they read; and all teachers do not use the same instructional methods or hold the same beliefs. Not surprisingly, diagnosticians who use the same instruments or procedures each time tend to make the same judgments about students each time. In Johnston and Allington's words, "How and what one knows . . . is bounded by the lens one uses to examine the child." (1991, p. 985) Using the same "lens" each time makes diagnosis a fairly simple process: Ask these predetermined questions, get these answers, and form these judgments. After a while, it can almost be done by rote.

This conclusion does not mean there are no procedures we can depend on to give us reliable information; if that were so, diagnosis books would not be written. It does mean that diagnosis must be flexible, and practitioners must be ready to use a variety of means to become informed about a child. In this book we have attempted to provide you with these means.

3. *Diagnosis means looking for strengths as well as needs.* Using the medical point of view, diagnosis may be seen as identifying all the student's deficits, and remediation as the job of repairing them—a negative and discouraging process. The student is given numerous tasks he or she cannot do successfully, and comes to fear further testing. The examiner may become overwhelmed by the growing list of things the student cannot do, and the teacher may feel woefully unprepared to deal with them. Diagnosis must be a process of discovering what the student can do as well as what cannot yet be done successfully or fluently. By learning what a child's strengths are, we can build instruction on success rather than on failure. When students are successful, they are more apt to approach other assessment tasks positively. Teachers are better able to develop a more balanced and realistic view of learners. Each student is a person with abilities as well as weaknesses.

4. *Diagnosis is the basis for instructional change.* When we discover what students do well and less well, we are in a position to provide instruction that will foster progress in learning. Diagnosis which results in labeling or categorizing students, rather than in instructional change, is merely an academic exercise that wastes time and resources. Nor does diagnosis result in final answers. It must be a continuous process of asking: Where is this student now in his or her development, and where should we go at this time? There are no final answers to these questions, for today's students will be different tomorrow. Diagnosis is never once-and-for-all. In the words of Calfee and Hiebert (1991, p. 292), "When the connection between assessment and instruction is close, then initial observations lead to intervention, followed by the next round of observation. In this situation, the purpose of assessment is not only to determine student performance, but equally to guide the teacher's instructional decisions."

5. *Students should participate as conscious partners in diagnosis and as deliberate agents of their own change.* Because the terms *diagnosis* and *remediation* came to us through medicine, they carry with them the unfortunate image of a busy professional dressed in white, working some cure—usually by means of surgery or drugs—on an inert patient whom he or she rarely bothers to talk to. Nowadays, however, this stereotypical doctor/patient stance is criticized in medical circles because it dehumanizes people—and separates them from participation in their own health. If this stance is not even good medicine, it certainly has no place in education!

Reading, and learning to read, require that readers use a complex set of strategies, many of them consciously and purposefully. It follows that assessment, or diagnosis, should involve readers as conscious and active partners. We want learners to know what they are doing—and what they need to work on, and why and how they need to work on it. Students need to understand and purposefully carry out the instructional activities that grow out of this assessment. Students must take responsibility for their own learning. Assessment and instruction should result in their understanding how to help themselves.

6. *We need both qualitative and quantitative information.* Standardized tests are given under controlled circumstances and yield numerical results that allow comparison of one person or group to another. They are widely used to assess group achievement, but have little diagnostic usefulness. Students' reading tastes, interests, and purposes have little to do with testing, but much to do with the success of instruction. In contrast, informal procedures more closely resemble real reading in and out of school. Informal procedures are basically exploratory, rather than comparative, in nature, since they allow an examiner to determine what a reader does more or less well during reading of a variety of types of materials for different purposes. Thus they yield information which is qualitative rather than, or in addition to, quantitative. Informal measures may be used by both classroom teachers and specialists, and may be used during ongoing instruction rather than requiring a separate setting. After all, it is the classroom teacher, rather than the outside specialist, who has the fullest and clearest perception of the student, as well as the responsibility for the student's instruction. Diagnosis and remediation are closely linked, and both require the active involvement of the classroom teacher.

Principles of Corrective Instruction

1. *Reading is its own best practice.* We should not only be building reading skills, but helping children become active, enthusiastic readers. This outcome occurs only when children read books for pleasure as well as for information. The traditional "skill and drill" orientation to remediation is being replaced by a more literature-based model where children learn to read by reading rather than by mastering skills. If we build up weak skills, but children still do not choose to read, then our corrective instruction has been for naught. "Remediated" readers who do not develop the habit of reading are likely to fall back into difficulty, like patients who are restored to health by surgery or treatment but then refuse to get out of bed. By finding and offering real books that children can and will read, and by making the process of reading whole books inviting and engaging, we help children become real readers.

2. *The best instruction involves children in their own learning.* We need to periodically ask ourselves: Why do *we* read and write? We read for pleasure, for escape, and to learn more about things and people. We write to communicate to others and to ourselves, to send and receive messages. We do not read to pass tests, to get candies, and to earn stars on a chart. We do not write to complete worksheets, to get grades, or to pass tests (except in graduate school, of course!). When children are reading what they want to read, and writing what they want to write about, they exert greater effort, sustain their attention longer, and challenge themselves in ways we would be hard pressed to require.

3. *Corrective instruction must involve all teachers who work with a child.* It does no good to encourage faltering writers to invent spellings for the words they want to use if in their classrooms they are required to look up and spell correctly all words in their compositions. It does no good to encourage children to read whole books in the classroom if in the reading lab they complete reams of duplicated worksheets. It does no good to recommend to a teacher that he or she use this method or that strategy if the teacher doesn't know how to use them. Where more than one teacher works with a child, remediation must be a group effort.

Collaboration helps everyone. Recently one of our remedial students, a fourth-grader who was seen daily on an individual basis, received additional help from a university-supervised tutor during school hours. At the end of the year, the tutor wrote a report about what the student could do and made recommendations about effective methods that should be used with the student. What the tutor did not know was that these same methods had been in nearly daily use all year with the student, along with some modifications of which the tutor was not aware. The tutor did not know this because he had never conferred with either the classroom teacher or the Chapter One teacher about what was already being done. In this case, the tutor spent a lot of time and effort reinventing the wheel!

4. *Diagnosis is continuous.* The initial assessments provide us only with a tentative direction in which to go. The proof of the pudding, so they say, is in the eating; the proof of our diagnostic hypotheses is in the teaching that follows. We may conclude from our original assessment that a student is weak in mastery of letter-sound correspondences, but find out that in spontaneous writing the student creates logical and readable invented spellings by isolating and matching speech sounds with letters. We may initially determine that a student is weak in the literal comprehension of test passages, but subsequently find out that when reading self-selected material the student's recall and understanding are accurate and detailed. What at first looked like a major weakness may yield to only a few sessions of instruction, while what looked like a strength may not hold up in everyday reading. In our day-to-day teaching we must constantly test and revise our initial judgments, modify our strategies, and re-create our estimates. Such ongoing decision-making and documentation are discussed in Chapter 5 on portfolio assessment, which follows later in this text.

SUMMARY

Teaching students to read is a central task of the schools. The task is getting harder, because the level of literacy demanded by the nation is going up and up. Reading is thus an economic issue and a social one. In the school setting, reading is an educational industry, a subject of instruction, an ability children partially develop for themselves, the cause of feelings of success or failure, a source of pleasure or embarrassment. Reading involves language and perception; reading is thoughtful, but reading is also an automatized skill. No wonder there is disagreement over reading policy and practice, in spite of so much that has been written about it.

Our task in this book will be to understand how people learn to read as well as how they often fail to learn. Our task is also to develop skill in discovering aspects of reading that students can and cannot do well, and to learn teaching techniques that will overcome problems and make each student a reader.

We begin by describing the learning-to-read process of each level of development with a preview of the problems that can occur at each level.

References

Calfee, Robert, and Elfrieda Hiebert. "Classroom Assessment of Reading." In *Handbook of Reading Research*, Vol. 2, ed. Rebecca Barr, Michael L. Kamil, Peter Mosenthal, and P. David Pearson. White Plains, NY: Longman Publishers, 1991.

Heath, Shirley Brice. *Ways With Words: Language, Life and Work in Communities and Classrooms.* New York: Cambridge University Press, 1983.

Johnston, Peter, and Richard Allington. "Remediation." In *Handbook of Reading Research*, Vol. 2, ed. Rebecca Barr, Michael L. Kamil, Peter Mosenthal, and P. David Pearson. White Plains, NY: Longman Publishers, 1991.

Kozol, Jonathan. *Illiterate America.* New York: New American Library, 1985.

Reading and Reading Problems

T his book is about assessing people's reading difficulties and helping to overcome them. We start, though, by taking a rather long
view of how people learn to read and what normally happens to
them as they progress from prebeginner status to advanced reader. Naturally,
the possibilities and problems readers face are different at different stages,
and this introduction will help us later by showing us what to expect as we go
about assessing and teaching for the reading problems students may develop
at different points in their lives.

We're going out on a limb a little by talking of reading *stages*, although
we are in good company (e.g., Chall, 1983). There's nothing sacrosanct about
those that follow; they're mostly a convenient way to organize our discussion. The stages into which we divide the process of learning to read are the
following:

- *Emergent Literacy*   Children in the stage of emergent literacy are discovering basic concepts about print—both reading and writing—and learning
to associate pleasure with books. Usually these children are found in
preschool through first grade.

- *Beginning Reading*   Children in the beginning reading stage know
enough about the act of reading and the nature of print to begin to learn individual words—learn a *sight vocabulary*—from their encounters with them.
These children are normally first-graders, but they may be younger, or older.

- *Building Fluency*   Children who are building fluency, usually in
grades two and three, can recognize many words automatically and are reading passages several sentences long without stumbling over words. They are
beginning to read with expression.

- *Reading for Pleasure/Reading to Learn*   Children in this stage, usually
from grade three on up, may be reading chapter books for pleasure and
homework assignments for learning. At this stage good and poor readers are
pulling apart dramatically in their ease of reading and in the amount of reading they do.

- *Mature Reading*   Mature readers are those who read and compare
many sources of information on a topic. They can "read against the grain" of a
text and use the reading experience as a way of generating original ideas of
their own. They also read with appreciation of an author's techniques. It's
true that many readers do these things in the lower grades; but we group
these abilities under "mature reading" because they become a problem if
high-school or college students don't have them.

Of course individual students will go through stages of reading at different rates, but if they vary too much from the norm, they will have a price to
pay. As you can see from these descriptions, in each stage students develop

new reading abilities, and new challenges are placed on those abilities by the curriculum. If students' reading development gets out of synch with the demands of the curriculum, they may find themselves in real trouble. In first grade, for example, children struggle to recognize words, while in fourth grade reading is normally fluent, automatic, and often purposeful: Fourth-graders are required to write book reports and read for homework. There are some children in fourth grade who still struggle to recognize words, and in that way their reading is like the reading of first-graders. Their situation is very different, however, because these troubled readers have fewer chances to practice reading using material written on their grade level than first-graders (Allington, 1983): That is, they will have an impoverished opportunity to get better at reading. Moreover, if they cannot easily read for information, they may find themselves competing with classmates who have a richer knowledge base. This is a recipe for failure.

Let us now take a closer look at these stages, beginning with the earliest one, *emergent literacy.*

EMERGENT LITERACY

The stage that once was called *reading readiness* or *prereading* is now known as *emergent literacy* (Teale and Sulzby, 1985). Emergent literacy refers to a child's growing discoveries about print: that writing is talk written down, that the print talks and not the pictures, that print is composed of a certain set of letters arranged "just so" on a page, and that those letters stand for spoken words in a certain way.

These concepts are so naturally learned by many children—usually those whose parents read to them every night—that in past years teachers launched right into some kind of reading instruction without taking much account of the orienting concepts about literacy children might already possess. Now, thanks to the research in the field of emergent literacy, we recognize this critical set of learnings children must have in place if they will profit from reading instruction. We know how to identify children who still need to develop emergent literacy concepts, and we have strategies to help them learn. We even have clear recommendations to give to families and volunteers in our communities to enlist their aid in helping all children get off to a good start in reading. These are real breakthroughs.

Now we will highlight the key developments of the stage of emergent literacy. But first, let us point out that much of this discussion will focus on writing as well as on reading. That's because children's discovery of how print works includes its production—writing—as much as its interpretation—reading.

Concepts About Print

In the following paragraph, Marie Clay, a pioneer in the field of emergent literacy, gives us a good introduction to what we mean by "concepts about print."

> Suppose a teacher has placed an attractive picture on the wall and has asked her children for a story, which she will record under it. They offer the text "Mother is cooking," which the teacher alters slightly to introduce some features she wishes to teach. She writes:
>
> > Mother said,
> > "I am baking."
>
> If she says, "Now look at our *story*," 30 percent of a new entrant group will attend to the *picture*. If she says "Look at the words and find some you know," between 50 and 90 percent will be looking for *letters.* If she says, "Can you see Mother?" most will agree that they can, but some *see* her in the picture, some can locate *M* and others will locate the word *Mother.*
>
> Perhaps the children read in unison "Mother is . . ." and the teacher tries to sort this out. Pointing to *said,* she asks, "Does this say *is?* Half agree that is does because it has *s* in it. "What letter does it start with?" Now the teacher is really in trouble. She assumes that the children *know* that a word is built out of letters, but 50 percent of the children still confuse the verbal labels *word* and *letter* after six months of instruction. She also assumes that the children know that the left-hand letter following a space is the "start" of a word. Often they do not. (Clay, 1975, pp. 3–4)

Concepts about print, then, include knowing that

1. a book has a front and a back, and a "right side up,"
2. we read the words in a book and not the pictures,
3. print is arranged left to right, top to bottom,
4. language is made out of words,
5. words are made out of sounds,
6. sounds are matched with letters,
7. there is a limited set of those letters,
8. the letters have names, and
9. other parts of print have names, too, like *sentence, word, letter, beginning,* and *end.*

Some of these concepts turn out to be more troublesome for young children than others. Three that have proved especially important are the *concept of word, phonological awareness,* and *knowledge of the alphabet.*

The Concept of Word

A popular way to ease children into reading is to teach them to memorize a catchy phrase or rhyme, and then show them the phrase or rhyme written down. It seems natural that a child who has memorized the words of a poem should find it easy to read the printed version, pointing at the words as she goes. In fact, it may not be. To do this supposedly simple speech-to-print matching (Morris, 1981) requires the child to know that the language she speaks comes in units of words, and know that those units correspond exactly to the clusters of letters on the page with spaces at either end. Only in late kindergarten or early first grade do many children develop this *concept of word* (Morris, 1981), and many children still don't have it even in early first grade—a cause of difficulty in learning to read.

It is easy to see why the concept of word should be important in learning to read. R. D. Morris has demonstrated that children who can point at words as they say them are more likely to learn words from seeing them in print. Other researchers agree (Ehri and Sweet, 1991; Reutzel, Oda, and Moore, 1989).

What other abilities support the concept of word? Morris (1989) found that children were more likely to voice-point (to point to a written word in a line of text that has been memorized at the same time they say the spoken word) accurately if they were able to recognize some beginning letters and associate them with sounds—that is, a child who knows the letter *T* and associates the sound /t/ with it will have an easier time pointing to word units in "Twinkle, twinkle, little star." On the other hand, Ehri and Sweet (1991) found that children who were aware that words were composed of individual sounds (see the following section) were better able to voice-point. For now, we can say that children's instruction in emergent literacy should develop all of these concepts: knowledge of letters and awareness of their sounds, manipulation of sound units in spoken words, and voice-pointing to develop a concept of word.

Phonological Awareness

Once children have a concept of word, they must next be able to break a word down into the sounds that make it up. For example, they must sense that the spoken word *cape* contains the sequence of sounds /k/,/ā/,/p/. Why is this important? The short answer is, that's the way our alphabetic writing system works. Written words, for all their irregularity, use letters to spell the individual sounds of spoken words. If a child is not able to sense the individual sound units of spoken words—units we call *phonemes*, she won't be able to "sound out" that word when she is trying to read it. But that's only part of the answer. Some researchers, such as Isabel Liberman et al. (1977) and Linnea Ehri (1978), believe that even when we have learned to recognize a word as a whole, the sort of memory process we use stores the word part by part, or phoneme by phoneme, with an awareness of the graphic representation or spelling of those phonemes. Thus, the more adept we are at breaking words into sounds, the more efficient we'll be at remembering those words for later recognition.

As we just saw, another aspect of phonological awareness should be an *awareness of letter-to-sound correspondences*: that is, knowing what sounds are usually represented by what letters. We are not saying that a child in the emergent literacy stage needs to know all of the possible relationships. At first we only care that she realize that such relationships exist. She is likely to see this first in the case of particulars: "The same sound and letter begin my name, Mary, and McDonald's."

Knowledge of the Alphabet

It is certainly not necessary for a child to know all of the letters of the alphabet in order to read, but research does suggest that it helps if she knows most of them (Walsh, 1988). For one thing, we know that the practice of invented spelling (see pp. 24–25) helps children develop phonological awareness and later word recognition (Clarke, 1988). Children need to know how to form letters and know their names in order to invent spellings.

A thorough assessment of children's emergent literacy will include an inventory of the letters they can recognize and produce. A sound instructional program will teach them the letters—at the same time that it has them doing more natural literacy activities such as listening to stories, reading picture books, producing early writing, and dramatizing narratives.

We cannot leave our section on emergent literacy without talking about two other key developments of this stage. The first is *emergent storybook reading*. The second is *early writing and invented spelling*.

Emergent Storybook Reading

We have described the aspects of emergent literacy as if they developed separately. In fact, these aspects develop naturally in the context of reading events: children are read storybooks and soon try to read storybooks themselves.

Elizabeth Sulzby has observed hundreds of preschool children of different ages reading storybooks, and she has discerned clear patterns of evolution in the strategies that younger to older children employ in such activities (Sulzby, 1985). These strategies, in turn, reflect children's growing awareness of decontextualized language, of the reality of words, of the speech-to-print match, and of some other learnings as well. The patterns are presented diagrammatically in Figure 2.1 (see page 19).

To summarize Sulzby's patterns very briefly, the youngest subjects (some as young as age two or three) read by pointing to the pictures and naming them. They treat the pictures rather than the print as the primary conveyors of meaning in texts; also, for them, reading consists of commenting on each picture as a separate exhibit. They do not attempt to weave a story across several pictures. Their commentary, also, is directed at the person reading with them. Reading at this stage is deeply embedded in conversation.

Figure 2.1

▬▬▬▬

Simplified Version of Sulzby's Classification Scheme for Children's Emergent Reading of Favorite Storybooks: Category Summaries

BROAD CATEGORIES	BRIEF EXPLANATION OF CATEGORIES
1. Attending to Pictures, Not Forming Stories	The child is "reading" by looking at the storybook's pictures. The child's speech is just about the picture in view: the child is not "weaving a story" across the pages.
2. Attending to Pictures, Forming *Oral* Stories	The child is "reading" by looking at the storybook's pictures. The child's speech weaves a story across the pages but the wording and the intonation are like that of someone telling a story, either like a conversation about the pictures or like a fully recited story, in which the listener can see the pictures (and often *must* see them to understand the child's story).
3. Attending to Pictures, Reading and Storytelling	The child is "reading" by looking at the storybook's pictures. The child's speech fluctuates between sounding like Mixeda story-teller, with oral intonation, and sounding like a reader, with reading intonation. To fit this category, the majority of the reading attempt must show fluctuations between storytelling and reading.
4. Attending to Pictures Forming *Written* Stories	The child is "reading" by looking at the storybook's pictures. The child's speech sounds as if the child is reading, both in the wording and intonation. The listener does not need to look at the pictures (or rarely does) in order to understand the story. If the listener closes her or his eyes, most of the time she or he would think the child is reading from print.
5. Attending to Print	There are four subcategories of attending to print. Only the *final* one is what is typically called "real reading." In the others the child is exploring the print by such strategies as refusing to read based on print-related reasons, or using only some of the aspects of print.

Source: From "Children's Emergent Reading of Favorite Storybooks: A Developmental Study." Elizabeth Sulzby, *Reading Research Quarterly* 20, 1985. Reprinted with permission of Elizabeth Sulzby and the International Reading Association.

Children eventually begin to form stories from texts, and this occurs before they pay attention to the print. The first stories are still highly conversational: ". . . . And do you know what she did then?" Indeed, in northern Mexico, where there is still a rich storytelling tradition, children have been found to show a prominent strategy of oral storytelling before beginning to attend to print.

Later reading attempts are conducted in voices that sound like people reading, though the children still orient themselves in the story by the pictures, not the print. But the idea is dawning that a book tells a certain story,

Figure 2.1 continued

CATEGORIES OF STORYBOOK READING

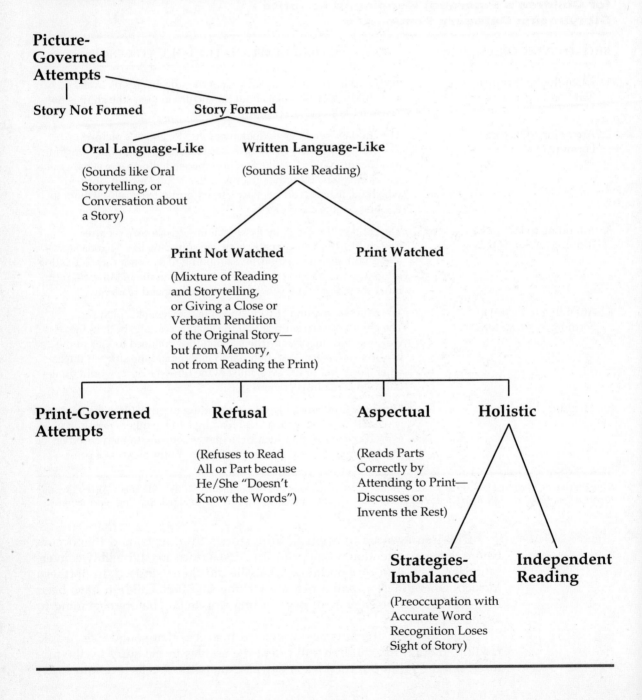

Picture-Governed Attempts

Story Not Formed   **Story Formed**

Oral Language-Like   **Written Language-Like**

(Sounds like Oral
Storytelling, or
Conversation about
a Story)

(Sounds like Reading)

Print Not Watched   **Print Watched**

(Mixture of Reading
and Storytelling,
or Giving a Close or
Verbatim Rendition
of the Original Story—
but from Memory,
not from Reading the Print)

**Print-Governed
Attempts**   **Refusal**   **Aspectual**   **Holistic**

(Refuses to Read
All or Part because
He/She "Doesn't
Know the Words")

(Reads Parts
Correctly by
Attending to Print—
Discusses or
Invents the Rest)

Strategies-Imbalanced   **Independent
Reading**

(Preoccupation with
Accurate Word
Recognition Loses
Sight of Story)

just so: in these words and no others. This reflects an awareness of decontextualized language, but it also prepares the children to start looking seriously at the print to see what part of the story it tells.

One of the first signs that children are looking to the print as a source of the spoken words comes as a refusal to read: they know they should be able to read the print, and they know they can't. Thus, a child who would have cheerfully trotted out a story the month before will now hesitate or refuse.

But practice with a favorite story—with, perhaps, some guidance in finger-point reading by a teacher—eventually enables children to match spoken words with written ones—and this leads to their learning the vivid ones and the ones that are often repeated. At some point a reading may consist of finding these known words—even at the expense of losing the thread of the story—before children actually succeed in reading the story by tracking along with the written words.

In summary, children's reading of a favorite story (defined as a story that has been read to them at least once, and that they, subsequently, have picked up and perused more than once) shows us the most important aspect of their understanding of the functions of print and the nature of the language that is represented in print. As a practical matter, storybook reading can provide a useful context for observing these concepts in action. Still more important, however, to give children exciting exposure to good books on their level, and then to encourage them to read these books in their own fashion, turns out to be a natural way to encourage the emergence of children's literacy, whether at home, in preschool, or in school.

Early Writing

Emergent literacy theorists have pointed to the pivotal role discovery plays in children's learning about literacy. In the following sections we demonstrate the discoveries children make—first, about how the writing system works; second, about the nature of print; and third, about the system of spelling.

How Writing Works

We have said that English has an alphabetic writing system, in which words are represented by a set of relations between letters and phonemes. Children have to discover these facts in order to learn to read and write.

Ferreiro and Teberosky (1982) investigated children's understanding of these issues by asking them to draw pictures and write captions under the pictures. When they questioned the children about the marks the children produced as they were "writing," the researchers identified stages that the development of writing goes through.

The first stage we might call *concrete writing*. A child draws a cat, and labels it.

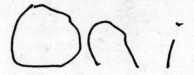

He draws a kitten, and labels it.

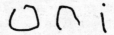

He draws a group of kittens, and labels them.

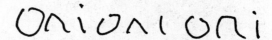

As you can see, the child believes there should be a concrete relationship between the thing he is labeling and the marks he uses. Names for similar objects (*cat* and *kitten*) should be similar. Names for big or numerous things should be big or numerous, and names for small and few things should be small and few. This *concrete strategy* bypasses any attempt to represent the spoken word for the thing and represents features of the thing itself.

A more mature child draws an alligator and writes the following:

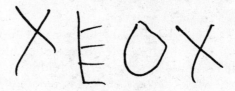

He draws a butterfly and writes the following:

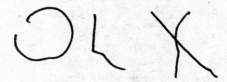

As you can see, the child is now trying to represent the names of the things. He is using marks to count out the syllables in the words *alligator* and *butterfly*. But there is no further relationship between the marks and the sounds of those syllables. In this *syllabic strategy*, marks are used as counters only.

A sightly more mature child draws a foot and writes the following:

fKtN

He draws a bird and writes the following:

BwCyh

As the beginning (left-hand) letter of each string shows, the child is now trying to represent a sound he hears in the name of the thing with a particular letter. No longer are letters mere counters; the child is thinking about writing as a way of finding correspondences between the sound-constituents of words and the letters of the alphabet. This *alphabetic strategy*, as we have already said, is essentially the one our writing system is based upon.

Learning the Features of Alphabet Letters

As Marie Clay's work (1975) has shown us, when children make marks on a page and call them writing, we can begin to tell what defining concepts they have in mind when they think of print. Often young writers create print by repeating the same move over and over. Clay called this idea the *recurring principle*.

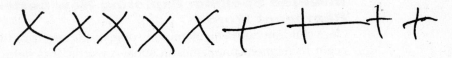

When the child learns to make a few discrete marks, she often uses the same marks over and over to generate a large amount of writing. Clay called this insight the *generative principle*: A small number of characters can be reproduced in varying orders to make a large amount of writing. The generative principle is, of course, the basis for alphabetic writing: Twenty-six letters can be combined and recombined to fill all the books in the Library of Congress.

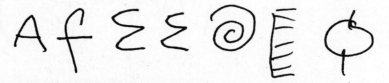

Once children know a few letters, they often begin to "fool around" with them, to draw them in different ways. Sometimes they happily produce letters they didn't already know; and sometimes they just seem to be testing the limits of the different ways they can make letters without changing them into something else. Marie Clay used the term *flexibility principle* to refer to the insights that come from exploring print by varying the forms of letters.

Psychologists of perception (such as Gibson and Levin, 1975) have shown that perceptual learning proceeds from whole to part and from gross distinctions to finer ones. We learn to tell birds from bugs, then robins from wrens, and gypsy moths from monarch butterflies. Clay found basically the same thing in children's writing. Children discover graphic principles related to the writing system as a whole before they master many individual letters. That being the case, then, if we give children opportunities in preschool and kindergarten to produce scribbles and other "pretend" writing we'll be making it easier for them to focus on individual letters when the time comes. In other words, scribbling and mock writing are useful early practices for learning to form—and recognize—letters.

Invented Spelling: Exploring How Letters Represent Words

Once children know the names of some of the letters of the alphabet, and can begin to segment phonemes in spoken words, it is natural that they should discover the alphabetic principle and begin to use letters to spell words by their individual sounds. So many children of age five or six do this, even

Figure 2.2

Invented Spelling by Annabrook, a Five-Year-Old, Not Yet Reading

I em GOWe 2 FRJYE OD
I hav a hED ac

Translation: "I am going to Virginia and I have a headache."

before they have learned to read in the conventional sense, that the phenomenon is now well known.

Thanks to the research of Charles Read (1986), Edmund Henderson (1992), and Henderson's students, the stage-bound set of discoveries by which many people learn to spell have been mapped out in detail. The stages are summarized in Box 2.1 (on page 26), but for now we should note that when children produce spellings such as those in Figure 2.2, they show that they:

- are segmenting the phonemes in words; and
- are actively exploring the relations between writing and reading, between letters and sounds.

When we look at the spelling of one child over a period of months, we see that even without being taught, her words take on more and more features of standard spelling, and that by reading and writing, she is discovering the spelling structures of the writing system. Capitalizing on this discovery process, many teachers offer children daily opportunities to write, representing ideas and words however they can—with drawings, scribbles, or invented spelling.

What Are Children Reading and Writing in This Stage?

The sorts of books that children at this stage can read successfully are simple, very predictable texts with few words and many supportive pictures. Little books fit the bill nicely; so do pattern books, alphabet books, and counting books (see Chapter 3 for a discussion of these books and their use).

Children's writing in this stage will encompass everything from **scribbles** with various graphic features showing up (see pp. 22–23), to **early phonemic spelling** (see p. 24).

Box 2.1
Stages of Invented Spelling

We used to think people learned to spell by memorizing thousands of individual spellings. Now we know that learners look for patterns in spelling that relate letters to sounds. As when they learn to talk, children learning to spell put forward their own ideas of how the patterns "work," and often make some bizarre-looking spellings in the process! Also like learning to talk is the fact that children seem to go through a rough set of stages in spelling development. These stages, which represent characteristic strategies for inventing their own spellings for words, are outlined below. You will note that these stages cover the range from preschool through high school.

Characteristics of Prephonemic Spelling
Phillip, Kindergartner

CHARACTERISTICS OF PREPHONEMIC SPELLING

Prephonemic spelling:

Is made up of letters and letterlike forms, such as numerals and incorrectly formed or made-up letters.

Is unreadable; letters and forms are used randomly, not to represent sounds.

Is usually arranged in horizontal lines.

May be made up of unbroken lines of letters or arranged in wordlike configurations with spaces between.

Shows that the child is aware that words are made up of letters and that print is arranged horizontally.

Is typical of older preschoolers, kindergartners, and many first-graders.

CHARACTERISTICS OF EARLY PHONEMIC SPELLING

Early phonemic spelling:

Is made up entirely of letters, usually in short strings of one to four letters; single letters are often used to represent whole words.

Represents the discovery of the alphabetic principle. Letters are used to represent some of the sounds in words.

Commonly features the use of consonants to represent initial sounds; sometimes

Box 2.1 continued

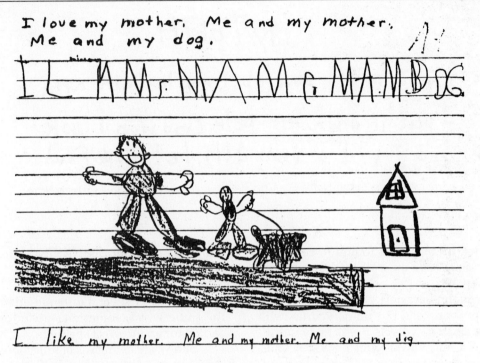

Characteristics of Early Phonemic Spelling

Brian, First Grade

final sounds and/or other important, clearly discernible sounds are represented too, but the spellings are very incomplete.

Shows the child's discovery that letters in print represent sounds in spoken words and indicates the beginning of the ability to segment phonemes.

Is typical of very beginning readers, some kindergartners, most early first-graders, and some older children just beginning to read.

CHARACTERISTICS OF LETTER-NAME SPELLING

Letter-name spelling:

Shows children's firm awareness that letters represent sounds, so the letters they use stand for sounds with no silent letters included.

Is still incomplete: Some sounds clearly evident in words are systematically omitted, such as m's and n's before consonants, vowels in unstressed syllables, and many short vowels until late in this stage; however, more sound features are represented than in earlier spelling stages.

Box 2.1 continued

My TEETH

Last nit I pold out my lustuth and
I put it ondr my pelr. And wan I wok
up I Fid a two dilr bel. The End.

Characteristics of Letter-Name Spelling

Billy's Spelling: Letter-Name

Uses the *names* of letters to represent sounds in words as well as the *sounds* of letters.

Is often characterized by: long vowels used appropriately, but unmarked (as with a silent *e*); short vowels predictably substituted by using vowel-letter names or omitted altogether; verb tenses and plural endings spelled as they sound: T, D, and ID; S, Z, and IZ; use of JR, GR, and CHR for sounds adults spell with *tr-* and *dr-*.

Is typical of beginning readers, who can read a little but are not yet fluent. Most first and many second graders fall into this group.

CHARACTERISTICS OF TRANSITIONAL SPELLING

Transitional spelling:

Is nearly complete; all phonemes are represented, long and short vowel sounds are generally spelled correctly or typically HED (head).

Shows an awareness of marking systems such as silent letters and consonant doubling but uses markers inappropriately:

RUNING (running), MAKKING (making), DUCKE (duck).

Is largely readable by others.

May show several different attempts at the same word, sometimes abandoning a correct for an incorrect spelling.

Shows an awareness of inflectional endings, but words are often spelled phonemically: PICKT (picked), WANTID (wanted).

Is typical of young pupils beyond the beginning reading stage and older ones who are still unfluent readers.

CHARACTERISTICS OF DERIVATIONAL SPELLING:

Derivational spelling:

Shows mastery of most of the phonemic and rule-governed spelling patterns, such as vowel marking and consonant doubling, that trip up transitional spellers.

Shows lack of awareness of relational patterns among words derived from the same source.

Is typical of older students and adults who have not read widely, written copiously, and studied word derivations directly.

Box 2.1 continued

Make a vest.
If you want to make a vest, you hare
to get some meatium-size
buttens and then some neadles
a in threds and then some
light Mateerial for the back
Make sure it is white mateea
and Make sure that the ves
is brown or tan then start
Soing. Make sure it has
no arms eather. Make sure it
has three buttens then you have
a rest to wear.
You will Know how to make a vest

Josiah

Characteristics of
Transitional Spelling

Source: Josiah,
First Grade,
Transitional Speller

definate   sergen   natchrel   revirse

version   nature   surgery

saler   sail   definition

Characteristics of Derivational Spelling

Learning Problems in the Emergent Literacy Stage

Emergent literacy is fascinating to observe, but it is also serious business. Children who successfully explore concepts about print during this period lay down a foundation that helps them profit from reading and writing instruction later on. Children who do not acquire foundational concepts about print may be doomed to permanent failure—unless extraordinary steps are taken to help them. One study has shown that nearly 90 percent of the first-graders who were behind their peers in reading were still in the bottom group four years later—but by then, the distance between them and the average readers was immense (Juell, 1988). This was in spite of the whole arsenal of special instructional services their school could bring to bear on them.

For this reason, in recent years intensive programs of early intervention such as Reading Recovery (Pinnell, 1989), Success for All (Slavin et al., 1991), and First Steps (Morris, 1993) have come into being. These programs, like hothouses for emergent literacy, have had notable success in heading off reading failure (Johnston, 1991). However, they also raise troubling questions for school personnel: Should the funds for special reading instruction be concentrated on children in the first few grades, where they might do the most good, or should they be used to support children at all levels of schooling? We wouldn't have to raise the question, of course, if we had adequate funding to provide support for readers at all grade levels. The dynamics of emergent literacy described in this section are certain to gain more attention in coming years as we strive to make all our children literate. Teaching strategies for helping children through the stage of emergent literacy are the subject of Chapter 3.

BEGINNING READING

Children reach the stage of beginning reading when they can learn to recognize words from their encounters with them. This stage is the beginning of true reading, but it comes after much prior learning. As we saw in the discussion of emergent literacy, before children can focus on printed words closely enough to learn them, they must be able to pay attention to spoken language and its parts, they must understand something about the way reading is done, and they must know a good deal about the nature of print.

An additional challenge in the period of beginning reading is to learn to recognize words and pay attention to their meaning at the same time. If all we do is teach children to recognize words, we will give them a distorted idea of what reading is, for reading is much more than identifying the words on a page. On the other hand, we can't get around the fact that children must learn to recognize words (and recognize them automatically) if they are to make progress in reading. In this section, we will consider word recognition, comprehension, and reading fluency.

Word Recognition

For years, reading teachers have debated whether it is better to encourage children to recognize words as wholes or to teach them to use *phonics*—the process of connecting letters and sounds. Research is now suggesting that the best approach is to honor what children are doing at different points in their development as they try to recognize words—or as Frank Smith wrote, "Figure out what children are trying to do, and help them do it." Indeed, recent studies show that children look at words differently as they gain experience in beginning reading.

Marsh, et al. (1981), found that children go through a series of stages in learning to recognize words.

Glance and Guess

Children who are reading very familiar text, such as a big book that the teacher has just read to them, or the lyrics of a song they know by heart, will glance at a word and identify it according to what makes sense. This identification is a form of guessing, based on context, perhaps on the shape of the word or other visual features. The word they call out is always drawn from words they have in their spoken vocabulary.

Sophisticated Guessing

With more experience, children begin to focus on a beginning or final letter in a word and use that letter-to-sound correspondence to narrow down their guessing. If the sentence says, "We went to the fire station," they might say "We went to the fire *store*." The word they guess is still supplied from words they know. If they didn't know the word, they wouldn't be able to sound it out.

Simple Phoneme-to-Grapheme Correspondences

As children get better at sounding out letters to sounds, their reading of unknown words may become bizarre: "We went to the fire *statone*." By now they may be so heavily involved in sounding out words that they forget about the meaning. Note that the letter-to-sound correspondences children use at this stage are based on small units, and the sounding goes almost letter by letter.

Recognition by Analogy

At a more advanced level, children decipher words not just on their individual letter-to-sound correspondences but on larger patterns. A child knows *night,* and she correctly reads the new word, *might,* because she recognizes the known pattern *-ight* in the new word. Traditionally, spelling units of this size were called *phonogram patterns.* More recently, Trieman (1979) has introduced the terms *onset* and *rime* to name the beginning element of a word and the phonogram pattern that follows it. For example, *C* or /k/ is the onset in *cat,* and *AT* or /æ t/ is the rime. Either way we describe these patterns, children who become familiar with them are more sophisticated at recognizing words and are very likely helped in their spelling, too (Temple, Nathan, Temple, and Burris, 1993).

Later Word Recognition

At a still more advanced stage, readers recognize unknown words by identifying known parts in them. On one level, this works with compound words—recognizing *playground* by reading *play* plus *ground.* On a still more advanced level, words are deciphered by the *morphemes* or meaningful word units they contain—as *equidistant* is broken into *equi-,* a word related to the known word *equal,* and *distant,* a known word. This later phase of word recognition surely carries from the middle elementary grades into adulthood.

Paying attention to the growth of children's word recognition can help us give them the help they need. For example, children at the *glance-and-guess* stage should be given plenty of supported practice reading simple and familiar text, according to ways we will describe in the next chapter. When they are reading many words (Russell Stauffer [1975] says 50 words), we can begin calling their attention to the words' beginning sounds and show them that words beginning with the same letter often begin with the same sound. We'll encourage them to write with invented spelling, too; when they want to spell words they don't know, we'll often encourage them to sound them out carefully—but remind them that the result should make sense.

When children have reached the point of *sophisticated guessing* we'll give them more practice identifying beginning sounds to consolidate their strength; and we'll also begin to call attention to sounds at the ends of words and in the middle. Their invented spellings will give them practice thinking about the relationship between sounds and letters.

When they reach the point of sounding out by means of *simple phoneme-to-grapheme correspondences,* we'll encourage the children to find those individual sound-to-letter matches, but also we'll begin to call their attention to phonogram patterns in words, especially by studying rhyming words or through word sorts (see Chapter 4). Once children expect to find familiar phonogram patterns in words, we can continue to discuss these patterns with them—again using rhymes and word sorts.

Any such sequence in our teaching should not be stressed to the exclusion of naturalistic approaches to literacy, though. We should still read poems and song lyrics with a group of children who are mostly reading words with a glance-and-guess strategy. Who knows? There may be a child in the group who will surprise us by discovering, well before we expected her to, that similar letter sequences make similar sounds.

We need constantly to remind all our children that reading is enjoyable and makes sense. As children get more engrossed in puzzling out words, they may lose sight of the larger purpose of reading. We should constantly remind children to ask themselves what makes sense, as they try to read unfamiliar words—even as they practice using their letter-to-sound decoding strategies. Expecting meaning, trying to decode, asking what makes sense: This is an important means by which children are learning to recognize words.

Normally, as children advance into second grade and beyond, their decoding strategies grow more sophisticated. They will take more complex patterns into account as they decipher words. At the same time, they will amass a number of *sight words,* words that they recognize instantly.

Sight Words

To read efficiently, readers must instantly recognize nearly all the words they encounter in print. They must have stored in memory a collection of remembered words that more or less equals the words they are likely to see. Obviously, it is easier to read by recognizing words than by connecting letters to sounds. If that point needs arguing, the following example should suffice:

> Ower entint heerizz tughshoa yugh wutta dissuhgrieuhbull choare iddizz tu sowndowt evrie wurd ennalign uvtegst, wunnbighwunn.[1]

But if efficient reading means recognizing words as wholes, why shouldn't we just teach whole words and skip decoding all together? The answer is the same as we stated earlier: Learning to break words into sounds and matching sounds with letters actually gives us a more efficient memory for recognizing words. Thus, people with sophisticated decoding knowledge, or *orthographic awareness,* are not only proficient at sounding out words in the first place, but they are also proficient at remembering them.

We should make sure that the materials students read are made up mostly of words they can read instantly. That is, the ratio of sight words to unknown words in a passage of text should be very high: about 20 known words to each unknown one (see Chapter 4). With remedial students, this point is particularly important. Unfortunately, it is seldom honored. As Allington's research has shown, the further behind grade level a student is found, the less likely he or she is to be placed in appropriate level text—that is, in text in which he or she can already recognize most of the words (Allington, 1983).

---

[1] "Our intent here is to show you how disagreeable a chore it is to sound out every word in a line of text, one by one."

Sometimes there is confusion between *sight words*—any words a reader can recognize instantly in print—and *basic sight words*—a term some authors use for certain high frequency words that are often taught to children.

A small number of words account for a high percentage of all running text. Just looking over this page will show you that words like *just, over, this, will, you, that,* and *like* are used again and again. Durr (1973) found ten words that accounted for one-fifth of all words used in a certain collection of juvenile books. A group of 188 words accounted for 70 percent of the running text in the same books. This kind of finding has led curriculum makers to compile lists of 100 to 200 words that all children should be taught to read.

This may be advisable, but there is a catch. These high frequency words are so common as to be bland, unmemorable, and rather hard to learn by themselves. A worse problem is that you can read these basic sight words and still not know what is going on in a passage. Consider, for example, the following passage, from which we have removed all of the words except for those on Eldon Ekwall's basic word list for first grade (1976):

_____ _____ and his _____ _____ _____ in the _____. They _____ in green. They _____ the _____ for _____ with their _____ and _____.

Pretty thin soup, wouldn't you say? Now, here is the same passage with the basic sight words taken out, and the other words put back in:

Robin Hood _____ _____ Merry men lived _____ _____ forest. _____ dressed _____ _____. _____ shot _____ deer _____ food _____ _____ bows _____ arrows. (Manning-Sanders, 1977, p. 1).

As we see, it is fairly easy to guess the high-frequency words if we know the low frequency words; but knowing the high-frequency words—the basic sight words—without the other words is not much help in understanding the passage.

Children are apt to learn low-frequency words with fewer exposures than they will basic sight words, simply because the former are more vivid. Since instruction in word recognition is generally better in a meaningful context, many teachers do not bother with teaching children basic sight word lists.

Comprehension in Reading

Surely comprehension—understanding what we read—is the whole point of reading; but the process of comprehension is not understood by all teachers. As Durkin's research has shown (Durkin, 1979), comprehension has not always been taught very well, either.

Comprehension involves *prior knowledge, knowledge of text structure,* and an *active search for information.* Let us describe each of these, and put them together into an understanding of reading comprehension.

Comprehension and Prior Knowledge

The simplest definition of *comprehension* is *understanding new information in light of what we already know.* The Swiss psychologist, Jean Piaget, argued many years ago that we understand new things and events we encounter by matching them with our store of mental frameworks that he called *schemes* or *schemata* (the singular is *schema).*

The same process is at work when we try to make sense of what we read. We use the words on the page to trigger our existing knowledge of whatever the words refer to, and in doing so, we often supply as much information as the words on the page do. Here is an illustration of what we mean:

This is an experiment. Read the passage below, then answer the questions that follow:

> Johnny was nearly in tears. It was his classmate Susan's birthday, and he'd forgotten to tell his mother. After school she hadn't been home, so Johnny had to come to the party empty-handed. Here he was, standing behind a cluster of children who were greeting Susan at the door. Inside beyond the door he could see the cake on the table, and brightly colored paper decorations taped to the wall and hanging from the ceiling.
>
> The other children now had moved inside. Susan turned and saw him.
>
> "Oh, hello, Johnny," she said. "I'm glad you could come."
>
> "Hi, Susan." Holding his hands behind his back he stepped forward, feeling his face blush bright red.

1. Retell this story in your own words without looking back at it.
2. See if you can summarize the story in one sentence.
3. What is Johnny so upset about?
4. Why is he empty-handed?
5. Describe the cake he saw inside on the table.

If you are like most readers, you began making some decisions about Johnny fairly early on. He is probably older than six and younger than 14. You probably decided, without thinking about it, that his problem is his lack of a present for Susan.

The point of the exercise, as you may have guessed, is to demonstrate how much of the meaning of the passage you supplied for yourself. Nowhere in the text is a *present* explicitly mentioned, nor is Johnny described. Yet readers have no trouble filling in this missing information. Indeed, they find it so natural, most are unaware they are doing it.

Current theories of how we comprehend text (Rosenblatt, 1978; Bartlett, 1932; Minsky, 1975; and Anderson and Pearson, 1984) stress the reader's active role in constructing meaning. According to one version called *schema theory,* readers have in their mind frameworks that organize their knowledge of the world. Schemata are abstract—that is, they are inexact enough to be called in to fit a range of new situations, and incomplete—they have slots in them that are available to be filled by the details in the text that is being considered (we say text, but this theory of comprehension can apply, of course, to events in the world as well). When we fit details from the text into the slots in our schemata (schema theorists call this process *instantiation)* we and the text jointly create the meaning.

In the case of the birthday party example, the text provided words about the characters and their actions, but the reader supplied his or her own understanding of the situation, the birthday party. The reader provided still more, however. To consider Johnny and Susan as characters, the reader demonstrated a set of expectations about narratives: namely, that they involve characters in causally motivated sequences of actions. Thus from the very beginning we want to know why Johnny is upset (and we can easily guess from the details we are given), and we want to know what will happen next.

Readers are thought to have both kinds of schemata—schemata that organize world knowledge, and schemata for text structure.

Schema Theory and World Knowledge

World knowledge refers to the things readers know that enable them to fill in the gaps when faced with text on birthday parties and the like.

We can make three points about world knowledge. First, while fourth-grade readers may know a lot about birthday parties, they may know little or nothing about Europe, or the way we elect presidents in America. If they encounter text about a country in Europe or a presidential election, they will not be able to fill in the gaps or organize the new information: They will not understand the text. Thus, the amount of background knowledge students have will affect their reading comprehension, a fact that had led E.D. Hirsch, Jr., to suggest that schools might attack reading problems by increasing the information content of the curriculum (Hirsch, 1987).

Comprehension and Text Structure

Becoming a good reader also requires that one be familiar with the *structure of the text* and be able to use that structure to guide the student's search for meaning. The text structure we're talking about can be as basic as sentence structure. That is, given the following sentence to read:

Shirley reached into her pocket and found a b_____.

a reader who is guided by awareness of sentence structure would supply *button, buck, bean,* or some other noun to fill the slot. The reader would know on some level that a noun must follow as the object of the verb *found* and the head word for the noun phrase denoted by the article *a* (though the reader surely would not be able to say so, in these terms).

Even beginning readers use larger structures than the structure of a sentence to help them understand what they read. The most familiar structure is probably the story. Consider this example:

THE DOG AND HIS SHADOW

Once there was a big brown dog named Sam. One day Sam found a piece of meat and was carrying it home in his mouth to eat. Now on his way home, he had to cross a plank lying across a running brook. As he crossed the brook, he looked down and saw his own shadow reflected in the water beneath.

He thought it was another dog with another piece of meat and he made up his mind to have that piece also. So he made a snap at the shadow, but as he opened his mouth the piece of meat fell out. The meat dropped into the water and floated away. Sam never saw the meat again. (McConaughty, 1980, p. 158)

The story of Sam, short as it is, nonetheless has all of the structural elements we expect in a simple story, and it has them in the right order.

It begins with a *setting* in which a character is introduced in some place at some time:

Once there was a big brown dog named Sam. One day, Sam found a piece of meat and was carrying it home in his mouth to eat. Now on his way home, he had to cross a plank lying across a running brook.

Next in the story comes an *initiating event,* which is either some occurrence or some idea that strikes someone and sets events in motion in the story, or that causes some important response in the main character:

. . . he looked down and saw his shadow reflected in the water beneath.

As a result of the initiating event, the main character has an *internal response:*

He thought it was another dog with another piece of meat . . .

He then sets a *goal:*

. . . and he made up his mind to have that piece also.

In order to achieve the goal the main character makes an *attempt,* some overt action to reach the goal:

So he made a snap at the shadow . . .

and this attempt has an *outcome:*

. . . but as he opened his mouth, the piece of meat fell out. The meat dropped into the water and floated away.

Following the attempt and outcome, there is a *consequence;* that is, some new action or situation results from the character's success or failure to achieve the goal:

Sam never saw the meat again.

There may be a *reaction*—an idea, an emotion, or some further action that indicates the main character's feelings about achieving or not achieving the goal, or a response that relates the events of the story to some larger set of concerns. "The Dog and His Shadow" did not include a reaction, but if it had, it might have looked like this:

Sam was indeed a sadder and wiser dog!

or like this:

A steak in the mouth is worth two in the brook!

Taken together, the elements of stories and the order in which they are presented are sometimes called *a story grammar,* because they describe story elements and their allowable orders in ways that remind us of sentence grammars, which do the same thing for the elements of a sentence. A schematic rendering of the structure or grammar of stories like "The Dog and His Shadow" is found in Figure 2.3. The grammar we just saw might be made more elaborate by making provision for episodes in it.

Episodes exist when a story is made up of more than one series of attempts and outcomes, as when the main character tries first one method to achieve the goal but fails, tries another method but also fails, then tries another method and finally succeeds.

Such is not the pattern of "The Dog and His Shadow," but it is the pattern of a great many other stories. When we consider the addition of episodes, and the interaction of more than one principal character, each having a goal,

Figure 2.3

A Diagram of the Structure of "The Dog and His Shadow"

Story = Setting + Initiating Event →

$$\text{Goal} \rightarrow \begin{Bmatrix} \text{Attempt} \rightarrow \text{Outcome} \\ \text{Attempt} \rightarrow \text{Outcome} \\ \text{Etc.} \end{Bmatrix} \rightarrow \text{Consequence } (\rightarrow \text{Reaction})$$

Key: = means "is made up of"
→ means "causes or leads to"
{ } mean "choose one or more of the enclosed elements"
( ) mean "you may choose or omit the enclosed element"

then even so-called simple stories like "The Three Little Pigs" can be shown to have a fairly complicated structure. Most—but not all—children come to school with an inner awareness of these structures—that is, they already have in their minds a very complicated and yet orderly idea of what stories should be like. Thus when they hear a reader or storyteller mention a time and place early in the story, they register these elements as constituting a setting. When a person or idealized animal is mentioned, they put this being down as the main character, and so on.

There is more to stories than story grammar, just as there is more to language than sentence grammar. Without an appreciation of structure, however, readers cannot tell how all the elements fit together and they will miss the significance of much that goes on in stories.

Other Text Structures

By the time they enter third grade, children have begun to encounter reading matter other than stories. Some readings will describe things while others will explain how certain things work or how to carry out a procedure. Later readings will give opinions and try to persuade the students to adopt certain attitudes and beliefs, while the students' own writings will still largely take the form of expressions of their personal feelings. Each of these purposes of writing tends to have its own structure, and each structure has a name. Material that describes is called *descriptive* writing. Writing that explains or gives directions is called *expository* writing. Writing that persuades is variously called *argumentative* or *persuasive* writing.

Far less research has been focused on these other text structures, but it is clear that

- knowing nonfictional text structures helps readers understand nonfictional text (Meyer, 1977);

- students who don't have a sense of these structures cannot comprehend text as well as those who do (Marshall and Glock, 1979);

- many older students lack an adequate sense of nonfictional text structures and hence do not know how to read nonfiction text (Marshall and Glock, 1979);

- many students who can read adequately in fictional text begin to founder at about fourth or fifth grade when the diet of nonfictional text is increased dramatically as reading is relied upon more heavily as a medium for learning other content (Richards, 1978).

Problems in reading nonfiction text are most acute in the content areas—science, social studies, health, and math—where students are expected to read nonfiction text and learn from it. We will devote a large portion of Chapter 6 to these problems, so our present discussion will be brief.

Comprehension: The Active Search for Information

Let's return to our birthday party example (please see page 35). Some readers won't understand that passage. Yes, they've been to birthday parties, and yes, they've heard stories before; but it won't occur to them to ". . . make the inferences required to weave the information given in a text into a coherent overall representation. . ." (Anderson and Pearson, 1984). In addition to having background knowledge and knowledge of text structures, these readers need to work on the thinking processes of comprehension—the processes we call the active search for information. Since many children may not have developed the habit of pursuing meaning actively, teachers will need to model this practice for them, and encourage them to seek meaning on their own.

In summary, *reading comprehension is the search for meaning, actively using our knowledge of the world and of texts to understand each new thing we read.* This one sentence identifies three elements of reading for comprehension:

- we need knowledge of the world to understand new things;
- we need to be familiar with the variety of text structures we're likely to encounter; and
- we need to seek meaning, and not wait passively for it to rise up from the page.

Reading and Writing at This Stage

In the stage of beginning reading, children still do not have an *independent reading level* (see p. 103); that is, there are very few books that they can pick up and read successfully without some support. They will continue to thrive in highly predictable text, supported by pictures—especially if it has been read to them first. Little books (see p. 82) and pattern books (such as Bill Martin, Jr.'s perennial favorite, *Brown Bear, Brown Bear, What Do You See?*) are good bets, so long as someone reads them through a few times first, so the children get the pattern. A great many simple books and pattern books are now available in big-book form—and these are surely one of the most glorious developments education has seen in recent years. Big books provide an excellent way for teachers to introduce a book to the whole class before children attempt to read smaller versions on their own. (Don't be surprised, though, when the children want to read the big book version to each other, exactly as you, the teacher, just did to them!)

Also effective at this stage are learner-generated materials, such as dictated experience accounts (see p. 59) class poems, and class songs (see p. 90).

Children's writing in the beginning reading stage will take the form of *letter-name spelling* (see p. 27). During this period you should see children representing more and more of the sounds they hear in words. Toward the end of this period, as children begin building fluency, you will see more and more standard spellings for vowel sounds and consonant digraphs showing up in children's repertoire. The spellings are still sound-by-sound, however, rather than syllable-pattern-by-syllable-pattern. That is, a child who can spell *went* correctly might still spell *bent* BET, because she doesn't yet think of *-ent* as a pattern that can show up in many different words.

Learning Problems in the Beginning Reading Stage

The problems children experience in the beginning reading stage usually center on word decoding, sight vocabulary, and comprehension. One noted researcher argues that these problems are related in a cause-and-effect sequence. Keith Stanovich (1986) used the term *Matthew effects* (inspired by the Biblical assertion that the rich shall get richer and poor shall get poorer) to describe a process by which students with initial difficulties see those difficulties compounded, while children who get off to a good start pile success upon success. More specifically, children who lack adequate *phonological awareness*—which, as we saw, should have been the outcome of the previous stage, emergent literacy—will have difficulty *decoding* words. Thus they will be slow to build *sight vocabularies;* and without adequate sight vocabularies, their *comprehension* will be limited. They will use up so much of their available attention deciding what the words are that they won't have enough of it left to concentrate on meanings.

If Stanovich's claims are correct—and a growing consensus of current research suggests that they are (see Juell, 1991, for a review)—then helping children to comprehend what they are reading will not be a substitute for helping them learn to read words accurately and efficiently. To be good readers, they have to be good at reading words. There seems to be no way around that. A great many children with reading problems at the beginning reading stage need help learning to decode words and developing a sight vocabulary.

Good readers also seek information, however. To make sure readers develop their comprehension side, we need to make sure they have background knowledge, see relationships between pieces of information, are familiar with structures of texts, and know how to seek information from texts.

BUILDING FLUENCY

If we may be permitted an analogy, then think of *beginning reading* as learning to balance on a bicycle and ride for short stretches without falling over. Think of *building fluency* as pedaling successfully for longer and longer stretches, though the bicycle is still not your main means of getting around.

In learning to read, children go through a period in which they are learning to orchestrate word recognition and comprehension and do both automatically and quickly. This is the stage of *building fluency*. Children usually go through this phase from the end of first grade through the end of second grade.

Their reading rate climbs dramatically during this time, from an average of 60 words per minute at the end of first grade, to about 110 words per minute towards the end of second grade (see Figure 2.4).

With the faster reading rate, children's comprehension improves. Why? Partly because as word recognition becomes automatic, readers simply have more concentration available to think about the meaning of what they've read. Also, the faster a reader goes, the more likely the reader is to "chunk" text for mental processing in increasingly meaningful units: words, then phrases, then clauses, then sentences, then arguments.

The main learning task of this period, then, is to practice, and practice, and practice reading. Knowledgeable teachers have moved beyond "Round Robin" reading activities, in which a group of eight or nine children take turns reading a few sentences each. The reason is simple: Children don't get enough practice reading in such arrangements. Allington's research (1983) has shown that in such traditional set-ups, most children in the primary grades spend only a few minutes actually reading every day. Since the goal is fluency, and fluency grows with practice, we need to provide children with many more opportunities to read. We will discuss strategies for fostering oral reading practice in Chapter 5.

As the graph in Figure 2.4 shows, the sharpest increase in children's rates of reading occurs during the period from the end of first through the end of second grade. Most students' reading rates continue to climb, however—at an average of 20 words per minute per year—every year thereafter through high school and college. This increase should remind us that building reading fluency continues as a goal of instruction throughout the school years. It does not end in second grade.

Reading and Writing at This Stage

Children at last have a fledgling *independent reading level* (see p. 104). That is, there are some simple books that they can pick up and read independently.

What kinds of books? One type are the books from a relatively new cate-

Figure 2.4

Reading Rate, in Standard Length Words per Minute.*

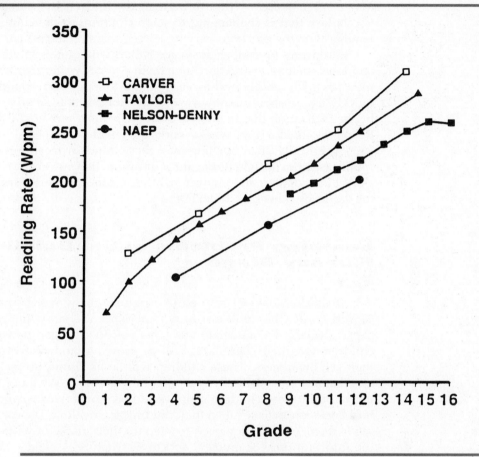

* Wpm. from grades 1 to 16, according to data reported in four different sources.

Source: Ron P. Carver. *Reading Rate: A Review of Research and Theory.* Fig. 1. New York: Academic Press, 1992.

gory, called *easy readers*. Examples of these books are Arnold Lobel's series about Frog and Toad, James Marshall's *Fox* titles, and Cynthia Rylant's *Henry and Mudge* books. Easy readers can be identified as collections of three or four short, catchy episodes per title; written in relatively short words which are often repeated; with layouts consisting of a few lines of print on each page accompanied by supportive pictures. Since they are available in inexpensive paperback versions, every first-, second-, and third-grade classroom should have a good supply of these books. Any school librarian will be able to advise on their selection.

Children in the fluency stage can also enjoy picture-story books—especially if the books have been read to them once or twice already. Books such as Mercer Mayer's *Just Me and My Dad* or William Steig's *Sylvester and the Magic Pebble* were written to be read to children by adults. They contain vocabulary that is challenging to some children, so the children had best be familiar with the plot before trying to read them on their own.

Children's writing at this stage is normally quite prolific. Their reading, and their spelling instruction, give them a larger writing vocabulary of words they can spell readily and a set of sound-to-letter correspondences they can quickly use to spell unknown words. Writing is still an adventure, unmixed by the realization that their style or their spelling may not be as developed as the professional writers whose works they read.

Specifically, their spelling may show trends from the *transitional stage of spelling* (see Box 2.1). In terms of composition, they are able to learn patterns—story plots, dialog, and characterization—from the stories they read, including works by other classroom authors.

Learning Problems in the Building Fluency Stage

If children haven't learned to recognize many words instantly by early second grade, they will not fully experience the spurt in reading rate and expressiveness we associate with this period. The gap between these slow children and their classmates will be growing; and, unfortunately, so will their self-awareness. These children will be beginning to feel like failures—and that attitude itself may compound the problem. We'll need to keep working to build these children's abilities to recognize words, and we'll want to find books on their level so they can practice reading. We can't neglect reading *to* them, either. They need to keep up their intake of written language for the information, vocabulary, and text structure it yields. Otherwise, their future hurdles will loom even higher.

READING FOR PLEASURE/READING TO LEARN

The phase of *reading for pleasure/reading to learn* may begin in late second grade or early third grade and last from then on (though most students will diversify their reading with what we call *mature reading* by the time they reach middle school, or even sooner). To return to our bicycle-riding analogy, children in this stage are reading to get somewhere. After students have built fluency in their reading comes this long period in which their ability is put to use, when we hope they *will* read a great deal, because they find reading both an enjoyable pastime and a source of information they wouldn't get otherwise.

The Benefits of Reading

At this point, reading becomes its own best teacher. Students who have the habit of reading are consuming dozens of books, thousands of pages, and hundreds of thousands of words a year. This reading practice equips them with an expanded vocabulary, familiarity with varied sentence structures, a broad knowledge of the forms of written language, and a passing acquaintance with most of the topics they are likely to come across in print. Until recently, few of us would have considered any of these to be components of reading ability, but now we realize that these achievements, all of them gained through practice in reading, probably make as much difference to a person's ability to read as any of the traditional skills of reading do.

Much of this difference has stayed beyond our direct control. Traditionally, children have done very little reading at school—only a few minutes per day, according to Allington's research (Allington, 1983). While many children do read outside of school, there are truly staggering differences in the amount of extracurricular reading any classroom full of children will do.

Figure 2.5 shows Keith Stanovich's interpretation of data on sixth-grade children's out-of-school reading collected by Wilson, Fielding, and Anderson

Figure 2.5

Variation in Amount of Independent Reading

	MINUTES OF READING PER DAY			WORDS READ PER YEAR	
PERCENTILE	BOOKS	TEXT	ALL READING	BOOKS	TEXT
98	65.0	67.3	90.7	4,358,000	4,733,000
90	21.1	33.4	40.4	1,823,000	2,357,000
80	14.2	24.6	31.1	1,146,000	1,697,000
70	9.6	16.9	21.7	622,000	1,168,000
60	6.5	13.1	18.1	432,000	722,000
50	4.6	9.2	12.9	282,000	601,000
40	3.2	6.2	8.6	200,000	421,000
30	1.3	4.3	5.8	106,000	251,000
20	0.7	2.4	3.1	21,000	134,000
10	0.1	1.0	1.6	8,000	51,000
2	0.0	0.0	0.2	0	8,000

Source: Keith E. Stanovich. "Matthew Effects in Reading." *Reading Research Quarterly* 21 (1986): 360–406.

(1986). We can reduce this data to one sentence: Assuming you teach a class of 30 sixth-graders from September to June, *your top three readers will read more words than your bottom three readers will read in 46 years!* And in one more sentence: *It will take the slowest reader in the sixth grade 591 years to read as many words as the top reader!*

These statistics have teeth. Stanovich's research shows that the good readers are gaining a wealth of information about the world and a wealth of vocabulary. This knowledge and vocabulary is what readers comprehend with: As the schema theory of comprehension predicts, we need to know a little bit about the topic already before we can learn something new about it. Readers who read a lot are going to know a little bit about a lot more topics—and will be better readers because of it (Hirsch, 1987).

What about those readers on the other end of the spectrum? Children who do not read so much will generally show depressed comprehension and overall inefficiency in reading. In practice, they will often be seen fidgeting instead of sustaining attention to reading tasks. They will show up without having read their assignments. Their oral reading will be halting and uncertain. Not so long ago, assessments of such students' reading behavior might have indicated they needed to develop this or that comprehension ability and to work on word recognition. Now we recognize that such judgments, while true, miss the larger point. To focus on the skill deficits of a person who doesn't read is like doing an expensive diagnosis of a car that's never used. Surely the car will have problems, and surely they must be fixed before it can be driven, but the problems will only return if the car is still not used. In the case of human beings who don't read, instruction in reading skills may well be called for—and reading diagnosis will help us decide when and what sort—but the real issue will be to get them to read.

Let us point out one more scary fact: *The students who read too little are the majority of our children.* Look again at Table 2.1. The amount of book reading done outside of school by the *median child* (50th percentile) was *only 4.6 minutes a day* in this sixth-grade sample. The lowest readers didn't read at all. As Paul Wilson concluded after collecting and studying these very data, "[W]e must face the fact that when we visit the typical elementary classroom, we find ourselves, at present, among nonreaders" (Wilson, 1992, p. 168).

Wilson went on to suggest:

> Knowing this, our first goal for school reading programs must be to cultivate literacy, to cultivate that headlong rush toward meaning that leads to large volumes of motivated voluntary reading (Wilson, 1992, p. 168).

In other words, reading instruction must begin by helping children learn to love reading. Make sure children have books available to them at school and at home—books that are interesting to them, books that are written on a level they can read easily—as well as incentives for them to read those books.

Reading for Information

After second grade, students are asked to learn from their reading. Learning from reading raises an unfamiliar set of problems. How are questions posed in texts? How are they answered? How are arguments set up in texts? How are they resolved? For those who up to now have thought of reading as pronouncing words aloud or of following a story line, these new tasks are real challenges. How will children learn to meet them?

Clearly, many children will not learn to learn from text without guided practice. That is, teachers need to *show them how to do it.* The best approaches for teaching children to learn from reading has us teachers—us skilled readers—figuring out exactly what *we* do as we learn from a text and demonstrating these very acts in front of our students. In other words, we use "Think-alouds" (Palincsar, 1986) to make our own thought processes explicit as we read and question our way through a text:

> This article is called "Desert Neighbors." Hmmm. The picture here doesn't show any houses around. Maybe the title means the article will talk about wild creatures who live near each other in the desert. That sound right? If so, I wonder which ones it'll mention? Anybody have any ideas? . . .

We also encourage children to "think aloud" as they read—both to encourage them to pursue meaning and also to show us how they are processing the information in the text. This sort of teaching goes under the general title of "cognitive apprenticeships" (Palincsar, 1986). In cognitive apprenticeships, teachers teach reading and writing as if these activities were, in Donald Graves' terms, "studio crafts": abilities to be taught through demonstrations by a master practitioner, followed by the learners' guided practice.

Explicit instruction may be used to teach students to learn from reading. Raphael's practice of QAR—Question-Answer Relationships (Raphael, 1984)—and Ogle's KWL—Know, Want-to-Know, Learn—activity (Ogle, 1986), are both means of teaching students to learn from reading. So are the various study guides for reading that were introduced by Harold Herber in the 1970s. All of these approaches will be treated in detail in Chapters 6 and 8.

Nonetheless, it is not enough that readers know strategies for learning from text. Readers also need a wealth of background knowledge, and a classroom in which knowledge is acquired, used, explored.

Response to Reading

When we speak of comprehension in reading, should we make a distinction between what readers do with fiction and what they do with nonfiction?

The literary critic Louise Rosenblatt (1978) suggests we should. There is a difference, she points out, between reading in which we take away literal information such as reading the schedule of hours the library will be open, and reading for more indirect enlightenment and vicarious pleasure, such as reading a novel. She calls the first kind *efferent reading;* the second kind she calls *aesthetic reading.*

In the moments when we are reading aesthetically, Rosenblatt believes, we are summoning up our own experiences and fantasies in response to the words in a book. The meaning of the text resides in just this event: It is a real-time experience of orchestrated thinking and revery, jointly created by the text and our minds.

Rosenblatt's position goes by the name *reader-response criticism,* and it raises interesting questions about the ways we should understand and teach reading comprehension. If a good part of the meaning of a text comes from the reader and not only from the book, then teaching reading for meaning means thinking about texts, bringing associations from personal experiences to the reading. It means that we should consider the students as authorities on their own understanding. It means that we cannot ever fully measure reading comprehension. It also means that the potential for misunderstanding among humans is very great—because the meaning of anything resides ultimately in what every individual makes of it. In fact, sharing books and discussing our responses to them turns out to be one of the best ways we have of building a community of understanding, or *an interpretive community,* as David Bleich (1975) has called it. Building community in this sense is the central task of the schools.

Teachers who take reader-response theory seriously arrange regular opportunities for students to read books, to say what the books make them think of, to write response journals about them, and to compare their responses with others.

Reading and Writing at This Stage

For children in the stage of *reading for pleasure/reading to learn,* there is a bonanza of books for them to read. Many new high-interest nonfiction books have been coming on the market—and if a school library hasn't gotten *lots* of new books in recent years, it may be missing out on a whole category of books that teach and expand children's curiosity. Especially suited to this age group are *chapter books,* in which a single story is sustained for 50 to 100 pages, with the support of occasional illustrations.

The high ratio of text to picture may make it difficult for some children to get into a book. So Wilson (1992) prompts teachers to help children learn strategies for choosing books they will enjoy. Having children recommend books to each other is one good way. So is the strategy of featuring different children's authors every few weeks: reading aloud from their books, inviting students to do reports and make posters from their work, and even writing them class letters. (The school librarian should be able to tell you which authors are most likely to respond.) It's best to feature authors who have written a string of books suitable for the same age group: authors like Beverly Cleary, Betsy Byars, Roald Dahl, E. Nesbit, Cynthia Rylant, Katherine Paterson, Virginia Hamilton, Gary Paulsen, or Avi. If students have enjoyed one of these author's books, they will know where to get others they will like.

As for writing, children in the reading for pleasure/reading to learn stage should be writing fluently for a variety of purposes. Thoughtful language-arts curricula have opportunities for children to use the following:

- *expressive writing,* as in journal entries, letters to pen-pals, rough notes written to themselves to explore a topic before giving it more formal treatment;
- *poetic writing,* not just poetry, but also stories for their own and others' enjoyment;
- *expository writing,* as in reports, directions for carrying out activities, and interviews with interesting people; and
- *persuasive writing,* as in arguments to persuade people for or against certain choices of action.

Children may choose for themselves the topics for writing, but the teacher should sometimes set up challenges for writing so that children write for different purposes and in different forms. We should show children models of other peoples' writings in each of the forms we're interested in. Here we mean "modeling" in both senses of the word: We should have examples around of things written in each form, and the teacher and other writers (including students themselves) should occasionally show *how* they write.

In terms of spelling development, students in this stage are spelling most words correctly. They may be struggling with the challenge of *consonant doubling* (that *bat + ing* is spelled *batting)* and of the spelling of *grammatical markers* (that the past tense of *wish, flow,* and *want* are all spelled with *-ed).* By the fourth or fifth grade, they will find a need to pay attention to the *derivational origin* of a word in order to spell it: knowing that *graph* and all its related words are spelled with *ph,* for example. (See pages 77–81 for more discussion of developmental spelling.)

Problems in the Reading for Pleasure/Reading to Learn Stage

Children who become adequate readers read a great deal, usually from about third grade on. It's certainly possible for people to get the habit of reading later than this; but our suspicion is that a price will be paid by what the person will have missed out on reading—especially the content reading that would have made that person's school studies more meaningful. The academic achievement of American students surely would not rank behind every other industrialized nation if even half of our students had the habit of reading.

Students who have difficulty in reading are especially likely to avoid reading. Therefore we must continue to work on their particular reading abilities and help them find materials that they *can* read and will *want* to read. We all need to become more imaginative and aggressive in providing interesting classroom libraries, family literacy projects that put books in homes and encourage parents to get involved in literacy, and community projects that distribute books and offer incentives for people to read them. But we must not limit these initiatives to the "problem readers." As we have argued in this section, *most* students do not read enough. We need to encourage all students to read: help them learn to choose books they will enjoy and even provide time in school for students to read. If Wilson's data reflect the time most children spend reading books, then we can greatly increase the national average if we have children reading books for just 20 minutes a day in school!

MATURE READING

Mature reading includes what is sometimes called *critical reading*, or arguing back with texts. It also includes what Mortimer Adler (1940) calls *syntopical reading*—that is, reading several sources on a topic to get a rounded picture of it. It further includes *aesthetic reading*, reading for an appreciation of the craft of good writing. Let's look at each of these in turn.

Critical Reading

Some years ago, parent groups asked the federal government to restrict the amount of violence and commercialism on children's Saturday-morning television programming. The government refused, giving an old response: *caveat emptor*, "Let the buyer beware." Since the "buyers" in this case were young children, the government's response raised the question:

> Should we teach our children to be critical of what they hear and read, so they can defend themselves against the manipulation of those who want their money or their loyalty for cynical purposes?

Many educators believe we should; thus the term *critical reading* is heard more and more these days. Critical reading means arguing back against books, and especially analyzing books for hidden biases, or even for their subtle sugges-

Box 2.2

An Example of Critical Reading

A mixed group of second- and third-graders are discussing the story, *Beauty and the Beast.*

"Suppose," says the teacher, "Beauty had been a boy in this story, and the Beast had been a girl."

A howl goes up from the class.

Alice looks troubled. "But then Beauty, the boy, would be *younger* than Beast, the girl. . ."

"So? Why would that matter? Besides, they don't tell you how old they are," says Alexander.

"But then, I mean, it's not right for a girl to ask a boy to go to the prom or something. . ." Alice still looks troubled.

"I've heard—this is what my Mom says—there's not a law against it or anything, but it's not right for a girl to ask a boy to marry her. This is what my Mom says. I don't know if it's true," says Charlotte.

"So why should that matter?" says Julian. "But I have another problem. The boys in the story are always the worse ones. I mean, the boys in the fairy tales just run up to a girl they don't even know and say 'Will you marry me?' "

"I know," adds Sarah. "I wish they'd say, 'Why no! How can I marry you? I don't even know you. I don't know what your *attitude* is!' "

"Boys in the fairy tales want to marry somebody they don't know anything about. I mean, they might not even *change their underwear!*" says Charlotte.

Allison takes a different tack. "I'm going to be a person who's the exact opposite of Beauty. Pretend there's a fire in here. You go up to that person and he says, 'So? Why'd you ask me? You help 'em!' But *Beauty.* . . You wouldn't have to tell her anything. She'd just go!"

"What does that have to do with how boys are and how girls are?" asks the teacher.

"Well, I'm not saying boys are *always* selfish. . . " Allison doesn't want to go further.

"What bugs me is that in the fairy tales, the guys are always doing things outside, and the girls are just basking around in their beautiful dresses," says Joanne. Several children nod.

Source: Charles Temple. "Suppose *Beauty* Had Been Ugly? Reading Against the Grain of Gender Bias in Children's Literature." *Language Arts* (March 1993).

tions that one or another sex or race or national group is superior to any other. Box 2.2 contains an example of critical reading.

Syntopical Reading

Mature reading also includes the practice of reading widely on a single topic, especially for the purpose of seeing how different groups respond to the same topic. The most vivid example that comes to mind is an experience with a freshman college seminar on 1492. On the topic of Columbus's trip, the students read materials written by Spaniards, by Native Americans, by Latinos, by Italian nationalist groups living in the United States, as well as by Columbus himself. Comparisons of these strikingly different readings told us a great deal about Columbus, but also gave us a greater appreciation of the points of view of each of these different groups of people who feel strongly about the Columbus legacy.

Syntopical reading is not just reading for information, but for nuances of the meanings, for the meanings of the meanings in their social contexts.

Aesthetic Reading

Another dimension of mature reading is *aesthetic reading*, savoring the artistry or examining the shortcomings of well-crafted or slapdash prose. A nice illustration of aesthetic reading is found in David Bleich's approach to reader response. Bleich first asks his students to retell a work they have all read, and he notes the variety in what students choose to include in their summaries. Then he asks students to name the most important parts of a work, and again he notes the effect of each reader's individual experiences and tastes in making such seemingly straightforward judgments—because there is invariably a lot of variety in what readers choose. Next, he asks students to comment on the most important *devices* in the work; he hears the students commenting on such things as voice, characterization, description, plotting, and irony—well before he has introduced the technical terms for these things.

A kind of aesthetic reading teachers and students sometimes do, often without realizing it's aesthetic reading, is to connect reading and writing. For example, some time after they have read and discussed *Maniac Magee,* by Jerry Spinelli, a teacher asks a fifth-grade class to reread the first chapter and lays out this challenge:

> Find all the tricks you can that the author used to make the story of Maniac Magee seem like a legend.

The students work in groups and come up with the jump-rope rhyme, the way the author introduced characters as if they were already famous, and the way the author mentioned several exaggerated versions of Maniac's background. After discussing those, the teacher then invites the students to use some of these devices in writing made-up legends of their own.

Now that we have described these three aspects of mature reading, it should be clear that these kinds of reading need not wait until high school or college. Indeed, the example of critical reading came from a second- and third-grade group. Children just as young are capable of making aesthetic responses to written works. Elementary-grade children can do syntopical readings as well. We only chose to call these activities mature reading because they strike us as the most mature kinds of reading we do—even though in many cases we begin doing them at an early age.

Reading and Writing at This Stage

As should be clear from the discussion thus far, the practices of mature reading—critical reading, syntopical reading, and aesthetic reading—can be applied to any sort of text. Of course as students grow in their reading maturity, they will seek out more challenging books. Our question is not so much what they read at this point but how they think about what they read.

In writing, demands will grow in school for students' writing to develop themes and arguments, to take positions clearly, and to provide details to support those positions. Students who have been encouraged to write often about what they really think, and have had their ideas taken seriously, should not have much difficulty meeting these later demands, but a great many students find these demands difficult or impossible to meet.

Problems in the Mature Reading Stage

Few students will be referred to a remedial-reading teacher for failing to read or write in the ways we have just described. We have included this discussion, though, because it is important for reading teachers to know where reading development is headed. The ultimate goal is not just that students understand what somebody else has written, but that they know where they stand on the author's claims, or be able to find an interesting interpretation of the work, and be able to state their positions clearly. Aspects of these goals, of course, might be included in our instruction at any level.

SUMMARY

In this chapter we described reading development as it progresses through five stages: *emergent literacy* (when children acquire foundational concepts about print), *beginning reading* (when children begin to recognize words and read with rudimentary comprehension), *building fluency* (when children learn to recognize so many words that their reading becomes more rapid and expressive), *reading for pleasure/reading to learn* (when children develop the habit of reading for pleasure, and also can reliably read for information), and *mature reading* (when students read critically, syntopically, and aesthetically). We expanded the description of each stage with a brief account of the sorts of books students are reading at each stage and the kinds of writing they do. Also included was a discussion of the problems associated with each stage. The rest of this text will be devoted to detailed accounts of assessment and instruction at each stage.

The next chapter begins with a detailed treatment of the stage of emergent literacy.

References

Adler, Mortimer J. *How to Read a Book.* New York: Simon & Schuster, 1940.

Allington, Richard L. "The Reading Instruction Provided Readers of Differing Abilities." *Elementary School Journal* 83 (1983): 548–559.

Anderson, Richard C., and P. David Pearson. "A Schema Theoretic View of Basic Processes in Reading Comprehension." In *Handbook of Reading Research,* ed. P. David Pearson, Rebecca Barr, Michael L. Kamil, and Peter Mosenthal. White Plains, NY: Longman Publishers, 1984.

Bartlett, Frederick. *Remembering.* New York: Cambridge University Press, 1932

Bleich, David. *Readings and Feelings.* Urbana, IL: National Council of Teachers of English, 1975.

Carver, Ronald P. *Reading Rate: A Review of Research and Theory.* New York: Academic Press, 1992.

Chall, Jeanne. *Stages of Reading Development.* New York: McGraw-Hill, 1983.

Clarke, Linda K. "Invented Versus Traditional Spelling in First Graders' Writings: Effects on Learning to Spell and Read." *Research in the Teaching of English* 22 (1988): 281–309.

Clay, M. M. *What Did I Write?* Portsmouth, NH: Heinemann Educational Books, 1975.

Durkin, Delores. "What Classroom Observations Reveal About Reading Comprehension Instruction." *Reading Research Quarterly* 14 (1978–1979): 481–483.

Durr, William. "Computer Study of High-frequency Words in Popular Trade Juveniles." *The Reading Teacher,* 27 (1973): 37–43.

Ehri, Linnea. "Beginning Reading from a Psycholinguistic Perspective: Amalgamation of Word Identities." In *Development of the Reading Process,* IRA Monograph no. 3, ed. Frank B. Murray. Newark, DE: International Reading Association, 1978.

Ehri, Linnea, and Jennifer Sweet. "Fingerpoint-reading of Memorized Text: What Enables Beginning Readers to Process Print?" *Reading Research Quarterly* 26 (1991): 442–462.

Ekwall, Eldon. *Diagnosis and Remediation of the Disabled Reader.* Needham Heights, MA: Allyn & Bacon, 1976.

Ferreiro, Emilia, and Ana Teberosky. *Writing Before Schooling.* Portsmouth, NH: Heinemann Educational Books, 1982.

Gibson, Eleanor, and Harry Levin. *The Psychology of Reading.* Cambridge, MA: MIT Press, 1975.

Henderson, Edmund H. *Teaching Spelling*, 2d ed. Boston: Houghton Mifflin, 1992.

Hirsch, Edgar Donald, Jr. *Cultural Literacy*. Boston: Houghton Mifflin, 1987.

Johnston, Peter A. "Remediation." In *Handbook of Reading Research*, Vol. 2, ed. Rebecca Barr. White Plains. NY: Longman Publishers, 1991.

Juell, Connie. Learning to Read and Write: A Longitudinal Study of Fifty-four Children from First through Fourth Grade. *Journal of Educational Psychology* 80, 437–447, 1988.

Liberman, I, Shankweiler, D., Liberman, A., Fowler, and Fischer, W. (1977). "Phonemic Segmentation and Recoding in the Beginning Reader." In ed. A.S. Reber and D.L. Scarborough *Toward a Psychology of Reading*. Hillsdale, NJ: Lawrence Earlbaum, pp. 207–225.

Manning-Sanders, R. *Robin Hood and Little John*. London: Methuen, 1977.

Marsh, G., Friedman, M., Welch, V., and Desberg, P. "A Cognitive-Developmental Theory of Reading Acquisition." In *Reading Research: Advances in Theory and Practice, Vol 3.*, ed. G. E. Mackinnon and T. G. Waller. New York: Plenum, 1981, pp. 199–221.

Marshall, Nancy, and Marvin Glock. "Comprehension of Connected Discourse." *Reading Research Quarterly* 14, (1978–1979): 10–56.

McConaughy, Stephanie. "Using Story Structure in the Classroom." *Language Arts*, 57 (1980): 157–165.

Meyer, Bonnie F. "The Structure of Prose: Effects on Learning and Memory and Implications for Educational Practice." In *Schooling and the Acquisition of Knowledge*, ed. Richard Anderson and Rand Spiro. Hillsdale, NJ: Lawrence Earlbaum Associates, 1977.

Minsky, Marvin. "A Framework for Representing Knowledge." In ed. P. H. Winston. *A Theory of Computer Vision*, New York: McGraw-Hill, 1975.

Morris, R. Darrell. "Concept of Word: A Developmental Phenomenon in the Beginning Reading and Writing Processes." *Language Arts*, 58 (1981): 659–668.

Morris, R. Darrell. "The Relationship Between Word Awareness and Phoneme Awareness in Learning to Read: A Longitudinal Study in Kindergarten." Appalachian State University, Boone, NC, 1989.

Morris, R. Darrell. "First Steps, An Early Reading Intervention Program." Appalachian State University, Boone, NC, 1993.

Morris, R. Darrell. "The Relationship Between Children's Concept of Word in Text and Phoneme Awareness in Learning to Read: A Longitudinal Study." *Research in the Teaching of English* 27, 2, May 1993 (pp. 133–154).

Ogle, Donna. M. "K-W-L: A Teaching Model that Develops Active Reading of Expository Text." *The Reading Teacher* 39 (1986): 564–570.

Palincsar, Annmarie S. "The Role of Dialogue in Providing Scaffolded Instruction." *Educational Psychologist* 21 (1986): 73–98.

Pinnell, Gay Su. "Reading Recovery: Helping At-risk Children Learn to Read." *Elementary School Journal* 90 (1989): 161–182.

Raphael, Taffy E. "Teaching Learners about Sources of Information for Answering Comprehension Questions." *Journal of Reading* 27 (1984): 303–311.

Read, Charles. *Children's Creative Spelling*. New York: Allen and Unwin, 1986.

Reutzel, D. Ray, L. K. Oda, and B. H. Moore. "Developing Print Awareness: The Effect of Three Instructional Approaches on Kindergartners' Print Awareness, Reading Readiness, and Word Reading." *Journal of Reading Behavior* 21 (1989): 197–217.

Richard, Jill. *Classroom Language: What Sorts?* London: Allen & Unwin, 1978.

Rosenblatt, Louise. *The Reader, the Text, and the Poem.* Carbondale, IL: Southern Illinois University Press, 1978.

Slavin, Robert E., Nancy A. Madden, Nancy L. Karweit, Lawrence J. Dolan, and Barbara A. Wasik. "Success For All: Ending Reading Failure from the Beginning." *Language Arts* 68, No. 5 (September 1991): 404–409.

Smith, F. *Understanding Reading.* New York: Holt, Rinehart, and Winston, 1975.

Stanovich, Keith E. "Matthew Effects in Reading." *Reading Research Quarterly* 21 (1986): 360–406.

Stanovich, K. E. "Are We Overselling Literacy?" In Temple, C., and Collins, P. *Stories and Readers: New Perspectives on Literature in the Elementary Classroom.* Norwood, MA: Christopher-Gordon, 1992.

Stauffer, R. G. (1975). *The Language-Experience Approach to the Teaching of Reading.* New York: Harper and Row.

Sulzby, E. "Children's Emergent Reading of Favorite Storybooks: A Developmental Study." *Reading Research Quarterly* 20: 458–481, 1985.

Teale, William, and Elizabeth Sulzby, ed. *Emergent Literacy.* Norwood, NJ: Ablex, 1986.

Trieman, Rebecca. "Onsets and Rimes as Units of Spoken Syllables: Evidence from Children," *Journal of Experimental Child Psychology* 39 (1979): 161–181.

Walsh, D., G. G. Price, and M. G. Gillingham. "The Crucial But Fleeting Skill of Alphabet Knowledge." *Reading Research Quarterly* 23: 108–122, 1986.

Wilson, P. "Among Nonreaders: Voluntary Reading, Reading Achievement, and the Development of Reading Habits." In Temple, C., and Collins, P. *Stories and Readers: New Perspectives on Literature in the Elementary Classroom,* ed. Charles Temple and Patrick Collins. Norwood, MA: Christopher-Gordon, 1992.

Emergent Literacy: Assessment and Instruction

F our out of five children make a host of useful discoveries about print before and during kindergarten. From being read to, from reading back favorite storybooks, and from attempting to make messages with pencils, these children pick up a range of concepts about print that enable them to grow as readers and writers with the help of normal tutelage. One out of five children are not so fortunate, however. These children do not have their early print concepts in place when they begin first grade, and things do not go well for them. Here is an account of one such child:

> Let me tell you about my 11-year old son. Billy started kindergarten, age 5 1/2, had done average work, went on to first grade. They waited till spring to tell me he was just immature; by now he was 7. I let them hold him back. I then started to watch more closely; halfway through the second year of first grade, he still couldn't read! They tested him (at my request); they said he had an attention disorder. They assigned him to special education; he went through second grade with a class of seven students in his room that were disabled. Billy didn't read but I felt he didn't belong there. Our doctor said they had made a mistake and he would not order Ritalin. I put him in one year of vision therapy, and three years of expensive tutors, and two more years in a Reading Study group at the University which is also expensive and wears us all out running back and forth. Now we wouldn't mind any of the above if some improvement had been made. At age 11 he's a normal all-boy child in every way; he shows a lot of common sense at home and play. Halfway through the fourth grade Billy does other subjects well, but he still isn't reading (Pinnell, Fried, and Estice, 1990).

Our task in this chapter will be to demonstrate first of all the techniques a teacher can use to find out what knowledge about reading a child brings into school. Secondly, we will explore ways to help every child's literacy emerge. The areas of emergent literacy we will consider include:

- oral language facility;
- storybook reading;
- a sense of story;
- the speech-to-print match;
- phonemic segmentation;
- letter knowledge;
- knowledge of spelling patterns; and
- sight word recognition.

In the pages that follow, we present techniques for investigating children's development in each of these areas, along with suggestions for helping children grow. The techniques center mostly around observing children as they are engaged in talking, and in reading or related tasks, and most require no more special equipment than illustrated reading books, paper and pencil (supplemented, sometimes, by a tape recorder) for taking notes, sharp eyes, and keen ears. For investigating some aspects of emergent literacy, commercially published materials exist that in our view simplify or add power to the teacher's unaided observations. We describe these materials and provide sources for them where appropriate.

We conclude this chapter with a discussion of new programs of early intervention. As the example of Billy makes depressingly clear, when it comes to helping children with reading difficulties, business as usual has not worked well enough.

A. ASSESSMENT OF EMERGENT LITERACY

ASSESSING ORAL LANGUAGE FLUENCY

As we said in Chapter 1, reading is an exercise in language use, and successful reading draws heavily on what children know about language. A reader needs to associate ideas with words, to use language elaborately to express fine shades of meaning that go beyond informal conversation, and to recognize the effects of grammatical structures on the meaning of word strings. In this section we describe two procedures that allow teachers to assess the oral language fluency of children in the context of activities that teach us as well as test. The first is the *dictated experience account,* an activity that we will return to throughout this chapter because it offers other diagnostic insights beyond the assessment of oral language fluency. The second of these procedures is *echo reading,* a sentence imitation task based in the language of books. We will also describe two more assessment approaches, each with a more limited focus. Marie Clay and her associates' *Record of Oral Language* (1982) deals with syntactical knowledge; Joan Tough's observational procedure identifies the functions to which children are able to address their utterances.

Dictated Experience Accounts

Dictated experience accounts are told aloud by a child and printed, exactly as spoken, by another person. One child can dictate a complete account, or a group can collaborate, with several children or each child contributing individual sentences.

Dictated experience accounts are a part of the language experience approach to beginning reading (Stauffer, 1980). Language experience is usually thought of as an instructional method, but dictations and rereadings have considerable value as diagnostic techniques for a small group or an individual child.

Materials

1. Individual account
   a. a stimulus (a hamster, arrowhead collection, picture book, or other concrete object or actual experience the child has just had)
   b. paper and pencil
2. Group story
   a. a stimulus (concrete object or event the group has just experienced together)
   b. an experience chart (a pad of large newsprint)
   c. a felt pen or crayon

Procedure

Whether with an individual or group, the dictated experience account starts with a concrete stimulus, which the children experience directly. The stimulus should be unique enough to (a) give the children an urge to talk about it and (b) enable them to remember it two or three days later when the dictation is reread.

After the students have enjoyed and discussed the experience, sit down with them and explain that together you are going to write an account of what has happened. You can begin by having the children talk about the stimulus and writing down some key words they use. Then ask each child to tell something about the experience and write down each one's contribution, including the child's name, like this:

THE STRIP MINE
John said, "We went and saw a strip mine."
Avery said, "It was real deep "
Sheila said, "I was scared we would fall in."
Bobby said, "They dig up coal with big machines."
Sue said, "My Daddy works on a strip mine."

Be careful to write down exactly what the children say, regardless of whether the sentences are complete or have errors in syntax, in order to preserve the integrity of their language. When it is all written down, read the whole account aloud two or three times, rapidly pointing to each word or line as it is read. Then ask the children to read the piece chorally with you. The idea is to have them memorize it so that the sentences become firmly anchored in their minds. When they have choral-read it twice or more and they seem confident, ask for volunteers to come forward and read a sentence, or the whole piece, if they can do so. As they recite the sentences, they should point to or underline individual words they know.

You can then make up a duplicating master of the group account and reproduce a copy for each child. These can be illustrated, reread many times, and as additional single words are recognized they should be underlined. Many children collect these accounts in booklets.

The dictated experience account can be done with one child, a small group of children, or a whole class. For diagnostic purposes it is best used with an individual or small group.

The activity can be spread over a number of days: the dictation one day, the choral and individual reading on the second day, and the distribution of copies to the children for individual reading on the third day.

What to Look for in Dictated Experience Accounts

When a child dictates an experience account, the teacher can get an indication of the child's fluency as a language user. Some aspects to consider are

- Does the child speak in sentences, or in single words and word clusters?
- Does the child use descriptive names for objects and events or many ambiguous terms like "it," "that," "this thing"?
- Does the child speak slowly and distinctly, repeating as necessary for the teacher to take the dictation, or blurt out or mumble sentences and then forget what was said?
- Does the child provide information that a reader who had not experienced the stimulus would need in order to reconstruct the event, or does the child assume that everyone has the same information about the event?

The more precise their terms are, the more inclusive their sentences, and the more their speech takes into account the listener's informational needs, then the more we would say that the children are speaking in an elaborated code. This speech style is closest to the language of books. Children who speak in an elaborated code will learn to read that language more easily than children who speak in a less elaborated code. Perhaps the best summary of the expressive use of language is this: a dictated experience story is "talk written down" (Allen, 1976); nevertheless, the more children's talk sounds like book language, the better their oral language prepares them for learning to read.

Echo Reading

Language fluency has two aspects that are particularly important. One is the expressive use of language, using elaborate sentences that make meanings adequately explicit. The expressive use of language can be examined informally by using the dictated story. The other aspect, the development of grammar or syntax, can be examined by using an *echo-reading* procedure.

We are not speaking here of a reading activity in the traditional sense, for of course we are assessing *prereaders!* In echo reading, the teacher reads a sentence aloud, and the child repeats or *echoes* the teacher's words, verbatim if possible, while looking at the line of print. The reading is not done independently but is accomplished in a highly supportive setting. What we are interested in is the precision with which the child can echo the teacher's words.

Syntax is a system of ordering and inflecting words within sentences and ordering sentences within utterances. The intuitive understanding of syntax helps in constructing and understanding sentences with many components. Syntax is a complicated topic, but in the present context of reading diagnosis we are concerned with only a minor aspect of it—namely, that syntactic development can limit the number of words a child can speak in a single sentence, which in turn can hinder the child's reading and discussion or written language, so it is a matter of concern in diagnosis.

Ordinarily by the time children are about five years old, their utterances are complex and lengthy, and counting the number of words in their sentences has ceased to be a worthwhile enterprise, as it was when they began talking. Some children, however, are still limited in the number of words they can comfortably handle in one sentence when they reach the first or second grade. When this is the case, it is sometimes hard to spot, since the paucity of speech may be mistaken for shyness. If the teacher does have a child who is a reluctant speaker, using echo reading is a fairly straightforward means of deciding if there is a lack of syntax.

The procedure for echo reading is as follows:

Materials

Select an eight-line passage from a book written at approximately a first-grade level. To record the echo reading, make a copy of the lines. To keep records on several students, type the lines, triple spaced, and duplicate a copy for each student.

Procedure

1. Sit down with one student at a time in a place that is relatively free of distractions.
2. Explain that you will read the lines aloud and that as you do so, you want the student to repeat the words you just read, exactly as you read them.
3. Read a line clearly, stop, and have the student echo it.
4. Repeat for each of the eight lines.
5. As the student echoes, record his or her words on your copy. You may it find it convenient to tape record these sessions and score the echo reading later.

Code the echo reading as follows:

1. Place a check mark (✔)over each word repeated correctly.
2. Circle words, word parts, or phrases that are omitted.
3. Write in words substituted for those in the line and draw a line through the words that were not repeated.
4. Write in words inserted in the line; use a caret (∧) to indicate where the insertion was made.

Here are some examples.

My new red wagon has (four shiny) red wheels. (correct and omission)

My ~~brother~~ *friend* and I pull things in it. (correct, substitution, and insertion)

Why is the ability to repeat sentences important? It is a curious fact of language development that children cannot accurately repeat a sentence that is more syntactically advanced than one they can produce spontaneously.

If you ask children to repeat a sentence more complicated than one they can produce themselves, they will normally simplify the sentence in the repeated version (Slobin and Welsh, 1971). Here, for example, are some sentence repetitions by young children between two and four years old.

1. *Adult:* Look at the doggy.
   Child: Doggy.
2. *Adult:* This boy is all wet.
   Child: Boy all wet.
3. *Adult:* The new bikes and roller skates are over there.
   Child: A new bikes are there and a skates are over there.

The link between children's ability to imitate sentences and the limits of their syntactic ability is fortuitous for language assessment. It enables us to get an idea of the limits of the complexity of their sentences by asking them to repeat sentences we read to them. Thus the method of echo reading can indicate whether a child's syntax is sufficiently developed to encompass the sentence patterns encountered in reading books written on a given level. Experience tells us that if the language patterns of a book do not lie within the children's control, they will be at a disadvantage in reading that book. And occasionally, reading teachers encounter children whose syntax is not adequate for any but the simplest books.

What to Look for in Echo Reading

One or two words deleted or substituted per sentence are not a cause for alarm, especially if the child substituted a familiar for a less familiar word such as *store* for *shop.* Similarly, if the child leaves off grammatical endings, plural markers on nouns, or tense markers on verbs, it is considered normal if he or she belongs to a dialect group that usually omits these endings. If, however, the child regularly leaves out important words or rewords whole phrases, it is more serious. In the previous examples, the first two show important elements omitted.

If children have a great deal of trouble with a basal reader, it is helpful to find out what they *can* successfully echo-read. It is easier to echo-read material written with predictable patterns of language, such as nursery rhymes, simple poems, and jingles. If the children are still having trouble even with this kind of material, you should observe whether or not they are taking advantage of the rhythm of the sentences. Do they repeat the sentences rhythmically? If not, make them tap their hands on the table along with you as they recite. Getting into the rhythm of the language will often help them repeat longer sentence patterns.

The important thing here is to find out what the children *can* do once the limits of their syntactic development have been found—that is, the length and type of sentence where their repetition falls below about 80 percent of the words, dialectical variances excluded. In these cases, their language in response to books will have to be drawn out before reading instruction can successfully proceed. Songs, poems, rhythm games and chants, and dictated experience accounts should all be used lavishly, as well as any simple books with a pattern (a rhyming or rhythmic element, as many books for young children have).

A Structured Sentence Imitation Task: *The Record of Oral Language*

While the level of difficulty of the echo-reading task (see p. 61) can be set to any level of text by the selection of the sentences out of which it is constructed, a more standardized version of the same task assigns kindergartners and first-graders high, average, and low levels of syntactical development. This assessment tool, *The Record of Oral Language* by Marie Clay and associates, also has provisions for pinpointing the kinds of sentence constructions (the *basic sentence patterns*), as well as specific transformations of these patterns (including *passives, imperatives, interrogatives,* and several types of *imbeddings*).

The Record of Oral Language is a test based on the same principle as echo reading. The groups of sentences to be repeated are carefully controlled for their form and their complexity, however, and they are arranged in three lev-

Figure 3.1

Sample Page from *The Record of Oral Language*

CLASS: _____ SCHOOL: _____ CHILD'S NAME: _____

DATE OF
BIRTH: _____ DATE: _____ AGE: _____ RECORDER: _____

THE LEVELS SENTENCES

Level 2 Part 1			Level 2 Part 2		
Type			Type		
A	*That big dog over there* is going to be *my brother's.*	☐	A	*That old truck in there* used to be *my father's.*	☐
B	*The boy by the pond* was sailing *his boat.*	☐	B	*The cat from next door* was chasing *a bird.*	☐
C	*The bird flew* to the top of the tree.	☐	C	*The dog ran through* the hole in the *fence.*	☐
D	*For his birthday* Kiri gave him *a truck.*	☐	D	*For the holidays* Grandpa bought us a ball.	☐
E	*Can you see what is climbing up the wall?*	☐	E	*The boy saw* what the man was doing *to the car.*	☐
F	*Here comes a big elephant* with children sitting on his back.	☐	F	*There is my baby* riding in his pushchair.	☐
G	*My brother turned the radio up* very loud.	☐	G	*The girl threw her book* right across the room.	☐

Total for Level 2 ☐

Enter 14 on the next page if all Level is credited.

Source: From Marie Clay, Malcolm Gill, Ted Glynn, Tony McNaughton, and Keith Salmon, *The Record of Oral Language* and *Biks and Gutches*, p. 20 (Auckland: Heinemann Publishers Ltd., 1982). Reprinted by permission.

els of difficulty. It comes bound in book form (the pages can be reproduced) with clear instructions for administering it and scoring the children's responses. Also provided is a detailed discussion of the syntactic structures being tested, the origins of the test, and the average scores of large groups of students for purposes of comparison. Because these students were all in New Zealand, however, it is inadvisable for American teachers to use these data *verbatim* in judging the performance of their students. A safer approach will be to administer the test to one or more whole classes of students and determine the range of scores that emerge.

A sample page from *The Record of Oral Language* is found in Figure 3.1.

Biks and Gutches

Knowledge of syntax has two aspects: the ordering of words in sentences and the inflections added to words that signal information (e.g., person, number, and tense of verbs, plurality in nouns, and comparatives in adjectives). *The Record of Oral Language* tests primarily the first sort of syntactical knowledge: sentence structure. Marie Clay and her associates have developed another test to investigate the second aspect of syntactical knowledge—word inflections. This test, derived from a famous experiment into children's knowledge of word inflections by Jean Berko (1958), is administered orally to one child at a time by the teacher, who reads an opening sentence that sets up a meaningful context, then pauses at a point where the child must supply a version of a word with its proper inflection (see Figure 3.2 for examples).

There is solid research evidence that the ability to use word inflections grows steadily along with, and can be an indicator of, general language development (Dale, 1972). However, the authors of *Biks and Gutches* report that the scores on their test vary widely with the size of the groups to which it is given and the dialect group to which the subjects belong. Rather than supply norms against which an individual child's performance should be judged, Clay et al. suggest that the test be used experimentally for the various purposes of gaining insight into this aspect of children's language growth in general, determining if children are making progress in language growth (which assumes the test will be given repeatedly at intervals throughout the year), and investigating how well speakers of other languages or dialects are acquiring the inflections of standard English.

ASSESSING STORYBOOK READING

As we saw in Chapter 2, the ways children perform when they pretend to read a favorite storybook can show us a great deal about their emerging concepts of literacy. Elizabeth Sulzby (1985) developed a research technique that can also be used to assess children's early reading knowledge. She chooses a book that she believes is appropriate for a child of a particular age and reads that book to the child at least twice, making sure that the child has become interested in the storybook. The reading of the book to the child may take place on several occasions over several days.

When it appears that the child is familiar with the book, she invites the child to "read" the book to her. She observes the child's pretend reading (or real reading) very carefully, and then characterizes it according to one of the strategies found in Figure 3.2.

In practice, she may carry out this procedure more than once with a given child—after all, the activity of pretend reading itself is a worthwhile lit-

Figure 3.2

Sample Questions to Test Syntactical Knowledge

Biks and gutches

11 This is a bik and here is another bik.
   There are two _____.   (biks)
12 There is a gutch and here is another gutch.
   There are two _____.   (gutches)

Open the door

The children said to the lady, 'Open the door.
4 The lady is _____ the door.   (opening)
5 But she is careful when she _____ it.   (opens)
6 Yesterday she nearly knocked the little girl over
   when she _____ the door.   (opened)

Source: From Marie Clay, Malcolm Gill, Ted Glynn, Tony McNaughton, and Keith Salmon, *The Record of Oral Language and Biks and Gutches*, p. 20 (Auckland: Heinemann Publishers Ltd., 1982). Reprinted by permission.

erary activity—to make sure she has found a strategy that the child seems to be using consistently. Sulzby's research suggests that children do use a particular strategy with some consistency, although they may revert to an easier strategy sometimes or experiment with a more difficult one on some occasions. On the whole, she found that children move in the direction from her earlier-named strategies to her later ones.

What does a child's use of these strategies tell us? If used repeatedly in assessment, Sulzby's categories eventually come to have meaning of themselves. In the meantime, as we noted in Chapter 2, the child's use of one or another strategy gives an indication of his or her understanding of the functions of print, of the decontextualized and highly structured language that print represents, and finally, of the form—including the spelling-to-sound code—that print embodies.

ASSESSING THE SENSE OF STORY STRUCTURES

A sense of story structures is an important aspect of prereading competence. Children should recognize a main character when one appears, sense a complication when one arises, and actively wonder how the main character will overcome the problems of the story. Children with a sense of story structure can make the most of the information that a story presents them. Those without this sense will not be able to tell an important event from a minor detail and may have little comprehension of a story even after hearing and understanding all of the words.

We suggest two procedures for assessing a sense of story. The first is a predictive questioning procedure known as the *directed listening-thinking activity*. The second is the *oral retelling of stories*.

The Directed Listening-Thinking Activity

This procedure, developed by Russell Stauffer (1980), is another assessment activity that also teaches, and the predictive questioning it employs fits well into the classroom instructional routine.

Materials

The teacher needs a storybook or picture book that has a good, strong plot with the elements of story structure described in the preceding chapter.

Procedure

The teacher reads the story aloud in parts, pausing several times just before some important event to ask the students to predict or guess what they think might happen next in the story, to summarize what they have found out in previous sections, and to determine what they still need to know. The aim is to get them to hypothesize about what *might* occur and what seems *most likely*. All predictions are accepted noncommittally regardless of whether they turn out to be correct.

The directed listening-thinking activity may be done with an individual, small group, or whole class. The spirit of friendly give-and-take and the proliferation of ideas the children generate make a group session preferable to an individual session.

What to Look for in the Directed Listening-Thinking Activity

Reading a story with the predictive questions of a directed listening-thinking activity demonstrates two aspects of children's orientation to stories. First is their attitude toward them; second is their sense of story structure.

1. When you announce the activity, which children come quickly and enthusiastically to the circle? Which ones do not? Over a number of trials, this is an indicator of expectations and attitudes toward books and reading.

2. When shown the cover or illustration of a book, do the children expect the cover to contain clues to the story? Do they expect the title to contain clues? Do they expect the pictures to give information? Their comments and predictions will reveal whether they have such expectations.

3. After a part of the story has been read and they are asked to make predictions:
    a. Do they make any predictions at all?
    b. If so, are their predictions:
       i. wild and random?
       ii. based on what might happen in real life?
       iii. based on story logic and story structures?
    c. Can they give a reason or justification for their predictions?

The answers to these questions will reveal the children's abilities to sense the structure of a story and use it to predict upcoming events. As we have seen, this is an important component of reading.

Oral Retelling of Stories

Another probe of children's awareness of story structure is to ask them to retell the story in their own words. Their retellings can be compared with the original for completeness and also analyzed for their story structure.

We can expect a youngster's retelling to have many of the structural elements of the original story: the setting, the initiating event, the goal, one or more attempts, or the resolution. One retelling, however, is not an accurate measure of sensitivity to story structure. A child may not like a certain story or feel like saying much on a given day. On the other hand, if a child on two or more occasions leaves out most of the structural elements in the retelling and does not venture good story-based predictions in the predictive questioning activity, it indicates that this child has not yet learned to function well with stories.

Happily, the solution follows the same process as the assessment: read and talk about lots more stories! It is through rich exposure to stories read aloud that youngsters abstract these structures and develop expectations about stories. Nothing can substitute for being read to daily. The predictive questioning group activity just described is an excellent vehicle for bringing children and stories together and helping them to develop a sense of story structure and language.

ASSESSING PRINT ORIENTATION CONCEPTS

Marie Clay's *Concepts About Print Test* (1979) assesses a number of aspects of a child's orientation to books and to written language that are not dealt with elsewhere. This test is highly recommended for kindergarten and primary grade teachers as well as for reading clinics. It comes with one of two reusable books and is available from Heinemann Educational Books, 361 Hanover Street, Portsmouth, New Hampshire 03801-3959.

The aspects of the *Concepts About Print Test* that are especially relevant to the present discussion of emergent literacy are:

- book orientation knowledge;
- principles involving the directional arrangement of print on the page;
- the knowledge that print, not the picture, contains the story;
- understanding of important reading terminology like *word, letter, beginning of the sentence,* and *top of the page;* and
- understanding of simple punctuation marks.

The assessment of orientation concepts about written language can be carried out by using a simple illustrated children's book, one that the child being tested has not seen before. *The Concepts About Print Test* has two specially made books (*Sand* and *Stones*), but teachers can get much of the flavor of the procedure with a book of their own choosing. The following are some concepts that can be tested and the procedures to use with them.

1. *Knowledge of the layout of books.* Hand the child a book, with the spine facing the child, and say, "Show me the *front* of the book." Note whether the child correctly identifies the front.

2. *Knowledge that print, not pictures, are what we read.* Open the book directly to a place where print is on one page and a picture is on the other (you should make sure beforehand that the book has such a pair of pages, and have it bookmarked for easy location). Then say: "Show me where I begin reading." Observe carefully to see whether the child points to the print or the picture. If the pointing gesture is vague, say, "Where, exactly?" If the child points to the print, note whether or not the child points to the upper left-hand corner of the page.

3. *Directional orientation of print on the page.* Stay on the same set of pages and after the child points at some spot on the printed page, say, "Show me with your finger where I go next." Then observe whether the child sweeps his or her finger across the printed line from left to right or moves it in some other direction.

Then ask, "Where do I go from there?" and observe whether the child correctly makes the return sweep to the left and drops down one line.

Note that a correct directional pattern is like this:

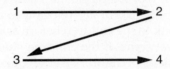

If the child indicates some other directional pattern, make a note of it.

4. *Knowledge of the concepts of beginning and end.* Turning now to a new page, say, "Point to the beginning of the story on this page," and then "Point to the end of the story on this page." Observe whether the child interprets both requests properly.

5. *Knowledge of the terms* top *and* bottom. Turning to another pair of pages that have print on one page and a picture on the other, point to the *middle* of the printed page and say, "Show me the bottom of the page," and then "Show me the top of the page." Then point to the *middle* of the picture and say, "Show me the top of the picture," and then "Show me the bottom of the picture." Note whether or not the child responds accurately to all four requests.

6. *Knowledge of the terms* word *and* letter. Now hand the child two blank index cards and say, "Put these cards on the page so that just *one word* shows between them," and then "Now move them so that *two words* show between them. Now move them again so that *one letter* shows between them," and then "Now move them so that *two letters* show between them." Make note of the child's response to all four requests.

7. *Knowledge of uppercase and lowercase letters.* On the same page, point to a capital letter with your pencil and say, "Show me a little letter that is the same as this one." (Beforehand, make sure that there is a corresponding lowercase letter on the page.) Next point to a lowercase letter and say, "Now point to a capital letter that is the same as this one." (Again, make sure that there *is* one.) You may repeat this procedure with other pairs of letters if the child's response seems uncertain.

8. *Knowledge of punctuation.* Turn to a page that has a period, an exclamation point, a question mark, a comma, and a set of quotation marks.

Pointing to each one in turn, ask, "What is this? What is it for?" Note whether or not the child answers correctly for each of the five punctuation marks.

In order to follow this assessment procedure efficiently, you will have to choose a book carefully and practice using the assessment questions enough times to become proficient. The procedure is easily carried out with Marie Clay's own test booklet, which is well worth the nominal cost.

The *Concepts About Print Test* was extensively reviewed by Yetta Goodman (1981), who has long been interested in what young children know about print and who has suggested several perceptive adaptations to the test. She recommended using a trade book relevant to the experience of the children rather than using Clay's *Sand* or *Stones*, which accompany the test. Goodman felt that the particular children pictured and their particular activities might not be culturally relevant to all. She also urged that teachers read the entire book to the children before asking the orientation questions because she found that some of the children she worked with became impatient with the interruptions of the story for the questioning.

It is advisable to make up a record sheet that provides for the quick recording of information yielded by the assessment. Clay's own test is matched with a scoring system. We believe, however, that it is sufficient simply to make a list of those print orientation competencies the children do or do not have. Then, as you work with them in simple trade books and basals, with dictated stories and by reading aloud to them, you can begin to draw their attention to the concepts they have not yet mastered: the direction of print, capital and lowercase letters, periods, and the like.

LETTER RECOGNITION

Everything in reading education is controversial, even the teaching of the alphabet. Most educators, however, believe that children who do not know the letters of the alphabet are at a disadvantage when it comes to learning to read. If your students do not have the ability to read, it is a good idea to verify with an alphabet inventory whether or not they can identify all the letters, both upper- and lowercase.

There are two reasons to go to the trouble of making up a special assessment device for the letters of the alphabet. The first is to test their recognition of letters out of the order in which they are usually recited. The *abcdefg* . . . routine is strong enough to cue an unknown letter by a known letter occurring before or after it. The *a-b-c* order, however, isn't very helpful when the letters are in words, and if a true test of letter recognition is to be made, the letters must be presented out of the normal order. The second reason for preparing a special letter recognition inventory is to test children's ability to recognize different typefaces. The lowercase letters *a* and *g* have alternate forms **a** and **g**, respectively, and children will sometimes fail to recognize both forms. Also, delayed readers have trouble associating handwritten letter forms with their printed counterparts. If this trouble is suspected, then the teacher can prepare a different version of a letter recognition inventory that mixes handwritten and typed forms of the same letters.

Materials

To prepare a letter recognition inventory, type a set of letters on sturdy paper with a triple space and below each letter. Then prepare a duplicator master of the same list. Score sheets can be run off from the master. (These can be combined with the sight word inventory to make up a single test.)

Here is a randomly ordered list of letters that can be used for testing:

d	f	t	g	n	b	e	h	l	v	o	y	m	a
a	r	c	q	z	u	s	j	p	i	x	k	w	g

F	W	D	T	N	R	A	C	G	Z	B	Q	E
V	J	O	Y	P	M	X	K	H	L	S	U	

Procedure

As you proceed from left to right across the line, point to each letter and ask the child to identify it. Enter on the record sheet only a notation of what letters were misidentified or unnamed.

Many beginning readers will have difficulty recognizing Z, Q, V, and perhaps one or two letters encountered out of sequence. Difficulty with *b, d, p, q,* and *g* is also common because of directional confusion. Children who confuse letters in isolation may still read them correctly in words, though they will be more uncertain than those who do not confuse them. Children who have difficulty identifying letters other than these are not likely to begin reading soon. They will need more experience with print and letters as a top priority.

ASSESSING THE SPEECH-TO-PRINT MATCH

As described in Chapter 2, the speech-to-print match or concept of word refers to one's ability to match spoken words with the same words as they appear in print. Children gain this ability only after they have acquired the following concepts about written language: (a) words are separable units; (b) printed words have spaces on either side that separate them from other words; and (c) words and syllables are not necessarily the same things. Therefore, dividing a line of writing up into its audible syllables or "beats" will not necessarily be an accurate way to separate the line into words (Morris, 1981).

The speech-to-print match can be assessed by informal means, either in a special *voice-pointing* procedure or as a follow-up to a dictated experience story.

The Voice-Pointing Procedure

This technique is best carried out by the teacher with one child at a time, although good results can be obtained with two or even three children at once.

Materials

You will need a short poem or a very memorable story, four lines long. A nursery rhyme, jingle, verse from a simple song, or similar material is perfect. Print or type the lines on paper or tagboard and triple space the lines. If large type is available, use that, because it helps the children to locate the printed words.

We have found that rhythmic children's stories like Martin and Brogan's (1971) *Instant Readers* work well with prereaders. These little books come in sets that include titles like *Brown Bear, Brown Bear, What Do You See?* and *Whistle, Mary, Whistle,* which have just the right elements of rhythmic, repetitious language and strong picture clues to make the lines easy to memorize and repeat. It is necessary for the child to learn to recite the lines confidently before the procedure begins, so choose some easily memorized text. Be sure that within the four lines you choose there are at least two words of more than one syllable.

Make a set of eight word cards, which you can use to see if the child already knows how to read any of these words from the text. For the word cards, choose two words from the beginnings of lines, two words from the ends of lines, and four words from the middles of lines. Two of the eight words chosen should be longer than one syllable. For example:

> *Twinkle,* twinkle little *star,*
> How *I* wonder *what* you are.
> *Up* above the *world* so high,
> Like a *diamond* in the *sky.*

Procedure

1. Use the word cards to pretest recognition of the words.
2. Recite the lines until the child has memorized them but has *not yet* seen them in print.
3. Read the lines aloud, pointing to each word as you read.
4. Have the child recite the lines and point to the words while doing so.
5. Read selected words aloud and ask the child to point them out.
6. Use the word cards to posttest recognition of those words; the child may now recognize some or all of them as a result of the activity.

The first and sixth steps, using the word cards, are intended to show if the child already knew any of the words before the exercise and if any of those selected were learned during the exercise. You should take note of the number of words recognized, if any, during steps 1 and 6.

The second step, memorizing the lines, is not timed or scored. It is important not to show the child the printed lines until after this stage is completed. Later on you will want to see how easily he or she can form associations between spoken words and printed ones, so it is important not to teach these associations inadvertently at this stage. Make sure that the child knows the lines before going on, inasmuch as children differ in how many repetitions they need to memorize the lines.

In the third step, you model the voice-pointing procedure. Read each line at a normal speed and point to each word as you read, but make sure that the child is watching your finger. Then, in step 4 ask the child to do the same thing, one line at a time. As each line is recited and pointed to, observe how accurately the child matches the spoken and printed words.

It is easier to keep track of the child's performance in step 5. This time you should call out the eight words that you put on the word cards, one at a time, and ask the child to point to them. It is to be expected that children will have to recite the entire line to themselves while searching for each word, so do not show them the word card but just pronounce the word and see if they can "count" across or between lines to find it. Keep track of how successful each child was in this search.

In the last step, scramble the order of the word cards and see if any of the words are now recognizable in isolation. Keep track of the child's performance on this posttest step.

At the conclusion of this activity, you should have:

- pre- and posttest scores of the child's recognition of words from the text in isolation;
- observations of the child's voice-pointing performance; and
- a score of the number of spoken words he or she could identify in the context of the printed lines.

What to Look for in the Voice-Pointing Procedure
This procedure directly tests three important components of beginning reading:

1. the concept of the word as a written unit in print;
2. the ability to recognize words in a meaningful context; and
3. the ability to learn new words from a supported reading activity.

Research with this procedure by Morris (1979), who developed it, has indicated that children tend to fall into three groups by their responses:

1. *One group of children performs poorly on word recognition and on the voice-pointing procedure.* The posttest scores of these children show little or no improvement over their pretest scores. They cannot yet reliably match memorized speech to memorized print, and they are not able to learn to recognize words even in a repetitious and highly supportive learning context like this activity. Until they develop a concept of word through more exposure to and experience with print, they will probably not profit from beginning reading instruction. The best program for these children is to read to them a great deal, to have them memorize rhymes and poems, and to practice the read-and-point routine.

2. *Another group knows some words in isolation.* These children can eventually identify words in context after they have learned to count through the line to the target word, reciting as they go. Their posttest scores on word recognition in context is higher than their pretest scores.

These children show some proficiency at pointing to words in a line, but two-syllable words usually throw them, which indicates an unstable word concept. Their word recognition in isolation posttest shows some improvement over the pretest, but they do not get more than half the words right.

This performance indicates that these children are making progress toward developing a concept of a word in print but that they need more practice at tasks similar to the testing procedure to help them develop this concept. You can accomplish this with any easily memorized text: dictated stories, poems, jingles, nursery rhymes, and songs.

3. *A third group of children may miss the words from the story on the pretest of word recognition in isolation.* The voice pointing of these children will be nearly perfect, however, and they will be able to correct any errors in voice pointing very quickly and confidently. Their posttest recognition of words in isolation is nearly perfect, which shows that they have learned several new words from this brief reading activity.

The children in this group are ready to begin formal reading instruction. The practice of reading new material with the support of a meaningful context produces new words for these children and rapidly expands their vocabulary in each new encounter with print. As they begin reading simple stories, they should have frequent experience with dictated stories and simple poems in order to reinforce their expectation that print matches speech and is predictable.

Using Voice Pointing with a Dictated Experience Story

Dictated experience stories provide excellent opportunities for teachers to test and develop a child's speech-to-print match. Earlier in this chapter we introduced the dictated story of "The Strip Mine" in which John dictates a sentence and the teacher reads the passage twice and then chorally reads it with the children. There is a good probability that John will remember his sentence, because he just said it: "John said, 'We went and saw a strip mine.'" He probably can recognize his own name, too. If the teacher asks him to read the sentence aloud he will be able to do so, perhaps even with his eyes closed! If the teacher asks him to point to his name, *John,* he should be able to do it. If she asks him to point to each word in the sentence as he says it, he probably will do so even though he may be a little hesitant. Now the question is: Can he point to a single word like *mine* or *saw?* If he can, he is showing signs of the speech-to-print match. He can recognize that bound configurations on the page correspond to spoken words in his head. This is how the sixth word, for example, in his spoken sentence comes to match the sixth word in his written sentence.

ASSESSING PHONEMIC SEGMENTATION BY MEANS OF INVENTED SPELLING

As we noted in Chapter 2, an important prerequisite for learning to recognize words is the ability to segment the word into its smallest constituent sounds, or *phonemes* (see p. 17). While a few words can be used as whole words before a child can segment phonemes, in order to begin to form generalizations about the ways groups of letters represent sounds (the basis of the *orthographic knowledge* we described in Chapter 2), a person must first be able to break a word up into its constituent parts.

The most natural way to observe whether or not a child has this ability is to ask him or her to spell words that he or she does not already know. By asking the child to spell unknown words, we ask the child to rely upon his or her *invented spelling,* the inner capacity to forge connections between letters and sounds. Children have an amazing intuitive ability to invent spellings, and we can learn very much about their word knowledge by looking at their invented productions.

A procedure for testing phonemic segmentation, then, is to have the child spell a list of words that you call out. Try a list such as the following:

bite	(three phonemes)
seat	(three phonemes)
dear	(three phonemes)
bones	(four phonemes)
load	(three phonemes)
fold	(four phonemes)
race	(three phonemes)
roar	(three phonemes)
beast	(four phonemes)
groan	(four phonemes)

Explain to the child that you want to see how he or she believes words are spelled. You're going to ask the child to spell some words you know the child doesn't know how to spell. After you call out each word (at least twice, and as many more times as the student requests), ask the student to try to spell each sound in the word. If the student says he or she can't, ask the student to listen to the way the word begins. What sound does it start with? Ask the student to write down a letter for that sound and letters for any other sounds he or she can hear. If the student is not sure how to spell a sound, ask the student to write a little dash (—).

After reading all ten words (fewer, if the test seems too arduous for a particular child), count the number of letters the child wrote for each word, and compare that to the number of phonemes in the word. A child who consistently writes three or four letters that show some reasonable connection to the sounds in the word appears able to segment phonemes. A child who writes nothing or strings together many letters indiscriminately is not yet able to segment phonemes, while a child who writes one or two reasonable letters per word is just beginning to segment phonemes.

A Spoken Test of Phonemic Segmentation

Invented spelling is a natural means both to assess and practice phonemic segmentation; but it does have one drawback. In order to demonstrate that they can segment words into phonemes, the children must also be able to match phonemes with letters, know what the letters look like, and know how to form them on paper. These latter abilities have nothing to do with segmenting phonemes: Hence, invented spelling both tests and exercises more than phonemic segmentation ability.

A procedure that does not depend upon spelling and writing is an oral test of phonemic segmentation developed by Hallie Kay Yopp (Yopp, 1988). This procedure is done with one child at a time, and it takes between five and ten minutes to administer. The test consists of a series of 22 one-syllable words. The child's task is to pronounce the words slowly to highlight the phonemes, after the tester shows the child how. Yopp's directions to the children work as follows:

> Today we're going to play a . . . word game. I'm going to say a word, and I want you to break the word apart. You are going to tell me each sound of the word in order. For example, if I say *old*, you will say *o-l-d*. Let's try a few words together. (Yopp, 1988, p. 166)

She follows with three more demonstration words: *ride*, *go*, and *man*. She praises the child if the child is correct, and corrects the child if he or she is wrong. Following the trials, she reads 22 words to the child and the child breaks the words apart one at a time as they are read. Again, the teacher gives praise or correction after each word. The words are as follows:

dog	lay	keep	race
fine	zoo	no	three
she	job	wave	in
grew	ice	that	at
red	top	me	by
sat	do		

Yopp gives the child a point for each word correctly segmented (there is no partial credit), so the scores can range from 0 to 22. When the test was given in the spring of the year to a group of 94 kindergartners in southern California—children with a median age of five years, ten months—the children got an average of nearly 12 items correct.

Yopp gives data that suggest that her task predicts children's ability to learn to sound out words more reliably than nine other phonemic segmentation tasks against which she compared it. Unfortunately, she did not compare her task against invented spelling. Mann, Tobin, and Wilson (1988), however, did find that invented spelling, when measured as a test of phonemic segmentation in kindergarten, significantly predicted reading ability in first grade.

Sight Word Recognition

Before children can read independently (that is, before they can make sense of text they have not dictated or heard read aloud), they must accumulate a number of sight words. Words that children recognize immediately are stepping stones that help them get through text that contains unknown words. Without sight words, reading is reduced to word-by-word decoding, and while this resembles reading in some superficial ways, it is not reading in a meaningful sense.

It is therefore important to see if children have begun to acquire some sight words. We cannot productively ask them to identify all the words they can recognize in print, however. We must instead construct a sample list of words they are likely to encounter in beginning reading, test them on those, and estimate from their performance what proportion of typical words they are apt to recognize as sight words in other contexts.

A *sight word inventory* can be made up by the teacher from early reading material. Here are the steps:

Materials

1. Get a copy of the earliest reading books that have simple sentences. These are usually preprimers and primers. You probably can omit the commercial readiness books, as they usually feature only single words.

2. Open the first book to a page approximately a third of the way through.
3. Select the fifth word on that page and every fifth word thereafter until ten words have been selected.
4. Eliminate any repetitions of words already selected and replace them by the sampling method in step 3.
5. Select ten words from each of the next readers, using the process outlined in steps 2 through 4.
6. Type or print (in large letters) each group of five words together on a piece of tagboard, arranging them in columns like this:

```
dog
sat
the
cake
boy
```

Don't label the lists according to the reading level; just arrange the lists in order, beginning with the easiest.
7. Make a ditto master of the word list and run off a copy for every child to be tested.

Procedure

This procedure is used with one child at a time. If you are right-handed, sit with child on your left. Put the tagboard with the word list in front of the child and a duplicated copy of the list by your right hand. (If you are left-handed, the placement is reversed.) Using two index cards, frame one word at a time to the child, asking, "What is this word?" "How about this one?" Put a check mark (✔) on your sheet next to every word the child recognizes. You can put an X next to any word the child does not know at sight but is able to figure out. Continue until all the words have been exposed unless the student becomes frustrated or unhappy with this experience, which may happen if the child knows only a few sight words. Use your judgment and stop if the child gets discouraged.

Record the percentage of correct identifications for each list on the score sheet, along with the date and the child's name, and keep the paper for later reference. As sight vocabulary grows, so will reading proficiency.

Basal readers differ quite widely in the number of new words introduced at each level, the number of times they are repeated, the syntactic complexity of the sentences, and the degree to which the sentences sound like natural language. Some primers use 40 or fewer words arranged in short, repetitious sentences; others have fewer vocabulary controls and feature 100 or more different words and fairly lengthy sentences. Some basal series teach a core of 10 to 20 basic words at the end of the readiness level so that children using preprimers have a few sight words established; in other series, the first words are introduced in the preprimers. Consequently, what constitutes an adequate score on the sight word inventory depends on what program you are using and where in the program the child is. We're not hedging; hard-and-fast criteria for everyone just cannot be established.

The best procedure is to look at your own students and their books. Try out the inventory with a number of children from all ability levels. Include some children you are sure can already read a little and compare their performance with the nonreaders. Using other informal assessments as well, determine what range of scores on sight words is associated with each group of children: those who have begun to read, those who seem to be about ready to begin, and those who are not ready to read at all even with help. Normally, children who have begun to read and are comfortable in preprimers and primers will recognize about 90 percent of the words in these books; those just beginning to read with help will identify about 70 percent of the words; and those who are not yet ready will identify fewer than 50 percent even at the earliest levels.

COGNITIVE MATURITY

When we have taken into account all of the factors we have associated with the readiness to learn to read—oral language fluency, familiarity with books and the purposes of reading, the sense of story structures, the speech-to-print match, print orientation concepts, sight word recognition, and letter recognition—is there not still some other underlying factor whose presence makes a child ready to read? If so, the best candidate would seem to be a maturing of the mind. Child developmentalists such as Elkind (1973) have argued that children must be capable of what Piaget called *concrete operational thought* before the several demands reading makes on the mind come within their power. We would not quarrel with that claim. Surely when children grow in all of the areas we have explored in this chapter, they have grown mentally. But growth in the particular is easier to nurture than growth in general. We can stimulate children's language, and give them daily rich experiences with stories and with print; and after months, perhaps many months, we can watch them grow to the point when they begin to read.

B. TEACHING FOR EMERGENT LITERACY

The techniques used to help each youngster's literacy emerge, whether in classroom or in clinic, should derive from two guiding principles: First, they should involve real reading and real writing in real contexts; second, they should respond to what the child knows and needs to know about reading and writing. In the following section we suggest activities that are related to each of these assessment areas.

READING STORYBOOKS

As you will recall from our discussion of emergent storybook reading in Chapter 2, by paging through and pretending to read favorite storybooks, in imitation of adults they have seen reading, children develop concepts about the form and function of written text, and the kind of language that is used in print. Since this is the case, good instruction for emerging readers will include providing individual books on their level, with simple text, that they will enjoy. The teacher introduces the books by reading them to a child or group of children more than once and then giving them to the children and encouraging them to "read" the books to friends or parents. Opportunities for such storybook reading should be provided on a daily basis for children on all levels.

LITTLE BOOKS

Christine McCormick and Jana Mason (1989) developed a simple but effective means of boosting young children's early experience with books. They created a series of "little books," each made from a single sheet of paper printed on both sides, cut in half horizontally, and folded (see Figure 3.3). One

Figure 3.3

A "Little Book"

book, called, appropriately, *Stop*, said

> Stop, car.
> Stop, truck.
> Stop, bus.
> Stop, stop, stop.
> Stop for the cat.

One line was written on each page, and each page had an illustration. The books were given to the mothers of low-income kindergarten children, a high percentage of whom could be at risk of reading failure later on. Each mother was encouraged to read the book to her child at least once, and then encourage that child to read the book on his or her own. Every six weeks or so during the year, McCormick and Mason mailed each family another little book, with the same instructions. The children thus received six books during the course of the year. When the children who had received the books were compared with a control group who had not, it was clear that the little books had helped them learn letters and develop a concept of word. They boosted the children's potential for learning to recognize words. The benefits of the little books were large in proportion to the amount of trouble they were to produce and share; thus, starting little-book sharing programs seems like a very good idea for kindergarten and first-grade classes with children who are not likely to have many books of their own at home.

TEACHING PRINT ORIENTATION CONCEPTS

How do we help children develop print orientation concepts? Don Holdaway (1979), a careful reader of his compatriot, Marie Clay, has tackled this question for us. He begins by noting that there are practical problems to be overcome in teaching groups of children about print. Books, after all, are usually just big enough to be read by one person. If a teacher tries to point out features of print to a group of children sitting around her, it's not likely that they will be able to see, say, the spaces between words if she uses a textbook to point them out. Besides, if she sits so that she is facing them, her book will be oriented upside down to them unless she holds it up so that it is upside down to her.

The solution, Holdaway proposes, is the "big book": a giant, three-foot-high version of the readers the children are using (see Figure 3.4). The teacher can place a big book on a chart stand where it can be readily seen by a group of children. She can have them read along with her as she points out features of print: where the text begins on a page; the left-to-right direction of reading; the return sweep; the spaces that demarcate words; and punctuation.

Figure 3.4

Teaching Print Orientation Concepts Using the Big Book

Source: Don Holdaway. *The Foundations of Literacy*, p. 65. Gosford, N.S.W.: Ashton Scholastic, 1979. (Reprinted by permission.)

In New Zealand, these big books are usually made by the teacher or a parent volunteer. They might be chosen to accompany a reading series of which the children have copies; that way the children can look for the features on the page in front of them that the teacher points out in the big book. Big book versions are also made up from favorite trade books. When children already know and are excited about the story line, they can more easily pay attention to the way print portrays the text, which is the point of this sort of lesson. After some initial resistance by American publishers, big book versions of children's books are now available from many sources.

TEACHING LETTER RECOGNITION

Many children enter kindergarten knowing most of their letters. Middle-class children are often able to point to and name all but *Q, Z, J,* and *Y*—unless, of course, their own names employ some of these letters—and also write a dozen or more letters. Some children, however, enter kindergarten knowing very few letters, and come to know letters in school only slowly and with difficulty (Ehri, 1989). While it may be possible to recognize a few words by memorizing their overall appearance (focusing on the "eyes" in *look,* for example), knowing the letters is necessary for learning to read appreciable numbers of words and to write using invented spelling.

Marie Clay's work (1975) and the work of Harste, Woodward, and Burke (1984) suggest that many children can invent their way to letter knowledge if they have models of print around them and are given early opportunities to write. However, by kindergarten, and certainly by first grade, those children who do not know most of their letters need more explicit teaching. Indeed, many studies show that children who know many letters in kindergarten are more likely to read by the end of first grade than children who know few (Walsh, 1986).

Research cited by Ehri suggests that children learn to recognize letters fastest when the letters are presented to them in a graphic display that combines the letter form with a picture of something whose name begins with that sound (see Figure 3.5 for an example). Note that in this method the letters are not drawn next to the picture, but rather as a part of the picture.

We also suggest making large cards to hang on the walls and flashcards to show to individuals or pairs of students. It will help further to send a set of cards home for extra practice (duplicate them on two sheets and have the children cut them apart). Encourage parents to buy and read alphabet books to their children. Better still, sell your parent-teachers' association on the idea of producing and giving away simple alphabet books throughout the community.

EXERCISES TO DEVELOP A CONCEPT OF WORD IN PRINT

The concept of word, as we have seen, is the important ability to relate words in the mind with words on the page. Research by Morris (1981, 1995) has suggested that children need to develop this ability before they will

Figure 3.5

Graphics for Teaching Letter Recognition

advance very far in their phonemic segmentation and their word recognition ability. Several of the tasks that we have already introduced in this chapter as assessment devices lend themselves quite well as instructional devices, too.

The Voice-Pointing Procedure

Once children have memorized a line of text, such as a line of a poem or of a song, the teacher can show them the printed version and encourage them to read it. The teacher usually demonstrates first, reading the text aloud and pointing to each word. Then the children follow suit, reading and pointing to the words. Occasionally the teacher asks the children to read an individual word that the teacher brackets between the teacher's hands or between index cards. Sometimes the teacher asks the children to read a word to which the teacher simply points.

Using Dictated Experience Accounts

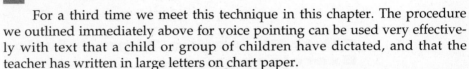

For a third time we meet this technique in this chapter. The procedure we outlined immediately above for voice pointing can be used very effectively with text that a child or group of children have dictated, and that the teacher has written in large letters on chart paper.

Another effective use of a dictated account goes as follows. Write a small version of text and duplicate it so that each child has two copies. Instruct the children to cut the paper so that each sentence is on its own strip of paper. Then they should cut these sentence strips into individual words. The teacher should circulate among them to identify the words they are cutting apart and encourage the children to identify them. Once the words are cut apart, the children should match the cut-apart words with the same words on the other intact sheet, laying each word above the intact word, so that it does not cover it.

Once children can do this sort of activity fairly easily, they can arrange the cut-apart words into sentences without using the intact words as a guide.

EXERCISES TO DEVELOP PHONEMIC SEGMENTATION ABILITY

For many children, the practice of writing freely and meaningfully using invented spelling provides all the phonemic segmentation exercise they will need.

Some kindergartners and first-graders may be reluctant to write with invented spelling. It is best to begin the year by encouraging the whole group to use invented spelling, in the following way. First, you should plan to have regular, at best daily, occasions for children to write and have meaningful and interesting topics for them to write about. In a pre-first-grade room, for example, the teacher read the children *Where the Wild Things Are* and *There's a Nightmare in My Closet*. After a discussion of monsters and nightmares, she passed out drawing paper and water colors , and invited the children to paint their own monster. Next the children were instructed to write the names of their monsters on the pages, and finally, to write what they do to defend or protect themselves from the monster.

Had the children not had plenty of experience by now writing with invented spelling, she might have kept the children in the group and asked them to think of a monster's name. Once they agreed on one, she might say, 'Long Arm Monster.' How are were going to write that? Who can think of a letter to begin it with? Long: luh, luh, luh." As each child thinks of a plausible letter, she can write it on the board—even if the result is LIG RM MISTR (one version of "long arm monster" in invented spelling). Several group demonstrations of this sort may be necessary before children will begin to use invented spelling; but before long, the children will find it natural to sound out words to write them. If they ask for help, they will be more likely to ask for the spelling of a sound than for the whole word.

Other Phonemic Segmentation Exercises

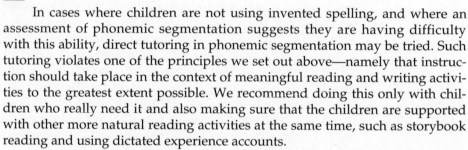

In cases where children are not using invented spelling, and where an assessment of phonemic segmentation suggests they are having difficulty with this ability, direct tutoring in phonemic segmentation may be tried. Such tutoring violates one of the principles we set out above—namely that instruction should take place in the context of meaningful reading and writing activities to the greatest extent possible. We recommend doing this only with children who really need it and also making sure that the children are supported with other more natural reading activities at the same time, such as storybook reading and using dictated experience accounts.

One effective procedure, described by Marie Clay (1986), is discussed in Box 3.1.

A more elaborate program to raise children's awareness of sounds in words was developed in Portugal by Ines Sim-Sim (Sim-Sim, 1994). Sim-Sim

---

Box 3.1
A Russian Device to Teach Phonemic Segmentation

In the 1950s, the Russian psychologist Daniel Elkonin, developed what are now the most widely used procedures for training children to segment phonemes. Elkonin was a student of the pioneer cognitive psychologist, Lev Vygotsky. Because he and his colleagues were among the first to determine that difficulties in hearing the sound constituents of words were more likely than distortions in visual perception to lie behind the reading problems of many children, they were searching for ways to teach this ability.

At first Elkonin worked at pronouncing words slowly and asking children to tap their fingers to count out the phonemes in the words. However, he soon realized that this task was too difficult for children. A colleague, P.J. Galperin, persuaded him that the training of a mental operation worked best if it proceeded by first making sure the children understood the task, then leading them to master the operation using concrete objects, then mastering the task using overt oral speech, then transferring the operation

Box 3.1 *continued*

to the mental level, and then having them carry out the task on an entirely mental level.

Accordingly, Elkonin drew up picture cards of words. For each word indicated by a picture, he made a matrix card—a long rectangle divided by vertical lines into horizontal arrays of squares, one square per phoneme of the word (see illustration).

He began the task by showing a child a picture card. Then, as he slowly pronounced the word, he pushed a small wooden token into a square for each phoneme of the word (at first the token was blank, since at this point he did not wish to complicate the task with letters).

After demonstrating the procedure several times, he then invited the child to look at a card, pronounce the word, and push one token onto a square for each phoneme heard. When the child could easily do this,

Elkonin removed the matrix card and had the child simply move a token for each phoneme the child heard in the word, without the guidance of the card. Later Elkonin removed the picture card, and finally, the tokens. At the end, the child was asked questions such as these: "How many sounds are in the word? In which position is such and such a sound when you count from the beginning? Which sound is first? Which is last? Which sound comes before (or after) such and such a word?" (Elkonin, 1973, p. 568)

Soviet teachers who tried Elkonin's task succeeded in twelve to fifteen short lessons to teach kindergarten children to segment phonemes. So successful was this procedure that it has been incorporated into the corrective teaching procedures promoted by Clay (1986) and Bryant and Bradley (1985).

(duck)   (dog)

Source: Daniel Elkonin. "Reading in the USSR." In *Comparative Reading,* ed. John Dowling. New York: Macmillan, 1973.

Box 3.2

Using Street Rhymes to Build Linguistic Awareness

The method used by Ines Sim-Sim begins with a street rhyme familiar to the children:

Miss Mary Mack
Dressed in black,
Silver buckles
Up and down her back.

It then follows these sequences of steps:

1. To make children aware of sounds, tell or sing the rhymes to the children until they know them by heart.
2. Repeat the rhyme without the word *black* and ask the children to supply the missing word.
3. Take the word *Mack* and ask the children which other words in the poem end the same way, in the same rhyme.
4. Ask children to think of other words that end in the same rhyme, *-ack,* and contrast them with words that do not rhyme, to give the children the concept of rhyme.

RAISING AWARENESS OF LANGUAGE SEGMENTS

1. *To raise children's awareness of the concept of a word:*
   a. Say the first line of a rhyme and ask the children to show (tap, count, sign) the number of words they hear in it.
   b. Ask the children to identify the first, middle, and last words in the line. Then ask them to repeat the line without pronouncing the first, middle, and last words.
   c. Ask them to substitute another word for the first, middle, or last word in the line.

2. *To raise children's awareness of the syllable:*
   a. Pronounce words to the children slowly, with the syllables segmented—*sil-ver, buc-kle.* Then ask them to rebuild them.
   b. Tell them a word (for example, *silver*), and ask them to segment it into pieces (*sil-ver*) by tapping, counting, and signing.
   c. Ask the children to name the first and last "piece", and then ask them to repeat the word without pronouncing the first or last "piece".

3. *To raise children's awareness of phonemes:*
   a. Say to the children words that begin with vowels or with fricatives (sounds such as /f/, /v/, and /s/), and ask them to pronounce the words slowly, emphasizing the first sounds. For example, if the words were *up* and *silver,* ask them to emphasize the [u] and the [s].
   b. Then say the word with the sounds separated—M . . . a . . . c . . . k—and ask the children to put them together.
   c. Next ask the children to do the opposite: That is, say the word *Mack,* and ask the children to pronounce the first sound [m], or the last one [k].
   d. Play a game in which children have to say beginning or ending sounds of words.

With all of these activities, when children can isolate vowels and fricatives, move on to lateral sounds, such as [r] and [l], and then to stop consonants, such as [t], [p], and [k].

Source: Ines Sim-Sim. "Reading Around the World: News from Portugal." *The Reading Teacher,* 1994. In press.

designed her plan to help teachers boost the early reading success of immigrant children from former Portuguese colonies in Africa, who had little home experience with books and who spoke a Creole version of Portuguese. Sim-Sim based her approach on street rhymes the children already knew; in the presentation in Box 3.2, though, we have substituted English-language rhymes and words for Sim-Sim's Portuguese-language examples.

"Making Words": Using Invented Spelling to Teach Spelling Patterns

Patricia Cunningham and James Cunningham have developed a structured lesson pattern that guides children in using their invented spelling strategies to help them discover spelling patterns in words. The approach promises to help children grow in phonemic segmentation ability and to develop awareness of patterns of letter-to-sound relationships. The Cunninghams' "Making Words" procedure is described in Box 3.3.

Box 3.3
A "Making Words" Lesson

STEPS IN PLANNING A "MAKING WORDS" LESSON

1. Decide what the final word in the lesson will be. In choosing this word, consider its number of vowels, child interest, curriculum tie-ins you can make, and letter-sound patterns you can draw children's attention to through the word sorting at the end.
2. Make a list of shorter words that can be made from the letters of the final word.
3. From all the words you listed, pick 12–15 words that include: (a) words that you can sort for the pattern(s) you want to emphasize; (b) little words and big words so that the lesson is a multilevel lesson; (c) words that can be made with the same letters in different places (e.g., barn, bran)

so children are reminded that when spelling words, the order of the letters is crucial; (d) a proper name or two to remind them where we use capital letters; and (e) words that most of the students have in their listening vocabularies.
4. Write all the words on index cards and order them from shortest to longest.
5. Once you have the two-letter, three-letter words together, order them further so that you can emphasize letter patterns and how changing the position of the letters or changing or adding just one letter results in a different word.
6. Store the cards in an envelope. Write on the envelope the words in order and the patterns you will sort for at the end.

Box 3.3 continued

STEPS IN TEACHING A "MAKING WORDS" LESSON

1. Place the large letter cards in a pocket chart or along the chalk ledge.
2. Have designated children give one letter to each child. (Let the passer keep the reclosable bag containing that letter and have the same child collect that letter when the lesson is over.)
3. Hold up and name the letters on the large letter cards, and have the children hold up their matching small letter cards.
4. Write the numeral 2 (or 3, if there are no two-letter words in this lesson) on the board. Tell them to take two letters and make the first word. Use the word in a sentence after you say it.
5. Have a child who has the first word made correctly make the same word with the large letter cards. Encourage anyone who did not make the word correctly at first to fix the word when they see it made correctly.
6. Continue having them make words, erasing and changing the number on the board to indicate the number of letters needed. Use the words in simple sentences to make sure the children understand their meanings. Remember to cue them as to whether they are just changing one letter, changing letters around, or taking all their letters out to make a word from scratch. Cue them when the word you want them to make is a proper name, and send a child who has started that name with a capital letter to make the word with the big letters.
7. Before telling them the last word, ask "Has anyone figured out what word we can make with all our letters?" If so, congratulate them and have one of them make it with the big letters. If not, say

something like, "I love it when I can stump you. Use all your letters and make _____ ."

8. Once all the words have been made, take the index cards on which you have written words, and place them one at a time (in the same order children made them) along the chalk ledge or in the pocket chart. Have children say and spell the words with you as you do this. Use these words for sorting and pointing out patterns. Pick a word and point out a particular spelling pattern, and ask children to find others with that same pattern. Line these words up so that the pattern is visible.
9. To get maximum transfer to reading and writing, have the children use the patterns they have sorted to spell a few new words that you say.

Note: Some teachers have chosen to do steps 1–7 on one day and steps 8 and 9 on the following day.

A SAMPLE "MAKING WORDS" LESSON USING ONLY ONE VOWEL

Letter cards:	u k n r s t
Words to make:	us nut rut run sun sunk runs/rust tusk stun stunk trunk trunks
Sort for:	rhymes s pairs (run runs; rut ruts; trunk trunks)

Letter cards:	o p r s s t
Words to make:	or top/pot rot port stop/spot sort sorts stops/spots sport sports
Sort for:	or o s pairs

Box 3.3 continued

Letter cards:	e d n p s s	Letter cards:	a c c h r s t
Words to make:	Ed Ned/end/den pen pens dens/send sped spend spends	Words to make:	art/tar car cat cart cars/scar star scat cash rash trash crash chart scratch
Sort for:	rhymes names s pairs	Sort for:	a ar rhymes
Letter cards:	a h l p s s	Letter cards:	i c k r s t
Words to make:	Al pal/lap Sal sap has/ash sash lash pass pals/laps/slap slaps slash splash	Words to make:	is it kit sit sir stir sick Rick tick skit skirt stick trick tricks
Sort for:	rhymes names s pairs	Sort for:	i ir sk rhymes

Source: Patricia Cunningham and James Cunningham. "Making Words: Enhancing the Invented Spelling-Decoding Connection." *The Reading Teacher* 46 (1992): 106–115.

C. EARLY INTERVENTION PROGRAMS

Do you recall the lament of Billy's mother at the beginning of this chapter? It may come as a shock to hear that the special help we make available for children like Billy often doesn't work. Research shows, however, that nine out of ten children who are not reading at the end of first grade may still lag far behind their classmates four years later (Juell, 1989). Special help may push them ahead by inches, but as we saw in Chapter 2, their classmates are sprinting ahead by miles.

Recently, a chorus of critics have pointed out shortcomings in our ways of helping slower readers, and are proposing bold new solutions. The chief criticisms of remedial programs are the following:

1. *They don't work well enough.* While they may move poor readers ahead, they do not close the gap between poor readers and the rest of the class.

2. *They make children miss other subjects.* Remedial instruction has usually required that children be taken out of their other school subjects to get special reading skill instruction. Missing the information in these regular classes contributes to children's academic problems and even holds back their reading growth.

3. *They start too late.* Traditionally, remedial programs wait until children are clearly lagging behind their classmates in reading—usually after first grade—before offering them special help. To wait that long may doom the children to permanent failure.

4. *They are not intensive enough.* Even teaching six children at a time, the smallest size of most remedial classes, may prevent a teacher from carrying out a careful diagnosis and giving each child fully responsive teaching and adequate amounts of real reading practice.

Perhaps the most promising solution proposed to date is early and intense literacy intervention. Reading Recovery (Clay, 1975), the most widely used program of this kind, targets the bottom 20 percent of the children in first grade and offers them one-on-one tutoring by an experienced and specially-trained teacher. The tutoring lasts half an hour a day, five days a week, and continues until the children reach the median level of reading ability in their classes—usually in 15 to 18 weeks. It is the hope of Reading Recovery advocates that the children will be able to advance with their classmates after the training is complete and will not need further remediation.

Reading Recovery instruction begins with a comprehensive assessment of a child's emergent literacy, followed by a period of informal teaching, called "roaming around the known," intended further to explore the child's concepts about literacy. Following the preliminary assessment period, instruction begins in earnest—though continuous assessment is built into every day's activities. Each day's lesson usually contains seven elements:

1. *Rereading of two or more familiar books.* Reading Recovery tries to keep the child immersed to the greatest extent possible in real reading and writing tasks. Reading books on the child's level is done every day. (More on this later.)

2. *Independent reading of the preceding lesson's new book while the teacher takes a running record.* A running record is a diagnostic procedure developed by Clay (1985). A child reads aloud and the teacher makes detailed notes of the accuracy and fluency of the reading. (Strategies for making a running record are presented in Chapter 4.)

3. *Letter identification using plastic letters on a magnetic board* (only if necessary). Many educators, including Fernald, and Bradley and Bryant, have commented on the value of multisensory techniques in beginning literacy instruction. Plastic magnetic letters offer a concrete medium in which a child can call the letters by name as he or she arranges them to spell out words or to copy other words written out by the teacher.

4. *Writing a story the child has composed including hearing sounds in unfamiliar printed words via "sound boxes"* (a phonological awareness training technique developed by Elkonin, 1973). Writing with invented spelling, as we saw in Chapter 2, has been shown to help children develop word and sound awareness, and awareness of letter-to-sound correspondences—in other words, to lay the foundation for learning to recognize words and to spell them. If a child cannot yet segment a word into its phonemes (see pp. 17–18), the child's invented spelling will be very limited. Hence the "sound box" may be used to develop phonemic segmentation ability.

5. *Reassembling a cut-up story.* A technique is included to help a child develop a concept of word (see page 17), and also to practice word-to-word matching. A story the child has dictated is cut into sentence strips; then these sentences are cut apart into words. The words are reassembled—first, by matching them to another intact version, and later, by reading the words themselves.

6. *Introducing a new book.* The teacher introduces a new book each lesson, and the child will practice reading it several times on the day it is introduced and on subsequent days. Though the Reading Recovery program does not mandate any particular set of books, lists of books graduated by difficulty level are circulated among teachers who are trained to use the program. One of the aims of the running record (see earlier) is to make sure that the child is reading with between 90 percent and 94 percent accuracy in word recognition (easier material won't teach the child new words; harder material will frustrate him).

7. *Practicing the new book.* Practicing may be done by means of echo reading (teacher reads a line—child follows) or choral reading (they read simultaneously). The teacher aims to get the child to read the text over and over again (Iversen and Tunmer, in press, pp. 15–16, after Clay, 1975).

Details on these strategies follow in the next two chapters. For now, let us note that these lessons (1) base instruction on careful assessment and teach children what they need to know; (2) give practice that develops letter recognition, the concept of word, phonemic segmentation, and other concepts about print; (3) offer the child extensive daily practice reading real text that is on the proper level; (4) include writing as well as reading in a literacy lesson.

Let us also note what they do *not* do. They do not explicitly teach letter-to-sound correspondences, but rather they leave it to the teacher and child to infer these correspondences indirectly. What would happen if they did?

Iversen and Tunmer asked a group of Reading Recovery teachers to add activities to teach letter-to-sound correspondences. Using the plastic letters already mentioned, the teachers asked the children to move around the letters to ". . . make, break, and build new words that had similar visual phonological elements." Here is an example of a lesson:

> The teacher made the word *and* with the magnetic letters and said, "This word says *and*. What does this word say?" The child responded "*and*." If the child was in any way unsure, the teacher provided a model using other magnetic letters. After the child made the word, the teacher asked, "What word have you made?" Following the child's response, the teacher jumbled the letters and

asked the child to make *and* again and then to say the word the child had made. This process was repeated until the child demonstrated that he or she could perform the task easily. The teacher then put *s* in front of *and*, drew the child's attention to what the teacher had done by running his or her finger underneath the word and said, "Look, if I put an *s* in front of *and*, it says *sand."* The teacher asked the child to say the new word. The teacher then removed the *s* and said, "If I take the *s* away it says *and*. You make *sand."* After the child made the word, the teacher asked, "What word have you made?" The teacher then asked the child to make *and*. This process was repeated with the words *hand* and *band*. The teacher then made *sand,* then *band,* then *hand,* and *and,* each time asking what the word was. The teacher then asked the child to make *and, hand, sand,* and *band*. At this point the teacher passed more of the control of the task over to the child by asking the child to use the letters to make the same words, each time telling the teacher the word the child had made. Throughout the task the teacher positively reinforced all correct responses with specific praise to provide reinforcement for the process in which the child was engaged as well as for the outcome. (Iversen and Tunmer, p. 17)

Iversen and Tunmer compared the performance of 32 children who received Reading Recovery teaching plus these explicit procedures to teach letter-to-sound correspondences to another group of 32 who received standard Reading Recovery teaching, and to still another group of 32 who received small group instruction in a Chapter I classroom. Children in the Chapter I classroom gained very little compared to the two other groups, which used one-on-one teaching. Both of the Reading Recovery groups were successful in moving the children up to the median reading ability range of their first-grade classes, and to sustain these gains at least through the end of the year. The group with the explicit instruction, however, reached the desired level of reading performance in two-thirds the time it took the regular Reading Recovery groups (in 42 lessons, on the average, instead of 57). This work should be tested further before these results are taken to be fully demonstrated. It is clear, though, that careful one-on-one intervention like Reading Recovery works, and the values of explicit word study in such programs are worth taking seriously.

SUMMARY

In this chapter, methods have been advanced to structure your observation of children's *emergent literacy*, a term that applies to preliminary reading and writing. The areas of emergent literacy stressed in the chapter were *oral language, storybook reading, the sense of story structures, print orientation concepts, letter recognition, the concept of word, phonemic segmentation,* and *sight word recognition.*

Oral language development can be measured by several means: The two tests by Marie Clay et al., *The Record of Oral Language* and *Biks and Gutches,* devices dedicated to the assessment of children's oral language fluency, were described in this chapter. We would suggest that teachers who are not adept at assessing children's language ability orient themselves to the task by using one or more of these devices. Once they know what they are looking for, they may be able to assess language ability informally while they are teaching: We suggested ways that the *Dictated Experience Story* might be used for this purpose.

The *assessment of children's storybook reading* can be done by having a child pretend-read a favorite storybook and categorize the results according to Elizabeth Sulzby's scheme.

A child's *sense of story structures* can be inferred in at least two ways. One method is the *directed listening-thinking activity,* in which children listen to a portion of a story and are asked to predict what might happen next. The predictions and comments can reveal whether a child has certain expectations about the structure of stories. Another method is to have children *retell stories* they have heard read aloud. Retellings can be analyzed to see if critical elements of stories were included in their proper order.

A child's ability to make the *speech-to-print match* in a memorized written sequence can be assessed by using the dictated experience story or some other easily memorized material. The *voice-pointing procedure* is used with either type of material to determine if children can match spoken and written words in a familiar portion of text and if a supported rereading activity helps them to recognize new words in print

A *phonemic segmentation task using invented spelling* was described for the purpose of investigating children's ability to divide words up into their smallest sound units, a necessary part of word knowledge related to the application of phonics.

Print orientation concepts can be assessed by using the *Concepts About Print Test* or by adapting this procedure in minor ways, such as varying the questions asked and the text used. The *Concepts About Print Test* represents a real reading experience with prereaders. It helps a teacher learn what a child knows about book orientation, directionality of print and pages, concepts of letters, words, spaces, and punctuation marks, and the communicative nature of print and pictures.

Big books, brought into popularity by New Zealander Don Holdaway, were suggested as an excellent aid for teaching print orientation concepts, since they enable children to read along with the teacher in a favorite story and notice features of the print as they do so.

The *acquisition of sight words* can be assessed informally by using a *sight word inventory* made up of words frequently occurring in beginning reading materials. Words are presented in isolation, but the presentation is untimed.

A similar inventory can be used to examine the *recognition of letters,* uppercase and lowercase.

The results of our traditional programs for remediating reading difficulties have been roundly criticized in recent years: Few have actually made normally successful readers of children with moderate to severe reading problems. New programs are being tried which bring to bear everything we know about emergent literacy on the lowest reading group of first-graders. One of them, the Reading Recovery program, focuses intensive one-on-one instruction on low readers until they are boosted to the middle of their classmates' performance range—where it is hoped they will stay. Programs such as this one show promise, especially when attention is given to developing children's word knowledge.

References

Allen, R. Van. *Language Experiences in Communication.* Boston: Houghton Mifflin, 1976.

Berko, Jean. "The Child's Learning of English Morphology." *Word* 14 (1958): 150–177.

Clay, Marie. *What Did I Write?* Portsmouth, NH: Heinemann Educational Books, 1975.

——*The Early Detection of Reading Difficulties, with Recovery Procedures,* 3d. ed. Portsmouth, NH: Heinemann Educational Books, 1986.

Clay, Marie, Malcolm Gill, Ted Glynn, Tony McNaughton, and Keith Salmon. *The Record of Oral Language and Biks and Gutches.* Portsmouth, NH: Heinemann Educational Books, 1983.

Cunningham, Patricia, and James Cunningham. "Making Words: Enhancing the Invented Spelling-Decoding Connection." *The Reading Teacher* 46 (1992): 106–115.

Dale, Phillip. *Language Development: Structure and Function,* 2d ed. New York: Holt, Rhinehart, and Winston, 1976.

Ehri, Linnea. "Research on Reading and Spelling." Paper presented at the George Graham Memorial Lectures. University of Virginia, Charlottesville, April 1989.

Elkind, David. *Child Development and Education.* New York: Oxford, 1976.

Elkonin, Daniel. "Reading in the USSR." In John Downing, ed. *Comparative Reading.* New York: Macmillan, 1973.

Goodman, Yetta. "Test Review: Concepts About Print Test." *The Reading Teacher* 34 (1981): 445–448.

Harste, Jerome, Virginia Woodward, and Carolyn Burke. *Language Stories and Literacy Lessons.* Portsmouth, NH: Heinemann Educational Books, 1984.

Holdaway, Don. *Foundations of Literacy.* Portsmouth, NH: Heinemann Educational Books, 1979.

Mann, Virginia, Paula Tobin, and Rebecca Wilson. "Measuring Phonological Awareness Through Invented Spelling." In *Children's Reading and the Development of Phonological Awareness,* ed. Keith Stanovich. Detroit: Wayne State University Press, 1988.

Martin, Bill, and Peggy Brogan. *Bill Martin's Instant Readers.* New York: Holt, Rhinehart, and Winston, 1971.

Mason, Jana, and Christine McCormick. *Little Books for Early Readers.* Charleston, IL: Pintsize Prints, 1985.

McCormick, Christine, and Jana Mason. "Use of Little Books at Home." In *Emergent Literacy,* ed. William Teale and Elizabeth Sulzby. Norwood, NJ: Ablex, 1986.

McCormick, Christine, and Jana Mason. "Fostering Reading for Head Start Children with Little Books." In *Risk Makers, Risk Takers, Risk Breakers,* ed. JoBeth Allen and Jana Mason. Portsmouth, NH: Heinemann Educational Books, 1989.

Morris, Darrell. "Concept of Word and Phoneme Awareness in the Beginning Reader." *Research in the Teaching of English* 17 (1981): 359–373.

Morris, Darrell. "The Relationship Between Children's Concept of Word in Text and Phonemic Awareness in Learning to Read: A Longitudinal Study." *Research in the Teaching of English* 27, 2, pp. 133–154, 1993.

Sim-Sim, Ines. "Reading Around the World: News from Portugal." *The Reading Teacher,* 1994. In press.

Slobin, Dan, and Charles Welsh. "Elicited Imitation as a Research Tool in Developmental Psycholinguistics." In *Language Training in Early Childhood Education,* ed. Celia Lavatelli. Urbana, IL: University of Illinois Press, 1971.

Stauffer, Russell. *The Language Experience Approach to the Teaching of Reading,* 2d ed. New York: Harper and Row, 1980.

Sulzby, Elizabeth. "Children's Emergent Reading of Favorite Storybooks: A Developmental Study." *Reading Research Quarterly* 20 (1985) 458–481.

Tough, Joan. *Focus on Meaning: Talking to Children to Some Purpose.* London: Unwin, 1973.

Vardell, Sylvia. "Reading Around the World: Zimbabwean and Texan Teachers Form a Partnership to Promote Literacy Through Original LIterature." *The Reading Teacher,* 1994. In press.

Walsh, Daniel, Gary Price, and Mark Gillingham. "The Critical but Transitory Importance of Letter Naming." *Reading Research Quarterly* 23 (1988): 108–122.

Yopp, Hallie Kay. "The Validity and Reliability of Phonemic Awareness Tests." *Reading Research Quarterly* 23 (1988): 159–177.

Informal Reading Assessment

I n this chapter and the one that follows, we discuss the assessment of student performance based on teacher judgment. According to Calfee and Hiebert (1991), there are basically two types or "tiers" of assessment: assessment designed for instruction, or "internal assessment," and assessment designed for external accountability, or "external assessment." Internal assessment includes teacher-made tests and procedures, observations, interviews, informal reading inventories, anecdotal records, and portfolio assessments. Such assessments are driven by teacher judgment. External assessment includes norm-referenced and criterion-referenced tests. Figure 4.1 contrasts the purposes, criteria and pragmatics of these two assessment models (from Calfee & Hiebert, 1991, p. 283). Chapters 4 and 5 deal with internal assessments; Chapter 9 deals with external assessments.

Assessment of student performance based on teacher judgment, or internal assessment, is growing. In the 1970s, public concern about accountability and educational outcomes spurred tremendous growth in the use of standardized tests to provide data for accountability and reduce subjective bias. Since then, however, several significant trends have occurred that have underscored the importance and practicality of classroom-based assessments. These trends include a growing emphasis on thoughtful, strategic literacy instead of the mastery of basic skills, the move toward the professionalization of teaching, and the growing agreement that thoughtful assessment requires a balance of information sources. Standardized testing is firmly entrenched in our schools and will probably be with us for a long time; but recent calls for the "redirection of assessment," such as that which appeared in the April 1989 issue of *Educational Leadership,* underscore the need for internally generated, classroom-based assessment devices and procedures.

In this chapter we discuss informal reading inventories, both commercial and teacher-made; informal word recognition inventories, which help teachers assess sight recognition and decoding skills; cloze and maze procedures, useful for matching readers with particular materials; and supplementary assessments of decoding skills and text readability.

LEVELS OF READING ABILITY

Parents, teachers, and students alike are concerned about reading levels, which are often linked to issues of retention, promotion, and graduation. Usually the statements and questions we hear about reading levels assume that a reader has one single reading level, but this is an oversimplification. Most readers who have progressed beyond beginning reading have three reading levels. Each level is appropriate for reading different kinds of texts and for different purposes.

Figure 4.1

Comparison of Assessment Instruments Designed for Different Purposes

Assessment Designed for Instruction	Assessment Designed For External Accountability
Purpose and Source	
Teacher-designed for classroom decisions	Designed by experts for policy makers
Combines several sources of information	Stand-alone, single index
Strong link to curriculum and instruction	Independent of curriculum and instruction
Criteria	
Valid for guiding instruction	Predictive validity
Profile reliability—strengths and weaknesses	Total test reliability
Sensitive to dynamic changes in performance	Stable over time and situations
Performance is often all-or-none	Normally distributed scores
Pragmatics	
Judgmental, quick turnaround, flexible	Objective, cost and time efficient, standardized
Performance-based, "real" task	Multiple-choice, recognition
Administer whenever needed	Once-a-year, sometimes twice

Source: Robert Calfee and Elfrieda Hiebert. "Classroom Assessment of Reading." *Handbook of Reading Research,* Vol. 2. White Plains, NY: Longman Publishers, 1991, p. 283.

The Independent Level

At this level of difficulty students can read text *easily*, without help. Comprehension of what is read is generally excellent, and silent reading at this level is rapid because almost all the words are recognized and understood at sight. Students have to stop rarely, if at all, to analyze a new word. Oral reading is generally fluent, and occasional divergences from the written text rarely interfere with comprehension.

The Instructional Level

At this level the material is not really easy but is still *comfortable*. Students are challenged and will benefit most from instruction. Comprehension is good, but help is needed to understand some concepts. The silent reading rate is fairly rapid, although usually slower than at the independent level. Some word analysis is necessary, but the majority of words are recognized at sight. Oral reading is fairly smooth and accurate, and oral divergences from the written text usually make sense in the context and do not cause a loss of meaning.

The Frustration Level

Here the material is *too difficult* in vocabulary or concepts to be read successfully. Comprehension is poor, with major ideas forgotten or misunderstood. Both oral and silent reading are usually slow and labored, with frequent stops to analyze unknown words. Oral reading divergences are frequent and often cause readers to lose the sense of what was read. Because of this difficulty, it is frustrating for students to attempt to read such material for sustained periods of time, and their efforts often fail. This level is to be avoided in instruction.

Figure 4.2 shows the characteristics of each level and some typical kinds of reading a student might do at each level.

The instructional level, where the student is comfortable yet challenged and will benefit most from instruction, is the level we usually mean when we refer to a student's reading level. The other two levels, however, are also very important. At the independent level we want students to read for pleasure, information, and enrichment. Reading assignments such as homework, tests, and seatwork should also be at the independent level so that they can complete it alone.

We want to be able to place a student at the instructional level with regard to materials for direct instruction, such as novels, basal readers, other textbooks, study guides, workbooks, skills activities, and worksheets that are read in class where the teacher can provide help and guidance. Therefore, it is necessary to determine what material represents the frustration level, even though trying to read these passages on an informal reading inventory is difficult for the student. Unless we explore the limits of the student's reading ability, we will not know how far he or she can go. The teacher has to see what strategies a student can use when pushed and what strategies continue to serve well. After the frustration level has been determined, a reader should never be assigned to read material that difficult.

Figure 4.2

Functional Reading Levels

	CHARACTERISTICS	TYPICAL READING

Independent Level:
  Easy
	Excellent comprehension
	Excellent accuracy in word
	  recognition
	Few words need analysis
	Rapid, smooth rate
	Very few errors of any kind
		All pleasure reading
		All self-selected reading
		  for information
		Homework, tests, seatwork,
		  learning centers, and all other
		  assigned work to be done alone

Instructional Level:
  Comfortable
	Good comprehension
	Good accuracy in word
	  recognition
	Fairly rapid rate
	Some word analysis needed
		School textbooks and basal
		  reader
		Guided classroom reading
		  assignments
		Study guides and other
		  work done with guidance
		Forms and applications

Frustration Level:
  Too hard
	Poor comprehension
	Slow, stumbling rate
	Much word analysis
	  necessary
		No assigned material
		Reading for diagnostic
		  purposes
		Self-selected material where
		  student's interest is very high
		  in spite of difficulty

The Listening Level

Although it is not an actual reading level, there is one more level that is important because it relates to a student's reading abilities: the listening level. This is the highest grade level of text material that a student can understand when he or she listens to it read aloud. The listening level provides an estimate of the student's present potential for reading improvement.

Most readers who have not yet reached their full potential as readers, who are still developing their reading skills, can listen to and understand text read aloud to them that they cannot yet read for themselves. This is most obvious with beginning readers, who can understand many books and kinds of text by listening to them, but may not yet be able to read independently. As students are exposed to text by being read to and their ability to read grows, the gap between what they can understand by listening and what they can read independently begins to close. By the time they become fluent, mature readers, there may be no difference at all; that is, they can understand material as well by reading it as by listening to it. But for students have not yet completed their development as readers, the listening level is usually higher than the instructional reading level. The listening level gives us an indication of how much their reading may be expected to advance at this point in time. We will examine the listening level more fully later in this chapter.

THE USEFULNESS OF READING LEVELS

In the past when almost everyone used basal readers or similar language arts materials of graded difficulty for reading instruction, the usefulness of reading levels was obvious. If Tommy's instructional level was late first grade, or Level 5 in his basal reader, then teachers knew that Tommy would be most appropriately placed in the Level 5 book or in materials of similar, but not greater, difficulty. If Tommy had completed all the stories in his Level 5 book, but could not read the next level book comfortably, he could be placed in a "supplemental basal" or other alternative materials until his instructional level advanced. The most common use of a student's instructional level was to place him or her in an appropriate basal reader.

Today far fewer teachers use basal readers for reading instruction. While many still do, many others use them only occasionally, picking and choosing the selections they want children to read, often omitting the accompanying skills material entirely. Many others use trade books and novels entirely, while the basal and workbooks gather dust on bookroom shelves. Do these teachers still need to know about students' reading levels?

We believe there is still usefulness in the concept of reading levels, even for those teachers who haven't touched a basal reader in years. Not everyone will agree; but you probably already know that in all of education, there is almost nothing that everyone agrees on! Trade books are still subjected to readability studies, and approximate reading levels are usually indicated somewhere on the back cover. Textbooks and classroom materials in subject areas like social studies, science, and health are still "grade-leveled" and reading levels assigned to them. Parents still want to know if their children are able to read as well as typical children in the same grade. When students receive special help in reading from Chapter One or other programs, their reading levels are among the first information required to document their progress.

It is certainly true that children functioning at a particular instructional reading level differ widely in the materials that they can and do successfully read. The importance of a reader's interest in particular materials or topics cannot be overemphasized; we all know of many examples of students successfully and enjoyably reading materials thought to be "too hard" for them just because they are fascinated by the topic. But while Jennifer may choose to read Beverly Cleary novels because all her friends love them, and so plow through one after another, we cannot count on her motivation to expand to other novels of the same level of difficulty. Likewise, Antoine may read anything he can get his hands on about hunting, his particular passion, but be stumped by materials of similar difficulty on other topics.

Students will often self-select very difficult materials because of interest in the topic or author, but may not be able to deal with assigned materials just as difficult. We should not discourage them from self-selecting "hard" books, but we need to know what they can read effectively for the many assigned materials we use. In most classrooms, much of what children read is still teacher-selected. Reading and reading instruction are not limited to the language arts block, but extended throughout the school day and across many topics and genres.

In the selections that follow we will describe a variety of materials and procedures that will help all teachers become more sensitive users of materials that are appropriate for all learners.

THE INFORMAL READING INVENTORY

An informal reading inventory (IRI) consists of text passages corresponding in difficulty to basal and textbook materials at grade levels from primer through secondary school, and sets of questions for each passage intended to test readers' comprehension and recall after reading. Passages and their questions are arranged in order of difficulty from easiest (primer and primary grades) to hardest (usually ninth grade or beyond). IRIs usually also contain either a word recognition inventory or lists of individual words arranged in levels like those of the reading passages. In addition, many commercial IRIs have supplementary tests such as phonics inventories, cloze tests, and spelling inventories.

Figures 4.3 and 4.4 show a student page and corresponding examiner's pages from a commercial IRI.

Many basal reading and language arts series provide an IRI to be used for placement within that series and for diagnostic use. There are also a number of commercial IRIs, most of them essentially similar, and a list of those follows at the end of the next section, "Selecting a Commercial IRI." Teachers can also make up IRIs, and instructions for doing so are included in the section, "Constructing an IRI" at the end of this chapter.

Teacher-made IRI passages are selected from basal readers or other school texts, while commercial IRIs have passages that are selected from

Figure 4.3

Commercial IRI Pupil Page

A DAY AT THE BEACH

The day was warm and sunny. Tanya and Melissa packed a lunch. They brought ham sandwiches, chips, and pickles. They brought lemonade to drink. They rode their bikes down the dirt road. Along the way they saw little animals run to get out of their way. Tanya and Melissa had found this beach two years before. They loved it because few people knew about it. Also, it was protected from the wind. Other beaches were so windy that people got windburn.

When they got to the beach they built sandcastles and lay in the sun. They swam as far out as they dared. They were careful to avoid the strong current which might carry them away. After their swim they had lunch. It tasted good, as food always does when eaten outdoors. The girls lay down on their blanket to rest. An hour later they awoke to red backs. Their skin hurt to touch. The girls packed up what they had brought and headed for home. On the way home Tanya rode over a rock. It put a hole in her front tire. For the last three miles, the girls walked. They were very tired and sore when they got to their homes.

Source: Lauren Leslie and Joanne Caldwell, *Qualitative Reading Inventory.* NY: HarperCollins, 1990, p. 119.

many types of trade books or that are specially written for the test. Usually they are only 50 to 250 words long, and they can be read comfortably in a few minutes. An IRI consists of a student's booklet of the reading passages and an examiner's copy of the instrument. The examiner's copy contains the reading passages and the corresponding comprehension questions with their correct answers. The example in Figure 4.4 also includes a score sheet for unaided retellings.

So that an examiner can assess oral and silent reading separately, a good IRI should have two or more different passages at each grade level. The passages should be from different stories but comparable in difficulty. To be most useful in testing children of various abilities and ages, the grade levels represented should range from preprimer or primer through at least sixth-grade text, preferably through ninth- or even twelfth-grade material.

Commercial IRIs have both advantages and disadvantages. They offer the teacher a complete set of word lists, passages, and questions already compiled and ready to reproduce and use. They feature multiple forms at each grade level, which allow the teacher to assess oral and silent reading or to retest later with new material. They are inexpensive and widely available.

Figure 4.4

Commercial IRI Examiner's Pages

LEVEL: TWO

Nongoal-Based Narrative
Concepts

beach _____(3-2-1-0)
protection _____(3-2-1-0)
current _____(3-2-1-0)
Free Association Score: _____ /9 = _____%
_____ FAM _____ UNFAM

Number of Total Miscues
  (Total Accuracy): _____
Number of Meaning Change Miscues
  (Total Acceptability): _____

TOTAL ACCURACY		TOTAL ACCEPTABILITY
0–5 miscues ___	Independent___	0–5 miscues
6–21 miscues ___	Instructional___	6–11 miscues
22+ miscues ___	Frustration ___	12+ miscues

Rate: 203 x 60 / ____seconds = ___ WPM

A Day at the Beach

The day was warm and sunny. Tanya and Melissa <u>packed</u> a lunch. They brought ham sandwiches, chips, and pickles. They brought lemonade to drink. They rode their bikes down the dirt road. Along the way they saw little animals run to get out of their way. Tanya and Melissa had found this <u>beach</u> two years before. They loved it because few people knew about it. Also, it was protected from the wind. Other beaches were so windy that people got windburn.

When they got to the <u>beach</u> they <u>built</u> sandcastles and lay in the sun. They swam as far out as they dared. They were careful to avoid the strong current which might carry them away. After their swim they had lunch. It tasted good, as food always does when eaten outdoors. The girls lay down on their blanket to rest. An hour later they awoke to red backs. Their skin hurt to touch. The girls <u>packed</u> up what they had brought and headed for home. On the way home Tanya rode over a rock. It put a hole in her front tire. For the last three miles, the girls walked. They were very tired and sore when they got to their homes. (203 words)

Retelling Scoring Sheet for A Day at the Beach
Setting/Background
_____ Tanya
_____ and Melissa packed a lunch.
_____ They brought sandwiches.
_____ They rode their bikes.

Events
_____ They saw animals.
_____ They loved the beach
_____ because few knew about it.
_____ When they got
_____ to the beach
_____ they built sandcastles
_____ and lay in the sun.
_____ They swam
_____ as far as they dared.
_____ After their swim
_____ they had lunch.
_____ They lay down
_____ on blankets.
_____ An hour later
_____ they woke
_____ to red backs.
_____ Their skin hurt.
_____ They headed for home.
_____ On the way
_____ home
_____ Tanya rode

Figure 4.4 continued

_____ over a rock.
_____ It put a hole
_____ in her tire
_____ front tire.
_____ The girls walked
_____ for miles
_____ three miles.
_____ They were very tired
_____ and sore
_____ when they got home.

Other ideas recalled including inferences
_____

Questions for A Day at the Beach

1. Name two things the girls brought to eat on their trip.
   Explicit: ham sandwiches, chips, pickles, lemonade (any two)

2. How did the girls get to the beach?
   Explicit: on their bikes

3. How did they know the way?
   Implicit: they'd found the beach two years before; they'd been going there for two years

4. Why did they go to this beach?
   Implicit: Because few people went there; or it was protected from the wind. If the student says, "They'd been there before," ask, "Why did they go again?"

5. Why were the girls careful to avoid the current?
   Explicit: so they wouldn't get carried away

6. Why did their skin hurt after their rest?
   Implicit: they got sunburned

7. Why did the girls have to walk home?
   Implicit: because Tanya's bike got a flat tire

8. Why were the girls tired when they got home?
   Explicit: they had to walk the last three miles

Number Correct *Explicit* _____
Number Correct *Implicit* _____
                              Total _____
_____ Independent: 8 correct
_____ Instructional: 6–7 correct
_____ Questionable: 4–5 correct
_____ Frustration: 0–3 correct

Source: Lauren, Leslie, and Joanne Caldwell. *Qualitative Reading Inventory.* New York: HarperCollins, 1990, pp. 126–127.

They do have shortcomings, however. IRIs that accompany a basal reading series are made up of passages from that series, and the students being tested may have previously read one or more of the stories from which the passages came. Therefore, their comprehension scores on those passages may be falsely inflated. Other commercial IRIs have passages that are specially written to conform to readability levels or passages selected from sources other than basal readers, but the quality of such passages varies widely. Also, some tests use short passages, which severely limit the number of ideas available to the reader and the number of questions that can be asked.

In addition to these disadvantages there are several others: Particularly at the lower levels, some passages are written in short stilted sentences that don't sound much like real language. Some carry on the same story from passage to passage, making it difficult to omit the lower levels or move to higher to a lower level during administration. Some are taken from the middle of a story, but no introduction is provided to help the reader understand what content preceded the passage. Some have fairly interesting passages, but they use factual recall questions almost exclusively while ignoring other aspects of comprehension.

For these reasons, students in reading diagnosis and assessment courses sometimes are taught to make up and evaluate their own IRIs. This is an extremely helpful practice, but making up an IRI is a challenging and time-consuming task. When teachers opt to buy a commercial IRI, they must use judgment and care in evaluating these instruments. The following section will help you consider the most important aspects of commercial IRIs.

Selecting a Commercial IRI

To chose the best IRI for your use, you must examine and compare several, then select the one you believe has the most strengths and will serve your diagnostic needs best.

We believe that the following aspects are of critical importance in choosing an IRI:

1. literary quality of reading passages;
2. clarity and relevance of questions;
3. balance of question types, including a range of comprehension skills and both explicit and implicit questions;
4. convenient format;
5. complete instructions, including examples;
6. balanced use of both narrative and expository texts, ideally featuring use of both types at each level; and
7. some means of assessing readers' prior knowledge of topics before passages are read for assessment.

Literary Quality of Passages

The heart of an IRI is the reading passages. When you consider an IRI, *read the passages*. Are they generally interesting, with topics that many children will likely know something about and be interested in? We cannot expect good comprehension of dull text.

Does the language sound natural? When there is dialogue, do the speakers sound like real people? Are descriptive passages colorful and memorable? At the upper levels and in nonfiction passages, is the language clear and straightforward? Are sequences and cause-effect relationships presented clearly? Are the words and ideas in the passages appropriate for the grade levels and ages for which they are intended? In the primary levels, is there some story or sequence of events present? If there are illustrations, are they necessary to an understanding of the passages? Keep in mind that all information should be presented in the text, not in the illustrations.

You may not expect brilliant prose in an IRI, but do look for one that has consistently interesting, clearly written, straightforward passages with natural-sounding dialogue, colorful descriptions, and topics that a wide range of students can recognize and understand. Look for passages that are complete in themselves; that is, they do not sound like paragraphs taken from the middle of a story, with preceding material omitted. This is an important consideration in IRIs that accompany basal readers, since the reading passages have been taken from basal stories, and they may be only part of a longer story.

Quality of Questions

Most often, the questions we ask are the primary means we have of assessing comprehension. (Retelling, or spontaneously recalling what was read, is another useful means that will be described later.) If the IRI questions we use are confusing, picky, or limited in the thinking skills they require, we will not get an accurate picture of the reader's comprehension. To get good answers, we must ask good questions.

Good questions should be clear and simple, should follow the organization of the passage, should tap the most important information conveyed, should call on a variety of comprehension skills, and should be answerable only after reading, not by general knowledge, prior experience, or illustrations. They should require elaborated responses, should call on both convergent and divergent thinking, and should not be answerable by yes or no without explanation or elaboration. They should not be repetitious. Vocabulary questions should feature passage-based contexts for the words; for example, "In the sentence 'Jim put the package on the bar,' what did *bar* mean?" is a better question than "What does *bar* mean in this story?" or "What is a *bar*?" We will say more about the accuracy and content of IRI questions in the section entitled "Comprehension Skill Patterns" later in this chapter.

Format and Instructions

In order for you to assess oral and silent reading comprehension separately, the IRI you use should have two different passages of equivalent length and difficulty for each level. Most commercial IRIs have three equivalent forms, allowing you to use a third passage for retesting or for assessing listening comprehension. The instrument's format should make it easy for you to locate and to use the appropriate passages and questions during the testing

Are the different forms and grade levels clearly labeled and easy to locate? Are pupil pages coded in some way so that the grade level of the passage is not apparent to the student? Is a record or summary sheet provided to help you summarize your observations, findings, and conclusions?

Are the directions for administering the IRI clear and concise? Are there directions for interpreting findings? Are there examples of students' responses for you to study and practice interpreting?

Types of Text and Prior Knowledge

Many commercial IRIs are made up entirely of fiction passages. However, students must read both fiction and nonfiction, or narrative and expository, texts effectively. A good IRI will have a balance of both narrative and expository material at each level. This allows us to systematically assess a student's reading of both these types of texts. It is not sufficient for an IRI to include both types of text, but have only fiction selections at some levels while including nonfiction at other levels.

Likewise, some means of assessing whether a reader has sufficient prior knowledge of a topic to read a passage with adequate comprehension is a very useful feature. Leslie and Caldwell's *Qualitative Reading Inventory* is an example of commercial IRI that includes this feature for every passage. Before a student reads a passage, the examiner asks him or her to tell something about two or three key terms or concepts from the passage and notes on the examiner's page whether the student knows a lot, some, a little, or nothing about the term or concept. The passage is then rated as familiar or unfamiliar before it is read, and if unfamiliar, a different passage is substituted. For example, in Figures 4.3 and 4.4, "A Day at the Beach," the student is asked to tell what *beach, protection,* and *current* mean in the context of a trip to the beach. Responses are noted in the box labeled "concepts" at the top of Figure 4.4. This quick assessment of prior knowledge before reading a passage saves time and effort, and prevents us from attempting to assess readers' comprehension of passages they know little or nothing about before they start.

If your basal reading series includes an IRI, you should examine it critically before you use it, just as you would if you were choosing a commercial IRI. Basal series IRIs have an important advantage in that they closely match the kind of text students read every day. This is because the IRI passages are usually taken directly from the reading books. However, this can have a negative effect, too; if the student being tested has previously read the material in class, her or his comprehension may be falsely inflated. The ideal basal IRI would feature test passages very similar to the text material in difficulty, quality of writing, and topical interest, but not taken directly from the basal readers.

Other factors, if present, may limit a basal IRI's usefulness. Story passages should be long enough to be fairly complete in themselves (not always the case when a portion of the text is lifted from a longer story or account). Questions should be asked by the examiner and answers recorded; students should not be given questions to read and answers to mark or write. As with all IRIs, questions should relate directly to the reading passage, not to illustrations or the information contained in the longer book passage.

All of these features will make it easier for you to use an IRI correctly and effectively.

Commercial IRIs include the following:

Bader, Lois A. *Bader Reading and Language Inventory.* New York: Macmillan, 1983.

Burns, Paul C., and Betty D. Roe. *Informal Reading Inventory,* 3d ed. Boston, MA: Houghton Mifflin, 1989.

Johns, Jerry L. *Basic Reading Inventory,* 4th ed. Dubuque, IA: Kendall/Hunt, 1988.

Johns, Jerry L. *Secondary and College Reading Inventory.* Dubuque, IA: Kendall/Hunt, 1988.

Leslie, Lauren, and Joanne Caldwell. *Qualitative Reading Inventory.* New York: HarperCollins, 1990.

Newcomer, Phyllis L. *Standardized Reading Inventory.* Austin, TX: PRO-ED, 1986.

Silvaroli, Nicholas J. *Classroom Reading Inventory,* 6th ed. Dubuque, IA: Wm. C. Brown, 1989.

Wiederholt, J. Lee. *Formal Reading Inventory.* Austin, TX: PRO-ED, 1986.

Woods, Mary Lynn, and Alden J. Moe. *Analytical Reading Inventory,* 4th ed. Columbus, OH: Merrill, 1989.

The following are computer-based:

Blanchard, Jay. *Computer-Based Reading Assessment Instrument* (grades K–8). Dubuque, IA: Kendall/Hunt, 1985.

Johns, Jerry L. *Computer-Based Secondary and College Reading Inventory* (grades 7–college). Dubuque, IA: Kendall/Hunt, 1990.

Box 4.1 shows a comparison of characteristics of four commercial IRIs.

The following sources will give you more detail about informal reading inventories and additional information and guidance in evaluating commercial IRIs:

Arno, Kevin S. "Test Review: Burns/Roe Informal Reading Inventory." *Journal of Reading* 33, no. 6 (March 1990): 470–471.

Bader, Lois A., and Katherine D. Weisendanger. "Realizing the Potential of Informal Reading Inventories." *Journal of Reading* 32, no. 5 (Feb. 1989): 402–408.

Cardarelli, Aldo F. "The Influence of Reinspection on Students' IRI Results." *Reading Teacher* 41, no. 7 (March 1988): 664–667.

Demos, E. S. "Evaluation/Testing Procedures in Reading." *Reading Horizons* 27, no. 4 (Summer 1987): 254–260.

Duffelmeyer, Frederick A., "Vocabulary Questions on Informal Reading Inventories." *Reading Teacher* 43, no. 2 (Nov. 1989): 142–148.

Duffelmeyer, Frederick A., and Barbara Blakely Duffelmeyer. "Main Idea Questions on Informal Reading Inventories." *Reading Teacher* 41, no. 2 (Nov. 1987): 162–166.

Duffelmeyer, Frederick A., and Barbara Blakely Duffelmeyer. "Are IRI Passages Suitable for Main Idea Comprehension?" *Reading Teacher* 42, no. 6 (Feb. 1989): 358–363.

Gillis, M. K., and Mary W. Olson. "Elementary IRIs: Do They Reflect What We Know About Test Type/Structure and Comprehension?" *Reading Research and Instruction* 27, no. 1 (Fall 1987): 36–44.

Harris, Larry A., and Rosary M. Lalik. "Teachers' Use of Informal Reading Inventories: An Example of School Constraints." *Reading Teacher* 40, no. 7 (March 1987): 624–630.

Helgren-Lempesis, Valerie A., and Charles T. Mangrum II. "An Analysis of Alternate-Form Reliability of Three Commercially-Prepared Informal Reading Inventories." *Reading Research Quarterly* 21, no. 2 (Spring 1986): 209–215.

Johnson, Marjorie Seddon, Roy A. Kress, and John J. Pikulski. *Informal Reading Inventories.* Newark, DE: International Reading Association, 1987.

Kinney, Martha A., and Ann L. Harry. "An Informal Inventory for Adolescents That Assess the Reader, the Text and the Task." *Journal of Reading* 34, no. 8 (May 1991): 643–647.

Martin-Rehrmann, James. "Test Review: Analytic Reading Inventory (ARI), Fourth Edition." *Journal of Reading* 33, no. 7 (April 1990): 564–565.

Michel, Pamela A. "Test Review: Secondary College Reading Inventory." *Journal of Reading* 33, no. 4 (Jan. 1990): 308–310.

Olson, Mary W., and M. K. Gillis. "Text Type and Text Structure: An Analysis of Three Secondary Informal Reading Inventories." *Reading Horizons* 28, no. 1 (Fall 1987): 70–80.

Pikulski, John J. "Informal Reading Inventories." *The Reading Teacher* 43, no. 7 (March 1990): 514–516.

Robinson, Richard. "An Interview with Dr. Jerry L. Johns." (Leaders in Reading Research and Instruction) *Reading Psychology* 11, no. 4 (1990): 335–346.

Box 4.1

Comparison of Features of Four Commercial IRIs

Inventory	Grade levels	Forms of inventory	Length of passages	Sources of passages	Use of pictures	
Analytic Reading Inventory (ARI)	Primer to 9th, 1st–9th for science and social studies	3 equivalent narrative forms; 1 social studies and 1 science form	varies: 50–352	Written for inventory. Some science and social studies passages from textbooks	No	
Basic Reading Inventory (BRI)	Preprimer to 8th	3 Forms: A for oral, B for silent, C as needed	50 words at preprimer; 100 words primer to 8th grade	Revised from earlier editions; original source not stated	No	
Classroom Reading Inventory (CRI)	Preprimer to 8th	4 forms in all: A & B for students in grades 1–6; C for junior-high students; D for high school and adults	Varies; 24 words to 157 words	Written for inventory based on readability	Yes	
Informal Reading Inventory by Burns & Roe (IRI-BR)	Preprimer to 12th	4 forms; all interchangeable	Varies; 60 words to 220 words	Primarily from graded materials in basal readers & literature books	No	

Source: John J. Pikulski, "Informal Reading Inventories." *The Reading Teacher* 43, no. 7 (March 1990): 515.

	Use of purpose setting questions	Number of comprehension questions per passage	Types of comprehension questions	Criteria for instructional level	Time needed for administration
	Discourages discussion before reading, but allows examiner discretion	6 for levels primer–2nd; 8 for levels 3rd–9th	main idea, factual terminology, cause and effect, inferential, conclusion	95% for word recognition; 75% comprehension	not stated
	Uses prediction from titles	10 for all levels	main idea, fact inference, evaluation, vocabulary	95% for word recognition (only "significant" miscues counted); 75% comprehension	not stated
	Yes	5 for all levels	factual, inferential, vocabulary	95% for word recognition; 75% comprehension	12 minutes
	Yes	8 for all levels	main idea, detail, inference, sequence, cause/effect, vocabulary	85% word recognition for grades 1 & 2; 95% word recognition for grades 3 & above; 75% comprehension	40–50 minutes

Teale, William H. "Developmentally Appropriate Assessment of Reading and Writing in the Early Childhood Classroom." *Elementary School Journal* 89, no. 2 (Nov. 1988): 173–183.

Wood, Nancy V. "Reading Tests and Reading Assessment." *Journal of Developmental Education* 13, no. 2 (Winter 1989): 14–16.

Administering an IRI

Giving an IRI takes about 30 to 50 minutes, depending on the student's reading ability. It does not all have to be done in one sitting. Often teachers giving an IRI in class during regular instruction time break up the testing into a number of short sittings, with the student reading one or two passages at a time and finishing the IRI over a period of several days. This allows you to give an individual test without taking too much time away from other students or activities. You will need a student copy of the passages or the appropriate books, an examiner's copy for recording, and pencils.

It is not necessary to begin with the lowest level passages. If you are testing to see whether a particular book or other material would be comfortable reading, begin there. If the student is successful, you may proceed to higher levels or stop. If he or she is unsuccessful, you should drop down to an easier level.

If your diagnostic purpose is more general, begin two or three grade levels below the student's present grade. For primary graders, begin at primer or first grade. If the student is not reading easily and experiencing immediate success at that level, drop back. If the first passage seems easy, go on to higher levels.

Steps to Follow

These detailed steps will make IRI administration most effective.

1. Start where you think the student will be able to read easily. (If you overestimated, you can drop back to lower levels.) Some authorities advocate giving the word recognition inventory (WRI) first in order to find out where to begin the IRI. This practice is discussed in "The Word Recognition Inventory."

2. Assess the student's prior knowledge of the passage topic by asking the student to tell you something about the topic or explain two or three key terms or concepts. If the student knows little or nothing about the topic of the passage, use a different passage for assessment.

3. Give the oral reading passage at that level first. Show the student where to begin reading and where to stop and say, "Please read this passage

out loud to me. When you are finished, close the book and I will ask you some questions about what you have read."

4. Follow the reading on your copy and carefully mark down the responses that diverge from the text. These divergent responses, which happen naturally when we read aloud, have been termed *miscues.* These miscues will be analyzed later in order to provide detailed information about the reader's use of phonic and structural analysis, syntax, and word meanings during oral reading. The marks used for oral reading miscues are listed and discussed in "Marking Oral Reading Miscues."

5. When oral reading is completed and passage is removed, ask the comprehension questions. Jot down key words or phrases from the student's answers. Don't hesitate to probe for more information or ask a student to explain or justify an answer.

6. Give the silent reading passage for that level. Show the student where to begin and stop reading. Tell him or her to read silently and close the book (or turn over the card) when finished. Then ask questions after the reading is completed.

7. If the student answered 50 percent or more of the comprehension questions correctly, proceed to the next level. (The scores may rise again at the next level.) If oral comprehension scores are low but silent comprehension is still above 50 percent, discontinue the oral reading but continue silent reading at higher levels until these scores also drop below 50 percent and remain there. If the student shows poor silent comprehension but oral comprehension scores are still above 50 percent, continue oral reading.

Reinspection and Retelling
Most often, readers' comprehension of IRI passages is assessed by asking comprehension questions and by expecting unaided recall (that is, answering without looking back to the passage). There are several problems inherent in this approach:

1. When *reinspection* (looking back to the passage) is not allowed, both recall and comprehension are being tested. Readers may comprehend but fail to recall information, resulting in our underestimating their comprehension (Baker and Stein, 1981).

2. Readers may fail to include information in a response because, to the reader, it appeared obvious, redundant, or secondary to other information. Reinspection tends to encourage more complete answers.

3. Recall without reinspection is more a test-taking skill than an everyday reading strategy. In classroom reading, students usually discuss material and answer questions with the material before them rather than with books closed.

It seems clear that when we do not allow readers to reinspect, or look back to, the IRI passage when they answer questions, we place a heavy burden on the process of recall and short-term memory (Rubenstein et al., 1988). According to Cardarelli (1988), "In the conventional administration of the IRI, comprehension diagnosis is inordinately influenced by the reader's ability to recall information" (p. 666). Thus, we must face the question of whether we are testing reading comprehension, which surely involves memory but involves other factors as well, or whether we are instead testing the reader's short-term memory. Our original purpose in using an informal reading inventory was to attempt to provide a setting for the assessment in which the reading was as natural as possible; real text read for real purposes. Rubenstein et al. make the point that "this method of testing runs counter to the way people ordinarily read" (1988, p. 4). In everyday reading, when we do not understand something we can look back at the text; even in ordinary classroom reading, students are most often asked questions with the text available to them.

Several studies have concluded that reinspection significantly affects students' ability to answer comprehension questions on IRIs. This particularly seems to affect poorer readers, and to help all readers effectively deal with inferential questions (Cardarelli, 1988; Kender and Rubenstein, 1977; Rubenstein et al., 1988). We agree with these and other writers who have urged that IRI procedures be changed to allow students to reinspect passages if they need to when answering inferential and higher-level comprehension questions.

The issue of whether or not to allow reinspection is an important one, and you can incorporate reinspection fairly easily into standard IRI administration. To do so, you should direct the reader to look back to the passage and locate some specific information after the retelling and questioning. Again, some commercial IRIs have so-called "reinspection items" included in the comprehension questions, but many do not. It is a simple procedure to direct the reader to "Look back and find the place where it says that . . ." or the like, noting which item is being used for reinspection, and take note of whether the reader is able to scan for the desired information or must begin reading all over again, and whether the information can be located successfully. One reinspection item per reading passage is probably enough.

Another issue involves the use of questions alone, rather than allowing students to retell, or to describe in their own words, what they remember from passages. By the very act of asking questions, we shape students' comprehension, cuing them to what we feel is important for them to remember and include in their answers. Because of this, an effective way to learn more about students' comprehension is to ask them to retell what they have read, and either record what each student tells you or use a checklist of all of the information in a passage, allowing the student to use his or her own words in recalling these items.

Some commercial IRIs have incorporated retellings into their comprehension assessment. Figure 4.4 shows an examiner's page from an inventory that does. You will see that both a checklist for retelling and a set of questions is included for each passage. Students are asked to "retell the story" without promoting or probes, before questions are asked. Retellings are not scored quantitatively.

Synonyms and paraphrases are acceptable, as readers are not expected to recall verbatim. The examiner decides if the retelling matches the information in the story. Information recalled may be checked off on the list, or items may be numbered in the order in which the reader recalled them. The latter method helps the examiner determine if the reader recalled information in roughly the same order as it occurred in the passage, or if the retelling was not sequentially ordered. Information included in a retelling that was not in the passage may be noted as well.

Retellings may be informally evaluated for completeness, accuracy, and inclusion of the most important information or ideas in the passage. These judgments contribute to our diagnosis and implications for instruction, although they are not included in determining overall reading levels.

Marking Oral Reading Miscues

While the student is reading the appropriate passages aloud, you must mark all of the *oral divergences from the text*, or *miscues*, on your copy of the passage. Miscues are counted to determine the reader's degree of oral reading accuracy and analyzed to determine what strategies the reader used to figure out unknown words during the oral reading. Miscues include substitutions of real or nonsense words, insertions of extra words, omissions of whole words or phrases, corrections made by the reader either at the time the miscue occurred or later during the reading, words "given" by the examiner, and word order reversals. Pauses much longer than normal and repetitions of words or phrases may also be marked but are not counted as word recognition errors when accuracy is scored.

Box 4.2 contains a simple coding system that will allow you to record all miscues accurately. Figure 4.5 shows a sample passage with miscues marked.

Assessing Listening Comprehension

When the student reaches a level of 50 percent or lower comprehension, functional reading has broken down. One very important aspect remains to be tested, however: the student's listening comprehension. The listening level, the highest level of text a reader can comprehend when listening to another read aloud, provides a rough estimate of one's potential for reading improvement. It is of great help in forming reasonable expectations for growth in reading and is quite easy to determine.

When reading comprehension scores indicate that the reader has become frustrated (scores 50 percent or less), read either of the next level passages aloud to the student and then ask the comprehension questions. Before you read, say: "You've worked hard and the last story was difficult. This time I

Box 4.2

A System for Marking Oral Reading Miscues

1. *Substitution of a word or phrase:* the student's word written over a word in text

   The *dog* doll fell from the shelf.

2. *Insertion of a word not in text:* a word written in over a caret or small arrow

   The doll fell *down* from the shelf.

3. *Omission of a word or phrase:* the omitted element circled

   The (big) dog ran away.

4. *A word given by the examiner:* parentheses placed around that word

   The climbers were assisted by (Sherpa) tribesmen.

5. *Miscue spontaneously corrected by the reader:* check mark next to original coding

   The big dog *doll* ✓ ran away.

6. *Reversal of order of words:* proofreader's symbol of inversion used

   "Let's go," (shouted Sally)

7. *Repetition of word or phrase:* wavy line under repeated element

   The climbers were assisted.

8. *Pauses longer than normal:* slashes for pauses, one per second

   The // controversial theory. . .

---

want you to listen carefully while I read the story. Afterward I'll ask you questions as I did before." Read normally rather than too slowly or with exaggerated expression. If the student gets more than 50 percent of the questions correct, read a passage from the next level. Proceed until you reach a level where the student gets 50 percent or fewer of the questions correct, then stop.

To summarize, the steps in administering an IRI are shown in Box 4.3.

Scoring an IRI

Scoring procedures for an IRI are often quite simple. Accuracy in oral reading and comprehension is scored by percentages, which help the teacher determine the student's independent, instructional, and frustration levels.

Because IRIs are often used to determine a student's independent and instructional levels, the criteria for setting these levels are very important. IRIs have been widely used since the 1940s, when Betts (1941, 1957) and others popularized their use and the criteria for setting levels were derived largely from clinical experience. For many years, the minimum instructional level criteria attributed to Betts (95 percent oral reading accuracy and 75 percent comprehension) were widely accepted.

Figure 4.5

Sample IRI Passage with Miscues Marked

A DAY AT THE BEACH

The day was warm and sunny. Tanya and Melissa packed ⓐ lunch. *lunches* They

brought ham sandwiches, *potato* chips and pickles. They brought lemonade to drink.

They rode their bikes down the dirt road. Along the way they saw *a* little ani-

mal(s) run to get out of their way. Tanya and Melissa had found this beach two

years before. They loved it because *five* few people knew about it. Also, it was

protected from the wind. Other beaches were so windy that *they ✓* people got wind-

burn.

When they saw the beach they built / sandcastles and lay in the sun. They

saw swam as far out as they dared. They were careful to avoid the strong current

which might carry them away. After their swim they had lunch. It tasted *so*

good, as food always does when eaten outdoors. The girls lay down on their

blankets blanket to rest. An hour later they awoke to red *the banks* backs. Their skin hurt to

touch. The girls packed up what they had brought and headed home. On the

way *home* Tanya rode over a rock. It put a hole in (her) front (of) tire. For the last three

miles, the girls walked. They were very tired and sore *sorry* when they got to their

homes.

Source: Lauren, Leslie, and Joanne Caldwell. *Qualitative Reading Inventory.* New York: HarperCollins, 1990, p. 126.

Box 4.3

Steps in Administering an Informal Reading Inventory

1. Begin the assessment one or two grade levels below the student's present grade or basal level or at a level you think will be easy for the student. Remember, you can move back as well as forward in the IRI if the reading is still too difficult. Assess the reader's prior knowledge of each topic before reading.

2. Administer the first oral reading passage. Code the miscues during the oral reading. You may taperecord the oral reading for greater accuracy if it does not distract or annoy the reader. Record the retelling. Ask the comprehension questions and record the gist of the answers.

3. Administer the silent reading passage at the same level. Ask the comprehension questions and record the gist of the answers.

4. If the student was not reading comfortably and successfully at this level, move back to a lower level and administer the oral and silent reading passages as before. Then continue to move forward in the IRI, skipping the level you already administered when you come to it.

5. If the student was reading comfortably at the level on which you began testing, continue to move forward in the IRI, giving oral and silent passages as above, until the comprehension scores drop to 50 percent or less.

6. When you have located the frustration level, read one of the next level passages aloud to the student and ask the comprehension questions as before. Continue assessing listening with one passage per level until the listening comprehension score drops below 50 percent. Then stop the IRI.

Today some authorities still use the Betts criteria, although 70 percent comprehension is most often used. The oral reading accuracy criteria, however have been challenged as too stringent, and 90 percent is widely accepted as the lower end of the instructional range for oral reading accuracy (Johns & Magliari, 1989; Powell, 1970).

Oral Reading Accuracy

For each oral passage of the IRI used, score the oral reading accuracy by counting the number of *uncorrected* miscues, which are shown in Box 4.1. Many people do not count miscues corrected by the reader, ourselves included. We believe that corrections show that the reader is monitoring whether the passage makes sense, a good strategy we want students to use. Some people count all miscues, however, whether corrected or not, and some commercial IRIs instruct users to do just that. Likewise, some count repetitions and even pauses as scorable miscues; we do not. In informal assessment there are some issues on which practitioners do not agree.

While you are learning to give and score an IRI, it is helpful to tape-record the oral reading so that you can replay it and be sure you caught all the miscues. It may also help you to make a check or tally mark at the end of each line of print, one for each uncorrected miscue in that line. It makes counting up easier.

To obtain a reader's total accuracy score, you need to know not only how many miscues occurred, but also how many words there are in the whole passage. In other words, what percentage of the total words does each individual word contribute?

Most commercial IRIs do all the arithmetic for you, providing a box or chart showing how many miscues represent the independent, instructional, and frustration levels for that passage. If you look back at Figure 4.4, you will see a box at the end of the passage. It indicates that the passage would be at the independent level for a reader making from zero to five miscues, at the instructional level for a reader making from 6 to 21 miscues, and at the frustration level for a reader making 22 or more miscues. (These scores do not reflect whether the miscues made sense within the passage or not; that issue is discussed in a section to follow. This discussion refers only to accuracy of the oral reading.)

If you are using an IRI that only gives you the total number of words in the passage, or if you are using a teacher-made IRI, you will have to determine the *miscue deduction* for each passage—that is, how much each miscue "counts" in percentage terms. To do so, count the number of words in a passage, if necessary. Then divide 100 percent (100.00) by the number of words in the passage. For example, the passage "A Day at the Beach" contains 203 words without the title.

$$203 \overline{\smash{\big)}\, 100.00} \quad .49$$

Each of the 203 words in that passage accounts for .49 percent, or about half of one percent, of the total. For each uncorrected miscue, then .49 percent will be deducted from the score. If the miscue deduction is not already figured for each passage in your IRI, you should do so and write the number on the examiner's copy of each passage.

When you know what the miscue deduction is for any passage, the rest of the scoring is easy. Multiply the number of uncorrected miscues by the miscue deduction, round off the resulting number to the nearest whole number, and subtract it from 100 percent. For example, if a reader made 13 uncorrected miscues:

.49%	100%
x 13	– 6%
6.37% (rounded to 6)	94%

By making 13 uncorrected miscues in a passage of 203 words, the reader made 6 percent miscues and, by subtraction, read with 94 percent accuracy.

The accuracy score is always expressed in whole numbers.

Write the percentage of accuracy on each oral passage or on a sheet listing all scores at each level. The oral accuracy scores derived so far will be used to determine whether each successive grade level represents the student's independent, instructional, or frustration level of oral reading.

The score criteria for oral reading accuracy are

Independent level: 97% or higher;
Instructional level: 90–96%; and
Frustration level: below 90%.

These criteria may still seem very high, but remember that the context of a sentence provides a powerful word recognition aid. In sentences, words are constrained by their grammatical usage and meaning. An unknown word in a sentence does not appear there arbitrarily, as in a list, but because it fits grammatically and semantically. The number of alternatives for any individual word is therefore small, and it is easier to recognize words in context than in isolation.

Reading and Listening Comprehension

Score the silent and oral reading comprehension questions separately for each passage and determine the percentage of questions answered correctly. Enter the scores on the record sheet. Repeat the same procedure for all passages read to the student. The generally accepted criteria for reading and listening comprehension scores are

Independent level: 90% or higher;
Instructional level: 70–90%; and
Frustration level: below 70%.

(In our discussion of administering IRIs, you were told to continue testing until 50 percent or less was attained. By doing so we can be sure that the frustration level has been reached.)

Keeping Track of Scores

After you have derived scores for oral reading accuracy, oral and silent reading comprehension, and listening comprehension, enter the scores on a record sheet, which can be stapled to the front of the examiner's copy of the student's IRI. Having all the pertinent scores and observational notes you made during the testing on one sheet aids in interpreting the student's performance. (Interpreting IRI results is discussed in the next section.)

A model score record sheet is shown on page 128. On this sheet are spaces for recording all scores from the IRI, notes and observations, information about the student such as age and grade, and scores from the word recognition inventory (discussed later in this chapter). Look at the score record sheet now, and read more about it in the next section.

Box 4.4

Criterion Scores for Establishing Reading and Listening Levels with an IRI

	ORAL READING	COMPREHENSION
Independent Level	97%	90%
Instructional Level	90%	70%
Frustration Level	below 90%	below 70%
Listening Level	—	70%

The necessary scores for determining the functional reading and listening levels from an IRI are summarized in Box 4.4.

These scores are generally agreed upon by clinicians and by makers of commercial IRIs. If the IRI you prefer to use specifies somewhat different score criteria, use those given in the IRI instructions.

Interpreting an IRI

As with all assessment procedures, the IRI scores are not an end in themselves. They should be interpreted and then applied in instructional planning. To do so, the student's functional reading levels must be determined.

Establishing Reading and Listening Levels

The scores derived from the oral reading and comprehension measures are used to determine overall levels. Scores for *both* oral reading and comprehension areas should meet the criteria for the instructional level in order to be sure the reader will be comfortable at that level. The necessary scores are shown in Box 4.4.

The child in Example 1 is reading comfortably at the preprimer (PP) level with accurate word recognition, excellent comprehension, and scores at the independent level.

At the primer (P) level, her oral reading accuracy is still good although she made more miscues, and comprehension is good in both oral and silent reading. Primer level is a good instructional level for this youngster, but beyond primer, both word recognition and comprehension break down. The first-grade level represents her frustration level.

The listening comprehension score of 80 percent at second grade shows that this youngster's potential reading level is second grade, which corre-

Example 1

Scores for an Eight-year-old Student, a Second-grader (in percentages)

		COMPREHENSION		
GRADE	ORAL READING	ORAL	SILENT	LISTENING
PP	97	100	100	—
P	94	75	80	—
1	88	60	50	—
2	—	—	—	80
3	—	—	—	60

sponds with her listening comprehension, to read at second-grade level but presently is able to read only primer level material, about two levels below her potential at this time.

The student in Example 2 began with the IRI passages at the second-grade level because of his age. If his performance at second grade has not been good, we could have moved back to lower levels. His scores at second grade in oral reading and both oral and silent comprehension show that he

Example 2

Scores for an Eleven-year-old Student, a Fifth-grader (in percentages)

		COMPREHENSION		
GRADE	ORAL READING	ORAL	SILENT	LISTENING
PP	—	—	—	—
P	—	—	—	—
1	—	—	—	—
2	99	100	90	—
3	94	85	80	—
4	91	70	70	—
5	86	50	55	—
6	—	—	—	90

can read material through the second grade independently. His scores on all measures at the third and fourth grades fall within the instructional range, and consequently we can say that fourth grade represents his highest instructional level. His instructional reading level includes both third- and fourth-grade material.

With all fifth-grade scores falling in the frustration range, we can conclude that fifth-grade material is too difficult for this youngster to read, but the 90 percent listening comprehension score at sixth grade shows his ability to deal with successfully on an auditory basis with material above his present grade. A fifth-grader with a fourth-grade instructional level is probably not experiencing serious difficulty in his present grade, but this youngster's listening comprehension score shows that he has the ability to read at least sixth-grade material. Thus he is not functioning at his full potential.

Deriving percentages of correct responses and using these scores to determine reading levels is called *quantitative analysis*. It shows *how many* correct and incorrect responses the reader has made. Although this analysis is useful, it is incomplete because it lacks the essential element of in-depth analysis of the student's responses. In order to determine what the reader knows and where help is needed, we must determine the strategies underlying the correct and incorrect responses. We have to look for patterns of strengths and weaknesses. From this perspective it is not so important *how many* correct responses the student made but rather *which* responses were right and *why*. This assessment is termed *qualitative analysis*, because it focuses on the quality of responses and the strategies the reader demonstrated. Quantitative analysis will aid us in determining the levels of difficulty of text the reader can deal with successfully. Qualitative analysis aids us in determining what the student has mastered and what skills and processes are lacking. Only when both kinds of analyses are accomplished can we develop a prescriptive program for a reader.

Analyzing Oral Reading

The context in which a word appears is a powerful aid to word recognition, but context is provided only by connected text. When we mark the responses during the oral reading of IRI passages, we can analyze word recognition within the real act of reading. Thus accurate marking and analysis are important.

Even very fluent readers make occasional miscues, especially when they have not read the material before. Some miscues change the meaning of the sentence or passage very little, while others change the author's meaning significantly and interfere with the reader's comprehension.

For example, let's say two readers read the first paragraph from "A Hot Day at the Beach" aloud. One reads:

> The day was *hot* and sunny. Tanya and Melissa packed *their* lunches. They brought ham sandwiches, chips, and *peaches.*

The other reads:

> The day was warm and *sandy.* Tanya and Melissa *picked* a lunch. They brought ham sandwiches, chips and *pirckles.*

Each reader made three uncorrected miscues. Their overall accuracy scores for this paragraph would be the same, but the first reader's miscues more nearly preserved the meaning of the paragraph, while the second reader's miscues made less sense and probably interfered more with her comprehension. *Hot* and *warm,* when discussing weather, are closer in meaning than *sunny* and *sandy.* Likewise, *packed their lunches* is closer to the original meaning of the sentence than *picked her lunch. Peaches* aren't much like *pickles,* but they are at least both likely picnic foods; *pirckles* is a nonsense word even though it looks and sounds more like the intended word. While both readers made three miscues, the first reader's miscues were somewhat "better," in the sense of preserving the intended meaning, than those of the second reader.

When analyzing miscues, we reread the passage as it was read by the reader, with all the miscues as we marked them, and decide whether each miscue significantly changes the meaning of the passage or sentence in which it occurs. We do not look only at the individual word, but at the miscue within the phrase, sentence, or passage context. Miscues which do significantly alter the meaning may be marked by circling them, marking them with a colored highlighting marker, or marking them "M. C." for "meaning change." If we were marking the paragraphs read in the foregoing examples, we would mark only *peaches* as a meaning-change miscue by the first reader, and all three of the second reader's miscues as meaning changes.

Then we can rescore the oral reading to arrive at a percentage of accuracy that includes only the significant, or meaning changing, miscues. Some commercial IRIs, such as Leslie and Caldwell's *Qualitative Reading Inventory* used in this chapter as an example, instruct users to do this with each passage read orally. Look back at Figure 4.5; you will see in the box after the passage that miscues are counted to arrive at two different scores: "Total Accuracy," derived by counting all uncorrected miscues, and "Total Acceptability," derived by counting only meaning-changing miscues. For this passage to be at the reader's instructional level, a reader could make up to 21 miscues, but only a maximum of 11 miscues that changed the meaning. If a reader made more than 12 significant miscues, the passage would represent a frustration level of difficulty.

By taking the extra time and effort to examine and evaluate the miscues occurring during oral reading, we can add greatly to our understanding of what the reader is doing during the reading. We can see more than just if the reading is highly accurate or not. We can see, through the miscues themselves, if the reader is using context and sense-making strategies to try to actively construct the author's meaning. Students who generally make "acceptable" miscues need a different kind of word-attack instruction to help them read more accurately than those whose miscues generally don't make sense.

An important issue in analyzing a reader's miscues is the role of non-standard English dialects in oral reading accuracy. As we have seen, simply counting all the miscues and deriving an accuracy score does not take into account whether the reader's errors make sense. Likewise, it does not take into account whether the reader may be "translating" standard English text into his or her own familiar, although nonstandard, oral dialect.

For example, let's say a speaker of Black English reads, "'This is my mother,' said Rose" as "This my mother, say Rose." Superficially it appears the reader has made two uncorrected miscues: the omission of *is* and the substitution of *say* for *said*; but the conventions of Black English may include both the omission of capular verbs in some contexts and the substitution of present for past verb tenses. The oral reading does not correspond exactly to the words in the written sentence, but it does represent an accurate translation of standard into nonstandard English, with no loss of meaning. It is important not to confuse dialect miscues with true word recognition errors, because doing so results in falsely underestimating the word recognition abilities of many dialect speakers. Likewise, it is not helpful to assume that all miscues produced by dialect speakers will be acceptable and not provide the help they may need to develop greater accuracy and automaticity in word recognition. By listening closely to the informal speech of your dialect-speaking students, you will gain enough familiarity with its conventions to recognize true dialect miscues, which are generally acceptable, from those that interfere with comprehension.

Analyzing Oral and Silent Reading Comprehension

By looking at oral and silent reading comprehension scores across several grade levels, we can determine if the reader has a marked strength or weakness in comprehension during either oral or silent reading and whether this pattern is consistent with what others of the same age do. We can also spot a pattern by looking at responses to the different types of comprehension questions within a grade level and across levels that tell us whether the student has particular strengths or weaknesses in recalling main ideas or details, forming inferences, and other comprehension skills required by the questions.

If readers consistently show better comprehension performance with oral reading and lower comprehension scores with silent reading, we can conclude that they have to hear themselves say the words aloud in order to understand. Such readers translate or recode print into speech sounds and derive meaning from the spoken words. This is fairly typical of beginning readers, especially those whose initial reading instruction has been primarily oral. When asked to read silently, they sometimes lose their places because they do not have their voices to help "anchor" them in the print. It is not surprising when they read aloud and show consistently better oral than silent comprehension, since oral reading is still so widely used in primary classrooms. If, however, we see a student older than about eight or nine reading this way, it is a matter of great concern. Beyond the primary grades, emphasis shifts to rapid, silent reading for meaning. An older student who has to read audibly may have much trouble reading the volume of material required in upper grades.

For readers beyond the beginning reading stage, silent reading tends to be faster than oral reading. Oral reading speed is limited by how rapidly we can speak clearly; about 200 words per minute is very rapid speech, and even very fluent oral readers do not read aloud that fast. However, fluent silent reading may vary between 200 and 400 words per minute, depending on the difficulty of the material, the reader's purpose for the reading, and whether or not the material is familiar. Fluent mature reading of challenging material proceeds at about 250 words per minute (Perfetti, 1985), while fluent mature reading of easy interesting material read for pleasure may be considerably faster. Thus, the reading demands of the upper grades require that students shift from the primary oral reading of beginning reading toward fluent silent reading with comprehension.

It is therefore a common finding that as children approach the end of primary grades, somewhere between the second and the fourth grade, they begin to shift toward more silent reading and characteristically show better comprehension after silent than after oral reading. This is a normal development finding; it certainly does not indicate that these older students show an oral reading weakness or that they should begin a lot of remedial oral reading! On the contrary, oral reading should be deemphasized and silent reading emphasized in the upper grades.

Comprehension Skill Patterns

If we go back to the comprehension questions following the IRI passages, and if we included a notation of *what kind* of question each one was, we can discern whether there was a particular type that gave a student consistent difficulty. This is an example of qualitative analysis. By systematically looking from one grade level to another, we can see what, if any, pattern emerges. Was there a kind of question—for example, inference questions—that repeatedly gave the student difficulty at different levels? Was there a type of question that the student consistently answered correctly across several grade levels? A typical pattern might be one where the student always got the main idea questions correct but had great difficulty with recall of important details; another might be that the student showed much ability to remember factual, explicitly stated information but had difficulty arriving at conclusions or forming inferences based on implied information. Looking for individual patterns in comprehension responses allows us to design appropriate comprehension activities for students according to their individual needs.

However, we must be quite certain that the questions really tap the comprehension skills they purport to. Schell and Hanna (1981) argue that too often comprehension questions on commercial IRIs ". . . are not always objectively classifiable and that the meaning of the various subskill groups may not be uniformly clear . . ." (p. 264). In other words, do IRI questions labeled as "main idea," for example, clearly and discretely call for comprehension of the main idea? Hanna and Schell demonstrated that even experienced teachers attempting to classify comprehension questions by type often classified questions quite differently from the authors of a particular IRI.

In a related study, Duffelmeyer and Duffelmeyer (1987) analyzed questions classified as "main idea" by the authors of three commercials IRIs and found that "the vast majority of questions on the three IRIs measure the ability to either state a reading selection's topic or recall some other aspect of the content. Topic questions are the most prevalent (63%) . . . Other questions are the second most prevalent (28%); most of these are either detail questions . . . or cause-effect questions" (p. 164). Duffelmeyer and Duffelmeyer note that there is an important difference between a passage's *topic*, or what the passage is about at the simplest level, and the *main idea*, or the most general point the author wishes to make about the topic. (Figure 4.6 on p. 136 gives an example of main idea and topic questions.) Another important finding of these authors is that none of the questions in the three IRIs that purported to assess main idea questions in the preprimer through second-grade passages were actually main idea questions; 70 percent called for statement of the topic. These authors point out that teaching children in the early reading stages to identify the topic but not the main idea, while teaching them to think that the topic and the main idea are synonymous, may have the result "that students would be less likely to learn how to identify the main idea" (p. 165). Duffelmeyer and Duffelmeyer strongly suggest that "IRI main idea questions cannot be taken at face value. It would behoove teachers to analyze any so-called main idea questions on the IRIs they use, to determine what skill(s) are actually being measured. Otherwise, the diagnostic information those questions yield is likely to be misleading" (p. 165).

Unquestioning acceptance of IRI question classifications, and indeed unquestioning acceptance of all IRI questions as "good questions," just because they appear in a published IRI, is unwise. Comprehension patterns can often be discerned, however, and helpful teaching strategies devised from these judgments *if* teachers continually use critical judgment when they use IRI questions.

Our best advice to you is, don't take either the quality of questions or the way the author classified them on faith. Read the passages and each of the questions, and consider carefully whether you think the questions are appropriately labeled by type. Then, if you discern a consistent pattern in a student's response to particular question types, consider your judgment as a "working hypothesis" about the student's needs.

Begin instruction based on your hypothesis that a student needs practice in particular areas, but continue to evaluate based on how the student responds to that instruction. Further teaching may reveal that what looked like a comprehension skill weakness on the IRI did not persist or that what looked like an area of strength did not continue to be a strength for the reader beyond the IRI, in real text. Only further teaching will reveal whether your judgments were accurate.

Patterns in Listening Comprehension

If students achieve 70 percent or better on the comprehension questions after listening to a passage read aloud by the examiner, we assume that they can deal successfully with similar concepts and vocabulary on an auditory basis, although they cannot read that level of material for themselves. We refer to the highest grade level at which the student had 70 percent or better as the student's *listening level.* This level is important because it helps us determine what we can *expect* this student to achieve and thus makes it possible to set reasonable instructional goals.

Most students who are not fluent, mature readers can listen to someone else reading aloud and understand material they cannot yet read successfully because most of them, especially the younger ones, are still learning and developing as readers while they have been competent listeners and language users for a lot longer. Therefore, their listening levels are somewhat above their instructional reading levels, which is predictable, for it shows that they are not yet able to read as well as they can think.

Some youngsters will have instructional reading and listening comprehension levels that are the same. Material too difficult for them to read is also too difficult for them to understand on an auditory basis. This is fine. What it shows is that they are reading just as well as they can and that at the present time there is not much room for improvement. These pupils are reading right at their potential, using all their ability to read as well as they do. They need support and further instruction, but if they are poor readers, they will probably make steady, but not spectacular, gains in reading. The listening comprehension level represents a sort of overall goal in reading improvement.

The listening comprehension level is dynamic, not fixed or static. As children grow older and have more experiences, they can understand more and more difficult material. The average seven-year-old can listen to and understand stories appropriate for second- or third-graders and understand them, but ninth-grade material would be too difficult conceptually. By the time the child is 12 or 13, however, ninth-grade materials may well be comprehensible because vocabulary, store of concepts, and experiences have grown in those five years. The listening level represents an estimate of *present* functioning. Establishing a student's listening level once and using it as an ongoing standard, however, is no more appropriate than expecting last year's instructional level to be the same next year.

The listening level should never be equated with or confused with IQ, but it does gives us some rough indication of whether a child's verbal intelligence is about average, or somewhat above, or somewhat below. Children with average verbal intelligence will usually have listening levels at or very near their present grade placement. Here are three examples, all second-graders:

Jenny's listening comprehension level is late second grade. Since she is in second grade, we infer that her verbal intelligence is roughly average for her age and that she has the necessary concepts and vocabulary to learn to read second-grade material successfully, although at present time she has a first-grade instructional level. Although her instructional level is low, she can improve her reading with appropriate instruction and support.

Matt has a listening comprehension level of sixth grade. He has the concepts and vocabulary to listen to and understand very advanced material, and he is obviously very bright. In spite of his potential, he is achieving at grade level, and has an instructional level of late second grade. Thus his achievement is average for his grade, although he has the potential for higher achievement. The finding that Matt is not performing at his full potential is not necessarily negative. If he is comfortable, motivated, and interested, there is no need for concern. If he appears apathetic, bored, or frustrated, then he certainly needs greater intellectual challenge.

Sandy has an instructional level of first grade, and his listening level is also first grade. Although Sandy's achievement is below grade level, it is in line with his present potential. Sandy may be a slow learner or of below-average verbal intelligence; he may have learned to read later than others or may have a limited background of experience with print. At any rate, his performance and potential appear to be in line at the present. Sandy needs much support and instruction, and as he becomes a more proficient reader, his listening level will increase. This in turn will make greater reading improvement possible.

Constructing an IRI

Creating you own IRI is a very challenging task. Selecting good passages and creating thoughtful, challenging questions will help you become much more aware of the comprehension process and become a more discerning user of all tests. However, it is not a task we recommend you undertake without expert help available. A team of teachers working together with the help of an experienced clinician or instructor is the best way to attempt such a task.

Constructing an IRI consists of two stages. The first is developing the material: selecting reading passages, creating comprehension questions, retelling outlines, and prior knowledge items for each passage, and making up both a reader's copy and examiner's forms. The second stage, often omitted in directions for IRI construction, is critically important: Try out and evaluate your instrument before you use it to make decisions about a student's reading. Commercial test makers call this "field testing," and it is as important for you to field test your own IRI as it is for the biggest commercial test maker.

Creating IRI Materials

The following steps will help you complete the first stage of IRI construction.

1. *Select passages for reading and listening comprehension for each book level, primer, (or preprimer) through ninth grade (or beyond).* Often, passages are selected from current basal readers. We recommend using a series other than the one you use for your ongoing reading instruction, because if you use passages from stories your students have already read, their performance may be inflated. Use an alternate series that is similar in format and difficulty to the one in current use; *don't* use an old, outdated series, for it may be considerably easier than current ones. Trade books may be used instead of basals, if you check the readability level of the material to make sure it is not too easy or hard for a particular level. Avoid using familiar stories students may have already read or heard.

Select three different passages at each grade level, so you can assess silent and oral reading and listening comprehension separately. Choose passages that are typical of that grade level in content and subject matter. Avoid passages with many unusual or technical topics. Keep all the passages at each grade level consistent in length: 100- to 200-word passages are best, with primary-grade passages shorter than higher-level ones. Avoid using the middle of a longer story, for important information may be lost by omitting the beginning. Do not use one long passage divided into two or three parts, as some experts recommend, for whatever is understood (or not understood) from one passage will necessarily affect comprehension of the subsequent parts.

2. *Write comprehension questions for each passage.* There is no "best" number of questions for a passage; the number of questions depends on passage content. Begin by reading each passage and creating a list of information you recall from the passage. Then develop a set of questions that tap this information, including not only direct recall of stated information but also questions that call for interpretation and evaluation. Main ideas, important supporting details, sequences, cause-effect relationships, inferred information, understanding of vocabulary, and interpretation of characters' feelings and motives are all aspects of comprehension. Figure 4.6 shows sample questions that call on a variety of comprehension abilities.

Include a reinspection item for each passage so you can observe how successfully a reader can scan for and locate specific information after an initial reading.

Here are a few guidelines that may be helpful in writing comprehension questions:

   a. Make sure every question can be answered or inferred from the selected passage, not from the pictures or general knowledge.
   b. Do not make all the questions literal comprehension questions; about half is sufficient.

Figure 4.6

Sample Comprehension Questions

Literal Comprehension (Answers to questions explicitly stated in passage)

TOPIC:
What event was this story about?
What might make a good title for this passage?

MAIN IDEA:
What was the most important thing the author said about dogs?
How would you describe in one sentence the information about dogs given here?

IMPORTANT DETAIL:
What kind of animal was Nitwit?
What did Bob do as soon as he got home?

SEQUENCE:
What happened after Jill heard the window break?
Where did the children go first?

CHARACTERIZATION:
What did Ms. Willis do that showed she was angry?
How did Bruce act when he saw Jamie again?

REINSPECTION:
Find the sentence that describes Ben's new bike and read it to me.
Find the place in the story where the children began to argue, and read it out loud.

Interpretation and Judgment (Answers to questions not explicitly stated in passage)

INFERENCE:
Why do you think Jim spoke roughly to the dog?
What makes you believe Cathy might enjoy flying?

VOCABULARY:
What did Rita mean when she said "I'm simply green"?
What is a "chopper" in this story?

PREDICTION:
What might happen if the delivery boy loses the package?
If Shana runs away, where might she go?

---

c. Formulate questions for each passage that require interpretation and judgment as well as literal comprehension (see Figure 4.4). However, you need not include every type of question for every passage.

d. Frame questions that call for understanding the most important events or concepts in the passage. Ask yourself, "What is the student most likely to remember after reading this passage?" Don't ask for unimportant details.

e. Keep the wording simple.

f. Avoid yes-no and either-or questions. They can be answered correctly 50 percent of the time by guessing. "Did Bob go to the zoo?" or "Did Bob go to the zoo or the park?" are poor questions. A better question would be "Where did Bob go?"

g. Avoid questions that require only one-word answers; encourage the reader to respond and explain in natural language.

h. Ask the questions in the order in which the information appeared in the story. If you don't, one question can give away the answer to a subsequent one.

Figure 4.7

Informal Reading Inventory Record Sheet

Student _____ Age _____ Grade _____

Date tested _____ Tested by _____

LEVEL	WORD RECOGNITION INVENTORY		ORAL READING		COMPREHENSION		
	Automatic	Decoded	Total Accuracy	Total Acceptability	Oral Reading	Silent Reading	Listening
PP							
P							
1st							
2nd							
3rd							
4th							
5th							
6th							
7th							
8th							
9th							

READING LEVELS   Strengths: _____

Independent _____   _____

Instructional _____

Frustration _____   Needs: _____

Listening _____   _____

Retelling: _____   Prior Knowledge: _____

_____   _____

Recommendation: _____

_____

_____

_____

For additional information about informal reading inventory questions see Duffelmeyer (1989); Duffelmeyer and Duffelmeyer (1987 and 1989); Johnson et al. (1987); Pearson and Johnson (1989); Peterson et al. (1978); Pikulski and Shanahan (1982); and Schell and Hanna (1981).

3. *So that you can use retelling as a comprehension check as well as questions, create a retelling outline for each passage.* Refer to Figure 4.5 for an example. A checklist format is easy to use. Include all the important information in phrases, in the order in which the information occurred in the passage. (Use your own recall to help you include the most important information.) Likewise, create two or three items for prior knowledge assessment.

4. *Make up a student's copy of each passage.* You will need only one, because it is nonconsumable. Reproduce the passage from the original source, making sure the reproduction is clear with good contrast. Cut away material surrounding the passage but leave related illustrations. Glue the passage onto sheets you can laminate or onto tagboard. Put the passages in order into a notebook or binder.

5. *Type examiner's pages for each passage.* Double space so you have room above each line to write in miscues. Include at the top of each passage the title, book, page number, and series from which the passage was taken. Also at the top, include your prior knowledge items and space to jot down what the student tells you about each one. Count the number of words in the passage and compute the miscue deduction for each by dividing the number of words into 100.00. Under the passage, type the retelling outline, leaving blanks for checking off, and the list of questions for each passage, leaving enough space between questions to write in the student's answers and your probes and observations. Code each question by type (MI = main idea, V = vocabulary, EX = explicit, IM = implied). You may include allowable answers in parentheses if you wish.

6. *Make up a summary sheet to record scores and observations.* This form allows you to compare performance across and within levels and to record your judgments and recommendations. Figure 4.7 is an example that can be adapted to include other information. (In Figure 4.7 we have included space for scores on the word recognition inventory, to be discussed in the next section.)

Testing and Evaluating Your IRI

A wise test user would never use a completely untried test and assume its value or accuracy without evidence that it did what it purported to do. So it must be with teacher-made IRIs. You can validate and test out your instrument in a number of ways:

1. Double-check the readability of every passage with a readability formula. (See "Assessing the Readability of Text" at the end of this chapter.) If a

Figure 4.8

A Word Recognition Inventory

Second	*Automatic*	*Decoded*	*Third*	*Automatic*	*Decoded*
1. old			1. thread		
2. toy			2. silk		
3. promise			3. tongue		
4. trade			4. sharp		
5. pieces			5. rough		
6. room			6. claws		
7. built			7. believe		
8. beach			8. crowded		
9. right			9. salmon		
10. packed			10. hid		
11. height			11. chief		
12. boards			12. whale		
13. measured			13. special		
14. branches			14. wool		
15. though			15. removed		
16. begins			16. lion		
17. push			17. wear		
18. ends			18. lunch		
19. front			19. curious		
20. morning			20. spin		

Total Correct Automatic ___/20= ___%
Total Correct Decoded ___/20= ___%
Total Number Correct ___/20= ___%

Total Correct Automatic ___/20=___%
Total Correct Decoded ___/20=___%
Total Number Correct ___/20=___%

LEVELS			
Independent	Instructional	Questionable	Frustration
18–20	14–17	10–13	below 10
90–100%	70–85%	50–65%	below 50%

Source: Lauren Leslie and Joanne Caldwell. *Qualitative Reading Inventory.* New York: HarperCollins, 1990, p. 88.

passage you selected has a higher readability level than you wanted, select another passage. Don't try to make a passage "easier" by rewriting, creating shorter sentences, or using different words. This may have little or no effect on the actual difficulty of the material (Hansell, 1976).

2. Have several readers try to answer your comprehension questions *without* reading the passage. Any that can be correctly answered in this way should be thrown out, for they call for general information rather than comprehension of the passage itself.

3. Ask other teachers to read passages and questions without knowing how you classified the questions, and to classify the questions themselves. If there is general disagreement about what types of questions some are, change the questions or create new ones so they are more clearly and directly classifiable as one type or another (main idea, sequence, inference, and so forth).

4. Ask a number of students to read passages and give you immediate oral retellings to see if what is typically remembered from passages is reflected in your retelling outlines and in your questions.

5. After making necessary changes in passages and questions, give your IRI to a number of students whose instructional levels and strengths and weaknesses you know about. Do the results of your IRI bear out what you already knew, or do they contradict? This kind of informal field testing will help you determine if your IRI is fairly accurate in placing students at instructional levels.

6. After you have given your IRI to some students and derived a tentative instructional level, cross-check this with a cloze procedure (see the section at the end of this chapter) made up from different text at the same readability level. If your IRI indicates a fifth-grade instructional level, for example, that reader should be able to adequately complete a cloze text for comparable fifth-grade material if she or he has been shown how to complete a cloze test.

THE WORD RECOGNITION INVENTORY

This instrument consists of graded lists of individual words that may often occur in text at a particular grade level. These graded word lists, usually primer level through grade six, are included in commercial IRIs and can be quite easily made up if you are constructing you own IRI or to supplement a commercial one. (Directions for WRI construction follow in the next section.)

The word recognition inventory, or WRI, is used to assess sight vocabulary and some aspects of phonic and structural analysis. Since the words appear in isolation, the WRI is not used to assess comprehension in context.

Some teachers also use the WRI to help them determine where to begin administering the reading passages of the IRI. For this purpose, the WRI is given first, before the IRI, and the examiner begins having the student read story passages at the grade level where he or she first began to miss some words. We prefer to give the WRI after the IRI, because we prefer to have the student begin reading connected text first, since that is our primary diagnostic purpose. This order is a matter of individual preference.

The WRI consists of a graded set of word lists for the student to look at and a corresponding set of examiner's pages for the teacher to mark and score as the instrument is administered. The student's copy contains only the words arranged in lists. The examiner's copy consists of the words followed by blanks for filling in what the reader said when errors in word recognition occurred.

The examiner may use a file card to cover each word, drawing the card down the list to briefly reveal each word as the student reads down the list; or the student may simply read the list independently. Words recognized immediately and accurately are checked off on the examiner's copy; words incorrectly identified or sounded out are noted in the blanks following each word. Some commercial IRIs have one column of blanks, some two; those that have two blanks after each word are providing spaces for the examiner to note if the word was recognized automatically or had to be decoded by the reader. Percentages of accuracy are derived for each list of words by counting the errors made. Figure 4.8 shows two levels of word lists from a commercial IRI.

Administering, Scoring, and Interpreting the Word Recognition Inventory

The WRI is easy to give and score, taking only a few minutes to administer. The student reads down the list of words. Words correctly and automatically identified are checked off in the "Automatic" column on the examiner's sheet. Errors are written in the same column. Second attempts or words unrecognized automatically that the student must decode or analyze are written in the "Decoded" column. Errors corrected on second attempts are checked off in the "Decoded" column. Each column is scored separately for each level. Some commercial IRIs, like the one shown in Figure 4.6, show you how to derive an independent, instructional, or frustration level from these scores. Most authorities use these criteria:

Independent level: 90 to 100% accuracy;
Instructional level: 70 to 85%; and
Frustration level: below 70%.

The point is really academic, since we are not interested in setting a functional reading level from reading word lists but rather in analyzing the student's word recognition strategies and assessing how well the student recognizes words automatically. Scores for each list may be entered on the IRI record sheet.

The size and strength of the student's immediate sight word recognition is inferred from performance on the "Automatic" portion of the instrument. A large and stable sight vocabulary forms the basis of fluent, effective reading. A reader with a stable sight vocabulary of common, frequently occurring words will usually score around 90 percent or better on automatic recognition of words at least at the lower grade levels. At any grade level, scores below 70 percent indicate that the student does not recognize enough of the words typical at that level to read fluently and effectively at that level of difficulty.

The responses on the "Decoded" columns give us information about the phonic and word-analysis strategies a student can use when he or she does not recognize a word immediately. Students who typically correct an initial error when decoding the word show us that though sight recognition is weak, decoding skills are solid. Students who make unsuccessful attempts to decode unrecognized words, but who typically preserve the initial consonant or blend sounds in their attempts, show us that they have a grasp of initial sounds but may be weak in decoding medial or final sounds. By looking for patterns in individuals' responses, both correct and incorrect, we can begin to determine what word-attack skills need to be reviewed or retaught in our instruction.

Constructing a Word Recognition Inventory

If you use a commercial IRI or one that accompanies a basal reading system, your test materials will include a word recognition inventory. However, if you choose to make up an inventory from a particular set of graded materials, it is easy to do so. Words must be selected from the "new words," or basal words, introduced at each successive grade level in a basal system. This ensures that each level of the WRI is made up of words that are appropriate for learning at that grade level of material and are not too hard or too easy. Basal words are selected for the WRI by *sampling;* that is, certain words from the total basal words for that level are selected in order to obtain a representative sample for each level.

To select the words, you need a teacher's manual for each successive level of a current basal series, primer through sixth grade. If you have constructed an IRI from a basal series, use the same series for your WRI. Find the list of basal words introduced in each level in the back of the manual.

Here are the steps to follow in constructing a WRI:

1. For *each* level, find how many new basal words are introduced. If your WRI lists have 25 words, which is typical, divide 25 into the total num-

ber of basal words in that level and round off the product to the nearest whole number. For example, in a level with 345 new basal words, 345 divided by 25 equals 13.8, rounded to 14.

2. Using the quotient from step 1 (in this example, 14), count and check off every *nth* word (here, every fourteenth word) in the basal list. If a checked word is a proper noun or non-English word, use the next word instead.

3. If you have not checked off 25 words when you come to the end of the list, keep counting and checking as you return to the beginning and continue as before until you have 25 checked. Make a list of these words.

4. Repeat steps 1 through 3 for each successive level. Cross-check your lists to be sure no word appears twice. If the words are arranged alphabetically, rearrange them.

5. Make a student copy of each list by typing carefully, leaving space between words. Lists may be laminated. Store with your IRI. Make examiner's copies by typing the lists with each word followed by two blanks headed "Automatic" and "Decoded" or the like. Your examiner's copies should look like the example in Figure 4.8.

SUPPLEMENTING INFORMAL ASSESSMENTS

A number of other assessment procedures and devices may be used to supplement informal measures and explore particular areas of students' reading in detail. These include procedures that help us obtain information about how readers attempt to construct meaning from text, procedures for determining the relative difficulty of texts, and commercial word recognition and phonics tests.

Helping Students Become Strategic Readers

We know that effective readers are actively involved in the process of comprehending what they read. They use strategies like previewing the text, creating predictions about the content, self-questioning, summarizing at various points in the story, and continually monitoring their own understanding as they read (Schmitt, 1990). Effective readers do not simply take in meanings found in text; they actively construct meaning for themselves by interacting with the text, reviewing what is already known, and integrating new information with prior information (Flood and Lapp, 1990).

When readers activate what they already know and integrate new information in ways that make sense to them, when they select and use appropriate strategies to help them understand and remember what they read, they are becoming *strategic readers*. When readers fail to use prior information or lack sufficient prior information to make sense of new information, when they over-rely on word-attack skills at the expense of context, or when they fail to monitor their understanding, they are not making progress toward becoming strategic readers. They may need a program of instruction that teaches them how and when to use effective strategies as they read.

Schmitt (1990) developed a 25-item multiple-choice questionnaire, called the "Metacomprehension Strategy Index" (MSI), that teachers can use to evaluate children's awareness of reading strategies in middle elementary grades and beyond. The MSI measures awareness of predicting and verifying, previewing, purpose setting, self-questioning, drawing from background knowledge, and applying "fix-up" strategies (Schmitt, 1990, p. 455). The questionnaire may be administered orally by the teacher or read silently by students. It can be given individually or in groups. Students respond to items indicating what would be good strategies to use before, during, and after reading. Here is an example item.

> Before I begin reading, it's a good idea to:
> A. Think of what I already know about the things I see in the pictures.
> B. See how many pages are in the story.
> C. Choose the best part of the story to read again.
> D. Read the story aloud to someone.
>
> —(Schmitt, 1990, p. 459)

After scoring students' MSIs, the teacher can determine which strategies students are aware of and which strategies students need to learn and practice using. Since the MSI is a self-report instrument, it may be that students *say* they use particular strategies but in reality fail to use them; teacher observation is necessary to determine if they really use what they say. The MSI appears to provide useful information about students' strategic awareness when combined with other diagnostic information.

Think-Alouds

Think-alouds, or readers' verbal self-reports about their thinking processes during reading, can be used to obtain information about how readers construct meaning from text (Wade, 1990). During a think-aloud a reader reads short portions of a passage, one or a few sentences at a time. After each portion is read, the reader is asked to tell what the passage is about, what is happening in the passage, or what clues the reader is using to understand the passage. Nondirective probes such as "Tell me more about that" or "Why do you think so?" are used to extend the reader's responses. The entire procedure is taperecorded, and the record is analyzed to determine whether the reader generates tentative hypotheses about the topic, uses information from the text to support hypotheses, relates information in the text to prior knowledge, integrates new with old information, and deals with conflicts between new and old information. Behaviors that may reveal use of strategies such as rereading, as well as indications of anxiety, uncertainty, and the like are noted by the examiner. Box 4.5 shows the procedure for administering and interpreting a think-aloud.

The Cloze Procedure

Figure 4.9 shows a portion of a cloze procedure. After the first sentence, you will find blanks in the text. Can you figure out what might make sense in each blank? (Only one word has been deleted each time.)

In a cloze procedure (Taylor, 1953), students read material from which words have been systematically deleted; that is, every *nth* word has been left out. Frequently, every *fifth* word after the first complete sentence is replaced with a blank, as in our example. Our aim is to see how accurately students can predict or infer the words that should fill the blanks, thus creating *closure*, or wholeness, in the passage.

A completely accurate prediction of every deleted word is almost impossible unless the material is extremely simple in content and vocabulary, but it

Figure 4.9

Portion of a Cloze Procedure

"When Emily Johnson came home one evening to her furnished room and found three of her best handkerchiefs missing from the dresser drawer, she was sure who had taken them and what to do. She had lived in _____ furnished room for about _____ weeks and for the _____ two weeks she had _____ missing small things occasionally. _____ had been several handkerchiefs _____, and an initial pin _____ Emily rarely wore and _____ had come from the _____ -and-ten. And once _____ had missed a small _____ of perfume and one _____ a set of china _____. Emily had known for _____ time who was taking _____ things, but it was _____ tonight that she had _____ what to do."

Source: Shirley Jackson, "Trial by Combat," in *The Lottery.* New York: Farrar, Straus, 1949, p. 35.

Box 4.5

Procedure for Administering and Interpreting a Comprehension Think-Aloud

I. Preparing the text

Choose a short passage (expository or narrative) written to meet the following criteria:

1. The text should be from 80 to 200 words in length, depending on the reader's age and reading ability.
2. The text should be new to the reader, but on a topic that is familiar to him or her. (Determine whether the reader has relevant background knowledge by means of an interview or questionnaire administered at a session prior to this assessment.)
3. The text should be at the reader's instructional level, which can be determined by use of an informal reading inventory. Passages at this level are most likely to be somewhat challenging while not overwhelming readers with word identification problems.
4. The topic sentence should appear last, and the passage should be untitled. Altering the text in this way will elicit information about the reader's strategies for making sense of the passage and inferring the topic.
5. The text should be divided into segments of one to four sentences each.

II. Administering the think-aloud procedure

1. Tell the reader that he or she will be reading a story in short segments of one or more sentences.
2. Tell the reader that after reading each section, he or she will be asked to tell what the story is about.
3. Have the student read a segment aloud. After each segment is read, ask the reader to tell what is happening, followed by nondirective probe questions as necessary. The questions should encourage the reader to generate hypotheses (what do you think this is about?) and to describe what he or she based the hypotheses on (what clues in the story helped you?).
4. Continue the procedure until the entire passage is read. Then ask the reader to retell the entire passage in his or her own words. (The reader may reread the story first.)
5. The examiner might also ask the reader to find the most important sentence(s) in the passage.
6. The session should be taperecorded and transcribed. The examiner should also record observations of the child's behaviors.

III. Analyzing results

Ask the following questions when analyzing the transcript:

1. Does the reader generate hypotheses?
2. Does he/she support hypotheses with information from the passage?
3. What information from the text does the reader use?
4. Does he/she relate material in the text to background knowledge or previous experience?
5. Does the reader integrate new information with the schema he/she has already activated?
6. What does the reader do if there is information that conflicts with the schema he/she has generated?
7. At what point does the reader recog-

Box 4.5 continued

nize what the story is about?

8. How does the reader deal with unfamiliar words?

9. What kinds of integration strategies does the reader use (e.g., visualization)?

10. How confident is the reader of his/her hypotheses?

11. What other observations can be made about the reader's behavior, strategies, etc.?

Source: Suzanne E. Wade, "Using Think Alouds to Assess Comprehension." *The Reading Teacher* 43, no. 7 (March 1990): 445.

is not necessary to fill in each deletion with total accuracy. If an adequate proportion of words to blanks is supplied, readers can usually employ their sense of what is going on in the passage to supply words that will complete the author's text. Can you give a "good guess" for each of the deleted words in Figure 4.9? You probably could fill in more than half of the blanks accurately but not every one. For some of the deletions, there are only one or two words that could possibly fit while for others there are more alternatives. The ninth blank, for example, occurs in the phrase, ". . . had come from the ___-and-ten." You probably recognized almost immediately the expression "five-and-ten" and would have trouble thinking of a better alternative. On the other hand, what about ". . . a set of china ___"? You could probably think of several good alternatives for that blank: *plates, figurines,* or *animals.* In spite of some uncertainty, the whole passage is not too frustrating or difficult to complete.

The cloze procedure indicates the extent to which readers are able to follow the sense of a reading passage. In fact, studies have shown that the percentages of correct words readers are able to supply in a cloze passage constitute as reliable a measure of general comprehension as much more elaborate devices (Bormuth, 1966; Jones and Pikulski, 1974; Rankin and Culhane, 1969).

There are two common purposes for using a cloze procedure:

1. to determine whether a particular piece of written text represents an individual's independent, instructional, or frustration reading level (placement purposes); and

2. to assess the quality of an individual reader's use of context as a strategy for understanding what is read (diagnostic purposes).

Using a Cloze for Placement

A cloze placement test is a fast and accurate device for determining whether an individual, group, or whole class can comfortably read a given book or other material. In classes where everyone must read the same required text-books, cloze results can help the teacher form groups for differential instruction. Where students are reading trade books and novels, cloze results are invaluable for determining if selections are easy, too hard, or just right.

When constructing a cloze passage, omit systematically every fifth word; that is, 20 percent of the words. Leaving 80 percent intact gives sufficient context for the reader to supply the remaining words. Deleting every fifth word in order ensures that words of all grammatical classes and levels of difficulty are sampled, not just all nouns or all long words, for example.

Constructing the cloze for placement. Here are the steps for constructing a cloze passage for placement purposes (Estes and Vaughn, 1985):

1. Select a passage the students have not read before, about 300 words long.
2. Leave the first sentence intact, to get the readers started. Then begin counting words, replacing every fifth word with a blank 15 spaces long. If any word to be deleted is a proper noun, leave it in and delete the next word. (Proper nouns are harder to predict from context than other words.) Continue counting until you have 50 blanks.
3. Finish the sentence in which the last deletion occurs. Type one more sentence intact.

Administering and scoring the cloze. Administering and scoring a cloze are simple:

1. On the blackboard, show the students how to complete the passage. Give example sentences and discuss how to use context clues. Let students work together on short passages for practice. This step is important because even good readers will do poorly if they are unfamiliar with the demands of the task.
2. Direct the students to use only one word for each blank and to try to use the precise word the author would have used.
3. Explain that no one will get each word correct and that about 50 percent correct is a good score. If the students don't know this in advance, anxiety can affect their performance.
4. Give ample time for completing the passage without rushing. The students should not use their books because we want to see if they can read and understand the material without aid.

In scoring, accept only the *exact replacement*. Studies (Bormuth, 1966; Miller and Coleman, 1967; Ruddell, 1964) have shown this to be the most valid scoring system for placement purposes. When you use this activity instructionally to teach the use of context clues or work on vocabulary, you may choose to accept synonyms or make other changes. The rank order of scores changes little, if at all, if synonyms are accepted, but interpreting the results can be difficult. Also, you may drive yourself crazy deciding what is "close enough."

Determine the percentage of correct responses, adding 2 percent for each correct word. (Don't count incorrect *spellings* as errors on the cloze.) You can judge more accurately by averaging each student's scores on two or more passages from the same text.

A score of 60 percent correct or higher indicates that the material is easy for these students and that the material can be used for *independent* reading. A score between 40 and 60 percent indicates that these students can comfortably read the material and that it is suitable for direct instruction because it represents their *instructional* reading level. A score below 40 percent correct indicates that the material is too difficult and that it represents the reader's *frustration* level (Bormuth, 1968a, 1968b; Rankin and Culhane, 1969).

The cloze procedure can be very useful in classes where a single text or set of materials is required, as is typical of many secondary level classes and some upper-elementary content area classes. It enables the teacher to determine quickly and accurately which students will find that particular material too difficult (Jones and Pikulski, 1974). It is an effective procedure for gathering information about students' reading ability in the first days of school, before their teachers get to know them, especially when a teacher has more than one class. If the same text or material is used year after year, the initial cloze can be used again and again, or shared by several teachers who use the same textbooks or trade books.

Using the Cloze Diagnostically

The cloze procedure can be used diagnostically to find out what students know, to help them focus on context clues, and to read critically.

For diagnostic purposes, it is not necessary to delete words systematically. Instead, *key words* can be deleted, words that convey much of the information. When used *after* a reading assignment, the cloze can show a good deal about the concepts and vocabulary that students have gained from the assignment. Used *before* the assignment, the cloze can show their need for vocabulary and concept development prior to the reading.

A reader's tacit grasp of syntactic structures can be explored by deleting words of a particular grammatical class, such as verbs, prepositions, or adjectives. If used on a regular basis, the cloze can help students focus on grammatical forms, learn concepts of parts of speech, become aware of context clues, and infer the meaning of new words. Simplified cloze activities can be made up from students' dictated experience stories and their own written productions. This approach will help reinforce recognition of sight words and can be especially helpful for youngsters having trouble recognizing those troublesome structure words (*the, is, there, at,* and so forth). The *oral cloze*, in which selected word are left out and suggestions solicited while the teacher reads aloud to students, can be very useful in encouraging critical listening and comprehension (Blachowicz, 1977).

Cloze activities are particularly worthwhile for students who have relatively good word recognition but poor comprehension. Because they help students focus on the meaning and sense of the material, these activities can be invaluable in helping the word caller improve reading and listening comprehension (Bortnick and Lopardo, 1973, 1976). (Chapter 6 contains more ways of using cloze activities in the section entitled "Cloze Procedures.")

Assessing the Readability of Text

Readability refers to the level of difficulty of the written text. Readability is most often assessed by the use of one of several mathematical formulas which have been developed to assess text difficulty. The concept of text readability is important, but controversial.

When we refer to a person's independent or instructional reading level, we operate from an assumption that reading material comes to us in perceivable gradations of difficulty and that these gradations affect all readers the same way. We do make this assumption; we make it every time we refer to a student's instructional reading level, or to the grade level of a basal or other text. Certainly it is apparent that third-grade text material is "harder" than that for first grade, or that ninth-grade texts are likewise more difficult than fifth. Text written at lower grade levels tends to feature shorter, more frequently occurring words, shorter sentences, syntactically simpler sentences and, to some extent, simpler or at least more obvious ideas. It is here, when we begin to talk about the difficulty or simplicity of the content of the text, how complex the ideas are, that we begin to walk on very shaky ground. For, of course, the difficulty of text content is relative to the reader's prior knowledge of the subject and the ideas presented. We know that 10 hypothetical students with approximately similar reading abilities and levels who were reading the same text would not read the text with the same ease or difficulty. They would have different reading and life experiences, and thus would have different schemata for the information conveyed by the text. Those readers with prior experiences and knowledge closely related to the subject of the text would have an easier time than those whose experience with the subject was more remote. This happens all the time, and it reinforces for us the notion that the difficulty of the text is related to the individual reader, not contained entirely within the text.

However, it is possible to find two text passages on the same topic that are quite different in terms of the effort required to read and understand them. This is referred to as *relative readability* (Hirsch, 1978). When we analyze two pieces of text on the same subject to account for the relative readability of each, we find that two factors interact to account for the differences between them: (a) the degree of familiarity, or frequence of occurrence in written language, of the words used in the passages and (b) the grammatical complexity of the sentences (Klare, 1974). These two factors form the basis for most of the readability formulas for estimating text difficulty. Since there is usually an inverse relationship between the familiarity, or commonness, of words and their length, the difficulty of individual words is usually measured by word length, by counting letters or syllables in words. The same is true of grammatical complexity; the longer a sentence is, in general, the greater the difficulty. Thus, readability formulas are built on the assumption that easy, or low readability text is made up largely of short words or short sentences, while difficult text with a higher readability level is made up of longer words and sentences.

Readability formulas have been in use for many years, and more than a dozen similar formulas exist. In recent years, emphasis on text comprehension and its relative difficulty as an interaction between the structure and content of the text and the reader's prior knowledge of the content has challenged the assumptions on which readability formulas are based, that is, that difficulty is contained within the text and not relative to the reader. However, in spite of this change in our fundamental thinking about text difficulty, readability formulas are still widely used in education, business, insurance, banking, advertising, government, law, the military and, of course, publishing (Fry, 1987). School librarians use readability estimates in purchasing books and selecting books for teachers to use in their classes. State and local textbook adoption committees use readability estimates to purchase textbooks and other printed materials. It is a rare textbook sales representative who cannot cite the readability level of his or her texts, estimated by several different formulas. The use of readability formulas is alive and well, in spite of recent challenges to their basic premises.

The readability formulas described below are comparable in accuracy, easy to use, and may be helpful in estimating the difficulty of materials.

The Fry Readability Formula

To use the Fry formula (Fry, 1977), follow these steps:

1. Select three 100-word passages from near the beginning, middle, and end of the book. Count proper nouns, dates (1978), numerals (5,380), number words (5th), acronyms (NATO), and symbols (+, &) as words.

2. Count the total number of *sentences* in each 100-word passage, estimating to the nearest tenth of a sentence in the case of an incomplete sentence at the end of the passage. Average these three numbers by adding them together and dividing by three.

3. Count the total number of *syllables* in each 100-word passage. Do so by reading the words aloud; there is a vowel sound in each syllable of a word. Do not be misled by word size; *idle* has two syllables but is short, but *through* has one syllable although it looks longer. For dates, acronyms, symbols and the like, count each character as a syllable: 1977 has four, GNP has three, = has one. Average the total number of syllables by adding the numbers for each sample and dividing by three.

Figure 4.10

Fry's Graph for Estimating Readability—Extended

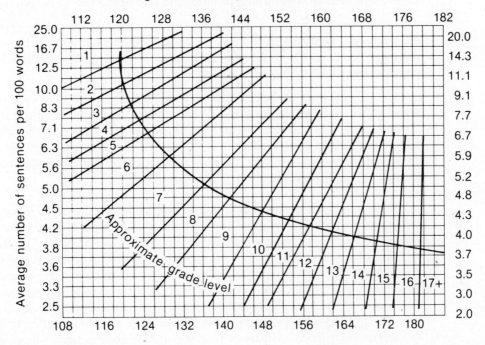

Average number of syllables per 100 words

Source: Edward Fry. "Fry's Readability Graph: Clarifications, Validity, and Extension to Level 17." *Journal of Reading* 21, no. 3 (Dec. 1977): 242–252.

4. Plot on the graph in Figure 4.10 the location of the average number of syllables and the average number of sentences. Most will occur near the heavy curved line on the graph. The perpendicular lines show the approximate grade-level areas. If the syllable and sentence averages fall outside or at the extremes of a grade level band, check your arithmetic for errors and if necessary recalculate using three new samples.

The levels yielded by the Fry formula are intended to be used as instructional levels. Students may be expected to read it with about 70 percent comprehension.

The Raygor Readability Estimate

This formula (Baldwin and Kaufman, 1979) may be used to estimate the difficulty of text at or above the third-grade level. To use it, follow these steps:

1. Select three 100-word passages as with the Fry formula, selecting passages from near the beginning, middle, and end of the text to be assessed.

2. Count the number of *sentences* in each sample, estimating to the nearest tenth of a sentence in the case of an incomplete sentence at the end of a passage. Average the number of sentences by adding the number for each passage and dividing by three.

3. Count the number of *words with more than six letters* in each passage. Average the number of "long words" by adding them and dividing by three. If one sample of 100 words yields very different numbers than the other two, select another passage. For example, if you see that two passages have about 25 or 30 long words and one has only four, add one more passage, count the long words in it, and average over four samples.

Find the point on the graph in Figure 4.11 where the average number of sentences and average number of long words intersect. The number of the band running across the chart tells you the grade level of the text. If the intersection falls in the areas marked "Invalid," do not try to interpret this finding. First, check your arithmetic and if necessary, do the procedure again with three more passages. If the same results occur, the text is so unusual that it does not conform to typical norms of grade level difficulty.

The grade levels yielded by the Raygor formula are intended to be used as *instructional levels*. Students reading at this instructional level may be expected to be able to deal with this text with about 70 percent comprehension.

Word-List Readability Formulas

Some of the older readability formulas use word lists of common English words rather than counting syllables or letters in words. The Dale-Chall (1948) and Spache formulas (1953) are examples. After counting the number of sentences in the three 100-word samples, the teacher checks each word individually against a list of common (or uncommon) words. Since this is a tedious and time-consuming process, the easier formulas were developed.

Computer Programs to Assess Readability

Readability estimation programs are now available for many computers. In the computer versions, a teacher types sample passages into the computer, which applies one or more readability formulas to the samples and displays the readability estimates of the passages within a few seconds. Some programs may also list rare words occurring within the passages. These programs make using readability formulas much faster than manual computation.

Figure 4.11

Raygor Readability Formula Chart

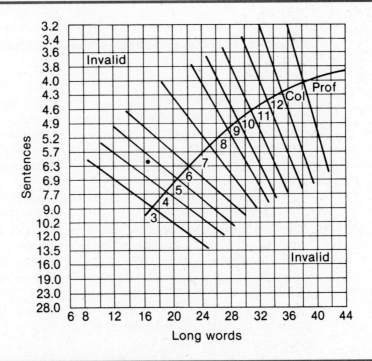

Source: From R. Scott Baldwin and Rhonda K. Kaufman. "A Concurrent Validity Study of the Raygor Readability Estimate." *Journal of Reading* (Nov. 1979): 148–153.

Such programs save time but may not make efficient use of the capabilities of computers. The current formulas are intended for manual use and are limited to syllable or letter counts and sentence length because these are easy to figure manually. More complex issues which affect text difficulty such as passage cohesion are ignored by current formulas because they are difficult to calculate manually. Yet computers are capable of much more complex and sophisticated analyses. It may be that in the future computer programs may be developed to assess more complex aspects of text difficulty than sentence length and word or syllable counts.

Readability formulas can be useful devices for estimating the approximate difficulty of text material, but they should only be used as approximations, never as absolute measures of text difficulty. Sentence length, word length, and familiarity of words used contribute to text difficulty, but readability formulas do not assess other critically important factors such as complexity of ideas presented, use of figurative language, paragraph cohesion, or the reader's ability to relate new information presented in the text to prior information she or he may (or may not) have.

Word Recognition and Phonics Tests

A number of commercial tests intended to test mastery of phonics skills and decoding are available. Usually they consist of letters and letter groups to identify and sound out, real words and pseudowords (nonsense words like *mif, drake,* or *faught*) to sound out using common phonic generalizations, and letters-plus-word-stems (like *p - in* or *s - ate*) to combine, or "blend," into pronounceable words.

Some commercial IRIs such as the *Diagnostic Reading Scales* (Spache), *Classroom Reading Scales* (Silvaroli), and the *Bader Reading and Language Inventory* include separate phonics inventories. A few standardized achievement tests, like the *Woodcock Reading Mastery Test—Revised,* the *Peabody Individual Achievement Test,* the *Gray Oral Reading Test—Revised* and the *Quick-Score Achievement Test* include phonics and word blending subtests. And another group of tests like the *Decoding Skills Test, Sipay Word Analysis Test, Botel Reading Inventory ,* and *Brigance Diagnostic Inventory of Basic Skills* are intended primarily for assessment of decoding skills and do not include other aspects of reading ability.

Tests like these may be useful for screening purposes, since they are fairly quick to administer and do not require analyzing the student's WRI responses. However, it is just this analysis that helps teachers develop the diagnostic skills and judgment they need to fully explore students' abilities. Commercial word-attack tests are adequate for screening purposes but should not be depended on to replace careful study of what a child can do. Please see Chapter 8 for fuller discussions of commercial tests.

SUMMARY

This chapter discusses the assessment of student performance based on informed teacher judgment. *Internal assessments,* designed for instruction, include teacher-made tests and procedures, observations, interviews, informal diagnostic procedures and so forth. *External assessments,* designed for accountability, include norm- and criterion-referenced tests.

Informal diagnostic procedures make possible *qualitative* analysis of reading behaviors as well as use of *quantitative* scores. They are useful in determining a reader's *independent, instructional,* and *frustration* reading levels and reading strength and needs.

An *informal reading inventory (IRI)* is individually administered for these purposes. IRIs consist of story passages for oral and silent reading at consecutive grade levels from primer through high school, and corresponding comprehension questions. During oral reading *miscues,* or divergences from the text, are recorded, counted to determine a reader's oral reading fluency, and analyzed to reveal word recognition strategies and use of context. Responses to comprehension questions are used to determine reading levels and reveal comprehension skills and strategies. *Retellings* may be used in addition to questions. When the frustration reading level is reached, subsequent passages may be read aloud to the reader to determine his or her *listening comprehension* level, an indicator of potential for reading improvement.

An informal *word recognition inventory (WRI)* consisting of graded lists of individual words may be used to assess sight vocabulary and decoding skills out of context. Sight recognition is assessed by *flashing* individual words for a very brief moment, and phonic and structural analysis skills are assessed by reexamining missed words in an *untimed* exposure.

Think-alouds, or students' verbal self-reports of their thinking during reading, may be used to assess students' use of strategies and attempts to construct meaning from text.

The *cloze procedure,* a passage in which words are systematically replaced by blanks for the reader to complete, is useful in determining whether particular material represents the reader's independent, instructional, or frustration level and in making judgments about his or her use of context. The *maze,* using multiple-choice responses instead of blanks, is an easier alternative to the cloze which has the same purposes. *Readability formulas* may be helpful in estimating the difficulty or grade level of text material. They may be computed manually or by a computer program. *Supplementary phonics tests* may be used to further study the reader's decoding skills.

REFERENCES

Baker, Linda, and Nancy Stein. "The Development of Prose Comprehension Skills." In *Children's Prose Comprehension: Research and Practice,* ed. Carol M. Santa and Bernard L. Hayes. Newark, DE: International Reading Association, 1981.

Baldwin, R. Scott, and Rhonda K. Kaufman. "A Concurrent Validity Study of the Raygor Readability Estimate." *Journal of Reading* 23, no. 2 (Nov. 1979): 148–153.

Betts, Emmett A. "Reading Problems at the Intermediate Grade Level." *Elementary School Journal* 40 (June 1941): 737–746.

Betts, Emmett A. *Foundations of Reading Instruction.* New York: American Book, 1957.

Blachowicz, Camille. "Cloze Activities for Primary Readers." *The Reading Teacher* 31, no. 3 (Dec. 1977): 300–302.

Bormuth, J. "Readability: A New Approach." *Reading Research Quarterly* 1, no. 3, (1966): 79–132.

Bormuth, John R. "The Cloze Readability Procedure." *Elementary English* 55 (April 1968a): 429–436.

Bormuth, John R. "Cloze Test Reliability: Criterion Reference Scores." *Journal of Educational Measurement* 5 (Fall 1968b): 189–196.

Bortnick, Robert, and Genevieve S. Lopardo. "An Instructional Application of the Cloze Procedure." *Journal of Reading* 16, no. 4 (Jan. 1973): 296–300.

Bortnick, Robert, and Genevieve S. Lopardo. "The Cloze Procedure: A Multi-Purpose Classroom Tool." *Reading Improvement* 13, no. 2 (Summer 1976): 113–117.

Calfee, Robert, and Elfrieda Hiebert. "Classroom Assessment of Reading." In *Handbook of Reading Research,* Vol. 2, ed. Rebecca Barr, Michael L. Kamil, Peter Mosenthal, and P. David Pearson. White Plains, NY: Longman Publishers, 1991.

Cardarelli, Aldo F. "The Influence of Reinspection on Students' IRI Results." *The Reading Teacher* 41, no. 7 (March 1988): 664–667.

Dale, Edgar, and Jeanne Chall. "A Formula for Predicting Readability." *Educational Research Bulletin* 27 (1948): 11–20.

Duffelmeyer, Frederick A. "Vocabulary Questions on Informal Reading Inventories." *The Reading Teacher* 43, no. 2 (Nov. 1989): 142–148.

Dufflemeyer, Frederick A., and Barbara Blakely Dufflemeyer. "Main Idea Questions on Informal Reading Inventories." *The Reading Teacher* 41, no. 2 (Nov. 1987): 162–165.

Dufflemeyer, Frederick A., and Barbara Blakely Dufflemeyer. "Are IRI Passages Suitable for Assessing Main Idea Comprehension?" *The Reading Teacher* 42, no. 6 (Feb. 1989): 358–363.

Estes, Thomas H., and Joseph L. Vaughn, Jr. *Reading and Learning in the Content Classroom: Diagnostic and Instructional Strategies,* 2d ed. Boston, MA: Allyn and Bacon, 1985.

Flood, James, and Diane Lapp. "Reading Comprehension Instruction for At-Risk Students: Research-Based Practices That Can Make a Difference," *Journal of Reading* 33, no. 7 (April 1990): 490–496.

Fry, Edward. "The Varied Uses of Readability Measurement Today." *Journal of Reading* 30, no. 4 (Jan. 1987): 338–343.

Fry, Edward. "Fry's Reading Graph: Clarifications, Validity and Extension to Level 17." *Journal of Reading* 21, no. 3 (Dec. 1977): 242–252.

Guthrie, John, M. Seifert, N. A. Burnham, and R. I. Caplan. "The Maze Technique to Assess , Monitor Reading Comprehension." *The Reading Teacher* 28, no. 2 (Nov. 1974): 161–168.

Hansell, T. Stevenson. "Readability, Syntactic Transformations, and Generative Semantics." *Journal of Reading* 19, no. 7 (April 1976): 557–562.

Hirsch, E. Donald. *The Philosophy of Composition.* Chicago: University of Chicago Press, 1978.

Johns, Jerry L., and Anne Marie Magliari. "Informal Reading Inventories: Are the Betts Criteria the Best Criteria?" *Reading Improvement* 26, no. 2 (Summer 1989): 124–132.

Johnson, Marjorie Seddon, Roy A. Kress, and John J. Pikulski. *Informal Reading Inventories.* Newark, DE: International Reading Association, 1987.

Jones, Margaret, and Edna Pikulski. "Cloze for the Classroom." *The Reading Teacher* 17, no. 6 (March 1974): 432–438.

Kender, Joseph P., and Herbert Rubenstein. "Recall Versus Reinspection in IRI Comprehension Tests." *The Reading Teacher* 30, no. 8 (April 1977): 776–779.

Klare, George R. "Assessing Readability." *Reading Research Quarterly* 10, no. 1 (Oct. 1974): 362–363.

Miller, G. R., and E. G. Coleman. "A Set of 36 Prose Passages Calibrated for Complexity." *Journal of Verbal Learning and Verbal Behavior* 6 (1967): 851–854.

Pearson, P. David, and Dale L. Johnson. *Teaching Reading Comprehension,* 2d ed. New York: Holt, Reinhart & Winston, 1989.

Perfetti, Charles A. *Reading Ability.* New York: Oxford University Press, 1985.

Peterson, Joe, M. Jean Greenlaw, and Robert J. Tierney. "Assessing Instructional Placement with the IRI: The Effectiveness of Comprehension Questions." *Journal of Educational Research* 71, no. 5 (May–June 1978): 247–250.

Pikulski, John J. "Informal Reading Inventories." *The Reading Teacher* 43, no. 7 (March 1990): 514–516.

Pikulski, John J., and Timothy Shanahan. "Informal Reading Inventories: A Critical Analysis," in John J. Pikulski and Timothy Shanahan, eds., *Approaches to the Informal Evaluation of Reading.* Newark, DE: International Reading Association, 1982.

Powell, William R. "Reappraising the Criteria for Interpreting Informal Reading Inventories." In *Reading Diagnosis and Evaluation,* ed. D. L. DeBoer. Newark, DE: International Reading Association, 1970.

Rankin, Earl F., and Joseph W. Culhane. "Comparable Cloze and Multiple Choice Comprehension Test Scores." *Journal of Reading* 13, No. 3 (Dec. 1969): 193–198.

Rubenstein, Herbert, Joseph P. Kender, and F. Charles Mace. "Do Tests Penalize Readers for Short Term Memory?" *Journal of Reading* 32, no. 1 (Oct. 1988): 4–10.

Ruddell, Robert. "A Study of Cloze Comprehension Technique in Relation to Structurally Controlled Reading Material." *Proceedings of the International Reading Association* 9 (1964): 298–303.

Schell, Leo M., and Gerald S. Hanna. "Can Informal Reading Inventories Reveal Strengths and Weaknesses in Comprehension Subskills?" *The Reading Teacher* 35, no. 3 (Dec. 1981): 263–268.

Schmitt, Maribeth Cassidy. "A Questionnaire to Measure Children's Awareness of Strategic Reading Processes." *The Reading Teacher* 43, no. 7 (March 1990): 454–461.

Spache, George. "A New Readability Formula for Primary Grade Materials." *Elementary School Journal* 53 (March 1953): 410–413.

Taylor, Wilson. "Cloze Procedure: A New Tool for Measuring Readability." *Journalism Quarterly* 30 (Fall 1953): 415–433.

Valencia, Sheila, and P. David Pearson. "Reading Assessment: Time for a Change." *The Reading Teacher* 40, no. 8 (April 1987): 726–732.

Wade, Suzanne E. "Using Think Alouds to Assess Comprehension." *The Reading Teacher* 43, no. 7 (March 1990): 442–453.

Portfolio Assessment

I n a prestigious reading clinic many years ago, two of the authors had just completed two days of work with an eight-year-old boy who had been referred for his reading problems. As we wrote up our findings for his parents and his teachers, we noted his scores on word recognition and comprehension measures, his reading rates in texts of varying difficulty, his hearing capacity, and his reading levels. Then a thought occurred to us: We really should tell them that he *loved* reading *Fox and His Friends.* So we did.

Of course we should have. Scores are important, and qualitative descriptions of readers' abilities and strategies are useful—but both are incomplete without describing what readers have actually accomplished in their reading instruction. Many teachers are using literacy portfolios as a means of putting together a rich description of a student's accomplishments in reading, and literacy in general—and also of involving the students in their own assessment.

WHAT IS PORTFOLIO ASSESSMENT?

A literacy portfolio is a collection of students' work or related artifacts that is carefully selected by students and (usually) teachers to represent the students' efforts, progress, and achievements (Northwest Evaluation Association, 1991; Farr and Lowe, 1990). In putting together portfolios, students are asked to think hard about what they have been doing and how they have been doing it. Their portfolios include records of their reflections on their own development as readers and writers.

Portfolio assessment thus serves six purposes that formal and informal reading assessments alone cannot:

1. *Portfolio assessment captures some measures that other assessments miss.* A portfolio may tell us, for example, how many books—and which books—a student read in a marking period.

2. *Portfolio assessment opens for us a window into the students' feelings and attitudes.* Portfolios let the students speak for themselves—commenting on what they like or dislike about certain texts or certain reading activities, and how they feel about their reading in general.

3. *Portfolio assessment is an excellent way to show parents and other teachers how a student or a group of students are doing*—and, again, what is shown is not just levels of ability, but the work itself that students have done, and how much and how well they have done it. Of course this tool invites the others—whether helping teachers, next years' teachers, or the parents—to support children in precisely those activities they are doing well, and to help them in other areas in which they need to do better.

4. *Portfolio assessment invites the teacher to become a researcher.* A full portfolio is evidence; it's data. It's a record of the steps and stages of children's growth in literacy, and it's proof of the effectiveness (or maybe the lack of it!) of certain activities and materials. Teachers can use this evidence to learn from their teaching and to strengthen their programs. They can share the contents of the portfolios with other teachers in building meetings and in professional conferences. They can write up gleanings from portfolios and submit them to professional journals, for the benefit of other teachers.

Perhaps most important of all are the portfolios' benefits for the students:

5. *Portfolio assessment motivates students.* Students are inspired if they can see their own progress, and portfolios show them very clearly how much and in what ways they have grown over time.

6. *Portfolio assessment invites students to become purposeful and strategic in their learning.* They are challenged to think about what they have been doing and how it has helped them. They think about what they can do to get still better at reading and writing.

Along the lines of the last two points, consider this quote from a ninth-grader:

> I like the portfolio because you get to see your grades, see what you did and didn't do. You see how your attitude was and how much work you did in all! You review your grades and ask questions (to the teacher). Therefore, you can see your mistakes and good habits, so you can fix whats wrong and keep doing whats right."

USING PORTFOLIO ASSESSMENT

It is useful to think of three stages in the portfolio process. The first is the *planning stage.* Here teachers reflect on their goals and objectives, and sketch out a blueprint for the kind of portfolios they want to build and how they will use them. The second stage we call *selection and reflection.* Here the students select *artifacts*—pieces of evidence to go into their portfolios. Their selections are guided by the blueprint that was made by the teacher during the planning stage. Students must think about their selections, must come up with clear criteria for their choices, and must be ready to explain in a conference and in writing why they chose each piece and what it says about their growth in literacy. During the third, or *conference stage*, students and teachers discuss the artifacts the students included and their reasons for including them. Students talk about how the classroom instruction is working for them and how they are doing, and teachers share their perceptions of the students' progress. The teacher and students may discuss grades at this point, if the teacher wants to use the portfolios in that way. As the last step in the process, the teacher and the students agree upon goals that the students will attain before the next conference, and discuss strategies for reaching those goals.

The Planning Stage

As you begin to use portfolio assessment, you must ask yourself what you want to achieve from your daily instruction. You must also ask what activities, from structured lessons to informal reading time, you offer to meet those goals. You must also ask yourself how you want to use the portfolio process. Figure 5.1 shows a list of questions you might ask yourself as you plan your use of portfolios. Let's look at each of these in turn.

1. *What are the teacher's goals for literacy instruction?* To set goals upon which to build a portfolio process means that you must make your own instructional goals explicit. In what ways do you want students to grow from being in your classroom? Do you want students to become better writers? If so, your portfolio blueprint should focus on student's growth in the writing

Figure 5.1

Questions for Planning the Portfolio Process

1. What are your goals for literacy instruction?
2. Which activities address the literacy goals you identified?
3. What artifacts or student works represent progress toward your literacy goals?
4. How can you facilitate student self-reflection?
5. How will grades be assigned?
6. How can you arrange the class schedule so that ample time is allotted to the portfolio process?

process over the year. Do you want students to become willing and competent learners as well as better readers and writers? Then your portfolio will be designed to help students understand their learning processes and the strategies they used to read and write.

You can clarify your instructional goals through self-reflection or through conferences with other teachers. Of course, some goals might come directly from established state or district curriculum guidelines.

2. *Which activities address the literacy goals you identified?* Adopting a portfolio process of assessment does not mean that you must abandon the classroom activities you were already using. It only requires that you find matches between the activities you use and the goals you have identified. For instance, if one of your instructional goals was to develop positive attitudes for reading, a matched activity might be sustained silent reading of a book or magazine that the student chooses.

You might review past lesson plans, textbook scope-and-sequence charts, teaching manuals, and student work folders to identify activity-goal matches between activities and goals. Where literacy goals are not addressed by existing activities, you may decide to modify some activities or develop new ones. Taking the trouble to find these matches is worthwhile, because it will make you aware of the opportunities you already provided for the students to meet your literacy instructional goals and let you see exactly where you need to make changes in your program.

3. *What artifacts or student works represent progress toward literacy goals?* Whatever goes into the portfolio should demonstrate the teacher's and the student's best thinking about what counts as progress toward meeting the instructional goals you have set. When those goals are not very concrete—for instance, "developing positive attitudes toward reading"—you can compile evidence of an indirect sort, such as the student's written reactions to books, notes written by the teacher about the student after a conference, records of books checked out of the school or classroom library, and accounts of the student's reading aloud to younger children.

When the goals call for a student to develop complex processes, entries to the portfolio can document the steps in those processes. Growth in the use of strategies for reading with comprehension, for example, can be documented by written K-W-Ls (K-W-L stands for "Know—Want to Know—Learn," and it is a teaching strategy described in Chapter 6), story maps, vocabulary exercises, and the like. Growth in comprehension can also be documented by means of written reports, critiques of books, or photocopies of entries in response journals. Comprehension may also be demonstrated in ways that do not leave tangible products: Dramatic enactments and oral presentations of novels are two possibilities.

A student's growth in the use of the process of writing can be documented by means of brainstorming lists and concept maps (for prewriting strategies), revised drafts (for drafting and editing), and final drafts (for publishing

Figure 5.2

Potential Literacy Artifacts

A partial list of potential artifacts includes, in no particular order:
- writing samples
- record of books read
- book projects (i.e., letter to the author, illustration of the book)
- interest inventory
- checklist of reading behaviors
- concept maps
- prewriting activity
- writing drafts
- evidence/notes taken during student-teacher conferences
- audio-taped oral reading
- a writing in progress
- reading logs
- reading response journal entries
- workbook pages
- teacher-made tests
- standardized tests
- favorite activity for the grading period
- evidence of reflection about the selections

and, perhaps, using a word processor). A list of possible literacy artifacts appears in Figure 5.2.

As a student selects these artifacts and, later, discusses them, he or she naturally becomes more aware of the strategies to be used to read purposefully or write systematically. At the same time, the teacher can observe how well the student seems to understand these strategies.

4. *How can teachers encourage students to reflect on their work?* The artifacts students select, and the reflecting on literacy processes they do, are guided by the questions the teacher puts to them. Your questions should give students guidelines for making judgments about what to put into the portfolios. The questions should also lead them to think in certain ways about activities related to the literacy goals. Your questions can challenge students to justify their choices, to choose artifacts intelligently, and to become aware of their own criteria for judging their work.

The questions should address the steps in becoming a competent reader, writer, and learner. For example, if you want to assess students' understanding of the process writing approach, you might ask questions that guide students to select examples of prewriting activities (e. g., a record of brainstorming) and describe why they used them and how the activities contributed to their final drafts. In this case, artifacts can represent significant steps in a process rather than the outcome of a process. Students' reflections on these steps provide benchmarks of progress and valuable feedback from which the teacher can make informed modifications to classroom activities. That is, if the students show little awareness of what prewriting is and why it is helpful, you have an indication that you may need to revisit this topic with the class.

No set of questions is ideal for all students, but all questions should make students think. You may thus word questions differently depending on whom they are for. Different questions may occur to you after you have gotten started. Changes and additions should be considered as part of the process rather than indications of poor planning. We have provided sample questions in Figure 5.3.

5. *How will grades be assigned?* Assigning grades to students' work is a necessary part of educational practice in most schools. Teachers who adopt a portfolio process as part of a literacy or reading program within a school are

Figure 5.3

Sample Questions That Foster Selection and/or Self-Reflection

- Select your best writing. Why do you think it is your best?
- Select your most important piece of writing. Put a star on it. Tell why you feel it was your most important.
- Select the activity that was most important to you this six weeks. Describe and tell why it was important to you.
- Tell why you think you echo read each day.
- Select a reading-response journal entry that represents your best writing. Tell what you think makes it your best.
- Of all the books you read this six weeks, which was your favorite? Tell what makes it your favorite.
- Pick a story you read that was hard for you to understand. Explain why you think it was hard for you.
- Explain why you think the teacher schedules a sustained silent reading period each day.
- Describe the K-W-L comprehension strategy. Do you think it helps you to understand a passage? If so, why? If not, why?
- Choose a prewriting activity that helped you the most when you wrote a draft. Put a "smiley face" on it and explain how it helped you.
- Select an unfinished draft. Tell why you didn't finish it. What problems did you encounter?
- Select your most effective piece of writing. What makes it effective?

rarely exempted from this practice. Scholars and practitioners offer different views on the appropriateness of grading portfolios and the methods for doing so. The typical grading environment observed in most schools separates instruction from testing or assessing. Within our blueprint, however, no such separation is made. If the blueprint for the portfolio process matches instructional goals with activities that indicate progress toward those goals, assigning grades becomes fairly straightforward. Grades are assigned during the portfolio conference phase, and they are, ideally, determined by consensus between the teacher and the students.

Teachers must continually act as aides to students' self-reflection, by monitoring the students' understanding and use of the grading criteria. For example, if work contained in a Reading Response Journal is to be graded, then the student and teacher must agree upon the criteria for assigning the grade. One teacher required students to write in each entry of their reading response journals brief summaries of the day's reading and personal reactions to that reading. Before assigning grades for their journals, she asked her students to go through and count how often summaries and reactions were included in the entries. Then they compared the number of summaries and reactions to the number of entries to determine how frequently the students completed the task. For this teacher, then, grades were assigned on the overall level of performance rather than on each entry in the journal.

The first task in a portfolio grading conference is to ensure that the student's criteria for judging the selected artifacts match the literacy goals established for the individual student and the course. Once the teacher and the student agree on the criteria for grading, a consensus grade can be reached. (It is important that the teacher, students, parents, and administrators share a common meaning for the grading scale.) In her portfolio process, Rief (1992) sends an informational letter to parents explaining the grading process she uses. We encourage this type of communication.

The preparation of a blueprint for the literacy portfolio process should include a plan for grading, with statements of criteria for evaluating artifacts and questions to guide the teacher and student toward a consensus.

6. *How can teachers arrange the class schedule to allow time for the portfolio process?* The blueprint for the literacy portfolio process should include a reasonable schedule, with time for students to select artifacts, reflect on their selections, and hold individual conferences with their teacher. If the portfolio conference is used to assign grades, the time for selection-reflection and conferences will likely come just before the end of grade reporting periods.

As the students begin to confer with you, there will be several days when holding individual conferences takes nearly all of your time. Students who are not engaged in conferences with you should be engaged in activities that isolate you from interruption as much as possible.

The time spent in conferences is well spent. It teaches and it motivates students. During the conference, the teacher models self-monitoring and metacognitive strategies. When students hold conferences with the teacher they set goals and identify strategies for reaching those goals. Teachers report that when students set goals and plan strategies to meet them, their motivation increases, and so does their performance level.

By including time for students to select and reflect on artifacts and hold conferences with the teacher, the classroom management plan becomes part of the blueprint for the portfolio process.

Once you have worked through the answers to the six questions we have just raised, you will be able to design a blueprint that will guide students in constructing their portfolios. We think that it is important for teachers to design their own portfolio blueprints if their own instructional goals are to be assessed. Blueprints should include instructional goals and objectives, guidelines for selecting portfolio artifacts, a plan for stimulating self-reflection, an organizational plan, and the criteria for judgment of the portfolio process and products.

Selection and Reflection

Once the blueprint for the portfolio process has been planned, students become actively involved in the process of selecting artifacts from their assorted works and reflecting upon them. The portfolio blueprint contains questions that help guide students as they make their selections, and write or dictate their reflections.

Sometimes the instructions to the students are stated fairly generally, and ask students to decide which ones of a range of classroom activities they judge as most important, helpful, or their best work. Here are some ways one teacher words such instructions:

> Look over the contents of your work folders and think about the different things you have done in class this six weeks. You have read each day, and written in your Reading Response Journals and Daily Journals. You have also participated in "5-Minute Workouts," K-W-L's, Concept Mapping, Computer activities and some of you have gone to the elementary school to read to the children.
>
> Choose the one thing you have done this six weeks that you feel was most important. Describe it and tell me why you think it was most important to you.

This teacher asked students to share their preferences and feelings about an artifact selected from among a wide variety of classroom activities. When given such an open selection and reflection task, student responses vary widely.

I like the computers. They are the funest and the most educated way of learning things. Because you get to push buttons.

The KWL helps me find out stuff I didn't know, let's me give opinions, and helps me remember what I read.

One of the most important things I did this six weeks was volunteering to read to the children at Songleaf. Because it helps some of the children to be successful in life and to reach their highest goal in life. The way it helped me was to reach my highest goal in life and help me to read better. I can read but not that good. When I read I put in words that aren't there. So reading to the children helps them and me at the same time. It teaches me how to read to my child.

The selection of an artifact can also be guided by more focused questioning. For example, in a kindergarten class, students regularly engaged in echo reading. In order to determine if the students understood the purposes of echo reading the teacher posed the following question:

Why do you think we echo read every day?

The young students' responses ranged from a general sense of the task—"for fun," to a more specific function of the task—"so we can hear reading." Here the teacher selected the activity for comments and the students provided their reflections on it.

Another way to guide artifact selection is to identify a part of the curriculum and ask students to select from among many artifacts reflecting on that part. For example, in one secondary reading class, the teacher presented the following selection task—"Select the most important writing and tell why it was important." Here writing was the part of the curriculum the teacher focused on, and the students were asked to examine a number of writings, make their selections based on their criteria, and state those criteria. The responses also ranged widely:

I put the star on the Christmas Poem we did in December I think it's my best writing because it's funny it was fun to do and I got to grades for but I didn't write it by my self me Billy and Anne Marie so I guess that why the poem was Perfect because friends help do it.

My most important work was my Halloween story It was called the scariest and most worst day ever I chose this story

because it was the first
book I wrote and it
became published for Halloween.
Many people read my story
and they liked it, and this
made me feel very happy
inside
         Didn't you like it?

The examples you have just seen show different degrees of specificity in guiding students' selections of their artifacts. Many of our examples are quite open and leave much of the criteria for selection and assessment to the students' own devices.

Some questions are aimed at classroom processes or activities that produce no concrete products. Still, students can be asked to make journal entries of reflections on their activities and then select from those reflections. In one case, a student chose to include in the portfolio a description of her reading to elementary school students. The artifact produced from this activity was the student's written reflection on her experience.

However specific the guiding questions are, teachers should take the opportunity to explain and model the process of selection and reflection. When the actual selection process begins, students must be encouraged to review *all* their relevant work. Once a selection is made, students may confer with peers to explain and justify their selections and criteria for the selection. These conferences help students to clarify their thinking as they reflect on their artifacts.

Reflection puts the students in a position that requires metacognition— thinking about their thought processes. They must be able to choose among artifacts for the ones that most nearly meet the selection criteria. The students must consciously state the criteria and describe those areas in which the selected artifacts met the criteria. Of course, students' willingness and ability to carry out these tasks independently will vary with the student's maturity, amount of practice with the tasks, the type of questions used to guide the process, and the degree to which the portfolio is an authentic part of classroom assessment practices.

These reflections will inform the teacher, students, administrators, and parents about the students' understanding of the process of learning this or that part of the curriculum. For example, in Response 1, the student doesn't demonstrate an awareness of the connection between activity and purpose. Surely the teacher will want to raise this issue in a conference with the student. On the other hand, in Response 2 the student mentioned a specific strategy (K-W-L) and indicated that he understood how to use the strategy and saw the reason for using it. Response 3 comes from a program in which middle- and high-school students read to first-graders in an elementary school. When reflecting upon her experiences, the student recognized the connection between reading to young elementary-school students and the way she might read to her own preschool-aged child. She has made a connection between school experiences and the real world. Now the teacher can seize on this "teachable moment" to extend the student's knowledge about emergent literacy—and bolster this young woman's *family literacy* in the process.

The students' reflections about their selected artifacts provide the topics for the culminating experience of the portfolio process, the conference. The questions that guide the selection and reflection process arise from the instructional goals of the classroom. The questions should model ways mature students think about their performance. If the students' selected works and their reflections are guided by meaningful questions, they will open the way to successful conferences in the final phase of the portfolio process.

The Conference Stage

Teacher:	Reggie, will you bring your work folder up to the desk for your conference?
Reggie:	I've done all my work, just give me an A this time. You know I always do everything!
Teacher:	Well, come on up here anyway, I want to see your successes!

[Reggie picks up his folder and approaches the desk with a bit of apprehension]

Teacher:	Reggie, let's see, you have selected your Reading Response Journal as the most important activity for this period. You wrote that the reason it was important was that you could tell others how you felt. Why is that important to you?
Reggie:	I don't really know, I just like being able to let people know how I feel.
Teacher:	Reggie, why is being able to tell people how you feel important to you?
Reggie:	I guess it's just that in lots of other classes, they just give you work and don't care how you feel about it. It makes me feel like people care about what I do and how I feel.

This interaction between Reggie and his teacher is not unusual in a portfolio conference. The teacher, in this interchange, has learned that Reggie really likes being able to share his feelings and that it is important that others care about those feelings. Although she has not learned much about Reggie's literacy level in this conversation, she has discovered a hint about how to motivate Reggie. This particular conference occurred early in the school year. The goal of the teacher in this conference was to find out which classroom activities were considered important by the students. Knowing this enabled her later to encourage students on days when they were less motivated. For example, if Reggie seemed reluctant to complete work, the teacher could suggest that he write his feelings in his journal. We will continue with our conversation with Reggie.

Teacher: Show me your Reading Response Journal.
[Reggie hands the teacher his RRJ]
Teacher: Let's see, you had 18 opportunities to write in your journal, and I see 12 entries. What happened to the others?
[Reggie looks through his RRJ and fidgets nervously]
Reggie: I don't know. I do them every time you ask us.
Teacher: Well, I don't see them here, could they be in your other journal?"
Reggie: Well, I guess sometimes I may talk to people at my table, but mostly I do it.
Teacher: I have noticed that you seem to get distracted by the others. What do you think you could do to write instead of talking?
Reggie: I guess I could just ignore them and write when I'm supposed to.
Teacher: That's a good idea, how can I help you do that?
Reggie: Maybe if you remind me if I start talking . . . OK?
Teacher: That sounds like something we could try.

In this part of the conference, the teacher addresses the quantity of work in Reggie's journal. The teacher notes that during the past work period Reggie had 18 opportunities to make entries; he only availed himself of 12. When asked to account for the missing entries, and presented with objective information, Reggie ultimately identified the problem: He gets distracted. The fact that Reggie identified his own needs empowered him to find a solution, which he did. We continue with the conference.

Teacher: Reggie, as I look at your journal entries, I see that you have included a brief summary and your feelings in each entry. That is exactly what I have asked you to do when you write in your Reading Response Journal. I can tell that you like to share your feelings, you can express them very well. If you were to assign a grade of A through F for your work in the Reading Response Journal, what would it be?

Reggie: C'mon, you're supposed to assign the grade, not me!

Teacher: But Reggie, I want to know how you would grade yourself. You know best what you have done and I want to know your opinion.

Reggie: O. K., D I guess.

Teacher: Why would you give yourself a D?

Reggie: Cause I didn't do all the work. I talk sometimes.

Teacher: I know you do get distracted, but what grade would you give yourself for the work you did do?

Reggie: I guess I'd give myself an A.

Teacher: I agree, when you do your work, you do it well. We also need to consider that you do sometimes get distracted. Overall, what grade would you give yourself for the work you did and the number of times you did it?

Reggie: C+.

In this portion of the conference, the teacher asked Reggie to evaluate himself against the traditional A through F grading system. Here, the teacher used the grading system as an opportunity to discuss two kinds of criteria: the quantitative (number of entries) and the qualitative (completeness of the entry). Often students will grade themselves more negatively than the teacher. Reggie did. Many students have never had the grading standards explained to them, so they are reluctant to assess themselves. Discussing grading standards gives teachers a chance to model self-monitoring that promotes metacognition. In the example, the teacher reminded Reggie of the key elements of a journal entry (summary and statement of feelings) and then pointed out the area in need of improvement (distractibility). We continue that dialogue.

Teacher: I think I would give you a B. You did make an entry most of the time and your entries were excellent. Now, what can we do to bring the B up to an A?

Reggie: I guess I'll just write every time.

Teacher: That is a good goal. You like writing about your feelings. What do you need to do to achieve that goal?

Reggie: I don't know.

Teacher: You said that you would ignore your friends during Reading-Response-Journal time and write. I think that will help you accomplish that goal.

The goal Reggie set for himself was to write in the Reading Response Journal every chance he got. He needed some prompting to address the basic problem of distractibility. Together, the teacher and Reggie found a way to boost the number of entries in the journal. Later the teacher will have an opportunity to confer with the others who sit at Reggie's table. Most likely, the same performance problem will surface in their journals, and actions can be taken to influence the performance of each student at that table.

This sample conference dialogue is focused on one activity, the Reading Response Journal. Other times, conferences will address a range of student activities within a classroom. Whether the conference is based on broadly defined criteria or more narrowly defined criteria, the students' written reflections provide the starting point of the conference.

If the blueprint for the portfolio process has been well designed, the conference will proceed more smoothly. Even though students may present issues that diverge from the blueprint, the teacher will always be able to return to the blueprint as a guide. An example of one blueprint is provided in the Reading Portfolio Record in Figure 5.4. The questions teachers ask and their responses to student input vary with the teacher's characteristics, those

Figure 5.4

Reading Portfolio Record

Student Name_____   Course Name_____   Grading Period_____

Birthdate _____   Current Grade Placement _____

Below is a written record of student reactions to their work and student-teacher assessment conferences.

A. Reading Response Journal
1. What you feel is important about your RRJ's?
2. Do you write in your RRJ each opportunity?
3. Do you include a summary about what you read?
4. Do you write your opinions or feelings about what you read or about why you didn't read?
Teacher Comments:

Reading Response Journal Grade_____

B. Writing Workshop
1. Put a star on the writing that represents your most important writing and describe why you believe this.
2. Show me evidence of prewriting activities (concept map or brainstorming).
3a. Show me an example.
3b. How do they help you write drafts?
Teacher Comments:

Writing Workshop Grade_____

Figure 5.4 continued

C. Class and Group Activities
  1. Group projects and whole class activities
     a. Describe the activity you liked best and tell why.
     Teacher Comments:

Grade_____

  2. Participation and ability to use K-W-L and other comprehension strategies
     independently
     a. Which strategy helped you the most and why?
     b. Show me the notes from the K-W-L's or other comprehension activities in which you
        have participated.
     Teacher Comments:

Combined Class and Group Activities Grade_____

D. Sustained Silent Reading
  1. What kind of material did you like to read most and why?
  2. Why do you think we read everyday?
  3. Do you read the entire SSR period? Why or why not?
  Teacher Comments:

Sustained Silent Reading Grade_____

E. Goal for Next Grading Period
  1. What do you want to accomplish this next six weeks?
  2. How do you plan to do this?
  Teacher Comments:

Teacher Signature_____ Date _____

Student Signature_____ Date _____

Source: Samuel Mathews, Josephine Peyton Young, and Nancy Dean Giles. *Student Literacy Volunteers: Providing Tools for Brighter Futures.* Pensacola, FL: The Educational Research and Development Center, The University of West Florida, 1992.

of the students, the teacher's instructional goals, and the goals for the portfolio conference. The conference is no more than a structured conversation between the teacher and the student about the day-to-day classroom activities. We do suggest that the conference be conducted in a formal setting so that it becomes a "special" time between the teacher and student, Although we present no formal script for the conference, there are some general guides that can shape the kinds of interactions that occur.

The guidelines we present show one of many possible structures. Our structure can either be used to elicit student assessment of specific works (e. g., a writing sample) or of an entire instructional area (e. g., a writing workshop). We encourage teachers to adapt the guidelines below to fit their own situations. Our guidelines are as follows:

1. *Explain and clarify the portfolio process.* Teachers explain the structure of the portfolio conference: the conference agenda and the responsibilities of the teacher and the student.

2. *Discuss preselected work and the student's reflections.* The beginning of the conference should focus upon the work(s) selected by the student and the students' reflections on them. These reflections include the student's assessments, and descriptions of criteria she or he used for selections and assessments. This gives the teacher and student a common point of departure for the remainder of the conference.

3. *The student provides an assessment (and grade when appropriate) of performance in the area of focus.* These assessments may be conducted against a personal best criteria. Regardless, once the student has provided the assessment, she or he should provide a rationale for the particular assessment. In the sample conference with Reggie, he used a criterion based on the number of entries when he assigned himself a grade of D on the first assessment.

4. *The teacher gives the student feedback to the self-assessment and criteria.* Here the teacher can ask the student to clarify any murky points in his or her self-assessment. The teacher may also think aloud and model rationales for assessment. Finally, the teacher can convey to the student that he has been understood. Students like Reggie often want to give up the opportunity to assess the themselves. In this step, teachers can demonstrate to students that their self-assessments have been heard and understood. This requires active listening on the part of the teacher.

5. *The teacher provides his or her assessment.* At this point in the conference, the teacher can confirm the student's own assessment and statement of criteria. In the conference with Reggie, the teacher stated that the quality of work was high but agreed with Reggie that the quantity of work was lacking. Again, the teacher can use this as an opportunity to model appropriate self-assessment and to point out to the student suitable criteria to be used in that assessment.

6. *The teacher summarizes the student performance in the areas of focus.* The role of the teacher at this point is to restate the strengths found in the student's work and the areas in which additional work is needed. This shows the student that the teacher was indeed listening and understood the student's input.

7. *Consensus is reached on assessment.* If the teacher's summary is accurate and the student is convinced that the assessment is based on valid criteria, then a consensus can be reached about the quality of the student's work. In Reggie's conference, there was negotiation, based not on power or control but on the degree to which the quantity and quality of his work met established criteria. Whether or not a grade is to be assigned, the student and teacher must agree on how much the selected artifacts represent progress toward the literacy goals of the classroom.

8. *The student and teacher set goals.* At this point in the conference, the student sets an instructional goal to be attained before the next conference. If the goal is set realistically and reflects literacy goals of the classroom, then during later conferences progress toward the stated goal is more meaningful, especially since the goal is set by the student. A major task for the teacher is to help the student set attainable goals. Goals that are unattainable will diminish the students' motivation in the long run. Goals should be based on the student's prior performance, and the ability of the teacher to support change in the student's work habits or to provide additional support in the form of strategies.

9. *Strategies for attaining the goal are identified.* The student, with support from the teacher, identifies ways to meet the established goals. In Reggie's case, the strategies revolved around classroom conduct and attempts to increase Reggie's resistance to distraction. In other cases, the strategies will include specific reading or writing strategies. One way to maintain the student's attention to the goal and strategies is to record both in a place the student will see them each day.

If the conference is to address only one selected artifact, then the work of the conference is over at this point. If a more comprehensive conference is undertaken, then the process moves to the next artifact selected by the student.

10. *The conference is ended.* The last step of the conference is a formal acceptance of the outcomes of the conference including any grades, goals, and strategies. One way to end the proceedings is for the teacher and student to sign and date the portfolio record. This formal acceptance indicates that both the teacher and student are satisfied with the outcome including assessments, goals, and strategies.

These guidelines provide a structure from which teachers can begin portfolio conferences with students. The goals of the conference encompass more than simply assessing students' work. They include modeling metacognitive strategies of self-monitoring, goal setting, and planning strategies to attain goals. The conference, like the entire portfolio process, should be integrated with instruction. The time spent in individual conferences should be viewed as time spent in individualized instruction. Teachers learn not only about their students' academic needs, but they often learn about personal and family issues. The conference is a special time between teacher and student and contributes significantly to the development of trust.

SUMMARY

We have described the three stages within the portfolio process. Good use of the *planning stage* requires that the teacher have an understanding of the literacy goals for the classroom and identify literacy activities that reflect progress toward those goals. The planning stage is also a time to address the ways students will select artifacts and reflect on their selections. The *selection and reflection stage* is the point at which students select artifacts that address progress toward a specified literacy goal and reflect upon the criteria for that selection. Finally, the *conference stage* culminates the portfolio process. This stage reflects the degree of success in planning, and selection and reflection. During the conference stage, the teacher and student discuss selected artifacts and the student's reflections about those artifacts, they reach consensus on assessments of those artifacts, and they set literacy goals and identify strategies for meeting those goals.

The portfolio process is one of several assessment strategies that fall under the label of "alternative assessments." As instructional efforts move toward higher level thinking and application of school learning in real-world settings, techniques such as the portfolio process are gaining more popularity. The only way to test it is to try it in your classroom.

There are several sources that will provide more in-depth coverage of the portfolio process and suggest other ways of using the process. We recommend creating your own blueprint for the portfolio process in your own classroom. Read and discuss ideas with your peers. Then begin simply at first, asking students to select and reflect upon a sample of work that reflects a single activity in your classroom. Once you feel comfortable with this, you can expand and modify the process as you wish.

References

Farr, Roger, and Kaye Lowe. "Alternative Assessment in Language Arts." In *Alternative Assessment in Language Arts: What Are We Doing Now? Where Are We Going?* ed. Carol B. Smith. Bloomington, IN: ERIC, in cooperation with Phi Delta Kappa, 1990.

Mathews, Samuel, Josephine Peyton Young, and Nancy Dean Giles. *Student Volunteers: Providing Tools for Brighter Futures*. Pensacola, FL: The Education Research and Development Center, The University of West Florida, 1992.

Meyer, Carol, Steven Schuman, and Nancy Angelo. *NWEA White Paper on Aggregating Portfolio Data*. Lake Oswego, OR: Northwest Evaluation Association, 1991.

Northwestern Evaluation Association. *Proceedings of the Fourth Annual October Institute: Alternative Assessments*. Lake Oswego, OR: Northwestern Evaluation Association, 1991.

Reif, Linda. *Seeking Diversity: Language Arts with Adolescents*. Portsmouth, NH: Heinemann Educational Books, 1992.

Sommers, Jeffrey. "Bring Practice in Line with Theory: Using Portfolio Grading in the Composition Classroom." In *Portfolios: Process and Product*, ed. Pat Belanoff and Marcia Dickson. Portsmouth, NH: Heinemann Educational Books, 1991.

6 Corrective Teaching Strategies

Chapter Outline

C hapters 6, 7, and 8 form a unit of material dealing with teaching strategies. Chapter 6 deals primarily with methods that support developing readers in regular classrooms and with corrective instruction in regular and special classrooms, including Chapter One classes, LD resource classes, and remedial tutoring classes.

Chapters 7 and 8 deal with reading instruction for older students; Chapter 7 concerns adolescents with reading problems, and Chapter 8 deals with strategies for supporting reading development in content-area subjects. You will find considerable overlap among these chapters; teaching methods or strategies referred to in one chapter may be recalled in another. Often the same or similar effective instructional techniques that help younger readers also help older poor readers. The means of helping these two groups of students are not mutually exclusive.

After you have completed your diagnostic assessments, you will know a great deal about the reading of your students. Now you are ready to begin the second stage in the diagnostic process: planning and implementing corrective teaching. Finding out what their present level of functioning is and what their strengths and needs are is not the goal, or the end, of the diagnostic process. This information is of no value if it is not used to develop teaching strategies that will further progress. In this chapter we discuss and demonstrate ways to use your diagnostic findings and judgments to plan instruction and to help students develop strategies for sight word recognition, word analysis, reading fluency, and reading and listening comprehension.

PLANNING FOR CORRECTIVE INSTRUCTION

Corrective teaching is instruction that is specifically directed toward supporting a reader's strengths while teaching and practicing skills and abilities the student is ready to acquire but has not yet acquired. Its purpose is to help students with reading or reading-related problems to overcome (and in some cases, compensate for) their difficulties and develop more balance in their reading strategies. Corrective teaching does not mean applying some preset prescription, method, or program, nor does it necessarily mean removing the youngster with a reading problem from his or her classroom, reading group or book, or "sending the student out" for special instruction; it may occur in the regular classrooms or in a special reading or resource class or both. Instead it means planning and goal setting for a particular reader within the context of ongoing instruction, taking into account his or her specific strengths and needs.

How does this differ from ordinary, everyday good teaching? In most ways, it doesn't, when everyday good teaching includes ongoing evaluation, utilizing students' strengths, needs, and interests routinely, and providing an appropriate balance of activities. What we call everyday teaching has two general underlying aspects that are somewhat different from corrective teaching, however. One is that most instruction is planned for group progress, and our everyday teaching is generally oriented toward the strengths, needs, and interests of groups rather than individuals. The other is that fairly well-balanced skills and fairly typical developmental progress are assumed. Because corrective teaching is directed toward those who have experienced difficulties in reading and who generally have not "kept up" with others their age in all aspects of reading, corrective teaching must be oriented toward the specific strengths and needs of these individuals. Successful corrective teaching is built around identifying pupils' strengths and needs and careful instructional planning, our next topics.

Identifying Strengths and Needs

We start planning for corrective teaching where the student is, not where the book, program, curriculum guide, or scope-and-sequence charts say that student "should" be. Where is the child now? What is our best estimate of her or his instructional level? What has been mastered? What can be done consistently and comfortably? We begin by making a simple chart of this information.

Let's consider the case of Jerry, a twelve-year-old fifth-grader. Jerry is a quiet boy who takes little interest in school and avoids contact with adults when possible. Jerry does just enough schoolwork to get by, and what he does is poorly done. Without overtly refusing to work, he is adept at stalling and other strategies to avoid reading and writing tasks.

Jerry was retained in second grade, resulting in his being a year older than many of his classmates. He has always been an unsuccessful reader and has received remedial reading instruction since second grade. In spite of this help, his reading progress has always been slow. At the end of fifth grade, as he approached middle school, he was given a fairly complete reading diagnosis. The findings of these assessments are shown as strengths and needs in Figure 6.1.

From our chart we can see that although Jerry is indeed a problem reader and is in considerable academic trouble, he has a number of strengths. It is very important to search for and list the things the student can do and enjoys doing, no matter how numerous the needs may be. Without rigorous attention to strengths and interests, we risk omitting the things the child does successfully, and we risk becoming discouraged about attempting to help her or him.

We proceed now to creating goals for instruction. What are Jerry's most critical needs for reading improvement? We select the factors that we feel will help him improve his reading most dramatically, as well as those strengths that we must not overlook in teaching, and create a list of goals, in order

Figure 6.1

Jerry's Strengths and Needs Chart

Jerry _____ , age twelve, entering sixth grade
Functional reading levels:
   Independent: primer
   Instructional: second
   Frustration: third
   Listening: fourth, possibly fifth
Strengths:
   Comprehension solid at his instructional level
   Working comfortably in low-vocabulary, high-interest material of second-grade
      readability
   Enjoys being read to
   Works cooperatively when he understands what the goal or outcome will be
   Listening comprehension at least two grades above instructional level (that is,
      shows potential for improvement)
   Has *some* sight vocabulary (although very small)
   Can use decoding, and context to some extent, to figure out words
   Has mastered most consonant and blend sounds
   Tries to make sense of what he reads
   Is interested in sports, cars, motorcycles, and outdoor life
Needs:
   Small sight vocabulary, particularly beyond primer
   Overusing phonics and underusing context in word recognition
   Miscues usually resulted in meaning change
   In phonics, has trouble with variant vowel sounds especially in medial position,
      and most polysyllabic words
   Reading rate slow and halting due to small sight vocabulary
   Very unsure of his ability to understand; says "I don't know" quickly
   Hesitant to risk a guess or prediction
   Avoids reading whenever he can and does no self-initiated reading
   Gives appearance of passivity and boredom, his response to failure and
      frustration

of importance for this particular student. From these, our activities will be developed.

Goals for Jerry's Instruction
1. Develop larger sight vocabulary.
2. Develop more effective word analysis skills, especially judicious use of context.
3. Improve reading fluency and rate.
4. Encourage active comprehension, making predictions, and risking

a guess.
5. Increase time spent reading.
6. Develop listening comprehension and story sense.
7. Encourage greater self-esteem and more positive attitudes toward reading.

Now we have clarified what Jerry can presently do, what he needs, and where we must place the most emphasis in our planning.

We are ready to select and devise activities that will fit our listed priorities, and to develop some general plans for Jerry's instructional time.

Following are generic types of activities to fit different purposes. In the sections that follow, these activities are discussed and described in detail. We will select from them as we develop a lesson plan for Jerry and others whose reading is like his.

To develop sight vocabulary:
dictated stories
predictable books
repeated reading
echo and choral reading
shared reading
sight word bank (or notebook)
To develop fluency:
repeated reading
choral reading with a group
practice reading in order to read to others
To develop word attack skills:
word sorting and categorizing
word families and letter substitution
confirmation exercises (in context)
cloze and maze procedures
To develop reading comprehension:
using predicting (directed reading-thinking activities)
developing awareness of prior information: prereading predicting, previewing, webbing
developing awareness of story and text structures
using story maps
retelling
reciprocal teaching and questioning
To develop listening comprehension:
being read to
interpreting stories and text listened to through drama, art, and movement
retelling stories and text listened to
summarizing and paraphrasing material listened to
storytelling

Planning Time and Achieving Balance

When we developed our list of priorities, we selected those areas we felt needed particular attention and emphasis. Our list of priorities helps us include what Jerry needs most right now: work on sight words, word attack, fluency, active comprehension, listening, and time spent actually reading. We will balance our instructional program by making sure that every day Jerry spends time working on the areas of greatest need and filling in around them the other things he will benefit from and enjoy.

Let's say that Jerry will have a 50-minute period each day for reading. We might plan to divide that time period into the following segments:

sight vocabulary, fluency	20 minutes
word study (that is, decoding, context, vocabulary development)	15 minutes
comprehension	15 minutes

This totals 50 minutes, but there is much we wanted to do that is left out. Fifteen minutes is about the shortest amount of time for a middle grader to work productively on most tasks. That means that we will decide what we must do every day and what we can do on alternate days to accomplish all we need and want to do. Since sight recognition is Jerry's foremost need, we should work on that daily. And since comprehension (which includes listening) is the goal of all reading, we must work on it every day too. We will have to plan our remaining time, and utilize a variety of activities, to achieve balance. We will also have to use our time flexibly, so that over a week we will have allotted enough time to each area.

Let's try mapping out a week's time, filling in activities as we go. Figure 6.2 shows how each day's and week's instructional time might be divided up so that Jerry would participate in a number of kinds of activities based on our priorities for him. This schedule would result in the following divisions of time weekly:

• sight vocabulary and fluency	85 minutes/week
○ reading and listening comprehension	95 minutes/week
△ word study	50 minutes/week
□ self-esteem and confidence	25 minutes/week

Jerry's time spent in pleasure reading and free writing could be extended by having him spend some time each day, say 15 or 20 minutes, doing these activities at home. He and a parent could keep a simple time sheet for this purpose.

The times we have listed are both arbitrary and approximate. Conforming rigorously to a schedule like this would certainly mean dragging some activities out and truncating others, and would serve no good purpose.

Figure 6.2

Sample Week's Lesson Plan

Key:	• sight vocabulary and fluency	Δ word analysis and vocabulary development
	○ comprehension	□ confidence and self-esteem

Monday
• Group or individual dictated story (transcribing, choral reading)	20 minutes
• Repeated readings—practice and timing	5 minutes
○ Silent reading and summarizing	15 minutes
Δ Sort words by phonic pattern	10 minutes

Tuesday
• Choral reading dictated story, identify sight words	10 minutes
□ Pleasure reading and/or free writing	10 minutes
○ Group Directed Reading-Thinking Activity (DRTA)	20 minutes
Δ Confirmation exercise	10 minutes

Wednesday
• Choral and individual reading of dictated story, identify sight words	10 minutes
• Repeated readings—practice and timing	5 minutes
○ Silent reading and summarizing	20 minutes
Δ Cloze procedure from DRTA	15 minutes

Thursday
• Review new sight words, put in word bank	10 minutes
□ Pleasure reading and/or free writing	15 minutes
• Practice story to read to younger students	5 minutes
○ Group Directed Listening-Thinking Activity (DLTA)	20 minutes
Δ Confirmation exercise	5 minutes

Friday
• Repeated readings—practice and timing	5 minutes
• Practice and read story to younger students	15 minutes
○ Silent reading and interpretation (drama, art, etc.)	20 minutes
Δ Sort words by meaning relations	10 minutes

We have listed times only to illustrate that it is important to plan in general how much time will be allotted to particular areas, so that the most time is spent on the most critical areas. Each week, different activities should be used, and some should be phased out as needs change and abilities develop. As Jerry's sight vocabulary grows, for example, dictated stories could be phased out and replaced with more directed reading and rereading of appropriate books, more directed writing, and word study.

Balance is achieved when available time is appropriately divided among activities requiring reading, speaking, listening, writing, and areas like drama and art. All areas should be included each week, and most every day. If you make a list of the activities you have planned in a week for a group, and label each activity by what process it primarily requires, you can see if you are including all aspects regularly. (No activity requires one process exclusively, since reading, speaking, listening, and writing are interrelated. Look for what an activity requires most.)

DEVELOPING SIGHT VOCABULARY

Individual words become *sight words* (recognized immediately without analysis) when they are seen repeatedly in meaningful context. Many youngsters acquire some sight words before school entry, and without direct teaching or drill, by looking at the same favorite storybooks many times over. First they learn what words are on the page as they hear the same story read to them again and again. Soon they can recite the words along with the reader; soon after that they can recite independently, role-playing reading as they turn the pages.

If at this point the reader casually points to the words as they are read, the child begins to associate the word spoken with its printed counterpart. This "speech-to-print matching" is an important foundation for learning to recognize words in print.

It is essential for readers to have a large sight vocabulary, so that they can move through print quickly and efficiently. As we have already seen, youngsters like Jerry who have only a small store of sight words are forced to read very slowly with frequent stops to figure out words, stops that interrupt their comprehension and interfere with their getting meaning. Many youngsters read poorly for this reason. Increasing their sight vocabularies is mandatory for their reading improvement. There are a number of means by which this can be accomplished.

Dictated Stories and Language Experience

Dictated stories are a part of the language experience approach to beginning reading (Allen, 1976; Hall, 1981; Nessel & Jones, 1981; Stauffer, 1980). An individual or a small group dictates an account to someone who writes down the account verbatim. The account is reread chorally until the students can recite it accurately and point to the individual words while reciting. Then parts, or the entire account, are read individually, and words that can be immediately recognized first in context, then in isolation, are identified. These new sight words go into the students' word banks, collections of sight words on cards or in a notebook.

It was long held that the value of dictated stories lay in the preservation of children's natural language, which may differ considerably from "book language." This is important, but the real usefulness of dictated words for developing sight vocabulary lies in the repeated rereading of the material. Students may reread dictated stories more willingly than other material because the stories concern experiences the students have had themselves. Rereading the stories chorally and independently, regardless of the topic or syntax used, reinforces the recognition of the words in other contexts.

As the students' sight vocabularies grow, and their word banks come to contain about 100 or more words, dictated stories can be phased out and selective rereading of other material, from books and their own writings, continued or expanded. Dictation works best as an initial means of establishing and fostering sight vocabulary.

When dictated stories are mentioned, some teachers of older poor readers associate the practice with very young children. They may immediately presume that older poor readers will be put off by what they assume is a juvenile practice. Although language experience is common in primary classrooms, it need not be reserved for little children. In fact, with many older and adult poor readers what they dictate may be about the only print they can read successfully. In Chapter 7 you will read more about the effective use of dictated material with adolescent poor readers.

With young children, you need a concrete "stimulus," or experience, to talk about: an object, picture, storybook or immediate event. With older students, past or future experiences, hopes, fears, reminiscences, content area subjects, and abstract concepts can serve as topics. Older students can usually move through the steps more quickly than younger ones, and can usually skip the voice-pointing step entirely. Older students often work best with this procedure individually or in pairs or threes rather than larger groups. A word notebook may replace the word bank card collection. And if the teacher presents the activity with a businesslike air and explains why it is being done, the experience need not feel like a juvenile one.

Figure 6.3 lists the steps in using dictated stories with younger and older students, in groups or individually.

Support Reading: Echo and Choral Reading

Support reading means helping readers get through text that is too difficult for them to read independently. Although students should never have to read material at their frustration levels without support, sometimes it is necessary for them to get through some difficult material. This is most often the

Figure 6.3

Steps in Using Dictated Stories

WITH YOUNGER PUPILS:
1. Present a concrete stimulus—an object or event—to discuss.
2. Encourage describing and narrating, so the students will have plenty to say about it.
3. Tell students you will help them write the story using a chart tablet, transparency, or the board.
4. Ask for volunteers to contribute sentences for the story.
5. Print the account verbatim, allowing students to make changes or additions. Read aloud what you have written, including amended portions.
6. Read the completed account to the group.
7. Lead the group in choral recitation, pointing quickly to the words as you read. Repeat until the whole account can be recited fluently.
8. Ask for volunteers to read one or more sentences alone, pointing to the words as in step 7.
9. Ask for volunteers to point to and identify words they know. Keep a list of these for review.
10. Provide individual copies of the story for rereading and sight word identification.
11. Any words a child can identify out of the story context can go into the child's word bank, to be used for sorting and other word study activities.

WITH OLDER PUPILS:
1. Work with groups of three or fewer.
2. Suggest, or allow students to suggest, a topic.
3. Lead discussion of the topic, encouraging as rich language use as possible.
4. Take the dictation as above, making minor word changes or additions as necessary to keep the story fluent. Cursive writing may be used instead of printing. Use a regular size sheet of paper if you wish.
5. Lead the choral rereading as above. Students may prefer to do more individual than group reading.
6. Provide an individual copy for each student, typed if possible, for practice rereading and word identification. Encourage rereading to a partner or someone else.
7. As individuals read to you and identify newly acquired sight words, have them enter the words in a sight word notebook. Older students may prefer a notebook to a traditional word bank.

case with older poor readers who are expected to get information from a content area textbook that is beyond their instructional level. If appropriate material at their instructional level is not available, you can help them through difficult text using support reading methods.

In *echo reading* the teacher reads a sentence or two aloud and the student immediately repeats what the teacher read while looking at, and, if necessary, pointing to, the words. Only one or two sentences, or even one long phrase, are read at a time to allow students to use short-term memory as they "echo." Older students may use specially prepared tapes, with pauses for repetition, to practice echo reading independently. Echo reading is an intensive support measure that is best used with short selections and material that is quite difficult or unfamiliar. Sometimes it may be sufficient to echo read only the beginning of a longer passage to get students started. One important characteristic of echo reading is that it allows the teacher to model fluent reading and the students to practice it.

Choral reading means reading aloud in unison. It is somewhat harder to choral read than to echo, so this procedure is best for material that is somewhat easier or for text that has been silently previewed or echo read first. Choral reading, with the teacher's voice leading and providing the model, is an excellent way of practicing oral reading without the anxiety of a solo performance. Complicated or unfamiliar text should be read aloud to the students first and may be echo read initially as well. Again, tapes can be used effectively for independent practice.

Choral reading is a superb way to enjoy poetry. Poetry deserves to be read aloud; many poems read silently are only pale shadows of what they are when rendered aloud. Add a little movement, a sound effect or two, and a bit of variety with voices (high/low, loud/soft, fast/slow) and you have more than a poetry reading—you have a Performing Art! Choral reading of poetry and prose is a low-anxiety experience; children's individual mispronunciations or lapses disappear into the sound of the collective voices, while everyone gets to experience fluent reading. It encourages the rereading of text which contributes to fluency and sight word acquisition, while students barely recognize that they have read the same text many times over. Choral reading has been shown to help particularly children who are nonfluent English speakers (McCauley & McCauley, 1992). Box 6.1 shows procedures for choral reading of poetry or other predictable text.

Predictable Books

Predictable books have a rhyming or repetitious element that make them easy to read, even for students who recognize few words at sight. The pattern of repeated words or phrases or the rhyme scheme helps readers remember and predict what words are coming next. It used to be that there were relatively few such books for beginners; even primer-level basals were written in straight narrative style, and for that reason dictated accounts and simple poems were often used in place of them. Today, however, the field of children's trade books has simply exploded, and there are many wonderful pre-

---

Box 6.1

Choral Reading Poetry or Predictable Books

---

1. Introduce the material by briefly discussing the topic with students.
2. Read the material aloud expressively.
3. Read the material a second time while children follow along in a large copy of the material (chart tablet sheet, transparency, or Big Book).
4. Choral read the material several times until it is very familiar.
5. Begin adding pauses, sound effects, movement, tonal variety or other expressive aspects to the reading.
6. Practice often so that all children feel very comfortable with it.
7. Ask children to suggest ways they can share their choral readings with others, and follow up on their ideas.

Source: Joyce K. McCauley and Daniel S. McCauley. "Using Choral Reading to Promote Language Learning for ESL Students." *The Reading Teacher* 45, no. 7 (March 1992): 526–533.

---

dictable books for young readers, many of them available in big-book format for group instruction. Some publishers, such as The Wright Group (19201 120th Ave NE, Bothell, WA 98011-9512) and the Rigby Publishing Company (P.O. BOX 797, Crystal Lake, IL 60039-0797) have built their product lines around the use of predictable books in both big book and individual book formats.

The growing popularity of the whole language approach and literature-based reading have contributed greatly to the widespread availability of predictable books for the classroom. A major emphasis of these approaches is to get children reading whole books, real books, right from the beginning of their instruction. A beginning reader's beliefs that "I am a reader" and "I can read a whole book by myself" are considered critical to his or her success in reading. Many books now available are so simple in text, so highly structured, that even prereaders can memorize the words and "read along" fluently and enjoyably. When they can do this, they are actually role-playing being successful readers. With repeated trips through the same books, they begin to be able to recognize words they didn't know they could read. When they begin to recognize these same words in other contexts, they are building their abilities to read independently.

In our work with beginning readers, we often introduce a new book either with a big-book version or with the text of an individual book printed on chart paper. We read the text to the children once or twice, pointing to each word as we read, and invite the children to join in the reading as soon as they are able to. After several trips through the text, most are able first to accurately recite the text, then to recite while pointing to each word. Individuals are invited to read and point to individual sentences, then to all of the text as soon as they want to (which is invariably right away!). We then provide either individual "little book" copies, or duplicated copies of the book with the text typed on each page for students to illustrate themselves. A few copies of these student-illustrated versions are laminated and remain in the classroom for independent reading, and the rest are sent home for reading. (For some students, these copies are the only books available at home. They are very precious to the students.)

Emerging readers need to have many books that they can "zoom through with joyous familiarity" (Martin & Brogan, 1972, p. 4) in order to see themselves as successful readers right from the start. Our beginning readers love to spread out in front of them all the books they can already read, and to read them over and over to themselves and each other. They love to keep charts of all the books they can read and add to their lists frequently. As the lists grow, and the collections of "their" books spread across their tables, so too does their confidence, their certainty that they are successful readers. We know that this confidence and certainty is a critical foundation for their growing literacy. Predictable books provide one of the very best means of encouraging emergent literacy.

Some predictable books repeat the same sentences or phrases over and over. Eric Carle's *Have You Seen My Cat?* (New York: Franklin Watts, 1973) is an example of such a pattern. On alternate pages, the sentences "Have you seen my cat?" and "This is not my cat!" repeat, as a small boy asks a variety of people from many cultures and finds a lion, a panther, and a cheetah, among other cats. On the last page, which reads "This is my cat!", he finds his own cat with a litter of newborn kittens. The inside back cover shows all the varieties of cats, labeled. Even the least-experienced prereader can recite this book and point to the words after only a few pages. Repetition makes it predictable. Bill Martin, Jr.'s *Brown Bear, Brown Bear, What Do You See?* (New York: Henry Holt, 1983) is another example, familiar to many teachers. Each left-hand page identifies a color and animal and asks, "What do you see?" On the right-hand page the animal answers, "I see a _____ looking at me," and identifies the next color and animal: a yellow duck, a blue horse, a green frog, and so forth. Again, the last page lists all the animals cumulatively with small copies of the larger illustrations. Like many others, these books are available in big book, standard trade book, and "miniature" versions. Eric Carle's *The Very Hungry Caterpillar* (New York: Philomel Books, 1969), *The Grouchy Ladybug* (New York: Harper & Row, 1977), and *The Very Busy Spider* (New York: Philomel Books, 1984) are other examples.

Some predictable books rely on rhyme rather than repetition. Nancy Shaw's *Sheep In a Jeep* (Boston: Houghton-Mifflin, 1986) is an example. Although it has few words, the hilarious antics of the sheep that go for an ill-fated joyride make it appropriate for a wide range of ages. It sounds like this: "Uh-oh! The jeep won't go. Sheep leap to push the jeep. Sheep shove, sheep grunt. Sheep don't think to look up front." It is a great source of rhyming words, those that share the same spelling pattern (sheep-jeep) as well as those that don't (grunt-front), and colorful sound words (splash! thud!). The rhyming adventures of the sheep continue in *Sheep on a Ship* (1989) and *Sheep in a Shop* (1991).

Predictable books also serve as jumping-off places for students to create their own original books. Changing the topic and illustrations, while retaining the original pattern, can result in wonderful original versions that children enjoy reading as much or more than the original version. For example, after mastering *Brown Bear, Brown Bear, What Do You See?*, a group of first graders created *The Vegetable Book*: "Green pepper, green pepper, what do you see? I see a red tomato looking at me . . ." and so forth. With the basic pattern written on chart paper and blanks for the color words and nouns, the group chose the vegetable theme and volunteered the word pairs to fill the blanks: brown pota-to, orange carrot, purple eggplant, for example. Each couplet was then printed on a separate sheet, and pairs were assigned to illustrate each page. The result-ing Big Book was stapled together and reread numerous times. Meanwhile the text was typed on individual pages with space for illustration, duplicated and stapled into individual copies. Each student then illustrated his or her own copy to keep. (During this time we brought in samples of the various vegeta-bles for exploring and tasting.) Another group followed the same procedure with *Have You Seen My Cat?*, creating their original *Have You Seen My Dog?* and illustrating it with different breeds and colors of dogs. (This effort involved looking at numerous books about dogs to learn about different breeds.) These books remained very popular all year for independent reading.

Both commercial and student-written predictable books are extremely useful for independent reading and as springboards for creative writing. They help students acquire and reinforce sight words while they provide successful reading practice for even the least fluent reader. Here are some predictable books you might use:

Abisch, Roy. *Around the House That Jack Built*. New York: Parents Magazine Press, 1972.

Barry, Katherine. *A Bug to Hug*. New York: Young Scott, 1964.

Becker, John. *Seven Little Rabbits*. New York: Walker & Co., 1973.

Bodecker, N.M. *It's Raining, Said John Twaining*. New York: Atheneum, 1973.

Bodecker, N.M. *Let's Marry, Said the Cherry and Other Nonsense Poems*. New York: Atheneum, 1974.

Brown, Margaret Wise. *The Important Book*. New York: Harper & Row, 1949.

Burningham, John. *Mr. Gumpy's Outing*. New York: Holt, Rinehard & Winston, 1970.

Carle, Eric. *Have You Seen My Cat?* NY: Franklin Watts, 1973.

Carle, Eric. *The Very Busy Spider*. New York: Philomel, 1984.

Carle, Eric. *The Grouchy Ladybug*. New York: Harper & Row, 1977.

Carle, Eric. *The Very Hungry Caterpillar*. New York: Philomel, 1969.

Charlip, Remy. *Fortunately*. New York: Parents Magazine Press, 1964.

Cohen, Carol. *Wake up, Groundhog!* New York: Crown, 1975.

De Regniers, Beatrice. *May I Bring a Friend?* New York: Atheneum, 1964.

Domanska, Janina. *Busy Monday Morning.* New York: Greenwillow, 1985.

Domanska, Janina. *If All the Seas Were One Sea.* New York: Macmillan, 1971.

Einsel, Walter. *Did You Ever See?* New York: Scholastic, 1972.

Emberly, Ed. *Drummer Hoff.* Englewood Cliffs, NJ: Prentice-Hall, 1967.

Fox, Mem. *Hattie and the Fox.* New York: Bradbury Press, 1986.

Galdone, Paul. *The Teeny Tiny Woman.* New York: Clarion, 1984.

Ginsburg, Mirra. *The Chick and the Duckling.* New York: Macmillan, 1972.

Hoberman, Mary Ann. *A House Is a House For Me.* New York: Scholastic, 1978.

Johnston, Tony. *Five Little Foxes and the Snow.* New York: Putnam, 1977.

Joslin, Sesyle. *What Do You Say, Dear?* Reading, MA: Addison-Wesley, 1958.

Joslin, Sesyle. *What Do You Do, Dear?* Reading, MA: Addison-Wesley, 1961.

Kalan, Robert. *Jump, Frog, Jump.* New York: Scholastic, 1981.

Keats, Ezra Jack. *Over the Meadow.* New York: Four Winds, 1971.

Kesselman, Wendy. *There's a Train Going by My Window.* Garden City, NY: Doubleday, 1982.

Kherdian, David, and Nonny Hogrogian. *Right Now.* New York: Knopf, 1983.

Krauss, Ruth. *What a Fine Day.* New York: Parents Magazine Press, 1967.

Langstaff, John. *Soldier, Soldier, Won't You Marry Me?* Garden City, NY: Doubleday, 1972.

Martin, Bill, Jr. *Polar Bear, Polar Bear, What Do You Hear?* New York: Henry Holt & Co., 1991.

Martin, Bill, Jr. *Brown Bear, Brown Bear, What Do You See?* New York: Henry Holt, 1983.

Martin, Bill, Jr. *Chicka Chicka Boom Boom.* New York: Simon & Schuster, 1989.

Martin, Bill Jr., and Peggy Brogan. *Bill Martin's Instant Readers.* New York: Holt, Rinehart & Winston, 1971.

Matthias, Catherine. *I Love Cats.* Chicago: Children's Press, 1983.

Mayer, Mercer. *What Do You Do With a Kangaroo?* New York: Scholastic, 1973.

McGinn, Maureen. *I Used to Be an Artichoke.* St. Louis: Concordia, 1973.

Mendoza, George. *The Scribbler.* New York: Holt, Rinehart & Winston, 1971.

Nolan, Dennis. *Big Pig.* Englewood Cliffs, NJ: Prentice-Hall, 1976.

Numeroff, Laura Joffe. *If You Give a Mouse a Cookie.* New York: Harper & Row, 1985.

Numeroff, Laura Joffe. *If You Give a Moose a Muffin.* New York: HarperCollins, 1991.

Pomerantz, Charlotte. *The Piggy in the Puddle.* New York: Macmillan, 1974.

Quackenbush, Robert. *She'll Be Comin' Round the Mountain.* Philadelphia: Lippincott, 1973.

Sendak, Maurice. *Chicken Soup with Rice.* New York: Scholastic, 1962.

Shaw, Nancy. *Sheep in a Jeep.* Boston: Houghton Mifflin, 1986.

Shaw, Nancy. *Sheep on a Ship.* Boston: Houghton Mifflin, 1989.

Shaw, Nancy. *Sheep in a Shop.* Boston: Houghton Mifflin, 1991.

Slobodkina, Esphyr. *Caps for Sale.* Reading, MA: Addison-Wesley, 1947.

Spier, Peter. *Bored—Nothing to Do!* Garden City, NY: Doubleday, 1978.

Supraner, Robyn. *Would You Rather Be a Tiger?* Boston: Houghton Mifflin, 1976.

Sutton, Eve. *My Cat Likes to Hide in Boxes.* New York: Parents Magazine Press, 1973.

Tolstoy, Alexei. *The Great Big Enormous Turnip.* New York: Watts, 1968.

Wood, Audrey. *King Bidgood's in the Bathtub.* San Diego: Harcourt Brace Jovanovich, 1986.

Wood, Audrey. *The Napping House.* San Diego: Harcourt Brace Jovanovich, 1984.

Zemach, Harve. *The Judge.* New York: Farrar, Straus, 1969.

Zolotow, Charlotte. *Someday.* New York: Harper & Row, 1965.

Zolotow, Charlotte. *Summer Is . . .* London/New York: Abelard-Schuman, 1967.

Shared Reading

For many, many years a staple of reading instruction has been the reading aloud of good literature to children. The teacher read the book aloud while holding the open book up so that the children could see the illustrations. This is still an excellent practice, but there was just one element missing: most of the time the children could not see the words on the page. Now we know that children need to see and follow the print as well as to see the pictures and hear the words. The widespread use of big books has added this missing element to reading aloud.

When everyone can see the print as well as the picture, all can share in the reading. Thus the practice of using big books when reading aloud is called "shared reading." A few years ago big books were rare; now there are hundreds being published, with more every month. Scholastic, Rigby, and The Wright Group are among the foremost publishers of big books. Several of the popular monthly "book clubs" offering low-priced children's paperbacks for individual purchase give away big books as prizes for large orders. Publishers like Scholastic often give away big books to participants in their teacher workshops. Teachers can buy special easels and tabletop stands to prop up big books during use, and durable hanging or freestanding storage boxes or pocket holders to store them.

Many big books are predictable, inviting children to recite or read along. Many have predictable elements, like the Gingerbread Man's repeated refrain ("Run, run, as fast as you can . . ."). Others are not predictable books, but are simply beautiful books to be enjoyed again and again. Using big books instead of their smaller versions encourages children to examine the print as well as the illustrations, to point to the words as they recite, and to eventually come to recognize the individual words both in the book and in other contexts. In emergent readers it encourages the development of print awareness, concepts of directionality and forms of print, and speech-print matching. In those already reading it encourages further print awareness and sight word recognition. Children of all ages enjoy and benefit from being read to, and using big books enhances this experience. Shared reading has an important place in both regular classroom and special reading instruction.

DEVELOPING READING FLUENCY

Poor word recognition and slow, word-by-word reading reduce comprehension. According to Allington (1983), lack of fluency is commonly noted as a characteristic of poor reading and can be taught but is often overlooked in corrective teaching. Allington proposed several hypotheses explaining why some fail to become fluent readers:

- Some children are not exposed to fluent adult reading models, or to prereading experience reciting memorized books.
- Good readers are more likely to be encouraged to "read with expression," while poor readers get more instruction on individual words and word parts.
- Fast learners are given more opportunities for reading, and hence more practice actually reading.
- Successful readers more often read text that is easy for them, while poorer readers more often are faced with frustration-level material.
- Successful readers do more silent reading, which provides practice and experience.
- Children's ideas differ about what good reading is, with poorer readers often viewing reading not as meaning getting but as "an accuracy competition." (p. 559)

Since reading fluency is an aspect of good reading that many students need to develop, methods that help students develop this skill are both useful and necessary. With greater fluency, readers can concentrate on comprehending what they read, develop greater self-confidence, and enjoy reading more.

Rereading

Rereading means reading the same material more than once. Rereading helps students gain fluency, bolsters students' self-confidence as readers, helps students recognize familiar words at sight, and helps students use phrasing to support the meaning of what they read. It need not mean drudgery for students, however. There are a number of ways we can integrate rereading into our teaching. Some are:

1. Have students read material silently before oral reading or discussion. If you will use predictive questions in your discussion, have them read silently up to a stopping point.
2. Encourage oral rereading for real purposes: to prove a point in a discussion, to role-play a dialogue, or to savor an effective descriptive passage, among other purposes.
3. Encourage the rereading of familiar or completed stories as seatwork or independent work, or during free reading of sustained silent reading periods.
4. Select or have students choose reading partners or buddies, then reread completed stories or books aloud to their partners.
5. Encourage children to take home familiar books to reread at home to family members. Since rereading is usually more fluent than the initial reading, children can "show off" their fluent reading at home this way.
6. Encourage rereading of favorite stories by revisiting old favorites when you read aloud to the class.
7. Have students listen to taped material, either professionally recorded or done by you or other volunteers. After listening and silently following along, have students imitate the reader as they listen, then eventually read the material alone. Tape-record their readings to self-critique.
8. Act out favorite stories using the technique of Reader's Theater, in which scripts are always read instead of memorized and recited.
9. Use choral reading frequently and perform for others.

Repeated Readings for Fluency

Repeated reading refers to a systematic practice of using timed oral rereadings to develop reading fluency. Described by Samuels (1979), the method involves helping the student select an instructional level passage and a reading rate goal, timing the first unrehearsed oral reading of the passage and successive readings after practice, and keeping a simple chart of the student's rate after successive timings. When the student is able to read the passage at or beyond the goal rate, a new passage of equal (but not greater) difficulty is begun.

This method of repeated reading is not intended to directly aid comprehension, but rather to help students acquire sight words and practice reading fluently and confidently. As they practice rereading their passages for timing, their reading rate for that passage climbs dramatically, and keeping a chart that shows these increases is highly motivating, especially for older poor readers.

Figure 6.4

Steps in Using Repeated Reading

1. Choose, or help each student choose, a fairly comfortable, interesting selection to practice reading. It should be too long to memorize: 100 or so words for younger children, 200 or more words for older ones. Trade books and previously read basal stories are good.
2. Make up a duplicated chart for each pupil (see Figure 6.5). Omit the accuracy axis if you want to simplify the task.
3. Time each reader's first, unrehearsed oral reading of the passage. Mark the chart for Timed Reading 1.
4. Instruct the readers to practice the passage aloud as many times as possible for the next day or two. Let them practice in pairs, independently, and at home.
5. Time the reading again and mark the chart for Timed Reading 2, and show the students how to mark their own charts.
6. Continue timing at intervals of several days. As the rate increases for the first passage, help each child set a new rate goal.
7. When the reader reaches the goal set, begin a new passage of equal (not greater) difficulty. Successive portions of a long story are perfect. Repeat steps 3 through 6.

Of course we are not surprised that their rates climb as they practice reading the same passage. What is surprising, and what is the real benefit of this practice, is that their reading rates also increase on each successive unrehearsed oral reading. The reason that this happens is that all that rereading has helped them acquire more sight words and helped them learn to read aloud fluently and confidently.

Figure 6.4 shows the steps in using the timed repeated reading method, and Figure 6.5 shows a partially completed chart.

DEVELOPING WORD ANALYSIS STRATEGIES

Immediate, accurate recognition of more than 90 percent of the words in running text is necessary for effective instructional-level reading. As students read more widely and sample various kinds of text, they will necessarily encounter words they do not recognize at sight. The role of teaching word analysis is to help students acquire efficient strategies for figuring out unrecognized words.

Figure 6.5

Sample Repeated Reading Chart

Name _Tony H._

X = rate
O = accuracy
# = tentative goal rate

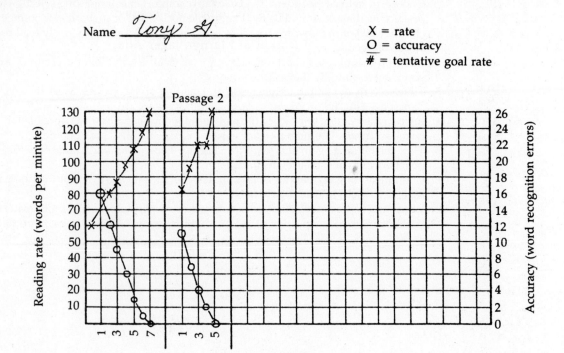

Timed readings

Teaching the "P" Word: *Phonics*

The "debate" over phonics versus other means of figuring out words not recognized at sight has gone on for more than a decade. "Some people," wrote Steven Stahl, "treat it as a dirty word, others as the salvation of reading." (1992, p. 618) It is hard to explain why a means of figuring out printed words engenders so much strong feeling. What do you think of when you think of "phonics"? Stacks of boring worksheets? Children mindlessly sounding out letters at the expense of the word's meaning? Children "barking at print"? Lists of isolated skills to be mastered in some hierarchy? The opposite of reading whole words? The simple solution to our children's reading problems, if only teachers would teach it properly? Phonics means these things to some people. If you think of people's beliefs about phonics as representing a continuum, then these positions occupy the opposite ends. Most teachers and parents' beliefs would lie somewhere toward the middle of both positions. Richard Allington wrote, "I am tired of oppositional polemics and politics, of us-versus-them groupings, of good-guys-and-bad-guys characterizations." (1991, p. 373) In recent years, though, it has seemed harder and harder to occupy the middle ground.

Recently the publication of Marilyn Jager Adams' provocative book, *Beginning to Read: Thinking and Learning About Print* (Cambridge: MIT Press, 1990) has prompted a renewal of the debate. In it Adams reinforces the notion that skilled reading requires rapid and accurate decoding as well as recognition of whole words. At the same time, she criticizes the mindlessness of much of the materials and methods used to teach phonics, and reiterates that phonics skills and knowledge are only useful in the context of real reading and writing for meaning. She writes, "Written text has both method and purpose. It is time for us to stop bickering about which is more important. To read, children must master both, and we must help them." (1990, p. 424). As a variety of position papers featured in *The Reading Teacher,* February 1991, reveals, Adams has been both praised and vilified for her work. Barbara Kapinus wrote, "Adams's book is required reading to be an informed participant in the dialogue." (1991, p. 379). Yetta Goodman charged that the purpose of Adams' book was "political" (1991, p. 378), and Jeanne Chaney wrote, "I feel that her overriding message for beginning reading instruction is disturbing," (1991, p. 374) and "Adams's book seems conspiratorial." (1991, p. 374)

Given the continuing nature of the emotional and certainly polemic debate about phonics, what is the average teacher or parent to think? Will students be harmed if we teach them phonics skills? Will they be harmed if we don't?

A growing and convincing body of literature exists which shows that good readers are able to use decoding skills rapidly and accurately, independent of the use of context, to recognize unfamiliar words in text (Adams, 1990; Ehri, 1991; Stanovich, 1980, 1991; and others). While there are hundreds of words that appear over and over in running text, and should be recognizable at sight for fluent reading, Adams (1990) estimated that 95 percent of the different words that children must read occur fewer than 10 times in a million words, or fewer than 10 times in a year's worth of reading (cited in Cunningham, 1990, p. 124). For this reason, all readers need to be able to decode letter patterns rapidly and accurately. According to Stahl, "The fact is that all students, regardless of the type of instruction they receive, learn about letter-sound correspondences as part of learning to read." (1992, p. 619)

What, then, should we teach as phonics? In Stahl's words, "There is no requirement that phonics instruction use worksheets, that it involve having children bark at print, that it be taught as a set of discrete skills mastered in isolation, or that it preclude paying attention to the meaning of texts." (1992, p. 618) Stahl (1992) described these nine components of effective phonics teaching.

Exemplary phonics instruction:

1. *builds on what children already know* about what reading is about, how print functions, what stories are and how they work, and what reading is for. This knowledge is gained by being read to, by shared reading of predictable books, by experience with dictated stories, and by authentic reading and writing tasks before reading begins. These are components of both whole language and traditional instruction in preschool, kindergarten and primary grades.

2. *builds on a foundation of phonemic awareness,* or a child's ability to perceive and manipulate sounds in spoken words. Phonemic awareness includes being able to think of words that rhyme, perceiving that some words have the same or very similar sounds at the beginning, middle, and end, and being able to segment and blend sounds in spoken words. A further explanation of phonemic awareness follows in a subsequent discussion.

3. *is clear and direct.* Good teachers explain exactly what they mean, while some phonics programs appear confusing and ambiguous. Some years ago debate raged about whether a phoneme, or letter-sound, had any existence outside of the spoken word. Teachers and programs influenced by this argument hesitated to pronounce any sounds in isolation, for example never explaining that *b* produced the /b/ sound at the beginning of words like *box, bear,* or *bed.* While of course we want to avoid inaccurate pronunciations like "buh-eh-duh" for *b-e-d,* more harm is done when we beat around the bush and never directly show at least the common and predictable consonant sounds.

4. *is integrated into a total reading program.* Phonics instruction should not dominate but instead complement the reading instruction children receive. The majority of time should be spent reading real texts, discussing them, acting them out, writing about them and interpreting them. Phonics instruction should spring from the words children need to read in real texts, not from a preset hierarchy of skills or a scope-and-sequence chart. Stahl suggests a *maximum* of 25 percent of instructional time to be spent on phonics. On many days even this will be excessive. In addition, the phonics skills taught should be directly applicable in the text being read at that time. A criticism of many basal phonics strands is that the skill being presented has only limited application in the accompanying story. Trachtenburg (1990) suggests using quality children's literature that features a particular phonic pattern to illustrate and practice the pattern, for example using *The Cat in the Hat* and *Angus and the Cat* to illustrate the short-*a* pattern. A fuller description of children's literature/phonics connections follows in a subsequent section.

5. *focuses on reading words, not learning rules.* Effective readers use patterns and words they already know that are similar, rather than phonics rules, when they decode. Most teachers already know that rules have so many exceptions that they are rarely useful, yet many phonics programs continue to stress them as though they were "golden rules." If a child can't decode *rake*, it is more helpful to point out that it has the same pattern as *make* and *take* than to cite the "silent *e* makes the vowel long" rule. Many poor readers can recite phonics rules fluently but cannot apply them in reading.

6. *may include onsets and rimes.* Onsets, or beginning sounds, and rimes, or the part of the word or syllable from the vowel onward, have long been taught under the more common name of "word families." Teaching children to compare words using onsets and rimes helps them internalize patterns and use known words, like *make* and *take* in the previous example, to decode the unfamiliar *rake.* It is certainly more productive than having children sound out letters in isolation.

7. *may include invented spelling practice.* It has been widely recognized that when children are encouraged to invent spellings for unfamiliar words they write, using the sounds in the words as they are pronounced, they practice decoding strategies within the context of real language use. Encouraging invented spelling has become a widely used and welcome aspect of primary literacy instruction.

8. *focuses attention on the internal structure of words.* Good phonics instruction helps children see and use patterns in words. Whether they use individual letter sounds, similar words with the same rime, or invented spelling, children are encouraged to look closely at the patterns in words. We learn to read and spell not word by word, but pattern by pattern.

9. *develops automaticity in word recognition.* The purpose of all phonics instruction is not to be able to sound out words, or bark at print, but to be able to quickly and accurately "unlock" familiar words so that the reader's attention may be reserved for understanding and enjoying what is read. Strict decoding-emphasis programs of the past, like DISTAR, encouraged children to learn to decode at the expense of comprehension; they failed because they created "word-callers" rather than effective readers. Effective phonics instruction today encourages automaticity in word recognition so that the mind may be freed for comprehension. That is what it is all for.

Phonemic Awareness: Building Blocks for Word Analysis

Phonemic awareness begins when children begin to learn to speak. As they talk, they naturally use the phonemes, or speech sounds, to produce and understand words. They spend little, if any, time thinking about sounds; instead they concentrate on getting and producing meaning. Even when they play with words, producing rhymes and silly word play, they rarely think about speech sounds. Indeed, phonemic awareness would not be very useful if it were not for the fact that our writing system uses letters and letter combinations to represent speech sounds in print. So phonemic awareness becomes important when children begin to read and write.

Most beginning readers realize that written words are made up of letters, but many do not realize that spoken words are made up of sounds, or phonemes. Phonemes have no real meaning like words do and may be very hard to isolate and manipulate in spoken words; but being able to do so may mean the difference between success and failure in beginning reading. Phonemic awareness has been shown to be a powerful predictor of reading success (Adams, 1990; Juel, 1988; and others). Griffin and Olson (1992) suggest three levels of phonemic awareness:

1. rhyming and recognizing rhymes;
2. segmenting the beginning sound (onset) from the remainder of the syllable (rime), as in /b/ - *ack*; and
3. Completely segmenting the phonemes in spoken words (/b/-/a/-/k/ and manipulating them to form new words, as in back-buck-duck-dull.

Griffin and Olson point out that many elementary classrooms already incorporate many of the activities that foster phonemic awareness: working with rhymes and word families orally, listening to and reciting rhymes, and encouraging invented spelling. They suggest these generic activities to foster children's phonemic awareness:

1. Using rhyming and alliterative literature. Many of the most popular children's books feature rhymes, such as *Jamberry* ("Hatberry, shoeberry, in my canoeberry") and *Sheep in a Jeep* ("Sheep shove, sheep grunt. Sheep forget to look up front."). Others, like the alphabet book *Animalia*, feature alliteration, or the repetition of initial consonant sounds, as in "Lazy lions lounging in the local library." *Don't Forget the Bacon!* plays with phonemes as a child repeats a shopping list but switches the phonemes around, so that "a cake for tea" becomes "a cape for me," then "a rake for leaves," and so forth. Daily experience with rhyming and alliterative texts helps children develop facility with spoken sounds.

2. Writing with invented spelling. Again, children are faced with the task of transforming words on the tongue into words on paper by mapping speech sounds to letters. Daily writing experience has been shown to benefit children who are lacking in phonemic awareness (Griffith and Klesius, 1990).

3. Segmenting language into words and syllables. Children need to be shown that words may be examined independent of their meaning. Clapping, marching in place, or tapping may be used to segment sentences or phrases

into component words, words into syllables, and syllables into phonemes. Similarly chips or counters may be lined up to represent these segments. Clay (1985) describes the use of matrix boxes to represent sounds, a procedure used in the Reading Recovery program. A picture card of a familiar word is presented, accompanied by a matrix of boxes, one box for each phoneme (not letter) in the word. The teacher pronounces the word slowly, articulating each sound while moving a counter into each box. The child joins in the process by saying the sounds as the teacher moves the counters, then by saying the sounds and moving the counters him- or herself. As facility is gained, the boxes are removed and the counters lined up, then the picture is removed, and the child works only with the spoken word and the counters. Later, similar boxes may be used to manipulate the letters representing the sounds. Invented spelling practice then follows, as children are encouraged to segment sounds in words they want to write, putting down letters representing those sounds in order left to right, without the use of boxes.

Connecting Children's Literature with Phonics Instruction

An important way to connect phonics instruction with authentic language is to integrate it with children's literature. Before and while children are learning about words, letters, and sounds, they need to be surrounded with a rich language environment. The richer the language environment, the more children learn about language, both spoken and written.

Phyllis Trachtenburg has described a "whole-part-whole" sequence integrating phonics instruction with children's literature (1990, p. 649) in this way:

1. Whole—read, comprehend, and enjoy a whole, quality literature selection.
2. Part—provide instruction in a high utility phonic element by drawing from or extending the preceding literature selection.
3. Whole—apply the new phonic skill when reading (and enjoying) another whole, high quality literature selection.

For example, the teacher reads aloud *Angus and the Cat*. Extension activities include dramatizing parts of the story or comparing the story to other dog-and-cat stories. The teacher then introduces the short-*a* sound and shows the students a printed portion of the story containing a number of short-*a* words, like *cat*, *that*, *back* and *glad*. The teacher rereads the story portion while emphasizing and underlining the target words. Students and teacher choral-read the excerpt several times, with emphasis on the target words. Students then work with a "word slotter," made of tagboard strips with a medial short-*a* and movable strips with beginning and ending consonants. Students experiment with moving the initial and final letters to create new short-*a* words. (Students could use linking letters, letter cards, or plastic letters as well.) Students then use a "sentence slotter" to construct sentences with short-*a* words. (Students could use word cards for this activity as well.) Finally, a new story is presented that also features many short-*a* words, like *The Cat in the Hat*. Choral and individual readings of the new book help reinforce the use of the phonic pattern in new text. The following is a list of trade books that feature short and long vowel elements, as suggested by Trachtenburg.

Short *a*

Flack, Marjorie. *Angus and the Cat*. Doubleday, 1931.
Griffith, Helen. *Alex and the Cat*. Greenwillow, 1982.
Kent, Jack. *The Fat Cat*. Scholastic, 1971.
Most, Bernard. *There's an Ant in Anthony*. William Morrow, 1980.
Nodset, Joan. *Who Took the Farmer's Hat?* Harper & Row, 1963.
Robins, Joan. *Addie Meets Max*. Harper & Row, 1985.
Schmidt, Karen. *The Gingerbread Man*. Scholastic, 1985.
Seuss, Dr. *The Cat in the Hat*. Random House, 1957.

Long *a*

Aardema, Verna. *Bringing the Rain to Kapitl Plain*. Dial, 1981.
Bang, Molly. *The Paper Crane*. Greenwillow, 1985.
Blume, Judy. *The Pain and the Great One*. Bradbury, 1974.
Byars, Betsy. *The Lace Snail*. Viking, 1975.
Henkes, Kevin. *Sheila Rae, the Brave*. Greenwillow, 1987.
Hines, Anna G. *Taste the Raindrops*. Greenwillow, 1983.

Short and long *a*

Aliki. *Jack and Jake*. Greenwillow, 1986.
Slobodkina, Esphyr. *Caps for Sale*. Addison-Wesley, 1940.

Short *e*

Ets, Marie Hall. *Elephant in a Well*. Viking, 1972.
Galdone, Paul. *The Little Red Hen*. Scholastic, 1973.
Ness, Evaline. *Yeck Eck*. E.P. Dutton, 1974.
Shecter, Ben. *Hester the Jester*. Harper & Row, 1977.
Thayer, Jane. *I Don't Believe in Elves*. William Morrow, 1975.
Wing, Henry Ritchet. *Ten Pennies for Candy*. Holt, Rinehart & Winston, 1963.

Long *e*

Galdone, Paul. *Little Bo-Peep*. Clarion/Ticknor & Fields, 1986.
Keller, Holly. *Ten Sleepy Sheep*. Greenwillow, 1983.
Martin, Bill. *Brown Bear, Brown Bear, What Do You See?* Henry Holt, 1967.

Oppenheim, Joanne. *Have You Seen Trees?* Young Scott Books, 1967.

Soule, Jean C. *Never Tease a Weasel*. Parents' Magazine Press, 1964.

Thomas, Patricia. *"Stand Back," said the Elephant, "I'm Going to Sneeze!"* Lothrop, Lee & Shepard, 1971.

Short *i*

Browne, Anthony. *Willy the Wimp*. Alfred A. Knopf, 1984.

Ets, Marie Hall. *Gilberto and the Wind*. Viking, 1966.

Hutchins, Pat. *Titch*. Macmillan, 1971.

Keats, Ezra Jack. *Whistle for Willie*. Viking, 1964.

Lewis, Thomas P. *Call for Mr. Sniff*. Harper & Row, 1981.

Lobel, Arnold. *Small Pig*. Harper & Row, 1969.

McPhail, David. *Fix-It*. E.P. Dutton, 1984.

Patrick, Gloria. *This Is. . . .*Carolrhoda, 1970.

Robins, Joan. *My Brother, Will*. Greenwillow, 1986.

Long *i*

Berenstain, Stan and Jan. *The Bike Lesson*. Random House, 1964.

Cameron, John. *If Mice Could Fly*. Atheneum, 1979.

Cole, Sheila. *When the Tide Is Low*. Lothrop, Lee & Shepard, 1985.

Gelman, Rita. *Why Can't I Fly?* Scholastic, 1976.

Hazen, Barbara S. *Tight Times*. Viking, 1979.

Short *o*

Benchley, Nathaniel. *Oscar Otter*. Harper & Row, 1966.

Dunrea, Olivier. *Mogwogs on the March!* Holiday House, 1985.

Emberley, Barbara. *Drummer Hoff*. Prentice-Hall, 1967.

McKissack, Patricia C. *Flossie & the Fox*. Dial, 1986.

Miller, Patricia, and Iran Seligman. *Big Frogs, Little Frogs*. Holt, Rinehart & Winston, 1963.

Rice, Eve. *"The Frog and the Ox"* from *Once in a Wood*. Greenwillow, 1979.

Seuss, Dr. *Fox in Socks*. Random House, 1965.

Long *o*

Cole, Brock. *The Giant's Toe*. Farrar, Straus, & Giroux, 1986.

Gerstein, Mordicai. *Roll Over!* Crown, 1984.

Johnston, Tony. *The Adventures of Mole and Troll*. G.P. Putnam's Sons, 1972.

Johnston, Tony. *Night Noises and Other Mole and Troll Stories*. G.P. Putnam's Sons, 1977.

Shulevitz, Uri. *One Monday Morning*. Charles Scribner's Sons, 1967.

Tresselt, Alvin. *White Snow, Bright Snow.* Lothrop, Lee & Shepard, 1947.

Short *u*

Carroll, Ruth. *Where's the Bunny?* Henry Z. Walck, 1950.
Cooney, Nancy E. *Donald Says Thumbs Down.* G.P. Putnam's Sons, 1987.
Friskey, Margaret. *Seven Little Ducks.* Children's Press, 1940.
Lorenz, Lee. *Big Gus and Little Gus.* Prentice-Hall, 1982.
Marshall, James. *The Cut-Ups.* Viking Kestrel, 1984.
Udry, Janice May. *Thump and Plunk.* Harper & Row, 1981.
Yashima, Taro. *Umbrella.* Viking Penguin, 1958.

Long *u*

Lobel, Anita. *The Troll Music.* Harper & Row, 1966.
Segal, Lore. *Tell Me a Trudy.* Farrar, Straus, & Giroux, 1977.
Slobodkin, Louis. *"Excuse Me—Certainly!"* Vanguard Press, 1959.

Source: Phyllis Trachtenburg, "Using Children's Literature to Enhance Phonics Instruction." *The Reading Teacher* 43, no. 9 (May 1990): 653–654.

Assessing Decoding Ability

Most often children's decoding ability is assessed by asking them to decode nonsense words that are similar to real words, such as *dap, rike, faught, blunch,* and so forth. The validity of such measures may be questionable, since such assessments are most probably the only time children are ever asked to attempt to read nonwords. In fact, teachers are cautioned against using nonsense words in teaching, since we are trying to help children make sense of the act of reading and apply sense-making strategies when they encounter unfamiliar words. Cunningham (1990) correctly points out that many children are confused by such a task and attempt to read nonsense words as real words, convinced that their teachers would never ask them to read something that makes no sense. Cunningham suggested an alternative to nonsense word decoding assessments which she calls "The Names Test," a list of first and last names of fictitious children. Each of the names is "fully decodable given commonly taught vowel rules and/or analogy approaches to decoding" (1990, p. 125). A student is asked to pretend to be a teacher reading a class list of students' names as if he or she were taking attendance (a task familiar to most students). A name is counted correct if all syllables are pronounced correctly, regardless of where the student places the stress or accent (for example, YO-lan-da or Yo-LAN-da). Errors are noted phonetically and analyzed to reveal what phonic patterns the student needs to review or learn. The Names Test and administration procedures are shown in Figures 6.6a and 6.6b.

Figure 6.6a

Procedures for Administering and Scoring the Names Test

Preparing the Instrument

1. Type or print legibly the 25 names on a sheet of paper or card stock. Make sure the print size is appropriate for the age or grade level of the students being tested.
2. For students who might perceive reading an entire list of names as being too formidable, type or print the names on index cards, so they can be read individually.
3. Prepare a protocol (scoring) sheet. Do this by typing the list of names in a column and following each name with a blank line to be used for recording a student's responses.

Administering the Names Test

1. Administer the Names Test individually. Select a quiet, distraction-free location.
2. Explain to the student that she or he is to pretend to be a teacher who must read a list of names of students in the class. Direct the student to read the names as if taking attendance.
3. Have the student read the entire list. Inform the student that you will not be able to help with difficult names, and encourage him or her to "make a guess if you are not sure." This way you will have sufficient responses for analysis.
4. Write a check on the protocol sheet for each name read correctly. Write phonetic spellings for names that are mispronounced.

Scoring and Interpreting the Names Test

1. Count a word correct if all syllables are pronounced correctly regardless of where the student places the accent. For example, either Yó/lan/da or Yo/lan´/da would be acceptable.
2. For words where the vowel pronunciation depends on which syllable the consonant is placed with, count them correct for either pronunciation. For example, either Ho/mer or Hom/er would be acceptable.
3. Count the number of names read correctly, and analyze those mispronounced, looking for patterns indicative of decoding strengths and weaknesses.

Using Context

In addition to rapid, accurate decoding, good readers use the context of an unfamiliar word to help figure it out. Most words have meaning in isolation, but some have no real meaning, only a function in sentences; who can define *the*, for example? Many other words, including some of the most frequently occurring words, have many meanings and only sentence context helps us choose the right one; for example, there are at least six different meanings for *run:* a rapid gait, a tear in a stocking, a jogger's exercise routine, a small creek, a sequence of events, and a computer operation. Sentences have more meaning than the sum of the meanings of their component words. For example, even if you know what *time, a, saves, stitch, in,* and *nine* mean, it is

Figure 6.6b

THE NAMES TEST

Jay Conway	Wendy Swain
Tim Cornell	Glen Spencer
Chuck Hoke	Fred Sherwood
Yolanda Clark	Flo Thornton
Kimberly Blake	Dee Skidmore
Roberta Slade	Grace Brewster
Homer Preston	Ned Westmoreland
Gus Quincy	Ron Smitherman
Cindy Sampson	Troy Whitlock
Chester Wright	Vance Middleton
Ginger Yale	Zane Anderson
Patrick Tweed	Bernard Pendergraph
Stanley Shaw	

Source: Pat Cunningham. "The Names Test: A Quick Assessment of Decoding Ability." *The Reading Teacher* 44, no. 2 (Oct. 1990): 127.

only when they are combined in a sentence, *A stitch in time saves nine*, that comprehension can occur. Sentences have meanings beyond the meanings of individual words; paragraphs and larger units of text have meanings beyond that of individual sentences. In language, the whole is indeed more than the sum of its parts.

Using these larger meanings to help make "educated guesses" about what an unfamiliar word might be involves using context as a word recognition strategy. It requires a reader to ask the mental question, "What would make sense here?" Several strategies may be taught to help students use context effectively.

Cloze procedures were described in Chapter 4 as a means of identifying students' reading levels in relation to a particular text. They are also helpful teaching tools for helping students use context. To complete a cloze passage, students must think along with the author, so to speak, using prior information, the meaning suggested by the entire passage, and grammatical and meaning clues provided by the words preceding and following the omitted words. Systematic practice with cloze procedures helps readers become sensitive to "context clues" and use them when reading.

For teaching, it is not necessary to delete every fifth word as you do when making a cloze passage for assessment. It may be better to delete fewer words and leave more of the text intact. Particular types of words, such as pronouns or verbs, could be deleted to highlight their function. Allow students to insert their best guesses, then discuss their choices. Discussion should guide students to consider how several alternatives may make good sense in one instance, while only one possible choice would make sense in another instance, and how different choices can lead to subtle but important changes in meaning. Cloze passages should be accompanied by discussion; their effectiveness is reduced if they are used as worksheets to be completed individually. Older students or more fluent readers may use text they have not read before, then compare their efforts to the original text. Younger students or less fluent readers may be more comfortable, and more successful, in text they have read or heard before, like dictated stories, predictable books, and familiar rhymes.

Confirming from text involves covering part of the text as it is read, predicting what might come next, then uncovering the hidden portions and proceeding. Whole words, parts of words following an initial letter, word groups or phrases may be covered, depending on what cues you want your students to use as they read the passage. Big books and stories put on transparencies or chart tablets work best for this activity.

If you are using a transparency, use a paper or tagboard strip to cover part of the text, have students read up to the covered part (and even a bit beyond it, in some cases), and predict what might come next. If you have covered a whole word, you might now uncover the initial letter or letters and have them predict again. Then slide the strip back and continue reading. At the end of the sentence have students tell what "clues" they used to help them guess. If you are using a big book or chart tablet, words can be covered with small notepapers with a sticky strip on the reverse, and phrases or lines with a tagboard strip held in place with paperclips. Keep the activity moving so students don't get bogged down, and don't cover too many words so that context is lost. It is better to do a little of this activity fairly often than to do it infrequently and beat it to death.

Word Sorting

Imagine a teacher working with a group of young beginning readers who have small collections of words printed on cards, words they recognize at sight that have been gleaned from dictated stories, familiar trade books and basal stories, signs, and labels. Such a collection of sight words is called a *word bank,* and today when the children come to the reading circle they bring their word banks along and sit on the floor.

The teacher tells the children to go through their word banks and group some of the words together on the floor in front of them. The words all have to go together in some way, and each child will have to tell how they go together. The teacher watches carefully as the students go through their words and sort them.

The first word in Tammy's word bank is *but.* After studying it for a moment, she shuffles through her cards and pulls out several more, arranges them in a line, and sits back with a satisfied smile. The words are

> but   ball   boy   brown   bananas

Chris studies his words intently after spreading them all out before him. With a good deal of muttering to himself he makes this group:

> butterfly   tomorrow   potatoes   Christopher

Alicia also spreads her cards out and makes several false starts as she tentatively puts words together, then changes her mind. Finally she appears to be satisfied with this grouping:

> puppy   grass   Mother   flower   hamster

Each child in the group has made a unique sort, because each child has somewhat different words in his or her word bank and because each has looked for a different sorting criterion. When told to "put together words that go together in some way," each has looked for certain word features.

What feature has Tammy used to categorize *but, ball, boy, brown,* and *bananas*? Obviously, they share the same beginning letter b. Tammy has also grouped her words by the same beginning sound feature, which she hears when she reads each word card aloud to the teacher. Tammy has attended to both letter and sound features in this sort.

Chris's words (*butterfly, tomorrow, potatoes, Christopher*) do not share the same letter or sound features. They do not start alike or have a similar vowel sound; two have a double consonant, but not all four. What feature do they share? They are all three-syllable words; Chris checked himself on this feature by pronouncing each word aloud. He attended to features of word parts, in this case the number of syllables in each word.

Alicia has apparently not used the same features as Chris or Tammy, for *puppy, grass, hamster, flower,* and *Mother* do not share the same number of syllables or a common affix, nor do they have a sound or letter feature in common. On what basis, then, has Alicia grouped them? She calls them all "living things," and we can see that she has used word meaning as the shared feature.

There are other word features the children might have used, such as grammatical features—the ways words function in sentences—what we know as parts of speech: for example, *car, mouse, tacos,* and *sea* are all nouns; *run, table, shoe,* and *light* can all be either nouns or verbs depending on how they are used; *happy, run-down,* and *fat* are all descriptive words. There are also spelling pattern features. *Mail, boat, shoes,* and *hear* all share the spelling feature of double vowels (vowel digraphs) as do *feet, sheep,* and *beer.*

The Importance of Classifying

In our example, the children were word sorting. To do this, they must study and compare words and determine the features several words have in common. The word sorting activity is based on principles of induction and discovery learning. The act of classifying stimuli into classes according to their common properties is one of the most basic and powerful operations of human thinking and is responsible for much of a child's natural learning ability, particularly the acquisition of linguistic concepts (Anglin, 1977).

Teachers can use this process productively in school to help children develop strategies for recognizing words in print and analyzing unrecognized words. We often forget that children come to school with five or six years of solid experience in looking for similarities in things, categorizing them, and drawing generalizations about how they work, but they have to be shown how to apply these thinking operations to the study of words in print (Gillet, 1980; Morris, 1982).

Words for Sorting

Since word sorts are done with words on cards, students need a collection of word cards with which to work. Their word banks are particularly good for this purpose because they contain words they recognize at sight. This growing collection of known words is perfect for use in word sorts, because the words must be quickly recognized before their components can successfully be analyzed.

A very quick way of helping children begin a word bank without using dictation is to give them a short story or passage that they can read fairly easily, have them underline each new word they can immediately recognize, and tell them to copy each word onto a small card. Then, working in pairs, they can run through each other's cards to weed out any words that are not quickly recognized. In this way they can develop collections of words they recognize and also accomplish the task of making the cards themselves, which is a time-consuming and tedious task for the teacher.

Using Word Sorts Diagnostically

There are two basic kinds of word sorts: those that call on *convergent* thinking and those that call on *divergent* thinking. In a *closed sort,* the feature that all words in a group must share is stated in advance. For example, the students are directed to search for words beginning like *stop,* having the same vowel sounds as *bake* and *sheep,* the same number of syllables as *feather,* or words that might be associated with a party. Students then search for words that fit the pattern. A closed sort helps them use convergent thinking.

In an *open sort,* which encourages divergent thinking, no sorting criteria are stated in advance. Instead, word cards are examined and categories formed as relationships suggest themselves spontaneously. In closed sorts, students search for instances of particular shared features; in open sorts they consider a number of features simultaneously, searching for those shared by other words. In both types of sorts, children are guided toward *discovering* similarities in words rather than being *told* or *shown* how they are alike (in contrast to some of the more traditional word study activities).

As instructional procedures, both open and closed word sorts are very useful in helping youngsters form generalizations about how known words work, which they can fruitfully apply when they encounter a new word. Word sorts are also a powerful diagnostic tool through which we can learn a good deal about what features of words children can perceive and how they go about learning new word analysis strategies.

Closed sorts. When teachers want to determine if children in the group can recognize certain features of words, they can use the closed sort, in which they specify what the children are to look for and illustrate the salient feature with word or picture cards as examples. The children then search their word banks and word card collections for one or more words with the same feature. Each child then holds up or lays down the cards simultaneously. A quick look around the circle at each child's offering will show the teacher which children have recognized that feature.

Let's say, for example, that a teacher of beginning readers wants to find out quickly what each child in a reading group knows about certain initial consonant sounds, but the teacher doesn't want to give the group a test. Using a diagnostic sort, the teacher uses the regular reading-circle time to determine this information. The children come to the circle with their word cards while the teacher brings a set of picture cards, commercial or homemade from magazine pictures. The teacher shows them one or more pictures of objects that illustrate the initial sound they will explore—for example, pictures of a *fox* and a *fire* to get at the initial consonant sound of *f*, or one picture for each of several sounds, like a *box*, a *mouse*, a *cake*, and a *hat*, to work on recognition of all four of those initial sounds. The teacher tells the children to find one or more words from their word banks that start with the same sound as these objects. The children identify each pictured object, and the teacher observes the words given as a match. (It is easier if the children sit on the floor so they can place their cards on the floor in front of them.) In this activity, pictures, not printed words, are used as exemplars so that the children must rely on an internalization of the sound feature rather than just matching initial letters visually (Gillet and Kita, 1979). The teacher can provide immediate feedback to each child, and time is used efficiently because all the children are involved simultaneously in the task rather than one child performing and the rest watching or waiting their turns. Any letter-sound feature can be assessed as well as any other feature of words. Number of syllables, meaning relationships, parts of speech, and structural elements like affixes are examples of categories that could be formed.

Open sorts. A related assessment activity, a little more open-ended, is the open word sort. A convenient format for this is a game in which students must "read each other's minds" by deducing the criterion another has used to form a group. In this game, each student begins with the same number of word cards; a dozen is an adequate number. Working individually, each child forms at least one category of words. Others must try to "read minds" by either stating the shared feature or, more abstractly, by finding words of their own to add to the category. During each phase of the activity, the teacher discovers what students know about words and what they still need to learn by observing the word groups formed and their attempts to "break" another category.

Individual sorts. Word sorts can also be used with one child individually, to see how well he or she is able to generalize from known words to similar unknown words. The student's word bank can be used or the teacher can make up a set of word cards.

Any closed or open sort format can be used. The teacher and student can also play the "read my mind" open sort game, in which the teacher forms a group and the student must find another word to fit it, then they reverse roles. This game demonstrates recognition of the shared feature.

The student's ability to generalize can be assessed in this way: the teacher groups several highly similar, easily recognized words like *my, by,* and *fly;* then the student is shown a similar but unknown word, perhaps *shy* or *cry* in this example. If the student can use the shared feature of the example words to figure out the new word, *the ability to generalize from the known to the unknown* is demonstrated. This generalizing is the fundamental aspect of all word analysis and decoding, an ability that appears only after children have begun to develop a stable store of sight words and have a clear concept of what a written word is.

The ability to group words by shared features is an important one to assess in beginning readers because if it is not yet developed, instruction in word analysis strategies will be largely misunderstood and confusing for the child. Decoding instruction should be put off until the youngster can do this kind of thinking.

DEVELOPING READING COMPREHENSION

In recent years reading comprehension has become a topic of enormous research interest, and new insights have been proposed that challenge much of the accepted wisdom about comprehension. Such challenges have sparked new controversies and in some cases have led to the development of new approaches in teaching comprehension.

A central issue in current comprehension research is the manner in which readers receive and process new information from print and the degree to which they must relate what is new to what is already known. That we learn by relating and associating new and old, or prior, information is not a new insight, but it is one that has increasingly been studied. Cognitive growth occurs when learners establish mental categories, or *schemata*, comprising concepts about objects and events sharing some general or specific features. As students experience new, unfamiliar things, they make comparisons to members of existing categories and either lump the new things with prior experiences or place them in a newly established schema. In this way established schemata become more complex, while new ones are established, providing more and more ways for learners to deal with new experiences. Only recently, however, has this process been directly applied to the acquisition of information during reading. Schema theory refers to a model of reading comprehension that takes into account what readers may already know and how they go about developing and adding to schemata as they read. In this model prior knowledge becomes critical to understanding and acquiring new information and meaning.

A second important issue is the presence of predictable organizational schemes in text and the reader's ability to perceive and use them. Recent study has shown that nearly all text we call "stories" are organized in similar, predictable ways, different of course in elaboration and detail but structured in basically similar ways. Studies by Stein (1978) and others have shown that students' understanding and memory of stories are enhanced when they have a set of expectations about how stories are structured and when what they read conforms to their expectations. Similarly there are characteristic organizational schemes present in well-written nonfiction text, structures that can aid readers in understanding and remembering information from the text if readers are aware of and use them.

A third issue concerns the nature of comprehension skills and the common practice of teaching them as separate entities. Recent thinking and research challenge this practice. Instructional programs have long been developed from the assumption that comprehension results from the mastery of a number of discrete skills, each of which can be taught and learned separately from the others. There has long been disagreement on just how many such separate skills exist, but most educators have at least agreed on the existence of such skills as getting the main idea, locating supporting details, differentiating between directly and indirectly stated information (usually called facts and inferences), drawing conclusions, recalling sequences, and understanding cause-and-effect relationships.

Traditional practice in both teaching and testing has been to present comprehension skills as separable entities, each of which may be learned and assessed in relative isolation from the others and mastery of which results in overall reading comprehension. The skills controversy centers around the question of whether such skills are actually separable and whether operations of comprehension are really different from one another, as well as around the question of whether meaning exists only in the text or in the reader's mind as well.

Current trends and findings in the study of comprehension have led away from the isolation of specific skills and toward the teaching of comprehension as an integrated process built around the reader's prior knowledge and schemata. In the sections which follow we will describe activities derived from this approach to comprehension.

Developing Prior Knowledge

Prior knowledge is what we already know or have experienced, directly or vicariously, that we bring to the act of reading. When we can somehow relate what we read to our prior knowledge we understand and remember more clearly. When we lack prior knowledge to relate to what we read, chances are that we will become confused, misunderstand, and forget what we read. In this situation we may also become disinterested in what we are reading, calling it boring or dull. And if our need is great to remember it, as in preparation for a test, we may resort to inefficient strategies like memorizing. Helping students develop, organize, and become aware of their prior knowledge is critical to improving their reading comprehension.

But there are two problems associated with prior knowledge. One is that we may lack sufficient prior knowledge about a topic, not having heard or read of it before. A second problem is that much of our prior knowledge about a given topic may not be readily accessible; it has been buried, so to speak, under other information and we can't summon it up and think about it readily. Because we can't bring it to mind immediately, we think we've forgotten it or never had it. Activities that develop prior knowledge center around helping students establish some basis for new information and helping them remember and organize prior knowledge that is not readily accessible.

Webbing

A simple way to help students begin to recall prior knowledge and form relationships is to use webbing, an exercise in which the teacher writes a topic or term on the board, students offer terms or phrases that may be related, and the teacher draws lines connecting associated terms with each other. In the following reading, terms and relationships are noted and the "web" may be revised to reflect new information acquired. The webbing exercise serves to help students remember old information related to the reading and to form expectations about what they will be reading.

For example, let's say that Ms. Brown, a fourth-grade teacher, plans to have her students read a nonfiction basal selection about how museums are organized and the jobs museum workers perform. She suspects that some of the students have never visited a museum and that the topic is relatively unfamiliar to many of them. She begins, then, with a web to explore with them what they already know.

First she writes *museum* on the board and begins a *brainstorming whip,* in which every student in turn offers a word or phrase related in some way to *museum.* Because some students look apprehensive, she suggests some questions to help get them started:

What is a museum for?
What are the names of some museums?

What might be in them?

What work do people do in museums?

As each student responds, Ms. Brown writes the response on the board around the key word. Because this is brainstorming, all responses are accepted without comment or evaluation. She notes that the first few responses appear to remind the others of things they may have forgotten and that many appear excited as their turn nears. After everyone has responded once, volunteers may offer other suggestions until their information begins to wane. Then she reads over all the suggestions from the board.

The next step is to help students organize this seemingly random collection of terms into categories. One way Ms. Brown could do this is to use different colors of chalk to draw connecting lines, but because there are a lot of items on the board, this may not help to clarify. So she selects one term, writes it below the web and says, "What other words go with this one?" Items are checked off and listed in categories, with students explaining why these items go together. These categories resulted:

paintings scientists mummies statues suits of armor rockets airplanes old cars Indian stuff animals and birds furniture old cars dinosaur bones

scientists guards guides

set up exhibits clean up take tickets tours

Smithsonian Museum of Natural History

Students then suggested names for these categories: things in museums, museum workers, jobs in museums, and names of museums. Ms. Brown then said, "We're going to read an article about how museums are organized and what kinds of work must be done. As you read, watch for mention of the names of famous museums, their collections, and museum workers' jobs. Let's see which of the things we mentioned are in the article."

After the reading was completed, Ms. Brown led her students in re-inspecting the web, adding to the appropriate categories items from the article they had not mentioned, and marking those not appearing in the article to look up in another source.

A webbing activity like this is effective for several reasons. One is that it encourages all students to draw on whatever prior knowledge they have, no matter how extensive or limited, and apply it to the reading task. Another is that hearing others' ideas often triggers a forgotten bit of information in another's mind, so that all benefit from sharing of information. A third is that seemingly unrelated information is directly organized so that relationships are sought and explored. A fourth is that prereading participation fosters curiosity and gives readers something to watch for as they read, and a purpose for reading. And a fifth is that the exercise helps the teacher realize what prior knowledge, if any, students have on the topic before they begin reading.

Previewing

Another way to help students organize their prior knowledge and develop expectations about what they are going to read is to let them quickly preview a reading selection and predict what kinds of information they may find in it.

When students preview a reading selection, they do not begin to read it, but rather they scan each page, looking at illustrations and text features such as boldface print and headings. The time allowed for this is very short so that they can get an overall general idea of the content, just enough to begin to predict about specifics. Depending on the length of the selection, two minutes or less are usually sufficient. Previewing is effective with both fiction and nonfiction, as we will see in these examples.

Mr. Talbott works with a group of fifth graders reading at a third-grade instructional level. He has selected a basal story for them to read and discuss that deals with events surrounding the celebration of the Chinese New Year. Because this holiday and Chinese-American customs in general are unfamiliar to his students, he uses previewing to help them form a basis for their reading. He tells the group to find the first and last pages of the story, and then to look at the title and the pictures but not to begin reading yet. He gives them 30 seconds to do so, telling the group when to begin and stop. Then he asks them to close their books and tell him what they saw in the pictures. He lists all the responses on the board:

> Chinese people
> a parade
> fireworks
> people in costumes
> people wearing masks
> some kind of big snake or dragon
> people inside a dragon suit
> some children looking scared
> people eating
> a building with a funny roof

Then he asks, "What do you think is going on in this story? What could be happening?" Again he lists responses:

party
celebration
parade
holiday

Then he introduces some terms from the story and encourages predictions about what they might mean and how they may be related to the story: festival, calendar, temple, parade, and feast. The students' predictions begin to form around the idea that a Chinese holiday celebration is occurring in which people prepare special foods, observe religious customs, wear ceremonial clothing, and participate in a street procession with costumes and fireworks. From this basis of information, Mr. Talbott guides his students to reexamine the illustrations and predict what might happen in the story: for example, who might the children be who are pictured several times? Why might they be frightened in this picture? What might happen at the end?

At this point, the students have developed a good basis of information and expectation, and are ready to begin reading. Their previewing has helped them develop a context for the story's events, introduced some of the story's key vocabulary, and helped them to set purposes for their reading.

Ms. Niles works with older poor readers from several grades. Five of her students must read an earth science selection on glacier formation, but prereading discussion reveals that both prior information and interest in the topic are lacking. She uses previewing to help overcome both problems.

First she asks the group to tell what they already know about glaciers. Other than that they are made of ice, her question is met with shrugs and blank looks. "All right," she says, "you have exactly two minutes to look over these pages and find out as much as you can, and we'll see who is able to gather the most information. Sally and Becky, you look at headings and boldface print. Maurice and John, you look at maps. Sam and Daniel, you look for topic sentences at the beginnings of each major section. Jessica, you look at photographs and their captions. All set? Begin!"

Ms. Niles has adapted the previewing task to fit the special informational demands of this selection and has given each student a specific task. She has also used a team approach and introduced an element of competition to arouse the students' interest in the task. After two minutes of silent study, she asks each student or pair to report on the specified area and begins listing terms, topics, and descriptions on the board under general headings. She compliments each responder on the amount of information gathered, without designating any "winner." After a quick review of the lists on the board, the students begin to read the selection, armed with an array of facts, terms, and concepts they had not possessed before, as well as with some confidence that they can read the chapter successfully.

Previewing is an effective means of helping students acquire some prereading information about topics of which they know little beforehand and set some expectations about the text that they can compare to what the selection conveys. The previewing time should be kept short and the discussion period should be conducted in an accepting, encouraging manner. Reading should begin when interest is aroused and some basis for reading has been established.

Developing Prediction

Closely related to the topic of prior knowledge is the process of prediction, in which students compare what they already know or remember to what they think they are going to read. Prediction requires that students relate their prior knowledge to the reading task at hand and form expectations they will apply to the reading. Thus, prediction forms the connection between prior knowledge and the new information coming in.

DRTA: Active Reading of Fiction

The directed reading-thinking activity, or DRTA, is a guided group discussion activity that focuses on the formation and testing of prereading predictions. In essence, it is a set of procedures for guiding prereading and postreading discussion. In a DRTA, children develop critical reading and thinking by predicting possible story events and outcomes, then reading to confirm or disprove their hypotheses. As described by Stauffer (1975), in a DRTA the students form a set of purposes for reading, processing ideas, and testing answers by taking part in a predict-read-prove cycle. The teacher *activates thought* by asking "What do you think?"; *agitates thought* by asking "Why do you think so?"; and *requires evidence* by asking "How can you prove it?" (Stauffer, 1975, p. 37). The DRTA format helps students to read more critically and with improved comprehension because it engages them in this process of fluent reading in a structured fashion, slowing down and making concrete the phases of the prediction process.

Students may be asked to form tentative hypotheses about a story from the title, cover art, or first illustration. They may be asked to look at other illustrations or to read the first sentence, paragraph, or page. They are asked to predict what might happen in the story and how it might end up, and to justify their predictions based on what they have seen, read, and already know or believe. At preselected points in the story they are asked to stop reading, review predictions and change them if necessary, form new predictions about upcoming material, and continue reading. Predictions may be recorded on the board to aid in recalling them later. Predictions which are disproved by later story events, or those students no longer think are likely, may be erased or crossed out. Students are continually asked to justify their positions based on what they have already read. They may reread orally to back up their points. The predict-read-prove cycle continues through the story; as students get closer to the end, their predictions become more convergent as more and more of the story is revealed. At the story's end, predictions and "clues" may be reviewed or other kinds of follow-up questions may be asked.

K-W-L: Active Reading of Nonfiction

K-W-L stands for the three questions readers should ask themselves as they read a nonfiction selection: "What do I *KNOW*? What do I *WANT* to learn? What did I *LEARN* from this? The first two questions are asked prior to reading; the third is asked following the reading. They correspond to the mental operations of accessing prior information, determining reading purposes, and recalling information (Ogle, 1986). The procedure has three steps.

Step K: Before reading, the teacher guides students in brainstorming what they already know about the topic of the reading. The teacher records this information on the board or on a transparency. After the brainstorming students are asked to use their prior information to predict what general types or categories of information they might expect to encounter when they read the passage. For example, if the topic is Columbus' voyage to the New World, and students have recalled prior information about three ships, cramped quarters, and inadequate food, they might be led by the teacher to identify categories of information such as "how they got there," "what the ships were like," and "what they ate and drank on the voyage." Since students often find this step difficult, the teacher needs to model and demonstrate this step numerous times until students begin to be able to perceive categories themselves.

Step W: As students complete the first step, disagreements and uncertainties will arise. These form the basis of the "What do I want to learn?" step. The teacher's role here is to highlight disagreements and gaps in prior information, raising questions that will help students focus on the new information they will encounter. Students should write down the specific questions they want to have answered, thus making a personal commitment to the information. Students may be given a K-W-L worksheet to use for notetaking, with the three questions as headings. An example of a completed worksheet is shown in Figure 6.7.

Step L: After completing the reading, whether they read the whole article or a portion of it, students should write down the information they recall from the passage. They should check their written questions to see if they found answers to them; some questions may require further reading or checking other sources. The teacher guides a discussion of the questions generated and the answers students found, including areas of disagreement; students refer to the passage to resolve disputes.

Carr and Ogle (1987) developed "K-W-L Plus," an enhanced K-W-L with two additional steps for secondary students. Following the reading and the use of the three steps, students engage in *concept mapping* and *summarizing*. A *concept map* is a graphic organizer that allows students to group pieces of information gleaned from the text, that helps students to see associations and relationships among various pieces of information. This process is considered

Figure 6.7

K-W-L Worksheet

Topic: _____ Crocodiles _____

K	W	L
What We Know	What We Want to Find Out	What We Learned

K — What We Know

eats people
eats meat
reptile
lays eggs
about 6 feet long
leaves its babies
solitary
vicious
has about 6 babies

W — What We Want to Find Out

do they eat people?
What do they eat?
How do they get their food?
How big are they?
How does it have its babies?
How many babies at one time?

L — What We Learned

Do eat people
Also eat bugs, fish, ducks, birds, antelope
Actively hunt with others
Herds fish with tail
Shares its food
Live in groups
6–15 feet long
most common 6–8 feet
female digs a nest
use same nest year after year
guards the nest
helps babies dig out
helps babies break shell
father crocodile helps can help break eggs
protects babies for 12 weeks

Categories of Information:

Diet
Size

Getting Food
Reproduction
Family Life

Figure 6.8

K-W-L Plus Concept Map

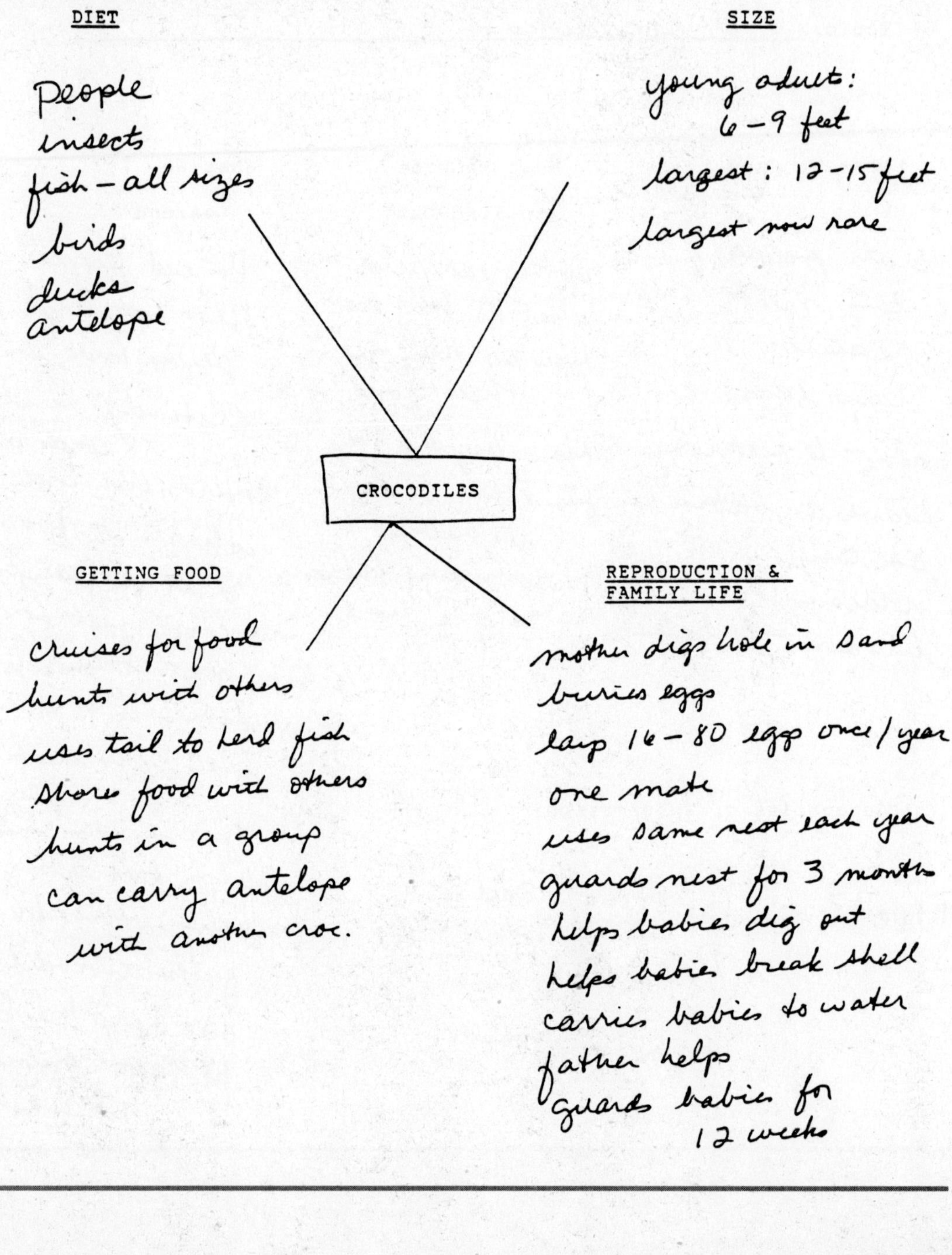

DIET

People
insects
fish — all sizes
birds
ducks
antelope

SIZE

young adult:
    6 – 9 feet
largest : 12 – 15 feet
largest now rare

CROCODILES

GETTING FOOD

cruises for food
hunts with others
uses tail to herd fish
shares food with others
hunts in a group
can carry antelope
    with another croc.

REPRODUCTION &
FAMILY LIFE

mother digs hole in sand
buries eggs
lays 16 – 80 eggs once/year
one mate
uses same nest each year
guards nest for 3 months
helps babies dig out
helps babies break shell
carries babies to water
father helps
guards babies for
    12 weeks

important because many students, particularly poor readers, acquire information from text only as isolated facts, failing to organize them into any coherent units of meaning. Practice in organizing information into main ideas or topics and supporting details improves overall comprehension. An example of a concept map is shown in Figure 6.8. The concept map is then used as the organizer for a written summary, which requires students to reflect on information gleaned and express it in their own words in a logical and readable form. Practice in *summarizing* helps students organize and include all important information from a text, not just that information they found most memorable or interesting.

Developing Awareness of Story Structure

As you may recall from Chapter 2, recent study (Applebee, 1978, 1980; Stein, 1978; and others) reveals that all texts we call stories contain characteristic elements, called story structures, that occur in a particular sequence and serve to relate the story's characters and events in a logical order. These structures include:

1. *setting*—a direct or implied statement that places the story in a physical, historical, or temporal context and introduces the protagonist.
2. *initiating event*—an action, idea, or situation setting the story's plot in motion.
3. *internal response*—protagonist's response to the initiating event, including the setting of some goal and decision to pursue some course of action.
4. *attempt**—an effort to achieve the goal.
5. *outcome**—a direct result of the attempt.
6. *consequence**—a result of the attempts to reach the goal and their outcomes. This may be an action, a change of behavior, or a state of affairs.

Some stories may have an optional final element:

7. *reaction*—protagonist's response to the consequence of the story's events, which may take the form of a change in opinion or belief, a statement of what has been learned, or a "moral."

Studies by Stein (1978) and others have shown that readers' understanding and recall of stories is influenced by their degree of experience reading or

---

*Sets of attempts, outcomes, and consequences make up episodes. A story may have many episodes or only one.

listening to stories, and by the presence and order of story structures in what they read. Those who have heard or read a variety of stories in the past develop a set of expectations about how new stories will unfold. When what they read is organized logically and well structured, readers appear to compare what they expect to what they read, and they mentally reorganize and remember depending on those comparisons. When they have few expectations, or when stories do not conform to their expectations, their understanding and memory of what they read declines.

These findings have important implications for teaching:

1. What students read should be well-written, clearly organized stories. Material made up of unrelated sentences ("Pam has a ham. Nick has a stick. Is the pig in a pan?") or "stories" that go nowhere, with little story line, should be avoided.
2. Teachers should draw students' attention to the structures in the stories they read and make them aware of similarities in story structure.

Story Mapping

A story map is a graphic representation of the parts of a story that shows how the story parts are related. Story maps "provide a practical means of helping children organize story content into coherent wholes" (Davis & McPherson, 1989, p. 232). "Story mapping," wrote Boyle and Peregoy, ". . . helps children use story grammar for comprehension and composing" (1990, p. 198). Story maps can be used to help readers perceive and understand plot structure and a variety of text structures such as literal and implied information, cause and effect, sequential ordering, and comparison and contrast. They are similar to other graphic organizers such as structured overviews, story diagrams, and webs.

Figure 6.9 shows a sample story map for the Aesop's fable, "The Crow and the Water Jug." This story map emphasizes the essential story structures described in the previous section: setting, initiating event or "problem," internal response or "goal," attempts and outcomes, consequence or "resolution." Figure 6.10 shows another kind of story map, devised by Boyle and Peregoy (1990). In this model, the essential story grammar is boiled down to SOMEONE . . . WANTS . . . BUT . . . SO. Under each of these headings, the teacher or students list the character or characters and their problems, the goals, and means of achieving them. Other story maps might compare the advantages and disadvantages of some story action, the causes and effects of certain story events, or aspects of the various characters in a story.

To construct a story map, first think about the kinds of information or story structures you want to emphasize in your lesson. Make some notes about how this information may be arrayed. For example, comparison and contrast may be illustrated by listing items in two vertical columns; sequential order of story events may lend itself to a linear or "timeline" arrangement;

Figure 6.9

Story Map for "The Crow and the Water Jug"

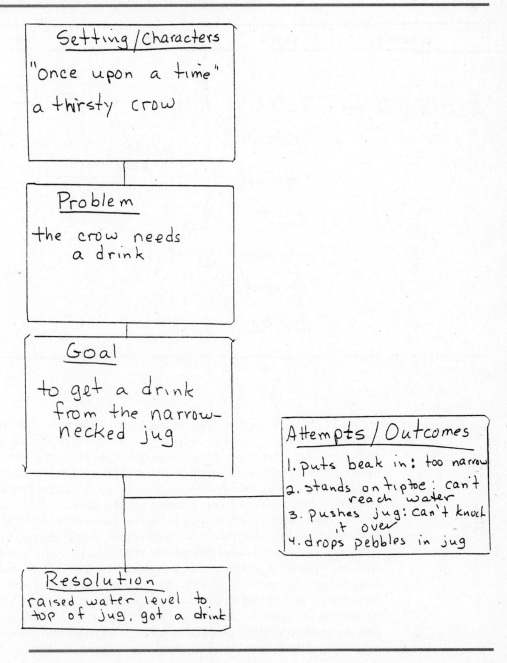

Setting/Characters
"Once upon a time"
a thirsty crow

Problem
the crow needs
a drink

Goal
to get a drink
from the narrow-
necked jug

Attempts/Outcomes
1. puts beak in: too narrow
2. stands on tiptoe: can't
   reach water
3. pushes jug: can't knock
   it over
4. drops pebbles in jug

Resolution
raised water level to
top of jug, got a drink

Figure 6.10

Story Map for "The Little Red Hen"

SOMEONE	WANTS	BUT	SO

Little Red Hen | help to plant tend cut thresh grind bake *the wheat* | the other animals won't help her | she does it herself

---

details of characterization may be illustrated by a web-style arrangement of circles connected to a central circle with short lines; or the comparison of two stories or characters may be shown by two intersecting circles, sometimes called a *Venn diagram*. Examine your story map to make sure it emphasizes the logical flow of information. Don't make it too technical or detailed; emphasize just one pattern of organization at a time.

To teach with a story map, it is best to start with a straightforward, literal map of story events. Introduce it after the story has been read to help students recall and reconstruct what happened. When students are somewhat familiar with the story map and its use as a postreading activity, you may begin using story maps as a prereading organizer. Students may be given some minimal information and asked to predict story events, or may be shown a partially completed story map and asked to predict what else might occur. Such pre-reading prediction has a positive effect on later recall and comprehension, just as it does with directed reading-thinking activities, K-W-L and other related prediction strategies. After reading a portion of the story, the story map may be modified, and students may continue reading and changing the map until the story is completed. Story maps may also be used as a postreading activity, with students reconstructing a map individually or in cooperative learning groups; they may also complete partially completed maps, which Davis and McPherson (1989) call "macro cloze story maps."

Retelling

We know that retelling stories helps children understand and remember stories and develop sense of story. Retelling requires readers or listeners to organize information and make inferences about it based on text information and their own prior information by constructing a personal rendition of the text. Thus, retelling focuses children's attention on relevant text information, sequences, and causes and effects. It requires that they organize that information into a coherent structure for retelling to another. Studies have shown that young children's story sense and story comprehension are significantly improved by practice retelling stories they have heard (Morrow, 1984, 1985, 1986; Pellegrini and Galda, 1982). Similarly, retelling has been shown to improve reading comprehension (Gambrell et al., 1985; Rose et al., 1984). You can use retelling strategies in your classroom to help all readers improve their story comprehension.

According to Koskinen et al. (1988), in its simplest form a retelling activity involves two students working together during direct instruction time or independent work time; one reads or listens to a portion of a text, or a whole story, and then teams up with a partner to retell the story. Since the listener's role is an important one and good listening is active, rather than passive, the listener is asked to provide helpful questions or comments to the teller and may be asked to complete a retelling reaction sheet.

Before students begin this activity, you need to model it so that students will have a clear understanding of what they are to do and why they are doing it. First, explain simply and clearly why retelling is a useful activity. Depending on the age of your students, you may say something like, "Retelling a story you have read or listened to helps you remember stories and helps you check to see if you understand what you have read or heard. It also helps you learn to be a good storyteller. I will show you what to do to practice retelling stories and how to be a helpful listening partner. Then you will have time to practice retelling with a partner."

Model retelling by telling students what you are going to do: "I'm going to read a short passage from this story. Then I'm going to retell it to you without looking at the story. I'm going to try to include all the important ideas and information. As I read it, listen for the important ideas."

Next, read aloud a fairly short passage from a story or nonfiction text, or a short, complete story. Afterwards retell the story or passage in a few sen-

Figure 6.11

Prompts for Encouraging Retelling

Narrative text

Who are the main characters?

When did the story take place?

Where did the story take place?

What important events happened in the story?

How did the story end?

Expository text

What is the topic of the selection?

What are the important ideas in the selection?

Source: From Patricia S. Koskinen, Linda B. Gambrell, Barbara A. Kapinus, and Betty S. Heathington. "Retelling: A Strategy for Enhancing Students' Reading Comprehension." *The Reading Teacher* 41, no. 9 (May 1988). Reprinted with permission of Patricia Koskinen and the International Reading Association.

tences, including the most important information, sequences, and the like. Then ask students for feedback on the retelling by asking them if you included all the important ideas, accepting their contributions or suggestions. Immediately following the modeling, students can read a short passage from a basal reader, textbook, or other material they all have. Guide them in group retelling by having volunteers retell to the group, using question prompts that are appropriate for the type of text with which they are dealing. (See Figure 6.11, Prompts for Encouraging Retelling.)

When children seem to have the idea of retelling, which may be after more than one model and group practice, create opportunities for students to practice retelling to a partner. In this practice, one student silently reads a passage or text for retelling, then retells it to a partner. Both students need not have read the same material; if the partner has not read the story and has trouble understanding it from the retelling, this is a good indication to the student that more practice retelling is needed. This is an excellent opportunity for students to read and share trade books they are reading in class, and it provides another important way for you to work trade books into your reading instruction. Students may practice reading and retelling during independent work time or free reading time. They should do this regularly, several times a week.

Retelling is more effective for both students involved if the listener has an active role. Good listening is active and responsive, not passive. The student who is the listening partner should have something to do besides just listen. With guided practice, the listening partner can learn how to ask helpful

Figure 6.12

Example of a Retelling Reaction Sheet

Name _____ Date _____

I listened to _____

Choose one thing your partner did well.

He or she told about the characters. _____

He or she told about the setting. _____

He or she told about events in the story. _____

His or her story had a beginning. _____

His or her story had an ending. _____

Tell your partner one thing that was good about his or her story.

Source: From Patricia S. Koskinen, Linda B. Gambrell, Barbara A. Kapinus, and Betty S. Heathington. "Retelling: A Strategy for Enhancing Students' Reading Comprehension." *The Reading Teacher* 41, no. 9 (May 1988). Reprinted with permission of Patricia Koskinen and the International Reading Association.

questions by using the prompts referred to in Figure 6.11, or by suggesting other important information that the teller omitted, if any. Students can also complete a retelling reaction guide, such as the one in Figure 6.12. This procedure focuses on positive responses rather than criticism, which is very important. Providing this task for listeners helps them set a purpose for listening and helps keep them focused on the task. Giving students systematic, structured opportunities to talk about what they have read helps develop comprehension and oral expression skills and provides teachers yet another way to incorporate fiction and nonfiction trade books in their regular instruction program.

Reciprocal Teaching

Reciprocal teaching (Brown et al., 1984) is a method for demonstrating and developing reading comprehension in a group setting. The teacher models a systematic way of approaching a passage by using a sequence of comprehension processes: summarizing, questioning, clarifying, and predicting. After the teacher models these processes in four steps, students take turns following the same steps and leading the others in discussing the passage read. This procedure is useful with any kind of text; it is particularly useful with nonfiction, which often contains a great many facts and pieces of new information. Here are the steps in using reciprocal teaching:

1. The teacher divides the passage to be read into fairly short sections; depending on the total length of the selection, one or two paragraphs at a time

may be sufficient. For long selections such as whole chapters, long chapter sections, and longer stories, several pages may be better. Or, she or he may wish to start the procedure with short sections, then make them longer as the reading progresses.

2. The teacher asks everyone to read the passage silently. To avoid having some students waiting for slower readers, she or he should assign the reading before the activity begins. In this case, all students should quickly re-examine and review the passage before the discussion begins.

3. After the reading is completed, the teacher models the comprehension process by following these four steps:
   a. *Summarize* the section in one or a few sentences.
   b. *Ask* the group one or two good questions, avoiding picky details.
   c. Identify a difficult part of the passage and *clarify* it by explaining, giving examples, drawing analogies, or making other clarifying statements.
   d. *Predict* what the next section might be about or what might be learned from it.

4. The teacher should repeat steps 1 through 3 until the pattern is familiar to all students. Afterwards, he or she can take turns leading the discussion steps previously mentioned: teacher-student-teacher-student, or teacher-student-student. The teacher modeling and continued teacher involvement is critical to the students' success with the procedure.

Here is an example of how a teacher might use reciprocal teaching with a nonfiction passage: Ms. Brown has chosen an article about penguins from a nature magazine to supplement a science lesson with her fifth graders. The article is three pages long, with lavish illustrations, so she divides the reading into passages of several paragraphs each. First, she distributes copies of the article with the stopping points marked on them. (If she were using a textbook, she would have each student locate the stopping point and mark it with a strip of paper across the page.) She directs students to read the first three paragraphs, which contain general information about penguins' habitat, habits, and diet. Then she models the use of the comprehension steps in this way.

First, I'll summarize this passage. In these paragraphs we read that penguins are large birds that are unusual because they do not fly, but they are excellent swimmers. Their wings are specially shaped like flippers to help them swim very fast and over long distances. They live in icy frozen areas of the world where there is little or no plant life. They live on a diet of fish.

I would ask these questions about these paragraphs:

In what ways do we know penguins are different from other birds? (Students answer that they do not fly, they swim very skillfully, they

live in icy places where there are no plants.)
- In what ways do you think penguins are like other birds? (Students answer that they have wings, other kinds of birds also eat fish, they lay eggs.)
- In what ways might their environment affect how they survive? (Students discuss the lack of plant life for making nests, the dangers of cold.)

"I thought that the paragraph telling about their environment was a little difficult. The passage used some difficult words like *barren, antarctic,* and *ice floes* which might need discussion. Let's write these on the board and discuss what each one means." (Discussion follows about the meaning of these terms; one student gets a dictionary and they refer to it.)

In the paragraphs to follow I predict that we will find out more about how penguins adapt to extreme cold temperatures and find out how they raise their young in this environment."

Ms. Brown then directs students to read to the end of the next section, and she again models these four steps. After the class reads the third section, she calls on a volunteer to follow the same steps: summarize, ask a couple of good questions, clarify a part or term, and predict what may be upcoming. When the article is finished, students briefly discuss the main points of the article and evaluate how well they answered questions and followed the steps in the comprehension process.

Reciprocal teaching helps students learn how effective readers approach challenging texts and helps them develop systematic ways of dealing with the information in them. After a number of repetitions, students may begin to internalize the comprehension steps and apply them independently to other text material.

Reciprocal Question-Answer Relationships

Successful readers use a variety of strategies to maximize their comprehension of text: They monitor their own comprehension, they self-question, they mentally summarize, and they seek relationships among ideas and facts presented in what they read. Unsuccessful readers often do not do these things; they tend to focus more on pronouncing the words and answering the teacher's questions, but they have few strategies for predicting what questions might be asked or for finding answers. Helfeldt and Henk (1990) propose an instructional strategy that helps at-risk readers use self-questioning to improve their comprehension. They call it ReQAR, reciprocal question-answer relationships. The procedure consists of four general steps: explaining what the students will do, reciprocal questioning (wherein students and teacher take turns asking each other questions about a passage just read and answering each other's questions), categorizing questions and their answers according to where the information is found ("in the book" or "in my head"), and finally combining steps two and three by combining reciprocal questioning and categorizing the answers. In this step students ask the teacher a question about the material, and the teacher answers it and categorizes the answer as "in the book" or "in my head"; then roles are reversed, with the teacher asking and the student or students answering and categorizing.

Helfeldt and Henk point out that ReQAR requires a high degree of student participation and that a lesson may span several days or longer. It would seem wise to break up both passages and steps into easily managed segments, at least until readers have had considerable practice with the procedure.

DEVELOPING LISTENING COMPREHENSION

Listening comprehension is related to reading ability in that students who are not yet fluent, mature readers can usually listen to and comprehend text that is read to them that they cannot yet read for themselves. The most common example of this is with emergent and beginning readers, who can listen to and understand a wide variety of materials but may not yet be able to read anything for themselves.

As students' reading abilities develop and their instructional levels go up, the gap between the instructional reading level and listening level may begin to close, and by the time they have become fluent, mature readers there may be no difference between what they can listen to and what they can read successfully. For much of the time before a student has reached this zenith in reading development, however, there will be a gap between these two levels.

Experience is an important factor in listening comprehension. Even if all other things are equal, a student who has been read to and whose school and home environments are rich in oral language (regardless of dialect or language origins) has an advantage over the student who has not had this experience. In the same way, students who can read fairly effectively have a greater store of information, concepts, and vocabulary than illiterate students or very poor readers, and the first group's listening comprehension levels are likely to be higher.

A student's listening comprehension level is important because it shows us how closely his or her ability to understand written text approaches the demands of the student's grade level, and gives us an indication of how much potential for reading improvement the student has at this point in time. We must remember that unlike IQ or other intelligence measures, the listening level is not fixed; as the student's reading ability improves and he or she reads more, the listening level also rises. Thus progress today paves the way for more progress tomorrow.

The Interaction of Listening and Reading Comprehension

There are several typical patterns in listening comprehension and reading. One is that a student may have a below-grade-level listening level and an instructional reading level that matches it. Take, for example, Sam, a fourth-grader whose listening and instructional reading levels are both at second grade. This means that Sam is presently reading about as well as he is able to, and that he lacks the verbal concepts and vocabulary to understand third- or fourth-grade text either by reading or by listening. To attempt to raise Sam's reading level without also developing his listening comprehension will likely result only in frustration, for he will be asked to do what is beyond his present capability. In Sam's case, listening comprehension must be fostered so that his reading ability can grow.

Another common pattern is exemplified by Elaine, also a fourth-grader. Elaine's instructional reading level is also second grade, but her listening comprehension level is fourth grade, and even includes some fifth-grade text when the topic is something she knows about. Elaine is a poor reader in fourth grade, but she already has verbal concepts and vocabulary appropriate to other fourth-graders and text typical of that grade. Elaine needs to develop her reading ability so that it more closely approaches her present listening level, which indicates that she has the present potential to improve her reading significantly.

Other patterns that occur less often are equally important. One is exemplified by Sarah, a fifth-grader. Sarah's instructional level is only about third grade, but her listening level is at seventh. Sarah is a poor reader in fifth grade, but she has the verbal capacity to understand much more difficult text. In Sarah's case this capacity far outstrips present performance, and she can benefit from intensive remediation. Her problems may lie in motivation, inappropriate instruction, or other factors that must be overcome. But she has the measured potential for at least grade-level reading achievement.

Consider, in contrast, the case of James, a ninth-grader in a remedial program. James is functionally nearly illiterate, with only a second-grade instructional level. His listening level is fourth grade. James may be classifiable as a slow learner; he is certainly verbally impoverished, and his illiteracy has kept his listening comprehension from developing. Still, because there is a gap between the two levels, he can improve his reading somewhat. And if he does, his listening comprehension is likely to increase also, which in turn will make possible further reading progress, assuming that James is motivated toward such improvement. In his case, both reading remediation and listening comprehension development are needed.

Strategies for Developing Listening Comprehension

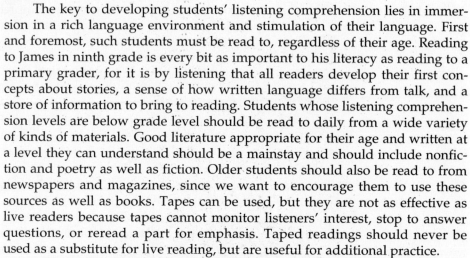

The key to developing students' listening comprehension lies in immersion in a rich language environment and stimulation of their language. First and foremost, such students must be read to, regardless of their age. Reading to James in ninth grade is every bit as important to his literacy as reading to a primary grader, for it is by listening that all readers develop their first concepts about stories, a sense of how written language differs from talk, and a store of information to bring to reading. Students whose listening comprehension levels are below grade level should be read to daily from a wide variety of kinds of materials. Good literature appropriate for their age and written at a level they can understand should be a mainstay and should include nonfiction and poetry as well as fiction. Older students should also be read to from newspapers and magazines, since we want to encourage them to use these sources as well as books. Tapes can be used, but they are not as effective as live readers because tapes cannot monitor listeners' interest, stop to answer questions, or reread a part for emphasis. Taped readings should never be used as a substitute for live reading, but are useful for additional practice.

A directed listening-thinking activity, or DLTA, is a good alternative to straight reading aloud. A DLTA is similar to the DRTA discussed previously in this chapter, wherein students make predictions about upcoming story events or, in the case of nonfiction, assert what they already know of a topic before reading and compare their predictions and assertions to what the text says. The only difference between a DRTA and a DLTA is that in the latter the material is read aloud to students. DLTAs are an effective means of monitoring listening comprehension and fostering interest in listening.

Immersion in a rich language environment also means that students should be actively engaged in oral discussions and conversations. They must be guided to do more than just answer questions, the most common form of classroom talk. They should also describe, summarize, persuade and argue, using as specific, vivid, and precise vocabulary as possible. Many of the typical composition activities suggested in reading and English books, such as making up stories, recounting real events and reminiscences, describing objects, persuading others to some action or belief, arguing for or against some course of action, and composing directions, are just as useful for oral language and listening development. Speaking and listening cannot be separated; they will develop together. Students with underdeveloped listening comprehension need daily experience with both.

Oral reading by students for other students can be useful, too, but must be used with care. All oral reading should be rehearsed and prepared by the reader beforehand. No one is served by listening to someone stumble through text. Material for oral reading should be read silently several times, then read aloud for practice before the final reading. Also, oral reading should be done for some purpose, not as an end in itself. Some material deserves to be read aloud and enjoyment of it is enhanced by being effectively read: poetry, vivid descriptions, and good dialogue are examples. The purpose of oral reading should be to share and enhance such material, not just to practice reading aloud.

And again we return to the point of teacher modeling. The teacher sets the tone and provides the model by which students judge what is useful and important. Without dominating activities, we must show students by our modeling what we want them to be able to do. We should prepare what we read aloud to the class so that our reading will be fluent and expressive. We should share portions of material we find appealing or especially effective with them and work to make our descriptions and summaries colorful and precise. We should exhibit interest in and curiosity about words and expressions and share with students interesting and unusual language in what we read. We should respond to students' efforts to use language more effectively with sincere interest, attention, and positive reinforcement. We should listen more to what they say than to how they say it, and we should respond first to their message.

The more direct experience with language students have, the more their language use will expand. The more it grows, the more their listening comprehension will improve. The more listening comprehension develops, the more they will be able to bring to reading, and thus their reading will improve. The roots of reading ability are buried deep in oral language, and we cannot overlook this foundation if we wish to help our students read better.

TIME SPENT READING

So far in this chapter we have concentrated on methods and issues related to reading instruction: helping students develop sight recognition of words, use word analysis strategies fluently and effectively, organize and apply prior knowledge to new information acquired from reading, and use a variety of reading processes and skills to become more fluent and comprehend better. It may be thought that effective reading lies in instruction, and indeed good instruction is an absolute requirement in helping children grow as readers. In spite of all the instructional techniques we apply, however, there is another factor that is critical: In order to become a good reader, a child must spend a lot of time reading.

This point seems self-evident. But how much time do children actually spend reading? A number of research studies have been conducted in attempts to determine this, and the results of these studies are shocking and disturbing.

Several major studies of children's independent reading have been completed in recent years. Vincent Greaney (1980) studied the out-of-school reading of 920 fifth-graders in 31 Irish primary schools and found that only 5.4 percent of out-of-school time was spent reading; mean reading time was only eighteen minutes per day, and this included reading books, magazines, newspapers, and comic books. Moreover, 44 percent of Greaney's subjects read no books at all during the time studied, while only 6.4 percent devoted at least an hour a day to book reading. Thus, a large proportion of subjects read very little or not at all, while a very small number of subjects read a lot. The amount of time spent reading, and particularly time spent reading books, was positively related to reading achievement.

Walberg and Tsai (1984) conducted a similar study with 2890 American thirteen-year-olds. They found that the median child in their sample read 7.2 minutes per day, and that the median child reported reading on about one day out of five. Like Greaney's results, 44 percent of the subjects in Walberg and Tsai's study reported spending no time reading for enjoyment, while only 5 percent reported spending three hours or more. These researchers also found that frequency and amount of reading were related to reading achievement.

The relationship between reading achievement and out-of-school reading time was also documented by Barr and Dreeben (1983) and Rosenshine and Stevens (1984). Anderson et al. (1988) studied the out-of-school reading time of 155 American fifth-graders. Average time spent reading books, magazines, and newspapers was 14 minutes per day. Variance between groups of children was extreme; those who spent the most time reading read nearly five times as much as those near the mean, and more than 200 times as much as those who spent the least time reading. Again, time spent reading and reading achievement were positively related.

From the results of their own and others' research, Anderson et al. (1988) concluded "that the typical child in the middle grades reads less than 25 minutes a day out of school. The amount appears to be considerably less than this in the United States, maybe as little as 8-12 minutes per day when all types of reading material are included, and maybe as little as 4-5 minutes a day when only books are counted. The amount of reading is almost certainly much lower than many have supposed" (p. 299). On the topic of book reading from the same research, Wilson et al. (1986) wrote, "The likely significance of our data on book reading, then, is that 50 percent of American fifth graders read from books for 4.6 minutes per day, or less. About 10 percent of the children we surveyed never read from a book the entire interval of our survey (8 weeks and 26 weeks)" (p. 77).

These findings and conclusions should shock us. They reveal, in these authors' words, "a bleak picture" (Wilson et al. 1986, p. 76). They offer convincing evidence that outside of school, a very large number of children read nothing at all; many children do very little reading, and only a few do very much at all. We already know that in spite of our instruction, children generally do not do very much reading of connected text in school; of the hours they spend in school, only a few minutes a day are usually spent actually reading text. Much of the reading time is spent instead listening to the teacher and others, waiting, filling in blanks, or reading single sentences on ditto sheets and other exercises, and waiting for others to finish reading. According to Allington and McGill-Franzen (1987) and Gaskins (1988), in a major study of poor readers' time on task in reading, poor readers spent "an alarming amount of time in unproductive ways" (Gaskins, 1988, p. 751). These researchers noted that it was "not uncommon" for teachers to allow five or ten minutes of reading group time to elapse before instruction began, to allow students to gather for reading group slowly, to prolong delays with disciplinary and managerial tasks, and to assign many pages of workbook or skills sheets during independent work time, reducing the amount of time poor readers could spend reading connected text. They also noted many instances of groups beginning reading with no introduction or anticipation activity, engaging in tedious oral round-robin reading with all but one student waiting their turns, early finishers waiting idly for others to finish, and over-lengthy "discussions" of story parts dominated by picky questions, so that students spent more time answering questions than reading. Of the reading that is done, by far the bulk of it is reading from basal readers and textbooks, not trade books. The conclusion seems inescapable: Most children, especially poor readers, do not read enough, either in school or out of it, to ever become proficient readers, in spite of instruction.

The situation is critical and dangerous. But the solution is within our means to employ. We *must* get children to read more, particularly real books (not school books). The two obvious fronts on which to attack the problem are at home and at school. They must be dealt with together.

Schools have never given much real effort to encouraging reading at home. Sure, we have sent library books home with children and encouraged parents to read to children and listen to them read, but most parents today still do not know how critically important this is and how crucial the home is to reading development. Most parents believe that enough attention is given to reading at school, and that reading in school is pretty much enough. We must convince parents that this is just not so. First, teachers, principals, and librarians must tell all parents directly, forcefully, and often that if children do not read books at home, every day or nearly every day, for longer than a few minutes, they will not grow as readers. Parents must be convinced that reading time at home is just as important as homework time, and more important than many at-home activities. All students in our schools should take home a trade book every day to be read as part of their homework or school preparation. Time should be allotted every day for this reading. Parents may occasionally listen to their children read, but the majority of the reading, at least beyond the beginning stages, should be done silently. Parents should help their children keep track of the books read and discuss them, at least in general ways, with their children.

Some teachers despair of ever having much effect on what goes on at home, but many of them have given up without a fight. Many parents do not emphasize reading at home, not because they don't care about it, but because they do not realize its vital importance. We must at least try, harder than we ever have, and assume success rather than failure.

Just as important and much more readily possible is to dramatically increase the amount of time children spend reading books in school. Probably the most obvious way, and one which many teachers are already doing, is to replace some of the time children spend reading basal stories, textbooks, and worksheets with time spent reading and discussing real books. Teachers usually worry that if they do so children will miss out on skills they need, but those teachers who have done so almost always find that their fears were not justified. Children seem to learn as much or more by reading as by being taught reading. Empirical data to back this up come from Collins (1980), who reported that in studies of matched classrooms in second through sixth grades, those students who did sustained silent reading in books moved faster through their basal programs than those who did not and showed no decline in spelling or English skills, even though as much as half an hour a day was given over to silent free reading. In addition, Manning and Manning (1984) reported that classes that did book reading and engaged in peer discussions and teacher-student conferences about the books had significantly better attitudes toward reading and produced significant gains in reading achievement over those that utilized traditional sustained silent reading practices. These results add weight to the contention that students must do more than just "drop everything and read," but must discuss and respond to the books they read as well.

Books can and should be used in all subject areas in every grade. It is particularly important, however, that students read real books as part of their ongoing reading or language arts instruction. When we spend heavily on basal readers and textbooks, we rob children of the opportunities they must have to develop real book reading abilities, as well as to develop lifelong reading habits, tastes, and attitudes.

For remedial readers, the case is even more imperative. These are the children who, in these studies, did not read at all out of school, the ones who could go for months on end without opening a book outside of class. Even in school, their plight is often not much different. In remedial reading and resource classes, the vast majority of the time is spent in skills work and reading from basal texts, often years below the children's grade level. To take time away from the teaching and practicing of skills seems to many teachers to rob these children of what they need. Perhaps more than any others, they need to read real books. How else will they ever want to do so, even if they can? If people learn to read by reading, then they must do so. There seems no alternative to this. We must use all our creativity and all our influence to get every student, especially the remedial reader, to read real books every day. Nothing less will do.

SUMMARY

Corrective teaching is directed toward supporting a student's strengths while teaching and practicing skills and strategies the student needs. From diagnostic data, strengths and needs are identified and priorities established. Instructional time is planned to fulfill priorities and provide instructional balance.

Readers develop *sight vocabulary* when they see the same words repeatedly in meaningful contexts. *Dictated stories* feature rereading until students achieve fluency and can identify individual words in and out of context. *Support reading* helps students get through difficult text and reinforces word recognition. Support reading includes *echo reading* and *choral reading*. *Predictable books* are useful because the same words appear repeatedly and help build readers' confidence.

Fluency contributes to comprehension and is developed when students *reread* material.

Word analysis strategies are needed when students do not recognize a word at sight. Although debate still rages over the role of phonics instruction in learning to read, a growing body of evidence suggests that good readers are able to use decoding strategies automatically and accurately during reading, thus freeing the mind for comprehension. It also suggests that all students learn letter-sound relationships as part of learning to read. Exemplary phonics instruction builds on what students already know about letters, sounds, and words, emphasizes phonemic awareness, is clear and direct, is integrated into a total reading program, focuses on reading words rather than learning rules, includes the use of onsets and rimes, focuses on the internal structure of words and develops automaticity in word recognition. *Phonemic awareness* is the ability to manipulate speech sounds in words; it contributes to the ability to rhyme and use phonics. Phonics instruction may be integrated with literature by using trade books that feature particular phonic patterns. Decoding ability may be assessed by using the *Names Test*. *Using context* is also an important word analysis strategy. *Cloze procedures* and *confirming* help students develop facility with context. *Word sorting* helps students apply phonic regularities by categorizing words sharing a similar word feature.

Recent research in *reading comprehension* has led to the development of teaching strategies focusing on readers' use of *prior knowledge, prediction,* and *story structures.* Activities like *webbing* and *previewing* help students activate and organize prior knowledge and prepare for reading. Activities like *directed reading-thinking activities, K-W-L* and *K-W-L Plus* help students use prediction as a strategy before and during reading. *Story mapping* and *retelling* aid students in organizing and understanding story structures. *Reciprocal teaching, reciprocal questioning* and *reciprocal question-answer relationships* activities help students improve comprehension.

Listening comprehension supports and promotes reading comprehension. The *listening level* provides an estimate of the reader's present potential for reading improvement. Means of developing students' listening comprehension include *reading to students, directed listening-thinking activities,* and *teacher modeling.*

Recent studies show that most students do little, if any, reading outside of school. Yet they also show a significant relationship between *time spent reading* and reading achievement. All students, especially poor readers, must increase their time spent reading; ways of doing so are discussed in this chapter.

References

Adams, Marilyn Jager. *Beginning to Read: Thinking and Learning About Print.* Cambridge: MIT Press, 1990.

Allen, Roach Van. *Language Experiences in Communication.* Boston: Houghton Mifflin, 1976.

Allington, Richard L. "Fluency: The Neglected Reading Goal." *The Reading Teacher* 36, no. 6 (Feb. 1983): 556–561.

Allington, Richard L. "Beginning to Read: A Critique by Literacy Professionals and a Response by Marilyn Jager Adams." *The Reading Teacher* 44, no. 6 (Feb. 1991): 373.

Allington, Richard, and Anne McGill-Franzen. *A Study of the Whole-school Day Experience of Chapter I and Mainstreamed LD Students.* Final Report of Grant #G008630480, Office of Special Education Programs, Washington, D.C.: U.S. Department of Education, 1987.

Anderson, Richard C., Paul T. Wilson, and Linda G. Fielding. "Growth in Reading and How Children Spend Their Time Outside of School." *Reading Research Quarterly* 23, no. 3 (Summer 1988): 285–303.

Anglin, Jeremy M. *Word, Object, and Conceptual Development.* New York: W.W. Norton, 1977.

Applebee, Arthur N. *The Child's Concept of Story: Ages 2 to 17.* Chicago: The University of Chicago Press, 1978.

Applebee, Arthur N. "Children's Narratives: New Directions." *The Reading Teacher* 34, no. 2 (Nov. 1980): 137–142.

Barr, Rebecca, and Robert Dreeben. *How Schools Work.* Chicago: The University of Chicago Press, 1983.

Boyle, Owen, and Suzanne E. Peregoy. "Literacy Scaffolds: Strategies for First and Second Language Readers and Writers." *The Reading Teacher* 44, no. 3 (Nov. 1990): 194–200.

Brown, Ann L., Annemarie Sullivan Palincsar, and Bonnie B. Armbruster. "Instructing Comprehension-Fostering Activities in Interactive Learning Situations," in *Learning and Comprehension of Text,* ed. Heinz Mandl, Nancy L. Stein, and Tom Trabasso. Hillsdale, NJ: Lawrence Erlbaum, 1984.

Carr, Eileen, and Donna M. Ogle. "K-W-L Plus: A Strategy for Comprehension and Summarization." *Journal of Reading* 30, no. 7 (April 1987): 626–631.

Chaney, Jeanne H. "Beginning to Read: A Critique by Literacy Professionals and a Response by Marilyn Jager Adams." *The Reading Teacher* 44, no. 6 (Feb. 1991): 374.

Clay, Marie M. *The Early Detection of Reading Difficulties,* 3d ed. Portsmouth, NH: Heinemann Educational Books, 1985.

Collins, Cathy. "Sustained Silent Reading Periods: Effect on Teachers' Behaviors and Students' Achievements." *Elementary School Journal* 81, no. 2 (Nov. 1980): 108–114.

Cunningham, Pat. "The Names Test: A Quick Assessment of Decoding Ability." *The Reading Teacher* 44, no. 2 (Oct. 1990): 124–129.

Davis, Zephaniah T., and Michael D. McPherson. "Story Map Instruction: A Road Map for Reading Comprehension." *The Reading Teacher* 43, no. 3 (Dec. 1989): 232–240.

Ehri, Linnea C. "Development of the Ability to Read Words" in *Handbook of Reading Research* Vol. 2, ed. Rebecca Barr, Michael L. Kamil, Peter B. Mosenthal and P. David Pearson, 383–417. White Plains, NY: Longman Publishers, 1991.

Gambrell, Linda B., Patricia S. Koskinen, and Barbara A. Kapinus. "A Comparison of Retelling and Questioning as Reading Comprehension Strategies." Paper presented at the National Reading Conference, San Diego, CA, December 1985.

Gaskins, Robert W. "The Missing Ingredients: Time on Task, Direct Instruction, and Writing." *The Reading Teacher* 41, no. 8 (April 1988): 750–755.

Gillet, Jean Wallace. "Sorting: A Word Study Alternative." *The Journal of Language Experience* 2, no. 2 (1980): 17–20.

Gillet, Jean, and M. Jane Kita. "Words, Kids and Categories." *The Reading Teacher* 32, no. 5 (Feb. 1979): 538–542.

Goodman, Yetta M. "Beginning to Read: A Critique by Literacy Professionals and a Response by Marilyn Jager Adams." *The Reading Teacher* 44, no. 6 (Feb. 1991): 378.

Greaney, Vincent. "Factors Related to Amount and Type of Leisure Time Reading." *Reading Research Quarterly* 15, no. 3 (1980): 337–357.

Griffith, Priscilla L., and Janelle P. Klesius. "The Effect of Phonemic Awareness Ability and Reading Instructional Approach on First Grade Children's Acquisition of Spelling and Decoding Skills." Paper presented at the National Reading Conference, Miami, November 1990.

Griffith, Priscilla L., and Mary W. Olson. "Phonemic Awareness Helps Beginning Readers Break the Code." *The Reading Teacher* 45, no. 7 (March 1992): 516–523.

Hall, MaryAnne. *Teaching Reading as a Language Experience,* 3d ed. Columbus, OH: Charles C. Merrill, 1981.

Helfeldt, John P., and William A. Henk. "Reciprocal Question-Answer Relationships: An Instructional Technique for At-Risk Readers." *Journal of Reading* 33, no. 7 (April 1990): 509–514.

Juel, Connie. "Learning to Read and Write: A Longitudinal Study of 54 Children from First Through Fourth Grades." *Journal of Educational Psychology* 80, no. 4 (Dec. 1988): 437–447.

Kapinus, Barbara A. "Beginning to Read: A Critique by Literacy Professionals and a Response by Marilyn Jager Adams." *The Reading Teacher* 44, no. 6 (Feb. 1991): 379.

Koskinen, Patricia S., Linda B. Gambrell, Barbara A. Kapinus, and Betty S. Heathington, "Retelling: A Strategy for Enhancing Students' Reading Comprehension." *The Reading Teacher* 41, no. 9 (May 1988): 892–896.

Manning, Gary L., and Maryann Manning. "What Models of Recreational Reading Make a Difference?" *Reading World* 23, no. 4 (May 1984): 375–380.

McCauley, Joyce K., and Daniel S. McCauley. "Using Choral Reading to Promote Language Learning for ESL Students." *The Reading Teacher* 45, no. 7 (March 1992): 526–533.

Morris, R. Darrell. "Word Sort: A Categorization Strategy for Improving Word Recognition Ability." *Reading Psychology* 3, no. 1 (Sept. 1982): 247–259.

Morrow, Lesley M. "Effects of Story Retelling on Young Children's Comprehension and Sense of Story Structure," in Jerome A. Niles and Larry A. Harris, eds. Changing Perspectives on Research in Reading/Language Processing and Instruction, Thirty-third Yearbook of the National Reading Conference. Rochester, NY: National Reading Conference, 1984, pp. 95–100.

Morrow, Lesley M. "Retelling Stories: A Strategy for Improving Young Children's Comprehension, Concept of Story Structure, and Oral Language Complexity." *Elementary School Journal* 75 (1985): 647–661.

Morrow, Lesley M. "Effects of Story Retelling on Children's Dictation of Original Stories." *Journal of Reading Behavior* 18 (Spring 1986): 135–152.

Nessel, Denise D., and Margaret B. Jones. *The Language-Experience Approach to Reading.* NY: Teachers College Press, 1981.

Ogle, Donna M. "K-W-L: A Teaching Model that Develops Active Reading of Expository Text." *The Reading Teacher* 38, no. 6 (Feb. 1986): 564–570.

Pellegrini, Anthony D., and Lee Galda. "The Effects of Thematic-fantasy Play Training on the Development of Children's Story Comprehension." *American Educational Research Journal* 19 (Fall 1982): 443–454.

Rose, Michael C., Bert P. Cundick, and Kenneth L. Higbee. "Verbal Rehearsal and Visual Imagery: Mnemonic Aids for Learning Disabled Children." *Journal of Learning Disabilities* 16 (1984): 353–354.

Rosenshine, Barak, and Robert Stevens. "Classroom Instruction in Reading," in *Handbook of Reading Research,* ed. P. David Pearson. New York: Longman Publishers, 1984.

Samuels, S. Jay. "The Method of Repeated Reading." *The Reading Teacher* 32, no. 4 (January 1979): 403–408.

Stahl, Steven A. "Saying the "p" Word: Nine Guidelines for Exemplary Phonics Instruction." *The Reading Teacher* 45, no. 8 (April 1992): 618–625.

Stanovich, Keith E. "Word Recognition: Changing Perspectives," in *Handbook of Reading Research,* Vol. 2, ed. Rebecca Barr, Michael L. Kamil, Peter B. Mosenthal, and P. David Pearson. White Plains, NY: Longman Publishers, 1991, pp. 418–452.

Stanovich, Keith E. "Toward an Interactive-Compensatory Model of Individual Differences in the Development of Reading Fluency." *Reading Research Quarterly* 16, no. 1 (Fall 1980): 3–71.

Stauffer, Russell G. *Directing the Reading-Thinking Process.* New York: Harper & Row, 1975.

Stauffer, Russell G. *The Language Experience Approach to the Teaching of Reading,* rev. ed. New York: Harper & Row, 1980.

Stein, Nancy. *How Children Understand Stories.* Urbana, IL: University of Illinois Center for the Study of Reading, Technical Report No. 69, March 1978 (ERIC: ED: 153–205).

Trachtenburg, Phyllis. "Using Children's Literature to Enhance Phonics Instruction." *The Reading Teacher* 43, no. 9 (May 1990): 648–654.

Walberg, Herbert J., and Shiow-ling Tsai. "Reading Achievement and Diminishing Returns to Time." *Journal of Educational Psychology* 76, no. 3 (June 1984): 442–451.

Wilson, Paul T., Richard C. Anderson, and Linda G. Fielding. "Children's Book-Reading Habits: A New Criterion for Literacy." *Book Research Quarterly* 2, no. 3 (Fall 1986): 72–84.

7 Adolescent Students with Reading Problems

T his chapter addresses the needs of adolescent students with reading problems. Adolescent students, whether or not experiencing reading problems, differ from younger students in several ways. Their differences are marked by:

- changes in peer groups;
- separation from family;
- the search for one's individual identity; and
- changes in cognitive processes.

By the time children reach adolescence, their teachers and peers expect them to be able to read and write independently. If adolescents lack the ability to read at grade level, they risk following behind their literate peers academically. This often leads to other problems with social relationships and can ultimately result in severe behavior problems and finally school dropouts.

For these adolescents, the tasks of the reading teacher often go well beyond instruction in comprehension, vocabulary, word attack, writing, and other skills associated with literacy. The first step is often simply rebuilding their trust in the educational system.

This chapter addresses ways of meeting the needs of adolescent students who have reading problems. First, we present the principles and theories which guide our decision making about assessment and instructional procedures. We then present three case studies which illustrate ways to deal with adolescent students who have reading, writing, and motivational problems.

GUIDING PRINCIPLES AND THEORIES

Our approach is based on four principles:

1. establishing trust,
2. providing literate role models,
3. reducing the feelings of learned helplessness or passive failure, and
4. legitimizing personal knowledge and experiences.

Establish Trust

The keystone for success with adolescent students with reading problems is the establishment of trust between the student and teacher. Without trust, students do not view the teacher, or anyone in authority, as a credible source of information. Erickson (1963) proposed that as early as infancy individuals begin to develop trust or mistrust in others. This early trust is based on having general survival needs met.

The family is perhaps the earliest influence—positive or negative—on trust. The trust established during infancy can be enhanced or diminished as people grow and have experiences outside the family. Their initial experiences with schooling also can enhance or diminish trust.

Many adolescent students with reading problems have a basic mistrust of authority whether from family or school experiences. Without this trust the outlook for subsequent positive social and academic development is poor (Erickson, 1963). However, trust can be established between adolescents with reading problems and their teachers. With this trust, teachers have a solid base upon which to address the problems of literacy for adolescents. Trust will foster risk-taking in the adolescents' writing and reading efforts.

Provide Literate Role Models

One reason children fail to develop the ability or motivation to read by the time they reach adolescence is the lack of literate role models in their lives. When we think back over our own academic histories, we often find that there were very few occasions in which we observed teachers reading silently. If adolescents have no literate role models in their homes and have had few opportunities to observe teachers or peers read silently, there is little reason to expect that reading will be a normal part of their lives.

To address the lack of role models for literacy, the classroom environment must be one in which reading and writing are pursued for pleasure as much as for formal school tasks. Children and adolescents model behavior they observe in trusted adults and peers (Bandura, 1986). This modeling extends beyond fashion and social behavior to the areas of reading and literacy in general.

Reduce the Feeling of Learned Helplessness or Passive Failure

Adolescents who meet with repeated failure due to the lack of literacy skills often resist the most well intentioned attempts at assessment or instruction. At the extreme, this results in learned helplessness. Learned helplessness is a sense that no matter what one does, nothing will help. We see this in adolescents with reading problems when they honestly believe that no amount of effort will bring about escape from a cycle of failure. They see all their attempts at success leading to failure. Harter (1986) proposed that children and adolescents who feel as though they have little or no control over their successes or failures in school often attempt to evade tasks which may result in failure. These young people tend to make excuses for their failures based on either an external or an internal source of failure or success. Some students will blame the test or the teacher for failure. This kind of helplessness provides some protection against an additional example of personal inadequacy and reflects the view that forces outside the students control their fates. Other students will sit quietly and whisper, "I knew I was going to fail, I'm just too dumb." This kind of helplessness represents a sense that internal forces are limiting the students' performances. Perhaps the most depressing combination of the reasoning behind success and failure in school is for students to attribute failure to the lack of ability (internal inadequacy) and success to the fact that the test was "so easy anyone could pass it," or "I was just lucky" (external control).

Johnston and Winograd (1985) used the phrase *passive failure* to describe the way students who have feelings of learned helplessness view the reading process. They suggest that readers who exhibit passive failure are not aware of the relationship between effort and success, attribute success in reading tasks to luck or simplicity of task, attribute failure to the lack of ability, and generally fail to persist in difficult tasks. Adolescents who are experiencing passive failure are not moved by simple cheerleader type statements like "you can do it, all you have to do is try." They have heard that statement, they have tried, and they have failed.

One way in which this learned helplessness and passive failure can be overcome is through modeling. Over time, modeling by a trusted and respected individual can be a strong motivation. If adolescents observe a trusted individual (e.g., a peer, a volunteer or a teacher) modeling literate behavior and successfully reading a book or tackling a difficult writing assignment, they are more likely to attempt tasks involving literacy. When these attempts are used as building blocks instead of measuring sticks, the adolescents begin to overcome passive failure and learned helplessness. Some of the building blocks include:

- being able to read a printed version of a short dictated story;
- coming to class;
- opening a book or magazine;
- asking for help reading a personal letter;
- listening to a story read to the class and asking questions; and
- attempting to write.

Some of these may appear insignificant. However, the goal is to recapture the adolescent as a learner and overcome passive failure.

Legitimize Personal Knowledge and Experiences

Classrooms today are much more culturally diverse than those of a decade ago. This trend will increase in the future as more students come to school with greater cultural and social differences. These differences also are seen between students and their teachers. This diversity may lead to the selection of inappropriate materials, inappropriate topics, and the misinterpretation of word meanings.

Adolescents with reading problems reflect this broad diversity of cultural and personal experiences and knowledge. Reading and writing instruction are particularly suited to the use of students' cultural and personal experiences to enhance instruction. A teacher can create opportunities for students to use their personal knowledge and experiences through self-selection of topics for writing, reading, and class discussion thus legitimizing personal knowledge and experiences.

In summary, adolescents with reading problems learn best in an instructional environment in which:

- a trusting relationship exists between the teacher and students;
- literacy is modeled;
- learned helplessness and experience of passive failure are replaced by a willingness to try and opportunities for success; and
- personal knowledge and experiences are valued and used.

These guiding principles lead us to an environment in which a variety of print material is available. It is structured to allow for teachers and other literate participants to model reading and writing. When possible, students select their own writing topics, reading materials, and classroom tasks. Within these tasks, there are ample opportunities for legitimate successes in which efforts are related to outcomes. Finally, the students and teacher develop a trusting relationship through a freedom to express feelings, ideas, and opinions in a nonevaluative atmosphere.

Develop a Learning Environment

Although not without controversy, the whole language philosophy is becoming more widely accepted as a means for empowering children and adolescents as learners (Weaver, 1990; Altwerger, Edelsky, & Flores, 1987). Our selection of the whole language philosophy is based on the guiding principles and theories we have described. One point to be made is that whole language is, for many, a philosophy which guides the creation of a learning environment, selection of instructional and assessment strategies, and materials. Whole language is not a specified set of strategies, exercises, or materials used in teaching.

Within the whole language philosophy, reading and writing are considered social as well as personal events. They are social in the relationship between the reader and the author of a text, the reader/writer and other members of a class, and the reader/writer and those who may be affected by the text. Reading and writing are also social events because when children observe others in their family or classroom reading or writing, they are more likely to read or write.

Classrooms which follow this philosophy provide many opportunities for sustained silent reading, reading aloud, free and guided writing, and class discussion. Davidson and Koppenhaver (1988) suggest that programs which have been successful in fostering literacy among adolescents:

1. spend a high proportion of time on reading and writing;
2. teach skills in context;
3. stress silent reading;
4. teach strategies for reading comprehension;
5. build on background information and experience;
6. integrate speaking and listening with reading and writing;
7. focus on writing;
8. use modeling as a teaching technique;
9. use involvement- or experience-based curriculum approaches that foster conceptual development;
10. facilitate discussions rather than lead them;
11. give students access to a wide variety of materials; and
12. use varied groupings and value collaborative learning. (pp. 184–189)

These characteristics are often observed in whole language classrooms. The methods by which each characteristic is realized and the specific strategies taught should be based on students' needs, interests, and abilities. Teachers typically can seize the teachable moment and create instructional lessons which are based on legitimate tasks such as preparing for drivers' license examinations, writing birthday cards for friends, or completing job applications.

Discussions of topics currently on the minds of adolescents also provide the basis for many literacy lessons in these classrooms. For example, child abuse, drug addiction, and teen pregnancy can be key topics for many readings, class discussions, and written and dictated compositions. In this way the whole language classroom provides not only an opportunity for fostering literacy but also for addressing pressing social issues in the lives of adolescents. It is within such a classroom that a variety of approaches can be implemented to address the complex needs of adolescent students with reading problems.

CLASSIFYING THE ADOLESCENT STUDENT WITH READING PROBLEMS

The earlier a child's problems are identified and addressed in an appropriate manner, the more likely it is that the child will succeed in school. Unfortunately, many reading problems are not diagnosed until high school.

For example, if a child happens to be a younger sibling of a notorious trouble-maker, any acting out by the child may be interpreted as a family trait instead of a symptom of academic difficulties. The child may be socially promoted through the elementary and middle school grades only to become frustrated at not being able to read high school material.

These adolescents with reading problems often fall into one of the following three classifications: *nonreader, disenchanted reader,* or *remedial reader.* A nonreader is one who lacks even the most rudimentary skills and strategies associated with reading. A nonreader has little in the way of sight vocabulary, often lacks even the most basic word attack skills, and cannot read and understand written text. This student may be able to comprehend when a teacher or peer reads aloud and may be truly motivated to learn.

The primary problem associated with a disenchanted reader is lack of motivation or the willingness to attempt the literacy tasks. This student often has had negative experiences associated with the social or behavioral elements of schooling or has experienced severe family or personal problems resulting in extreme emotional distress. In many ways, a disenchanted reader is the most difficult to understand, assess, and affect positively. This reader is often resistant to assessment procedures and foils even the most well intentioned attempts to motivate. A remedial reader may be able to recognize some sight words and may possess some limited word attack skills. In the majority of cases, however, a remedial reader experiences great difficulty in reading and comprehending grade-level texts. This student may be able to recognize enough words to perform at a minimal level on multiple choice tests, but probably will experience great difficulty in tasks which call for higher level thought processes such as comparisons, finding the main ideas, and forming inferences.

As you will find in our case studies, patience and creativity are necessary to successfully address the needs of adolescents with reading problems. The three case studies we will present provide insights into the assessment and instructional procedures which address the needs of adolescent nonreaders, disenchanted readers, and remedial readers.

Peter: A Nonreader

Peter is a 19-year-old nonreader who attends a secondary school which used to focus on vocational education but now functions as an academic alternative dropout prevention center. This section includes impressions about Peter which are based on his ninth-grade reading teacher's observations and discussions with his other teachers. Much of this information was informal but was useful for meeting his academic needs and creating an environment in which he could learn to read and write.

Peter was referred to the reading teacher for help in social studies and science. At that time he was 16 years old and had been enrolled at the school since he was 13.

The teachers reported that Peter was a very sincere and caring individual. He openly expressed love for his family; however, his family did not always value school as an essential activity in Peter's life. Because of his admiration for his family members, Peter strove for their approval and acknowledgment. Hence, Peter often seemed less than enthusiastic about school. He had a handful of friends and developed strong attachments with his girlfriends; however, he never allowed them to uncover his "secret" of illiteracy.

Peter met with continued failure throughout his years in school. He had developed an uncanny ability to "escape" from the risk of failing, and he developed tricks for distracting a teacher's attention from the real academic problems. Such behaviors are common to many adolescents with reading problems.

Peter used several techniques to effectively avoid reading and writing. One very effective one was using his charm and his gift of gab. Peter's favorite topics were himself, his cars, his jobs, his girlfriends, and his family. Some conversations helped to develop the rapport needed to work effectively with him, but some discussion time was used to escape academic pursuits. Invisibility was another method Peter used to escape school. Often he would sit quietly in a corner or the back of the room. When the teacher finally discovered him, he would smile coyly at the teacher as if to say "so you caught me . . . it's too late now!" Another technique he mastered was misbehavior—confronting teachers or disrupting class. Disruptive behavior could be caused by having his "secret" illiteracy exposed, being teased by a classmate, or by having family problems.

The most self-destructive method Peter used to avoid failure was simply not coming to school. The reading teacher noted that he dropped out of school during the second semester each year for the last four years to work with his father. We have presented this sketch of Peter to acquaint you with a fairly typical adolescent non-reader. The next "picture" of Peter is based on informal and formal assessments.

Assessment of Peter's Reading Skills and Levels

The reading teacher spent the first two sessions getting to know Peter and previewing his content-area textbooks. He was required to read high-school level texts, and his teachers reported that Peter experienced great difficulty. Peter blamed his academic problems on his teachers. This external orientation is typical of students who feel powerless and lack the confidence to even attempt academic work (Harter, 1992; Johnston & Winograd, 1985). When the reading teacher first began to tutor Peter using a high school textbook, he refused to read orally or silently, and began moving around the room. This refusal and avoidance was an indication that Peter felt defeated and required nurturing if he was to progress. After much prodding, he attempted to perform the oral reading task, but he was unable to read the passage. The reading teacher then offered to read selections of the text to him and ask him the end of chapter questions orally. This accomplished two goals. First, Peter was exposed to the content area material, and second, the reading teacher was able to assess his listening comprehension. With exchanges like these, Peter began to trust the reading teacher.

Peter and the reading teacher discussed his dilemma, and Peter agreed to take several reading tests so that a plan could be developed to improve his literacy skills. Testing began with a Word Recognition Inventory (see Chapter 4). He was able to pronounce 50 percent of the primer words on the automatic presentation. When given time to decode the unknown words on the primer list, he decoded three additional words raising his score on the primer level word list to 65 percent. The test indicated that Peter had very few sight words, and his ability to use phonetic decoding was extremely limited. Asked if he could read, Peter responded no and looked down at the table. When asked if he was ever placed in any special reading classes, he could not remember.

Next, Peter was asked to read the primer passage of an Informal Reading Inventory (see Chapter 4). His oral reading was laborious. When he did not know a word, he would say the beginning consonant sound, then make a guess at the rest of the word, or he would not attempt to pronounce the unknown word at all. He required more than five minutes to get through the 32-word paragraph. He yawned, fidgeted in his seat, got up, and said he really didn't want to go on. Because of his extreme frustration, the reading teacher read the passage to him. He was able to answer 80 percent of the comprehension questions correctly. Peter refused to attempt to read another primer level passage silently. He would, however, listen to the passages read to him. His listening comprehension level was assessed to be at least at the seventh grade level. This was consistent with the initial assessment using content area texts. Peter's listening comprehension score demonstrated Peter's potential to become literate.

The reading teacher had discovered one of the many children who reached high school without being able to read. In order to obtain more information about Peter's academic past, the reading teacher referred to his cumulative record file. The decision to use the academic history found in the cumulative record as a final source, instead of an initial source, of information was a conscious decision. By first learning about Peter as a person, then assessing his reading in an informal manner, the reading teacher's initial judgments were less likely to be influenced by some expectation of failure or problem behaviors.

Peter's School Records and Academic History

The first entry in his cumulative record file was Peter's elementary cumulative record form. (There are various types of information contained within cumulative records and this information differs from state to state.) Within this record the teacher found early school pictures of him, a yearly evaluation of personal characteristics, a list of schools attended, psychological assessments, and teachers' anecdotal records and comments. The teachers' comments about Peter included such information as, "Peter has spent two years in kindergarten. He is a nice child but sometimes he can act ugly." The reading teacher discovered that Peter repeated first grade and had attended six schools by the time he entered second grade. In second grade, Peter was referred for psychological testing. At the time of testing, he had been in school four years, and was 8 years, 11 months old.

Peter was referred for testing because he was working below grade level and was unable to cope with the learning process in the classroom. He was said to be disruptive in class, made inappropriate remarks, and talked to himself. He reportedly walked around the room at his own discretion and did not function as a group member. One early entry indicated that he could not retain information and could not sequence. A family interview revealed that Peter's mother and father were divorced when he was 5 years old, and his mother was remarried and divorced again at the time of the interview. Peter's father lived out of town. His mother attributed Peter's behavior problems to the divorce and the adjustments after biannual paternal visits.

Peter took two intelligence tests. The scores on these tests indicated that he was functioning in the borderline range (see Chapter 9). These scores predict the likelihood of Peter having difficulty becoming literate, but did not qualify him for special-education services. He was re-evaluated at age 10 years, 5 months while in third grade. These results were generally similar to the ones reported earlier. Again, he did not qualify for any special services, but recommendations were made to explore the possibility of vocational training. Peter repeated third grade, and his behavior was reported as very disruptive.

The third-grade teacher worked individually with Peter as much as possible, and a fifth-grade student came into the classroom to tutor him. He also attended a Chapter One reading program for remedial reading instruction. During this year Peter was also tested by a reading specialist who concluded that Peter had an "extremely severe reading disability." Using a standardized reading test, Peter's instructional reading level was found to be early first grade. The reading specialist stated that he had good listening comprehension and knew almost all his beginning consonant sounds. Peter did not however, apply this knowledge to decoding unknown words. The reading specialist recommended several strategies to Peter's teacher, which included reading aloud to him, echo and choral reading, and language experience activities. In addition, a behavior technician was placed in the classroom to conduct a behavior modification program for Peter. This technician also provided him with individual academic tutoring. With this individualized intervention, Peter's behavior problems were significantly decreased.

Little more information was found in Peter's cumulative folder. He went on to fourth grade and at the end of that year was administratively promoted to the alternative secondary school which could provide him with vocational training and basic academics. He was 13 years old. His report cards show he failed his academic courses but passed his vocational training.

To summarize, this portrait of Peter was based on initial impressions by a reading teacher, informal assessments, and a review of his cumulative school record. These data showed that Peter was a student who became "invisible" in a group, frustrated easily, and knew he did not have adequate reading and writing skills. He moved frequently as a young child and had experienced family problems. He continued to perform poorly on tests of reading, but his listening comprehension scores and IQ scores indicated he had the potential to become literate. Peter's behavior showed a significant improvement when a behavioral technician worked individually with him. Based on the initial contact with the reading teacher, Peter's test scores, and his positive experiences with the behavioral technician, individual tutoring by his ninth-grade reading teacher was continued.

Development of an Instructional Plan

The reading teacher's sessions with Peter included tutoring in content areas, reading to him, writing, language experience activities, word study activities, repeated readings, and sustained silent reading. The reading teacher met with him one period each day for individual tutoring. She read the required high school text to him, and he dictated the answers to the end-of-chapter questions. They discussed the text using a modified DLTA. A description of the DLTA appears in Chapter 3. It is important to point out that often particular strategies must be modified for individual students' needs. In this case, a nonfiction text was used. The reading teacher would read the section heading to Peter and ask "What do you think the author might write about next?" or "What would the author want you to know?" This modification can be used with virtually any content area text.

Content-Area Directed Listening-Thinking Activity (DLTA)

The procedure for a DLTA with content area material is basically the same as that for a Directed Reading Thinking Activity (DRTA) explained in Chapter 6, except the material is read aloud to the student. Stauffer (1975) developed the DRTA technique to assess young children's sense of story and prior knowledge, and to provide a means to monitor and increase listening comprehension. Using the DLTA procedure with content-area text provides remedial or nonreaders access to the information in a text too difficult for them to read. The DLTA provides a model for good reading and study-skill practices, and provides much needed comprehension support for the older students. It can be done individually or with a small group.

The first step in the procedure is to preview the section or chapter to be read. Together the teacher and the student look at the title, headings, subheadings, illustrations, and end-of-section questions. They discuss possible topics to be covered in the text and make predictions about the content. During this time the teacher may probe to activate any information the student already knows about the topic. After predictions are made, the teacher reads the text to the student. The teacher selects stopping points within the text and directs the student to confirm, discuss, question, and make further predictions about the text.

The amount of text covered between stops for predicting is determined by several variables. They include listener attention, the amount of the student's prior knowledge about the topic, and the difficulty of the text being read. In addition to the amount of text included between stops, the teacher should set the length of the entire session so the student does not become bored with the task and so the amount of information is not overwhelming. When the teacher previews the text, points of closure should be noted so that sessions can end at a logical point. Time should be allocated for a discussion and review of each session. This review might address the end-of-chapter questions or specific assignments which may be required. The content area DLTA is a strategy which can be used by teachers, teachers' aides, or classroom volunteers. A summary of this procedure is presented in Figure 7.1.

In Peter's case, the DLTA was successful. His content area teachers required that the end-of-chapter questions be answered and gave examinations based on those questions. Peter successfully passed oral examinations on those chapters which were included in the DLTA.

One of Peter's goals was to learn to read and write well enough to function in society (i.e., read road signs and newspapers, apply for jobs, read directions, and write lists or notes). To do this the reading teacher adapted the language experience approach to Peter's needs (Allen, 1965; Hall, 1981; Stauffer 1980).

Language Experience Approach with Adolescents

The reading teacher found dictation to be a way for Peter to express himself. By giving Peter an outlet for his knowledge, he became more confident in

Figure 7.1

Directed Listening Thinking Activity

1. Preview the section. Read and examine titles, heading, subheadings, illustrations and end of section questions.
2. Discuss possible topics to be covered, making predictions about content.
3. Probe for prior knowledge about the topic.
4. Read text aloud to designated stopping points.
5. Confirm, discuss, question and make further predictions.
6. Read text aloud to next stopping point.
7. Repeat procedure.

himself as a knowledgeable individual. Peter selected topics that were simple retellings of experiences he had on the job or at home with cars or friends. To motivate him to dictate, the reading teacher assumed the role of secretary and would write whatever Peter wanted her to write. An important characteristic of this dictation is the verbatim transcription of the student's words. Once transcribed, the reading teacher echo-read (see Chapter 6) the dictation with Peter. He then read the dictation to the reading teacher. With increased fluency and confidence, Peter began editing his own work as he read. During daily silent reading time, Peter would self-select his dictations to reread. Periodically, these dictations were reread orally by Peter or were used as text for additional echo reading. Peter was also asked to point to the words as he pronounced them (voice pointing) to help him pay attention to the words.

One of the most important dictations consisted of a day-by-day description of his brick masonry class (Figure 7.2). Peter was motivated by the class and wanted to complete it so he could get a job. This required a passing score on written tests. By reading and rereading his dictations about the class content, he was able to learn not only important vocabulary words but also orally rehearse procedures necessary in brick masonry. Peter passed his written examinations and finally began to recognize the connection between spoken words and written words. In addition, the study skill of rehearsal was made meaningful to him.

As Peter became more confident, he would dictate longer passages. His dictations were directly transcribed by the reading teacher using a computer program which recorded, printed, and analyzed texts for new vocabulary and word frequency. The reading teacher found dictation to be a way for Peter to express himself and to build confidence in himself as a knowledgeable individual. Figure 7.3 provides guidelines for using LEA with adolescent emergent readers.

Repeated Readings

For Peter, repeated readings helped to develop sight vocabulary, reading fluency, and confidence. In his case the repeated readings of his own dictations helped him acquire much needed job-specific sight words. As described in Chapter 6, repeated readings of text from content area or repeated readings from short stories are appropriate for any reader struggling with sight words. Elementary textbooks may be a good source of reading material for students like Peter. With these materials, photocopies or retypings can be used to avoid revealing their low levels. A teacher may choose to write original text adapting material from content or vocational texts.

Another method employed to increase sight words and oral reading fluency is taped readings. Students listen to tapes and follow the text with their fingers and eyes. The tapes are available commercially or can be recorded by the teacher or a volunteer.

With students like Peter, the temptation is to abandon these support activities too soon. Even though progress is observed, making up years of fail-

Figure 7.2

Peter's Dictated Text

Thursday, Sept. 13, 1990

My class is brick mason at George Stone from 11:00 to 2:00 and we are working on a house. My work is laying bricks, making mud, and a little bit of measuring, a little bit of math. Mud is sand, mortar mix, and water. It is used with a trowel. It makes the bricks hold up. We started to work as soon as I got there. I like getting an education doing something I can fall back on.

Friday, Sept. 14, 1990

I learned what the face of a brick was. It is the front side of the brick. The front will be coated with a white powder so you know what side is the back side. The face side is out. Laying a brick straight up and down means laying them like soldiers when it is the last topping of the house.

Figure 7.3

Language Experience Approach (LEA) with Adolescents

1. Work with groups of three or fewer.
2. Suggest, or allow students to suggest, a topic.
3. Lead discussion of the topic, encouraging as rich language use as possible.
4. Take dictation, making minor word changes or additions as necessary to keep the story fluent. Cursive writing may be used instead of printing. Use a regular size sheet of paper if you wish.
5. Lead the choral and/or echo rereadings of dictations. Students may prefer to do more individual than group reading.
6. Provide an individual copy for each student, typed if possible, for practice rereading and word identification. Encourage rereading to a partner or someone else.
7. Provide each student with several typed copies of the dictation. Have him or her cut the story apart and paste it back together. Depending on the ability of the student use one copy as a guide. An alternative to this is to ask the student to cut it apart and create a "new" story.
8. Make a word bank or word list of words they know. Words which the students identify out of story context can go in their word bank/list. Older students often prefer to keep their words in a notebook. Students can read their list of words, do word sorts with their words, and get a running total of the number of words they know.
9. Have students circle all words they know or identify words of like classifications (e.g., underline all number words).
10. Students may choose dictations for sustained silent reading text.

ure in school requires time. These support activities must be conducted frequently until nonreaders can begin independent reading.

Word Sorts

Once Peter acquired some sight words, additional activities using word sorting were conducted, providing him with concrete ways for learning about words. In addition to sorting words based on phonetic features, word sorting can provide practice in recognizing similar suffixes, grammatical categories (e.g., nouns or verbs), and meaning categories (e.g., animals or colors).

The open sort was particularly motivating for Peter. This type of sort, and word sorting in general, are discussed in Chapter 6. During open sorts Peter was quick to discover ways to classify words. He often used words from his dictations about brick masonry as a source of words for sorting. Peter could sort his vocational vocabulary into such categories as types of brick or words associated with the process of laying brick. As Peter became more confident in his abilities with word sorting, he would often identify categories for sorting and attempt to fool the teacher by asking her to guess the category. This allowed Peter to assert some control over the task and to maintain his interest in the activity.

Journal Writing

Journal writing was used with Peter to provide another experience with print and to provide the teacher with an assessment tool. From Peter's writing samples, the teacher could note progress in the use of sight words, gain insights into his knowledge about letter/sound relationships, and assess his awareness of print and text structure. Peter knew that words had boundaries and that each word had a meaning. His writings were similar to other beginning readers/writers in that he only wrote words he thought he could spell correctly and usually wrote from his own point of view. One writing reflected his feeling for his father.

> I love to work with my dad and I love my dad.

In order to encourage risk-taking with print, invented spellings were encouraged when Peter was unsure of a word.

Any teacher can encourage learners by unconditionally accepting their first drafts and by making specific positive comments about the writing. For instance, Peter wrote:

> I have a girl friend naum lori she a good girl but she is moving to texs this sumr but that is life but it gos on.

The teacher comment could be, "Peter, I'm sorry your girlfriend is moving to Texas. I'm sure you will miss her. I like the way you expressed your feelings." In this way, the teacher reinforces the content of Peter's writing without critiquing his spelling.

Another method used to encourage Peter to write was simply to discuss experiences in his life. The reading teacher would retell Peter's story, emphasizing the story's importance, content, and relevance. Then, Peter was told in a calm and pleasant voice to write down what he had said. If necessary, the reading teacher reminded him of information to be included in the writing.

These discussions also gave the reading teacher an inventory of topics which interested Peter. The topics were noted on a topics list in his journal.

One of the motivational strategies used to encourage Peter to write was the parallel writing which took place between him and the reading teacher. Each day when Peter wrote, the reading teacher also wrote in a journal. During the writing time, Peter would observe the reading teacher having similar difficulties choosing a topic, deciding what to write, and figuring out how to spell difficult words. This served as a model for what all writers do and helped Peter feel that he wasn't the only one who experienced difficulty writing. At the end of each writing time, the reading teacher and Peter would share their respective writings and request clarifications when needed. They responded to some part of the writing with a positive comment. This sharing led to the development of trust and respect between Peter and the reading teacher. Peter's written interaction with the reading teacher built his confidence in himself as a writer. With this confidence came a willingness to edit for content and produce longer and more descriptive passages.

Summary of Peter

Peter represented an adolescent who had progressed through eleven years of school without learning to read. His progress in a whole language environment was slow but steady. The use of individual tutoring was indicated given Peter's academic history and his unwillingness to share his secret of illiteracy with others. By reading aloud to Peter and asking questions about the content, the reading teacher was able to assess Peter's listening comprehension and present content-area information to him. The fact that the content area interested Peter provided motivation to learn. His dictations were used to establish more sight vocabulary and provide a successful reading experience once Peter could read them to the teacher. By writing and reading with Peter, the reading teacher provided a role model for literacy. By addressing the problems of lack of trust, absence of role models, learned helplessness, and the need for validation of one's personal experiences, the reading teacher was able to move Peter along the path toward literacy.

Jayne: A Disenchanted Learner

Jayne was referred to a high-school reading class during the first month of the school year. She was a 15-year-old ninth-grader who was not progressing in her classes. When given a standardized reading test, Jayne scored in the average range. Taken as a single indicator, this score would not place her in a reading class, but given her lack of achievement in other classes, she was enrolled. Attempts to communicate with Jayne were largely unsuccessful. She seemed to rebel every time conversations were initiated.

Jayne's entire demeanor appeared "closed" to adult intervention. She wore black jeans, T-shirts, denim jackets, and a black baseball hat every day.

Jayne was overweight and seldom smiled. Unlike Peter, Jayne's history was largely unknown. She was an example of the many students who reading teachers see because they have become disenchanted with school, and refuse to read and write. As in Peter's case, Jayne's refusal to read or write in her classes could be interpreted in several ways. Jayne's reading test scores indicated she was capable of reading her content-area texts, but for some reason, she chose not to read them. Cases like Jayne are often more difficult to address than a student who wants to read but hasn't learned—she could read but would not! Jayne's case study differs from Peter's in another way. Peter's difficulties were addressed in an individualized tutorial arrangement. Jayne's needs were addressed in a large-group, whole class environment.

The reading class Jayne entered was part of the regular curriculum at an alternative secondary school and was based on whole language philosophy. The class met each day for 50 minutes. Twenty to 25 students were enrolled in the class. Most were ninth- or tenth-grade students who scored at or below the twenty-fifth percentile on a standardized reading test. Others in the class were middle-school-aged expectant or teen mothers or students who had been recommended by teachers because of poor academic performance. Because of an open entry and exit policy at the school, new students enrolled each day and others withdrew.

Upon entry into the reading class, each student received a Unit Management Sheet (Figure 7.4) which outlined the requirements of the course. The students were required to complete all the activity sheets listed. (Sample activity sheets are shown in Figures 7.5 and 7.6.) Additional requirements included participation in whole class discussion, strategy instruction, and cooperative learning activities. Each student was also required to read a certain number of books, to write each day, and to publish at least one composition. Records of completion of these activities were recorded on the Teacher Record of Student Progress Sheet (Figure 7.7). Requirements were modified to meet individual needs.

The Unit Management Sheet was part of each student's work folder and provided a personal guide through the completion of the course. This system allowed the students to be accountable for the management of their own learning. Students made choices among class activities and were free to work at their own pace. These activities addressed literacy skills necessary to function in society. Skills such as using classified ads, reference materials, and maps were included.

Sustained Silent Reading

Jayne's reading class began each day with 10 to 20 minutes of sustained silent reading. Although the class had a variety of reading materials available, students also were allowed to bring books or materials from their homes. The classroom materials included copies of the daily newspaper, paperback books, high interest/low vocabulary adult readers, magazines, children's books, and picture books.

Figure 7.4

Student Unit Management Sheet Reading

Student Name _____ Grade _____

Birthdate _____ Enrollment Date _____ Ending Date _____

	Newspaper Study Unit	
Activity Sheet	Grade	Date
1. 5 W's and H	_____	_____
2. Main Idea	_____	_____
3. Classified Fact/Opinion	_____	_____
4. Word Groups	_____	_____
5. Following Directions	_____	_____
6. Classified Search	_____	_____
7. Other _____	_____	_____
Newspaper final grade	_____	_____

	MAP READING UNIT	
Activity Sheet	Grade	Date
1. Where do you live?	_____	_____
2. Where in the World is Carmen Sandiego? or Where in the USA is Carmen Sandiego? (you must solve three mysteries)	_____	_____
3. Plan a trip: (Panhandle Trip or Miami Trip)	_____	_____
4. Using compass directions	_____	_____
5. Compass Points	_____	_____
6. Reading chart, graphs, diagrams & schedules	_____	_____
7. Other to be determined	_____	_____
Map Unit Final Grade	_____	_____

	Reference Unit	
Activity Sheet	Grade	Date
1. Time Line—"Famous Person"	_____	_____
2. Time Line—My Life–Past, Present & Future	_____	_____
3. The Yellow Pages	_____	_____
4. Using the dictionary	_____	_____
5. Field trip to UWF Library or Field trip to Pensacola Public Library Write a description of the field trip in black journal (prewriting concept map must be used)	_____	_____
6. Other activity	_____	_____
Reference Final Grade	_____	_____

Source: Samuel R. Mathews, Josephine P. Young, and Nancy D. Giles. *Reading and Writing: Providing Tools for Brighter Futures.* Pensacola, FL: The Educational Research and Development Center, University of West Florida, 1992.

Figure 7.5

Activity Sheet: Search the Classified Pages

Name _____   Date _____

SEARCH THE CLASSIFIED PAGES

1. How many pages are in the classified section?_____

2. There are many different categories in the classified section. Categories help you
   locate particular items you may wish to buy. For example if you wanted to buy a
   German Shepherd, you would look under the category "Pets." List five categories
   from the classified section in the newspaper.

   _____

   _____

   _____

3. Here are some items you wish to sell. In which category should each item be
   advertised?

   ITEM   CATEGORY

   a 1967 Mustang   _____

   refrigerator   _____

   used children's clothes _____

   computer   _____

   lawn mower   _____

4. Suppose you were given $500.00 to move out to your own apartment. You have
   an old chair and some dishes your Mother was kind enough to loan you until you
   were able to buy them yourself. Your task today is to locate an apartment in the
   classified ads and furnish it. The $500.00 is for the furniture. Your family will pay
   the rent, but they will not pay over $200.00 a month. You may not rent a furnished
   apartment. List what you would need. Look for the items in the classifieds or ad-
   vertisements and write down the price you would pay for the item and the phone
   number of the place of purchase. You may, however, move out with two friends
   each of whom have the same amount of money.

   ** use the back of this paper **

Source: Samuel R. Mathews, Josephine P. Young, and Nancy D. Giles. *Reading and Writing:
Providing Tools for Brighter Futures.* Pensacola, FL: The Educational Research and Development
Center, University of West Florida, 1992.

Figure 7.6

Activity Sheet: Where Do You Live?

Where do you live?

1. Write directions to get to your school from your house. Include the name of the streets you must travel, the direction (north, south, east, or west) you must go on each street and the approximate number of miles on each street. Refer to the city map for this information.

2. Draw a map to your house using city maps for reference and graph paper.

Source: Samuel R. Mathews, Josephine P. Young, and Nancy D. Giles. *Reading and Writing: Providing Tools for Brighter Futures.* Pensacola, FL: The Educational Research and Development Center, University of West Florida, 1992.

Figure 7.7

Teacher Record of Student Progress
Reading I & II and Middle School Reading

Student Name _____ Course _____

Newspaper Study Unit	Grade _____	Date Completed _____
Map Reading Unit	Grade _____	Date Completed _____
Reference Materials Unit	Grade _____	Date Completed _____
Publish a Writing Selection	Grade _____	Date Completed _____
Reading Response Journal	Grade _____	Date Completed _____
Writing Workshop	Grade _____	Date Completed _____
Class and Group Activities	Grade _____	Date Completed _____
Sustained Silent Reading	Grade _____	Date Completed _____

RECORD OF BOOKS READ

TITLE	TYPE OF BOOK	DATE COMPLETED	BOOK CONFERENCE/PROJECT
1.			
2.			
3.			
4.			
5.			
6.			
7.			
8.			
9.			
10.			
11.			
12.			

Type of Books:
A type book = less than 100 pages; B type book (Standard Book) = 100–150 pp.; C type book = over 150 pages
• For 1/2 Reading credit a minimum of 3 B type books, 6 A type books, or 2 C type books must be read and the student must demonstrate comprehension of the book in the form of a book conference and/or book project.
• For 1 Reading credit a minimum of 5 B type books, 12 A type books, or 3 C type books must be read and the student must demonstrate comprehension of the book in the form of a book conference and/or book project.

Source: Samuel R. Mathews, Josephine P. Young, and Nancy D. Giles. *Reading and Writing: Providing Tools for Brighter Futures.* Pensacola, FL: The Educational Research and Development Center, University of West Florida, 1992.

In Jayne's case, the freedom to be able to read what she chose during sustained silent reading increased her participation in the class. She began by reading the newspaper each day. On some days she looked at picture books and on others she read short stories. Jayne's interest in the 1960s culture and heavy-metal music led her to a biography of the late Jim Morrison. This book was very long and probably would not have been selected by the remedial readers in the class. Jayne demonstrated through written and oral discussions (book conferences) that she could read the book with a high level of understanding. For example, she discovered and explained to the teacher interesting parallels between Morrison's life and Ozzy Osbourne's life. At one point, Jayne wrote a letter to Ozzy Osbourne warning him of the dangers of following Morrison's lead in drug and alcohol abuse.

Book Conferences

Book conferences are excellent means for students and teachers to share their feelings, opinions, and knowledge acquired through their readings (Atwell, 1987). Through guided discussions, a teacher can lead readers to a better understanding of what they have read, relate text to personal experiences, and give readers ideas about books or articles to read in the future. These conferences can be simple retellings or discussions generated by specific questions. Questions such as those in Figure 7.8 provide an informal way to evalu-

Figure 7.8

Book Conference Questions

1. Why did you choose this selection to read?
2. Who are the main characters in the story? Which one is most like you? Explain.
3. Tell me about the book in three or four sentences.
4. What was your favorite part? Explain why you selected this part.
5. Would you recommend this book to anyone else? Why or why not?
6. What do you think the author had to know to write this selection?
7. What do you think the author was trying to tell the reader in this selection? Explain why you believe this.
8. Do you think the main character handles situations the way you would? Give an example from the book.
9. Were there any words you didn't understand? What did you do when you came to these words?
10. Did your book have illustrations? What did you like about them? What part did they play in your understanding of the selection? Explain.
11. What information did you gain from reading the selection?
12. Do you think this story could really happen? Why or why not?

Source: Samuel R. Mathews, Josephine P. Young, and Nancy D. Giles. *Reading and Writing: Providing Tools for Brighter Futures.* Pensacola, FL: The Educational Research and Development Center, University of West Florida, 1992.

ate students' general understanding of the selection. When students like Jayne are encouraged to openly express and discuss their feelings and opinions, mutual trust and respect develops.

Reading Response Journals (RRJ)

Followed sustained silent reading, Jayne's class participated in some form of writing. Several days each week, the class, including the teacher and any classroom volunteers, wrote in an RRJ about the materials that they read and their reactions to them. This writing allowed the students to report on what they read and provided the teacher with a record of the students' participation and understanding of their chosen texts. Students in Jayne's class were told to write brief summaries of what they had read and their personal feelings and reactions to the text. (Other prompts are listed in Figure 7.9.)

Figure 7.9

Other Prompts for Reading Response Journals

CONDENSED FROM NANCIE ATWELL'S (1990) *COMING TO KNOW: WRITING TO LEARN IN THE INTERMEDIATE GRADES*.

* What did the author have to know about to write this story?
* Finish this sentence: I love the way the author . . .
* Tell about your favorite character in the book you're reading. What kind of person is your character, and why is he or she your favorite?
* How did you get to know the main character in your story? (Through what he or she said or did? Through description? How?)
* Tell what the setting was like in the book.
* Have you ever been to a place like the one described in the book?
* Is the setting of your story more or less important than the characters? Why do you think this is so?
* Tell the main things that happened in the story.
* Were you able to guess what was going to happen at the end? How?
* Write another way your story might have ended.
* Do you think the title of what you read is appropriate? Explain. Give details to support your answer.
* What kind of person do you think would like the book you're reading?
* Would you recommend your book to another? Why or why not?
* Write a letter to someone who says he or she doesn't like to read, convincing him/her to read your book.
* How does this book or story make you feel?
* How would you advertise this book?

After writing their entries, class members exchanged journals and responded to each other in writing. This exchange fostered the notion of writing as a form of communication and began building a trusting relationship among class members. Students were encouraged to respond to others' entries in positive ways. To do this, the teacher modeled examples of positive responses. The students then monitored each others' responses and explained to new students about RRJ etiquette. Students were taught to respond to what a writer had said, not how it was said. The students were held responsible for exchanging journals and getting written feedback. Part of their reading grade was based on the participation in the writing and exchanging of the RRJ.

Jayne participated in the RRJ. She quickly learned to use the RRJ as a form of interpersonal communication about what she read and how she felt. An example of this communication follows.

Teacher: In your RRJ's, write a brief summary about what you read. Then write your feelings, reactions, or thoughts about the way what you read relates to your life. After you finish, exchange with someone at your table and write them back. Sign your name after your response and pass the journal back to its owner. Remember, your journal entries are not graded for spelling, grammar, or structure.

Jayne:

I read a little bit of the jim morrison biography, it was really cool. It was talking about ALL these ramors going round about him being dead and he wasn't.

I really like this book because it tells more about his life than anything eles. And in more detail its a really good thing to read even if you don't like the doors because it tells about his poetry too, and its almost like Fiction sometimes in the book.

Response by adult volunteer (Nancy):

I used to listen to the Doors. I liked their music when I was in high school. He was a good looking guy. I remember that some of the other members of his group thought he was crazy What do you think?

Nancy

No he had a rough childhood and he was drunk or drugged all the time.

I didn't know he had a rough childhood. Do you think that is the reason for him doing drugs? Nancy

On another day Jayne wrote and a student responded:

I read about Jim Morrison in this old circus weakly 1978. It was real interesting?

Sounds real intresting to bad I wasn't the one reading it.

Angie

In addition to providing Jayne with an opportunity to communicate with others about what she had read, the RRJ also provided her a place to express negative feelings about reading and writing.

I did not read to day.

Response by adult volunteer:

It seems today was one of those days. No one felt like reading very much. I don't want to nag either, but you need to just read something and quickly jot down the main idea of it. Bring one of yous books. I know you're busy at home, but you have some spare time in here to read. Lisa

To summarize, RRJ's serve many purposes. They provide the teacher with diagnostic information about the students' reading comprehension—the depth of their understanding and interpretation of the reading, their written communication abilities, and glimpses into their personal experiences, background, and beliefs. These written and dated entries also helped the teacher determine a grade for Sustained Silent Reading by providing written documentation of student participation.

For the students, writing in RRJ's helped them discover that writing was a valid form of interpersonal communication and that what they wrote was important to others. Reading Response Journals also provided students with a record of what they had read. The exchanges among students fostered class cohesion and built mutual trust and respect for each other as learners.

Journal Writing and Process Writing

In addition to the writing in RRJ's, the students in this secondary reading class wrote original works in composition books with sewn bindings. These books are excellent for writing journals because the bindings discourage students from tearing out unwanted drafts. This process helps the student become aware of the concept of drafting. Writing journals were used for free writing, structured prewriting exercises, and other process writing steps. In this journal, entries remained confidential unless writers wished to share their work.

Free Writing

Free writing allows students the opportunity to express their thoughts, feelings, and ideas in a nonthreatening context. It is purely for self-expressions or a first draft in a process approach to writing. Allowing students to choose topics to write about encourages disenchanted learners to write about topics in which they possess knowledge and have an interest. Free writing also helps students begin to feel comfortable as writers. Some points to remember about free writing:

- Writing is typically not graded.
- Students choose the topics.
- Teacher comments are on content only!
- If students do not wish to share their writings, they should not have to do so.
- Teachers must respect students' wishes for confidentiality.
- Verbal discussion of topics during free writing time is OK.

Free writing is not an activity readily picked up by students who customarily have been given topics to write about. Encouragement and verbal probing of interests, talents, experiences, and knowledge usually helps motivate them to write.

Jayne's journal writing allowed her to vent her frustrations and opinions without being concerned about others' reactions. Our first insight into Jayne's views about school are reflected in her first journal entry:

Monday

Today, for me, was a very bad day, but it was just like any other school day so I'm use to it all. The thing that makes it so bad is having to wake up befor noon. It really makes me feel kinda sick, literally sick.

Jayne was not happy to be at school and she was willing to share those feelings with others.

Jayne used writing to express her opinions and feelings on a regular basis. Although her feelings were generally negative, she did express herself well and usually grounded her feelings with some rationale. For example, one day Jayne stomped into the classroom and asked for her journal. Jayne looked very angry so the teacher gave her the journal immediately.

I am sick of hearing all the people who are looking out for my best interest, and doing things that THEY think are good for me.

I'm also sick of the goverment letting people, who don't know who I am or what I'm about, make decisions for my life.

Other opinions she expressed were about world events. The day after the Persian Gulf War began, the class wrote about their feelings on the war. On this occasion, the teacher asked for students to volunteer to read their entries to the class. Jayne and many others shared their writings. Many other students' writings were equally as strong since many had relatives in the military and utilized this activity to express their personal concerns. The students responded passionately to each others' writing.

This activity represented a turning point in writing for many students who had once been afraid to share their written works with anyone. They felt comfortable enough with their writing and each other to share. A student suggested a special edition newspaper of their works about the war. To publish their writings, the students wrote and revised several drafts of their pieces, conferred together to clarify and extend their writings, edited their own and each other's work, and published their final products. This writing process is described in the next section.

The Writing Process

Although for the purpose of the special-edition newspaper, only one revision was made, the students developed an insight into the process all writers must go through in order to publish. The edited writings were typed using a desktop publishing computer program. The next day students edited for typographical errors and misspellings. By the afternoon, the Special War Edition of the newspaper was distributed to the student body.

The newspaper experience affected Jayne in an interesting way. She chose to interview several students about their feelings and wrote a second article for the paper based on these interviews. This activity stirred something in Jayne. It gave her a cause she could relate to her interest in the 1960s. After this publication, Jayne was anxious to write and to publish again. She joined the newspaper staff and quickly completed her reading class. For Jayne, the experience with the newspaper served to move her closer to the school in general and the acts of reading and writing in particular.

Any writing opportunity, whether a special edition newspaper or a daily journal entry, provides students like Jayne an option for engaging in the process approach to writing (Figure 7.10). The writing process begins with the prewriting activity which includes the selection of a topic either by individual students or by the class at large. (The process is also effective with a teacher-selected topic, although the selection of a topic must be made with the population of students in mind.) As part of the prewriting activity, students brainstorm for ideas to include in their writing. When this step is completed, students write first drafts without concern for mechanics or spellings. During this second step of the process, the primary concern is to put pen to paper or fingers to keyboard and produce prose. The third phase of process writing is sharing. In this phase, students share their works by reading aloud to their peers, a volunteer, or a teacher. The listener points out areas of strength and asks questions which will help clarify or expand the writing. The fourth step is the initial rewriting or second draft. In this draft, additional information is included as needed, and changes are made for clarification. As changes are made, the writer may enlist others' feedback for clarity and completeness. The fifth step is the editing phase in which mechanics and spelling are stressed. Students may use spellchecker programs with word processors, dictionaries, or other sources for help. Once the students complete the editing step, they begin the final step, publishing. In this step, they may choose to share their writing with others in the form of newspaper articles, entries in a class book,

Figure 7.10

Six Steps to Writing: A Process Approach

1. Prewriting: Writers generate or select a topic and brainstorm ideas for the text;
2. Drafting: Writers complete first draft without concern for mechanics or spelling;
3. Sharing: Writers read their draft aloud to another who responds with questions for clarification or expansion;
4. Revision: Writers reread their draft and revise based on questions and areas in need of change;
5. Editing: Writers edit for mechanics and spelling;
6. Publishing: Writers complete the final draft of their work and if desired, distribute their work to others. (Statement about publishing student works and citation)

NOTE: Throughout the process, conferencing between writers and readers/listeners is critical to the quality of the finished products.

(These steps were adapted from the works of Graves, 1985; Calkins, 1986; & Atwell, 1990)

Source: Condensed from Samuel R. Mathews, Josephine P. Young, and Nancy D. Giles. *Reading and Writing: Providing Tools for Brighter Futures.* Pensacola, FL: The Educational Research and Development Center, University of West Florida, 1992.

or letters and cards. The key to the success of the writing process approach is constant interactions between writer and reader/listener about the text. This ongoing conferencing is crucial and will promote cooperative learning. Figure 7.11 presents guidelines for these conferences.

Concept Mapping: A Prewriting and Postreading Strategy

Although Jayne had become motivated to express her feelings in writing and was beginning to participate more actively in class activities, she still needed to acquire strategies for organizing her thoughts and for analyzing others' thoughts. One such strategy which was used as a prewriting activity in the

Figure 7.11

Guidelines for Conferencing During the Writing Process

A. Guidelines for reader/listener comments:
1. Respect the writer's integrity as a person;
2. Be tactful!
3. Give encouragement;
4. Find something positive about the writing and express it to the writer;
5. Emphasize meaning as the most important element of the writing.

B. Sample comments to make to the writer after hearing/reading the writing
1. I understand you to be saying _____.
2. I understand your main point to be _____.
3. What I like about this piece is _____.
4. I would like to know more about _____.

C. Questions to help writers read their works critically:
1. Do you like what you have written? What part do you like best?
2. Does it say what you want it to say?
3. Did you include everything you wanted to say?
4. Does it make sense to you?
5. Is each new idea presented in logical order?

D. Questions and ideas for editing the final draft:
1. What words do you think are not spelled correctly?
2. Underline the words you think are not spelled correctly and look each one up in the dictionary.
3. Read each sentence aloud.
4. Does each sentence express a complete thought?
5. Does each paragraph contain one central idea?
6. Are capital letters and punctuation used correctly?

Source: Samuel R. Mathews, Josephine P. Young, and Nancy D. Giles. *Reading and Writing: Providing Tools for Brighter Futures.* Pensacola, FL: The Educational Research and Development Center, University of West Florida, 1992.

classroom was concept mapping. The steps for constructing a concept map are described in Figure 7.12.

This strategy has been shown to be useful for improving not only the organization of written material but also reading and listening comprehension (Novak, 1984; Heimlich & Pittelman, 1986). Jayne was not willing to use someone else's ideas. The use of a concept map as a strategy was somewhat of a compromise because the strategy was general but the resulting structure was based on her own ideas of how a certain set of facts might be organized. So she used this strategy and participated in class activities when concept maps were constructed.

Again, Jayne used the concept map to express her personal feelings when the topic of "running away from home" was suggested. Her concept map (Figure 7.13) indicates that she was able to organize her ideas in a logical and hierarchical form.

The concept map Jayne created is an example of an organizational scheme which is helpful during the prewriting step in the writing process. This same scheme is useful when attempting to organize ideas acquired from reading text (Novak, 1984). As a prewriting activity, concept maps represent a means of organizing concepts into topics and the topics into supporting facts.

Figure 7.12

Constructing a Concept Map as a Prewriting Activity

1. Identify a topic: Independently, in small groups, or as a class students select a topic with guidance from the teacher.
2. Brainstorm: Students generate ideas related to the topic. A student, volunteer, or teacher may act as class scribe.
3. Categorize: Students identify ideas which go together in some meaningful way and group them under category names (e.g., collie, doberman, and boxer can be categorized as dogs).
4. Graph: Begin with the topic. Draw lines radiating from the topic to each category name and from each category name to appropriate members or ideas. When possible, words representing the relationships among ideas, category names, and topic should be written on the connecting lines.
5. Discuss: Describe how the concept map might be put into sentences, paragraphs, and larger text units.
6. Writing: Students begin writing their first drafts from the concept maps.
NOTE: At each point in the process, additional ideas and revisions in the map can occur.

Source: Samuel R. Mathews, Josephine P. Young, and Nancy D. Giles. *Reading and Writing: Providing Tools for Brighter Futures.* Pensacola, FL: The Educational Research and Development Center, University of West Florida, 1992.

Figure 7.13

Concept Map: Running Away

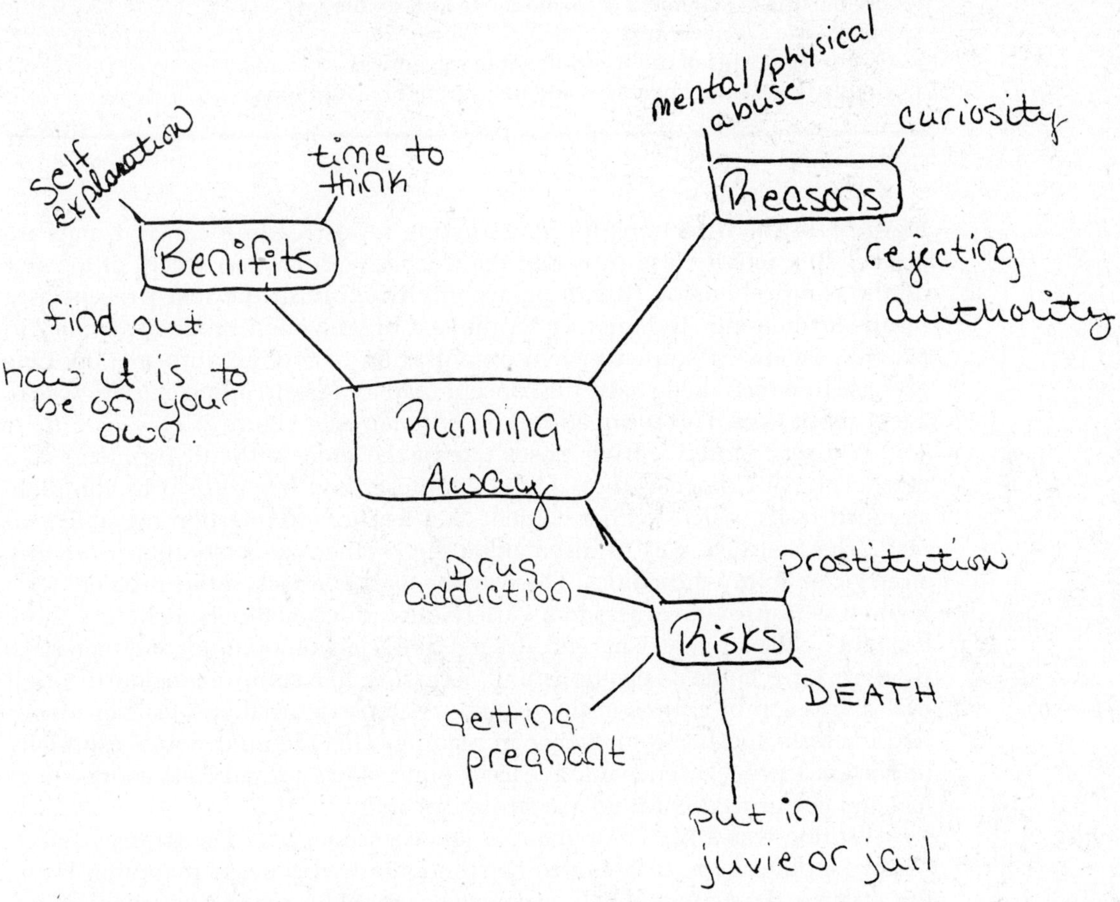

The map provides a visual guide to follow while writing. Each topic can become a paragraph and each supporting detail a sentence. Categorization of the supporting details occurs early in the mapping process and the relationships among the details, topics, and concept can be identified. The use of the mapping procedure also stimulates the students to recall and organize their prior knowledge about some topic. In Jayne's class, the generation of concept maps was conducted as a class, small group, and individual activity.

As a postreading activity, mapping allowed students in Jayne's class to formalize their organization of information acquired from reading text. (In

Figure 7.14

Steps in Constructing a Concept Map as a Postreading Activity

1. Use the title or statement of theme as the topic of the map.
2. Brainstorm about the text.
3. Group the results of brainstorming into categories.
4. Graph, using category names and items from brainstorming.

Figure 7.14 the directions for constructing a postreading concept map are given.) This activity also provided the teacher with an assessment of the students' comprehension. It can be accomplished with the text present as a means for helping students extract the text organization or from memory to provide a view of students' own organization of the text information. One exercise in which Jayne used the concept map as a postreading activity was in a text about trees. Her postreading concept map is in Figure 7.15.

A disenchanted learner poses one of the more difficult problems to a teacher. In our discussion of Jayne, we described her refusal to complete assigned tasks which led her content-area teachers to question her ability to read. The first task was to disentangle the problem of motivation from any strategic or ability difficulties. The way the teacher attacked this problem with Jayne was to provide access to a variety of reading materials including those brought by the student. This encouraged free selection of topics and materials. By observing Jayne's selections and assessing her comprehension through oral discussion or entries in the reading response journal, her teacher identified interests and her competence in reading. This identification is especially important since a disenchanted learner often views formal tests as meaningless and performs accordingly regardless of ability.

Writing was a key component of Jayne's school day. The strategy selected for helping Jayne to organize her thoughts was concept mapping. Using this strategy, Jayne was able to organize her thoughts using our organizational scheme. In the reading class, Jayne was allowed some control over instructional choices. Once her initial work was published, she was willing to revise her drafts to achieve cohesion and improve her mechanics. This empowered her to become an independent learner, and Jayne became an integral and contributing member of her class.

Sherita: A Remedial Reader

This case study follows Sherita, a remedial reader, through two years of reading courses. We will discuss remedial reading and writing strategies, and informal assessment measures used in the reading classroom. Sherita attend-

Figure 7.15

Concept Map: Trees

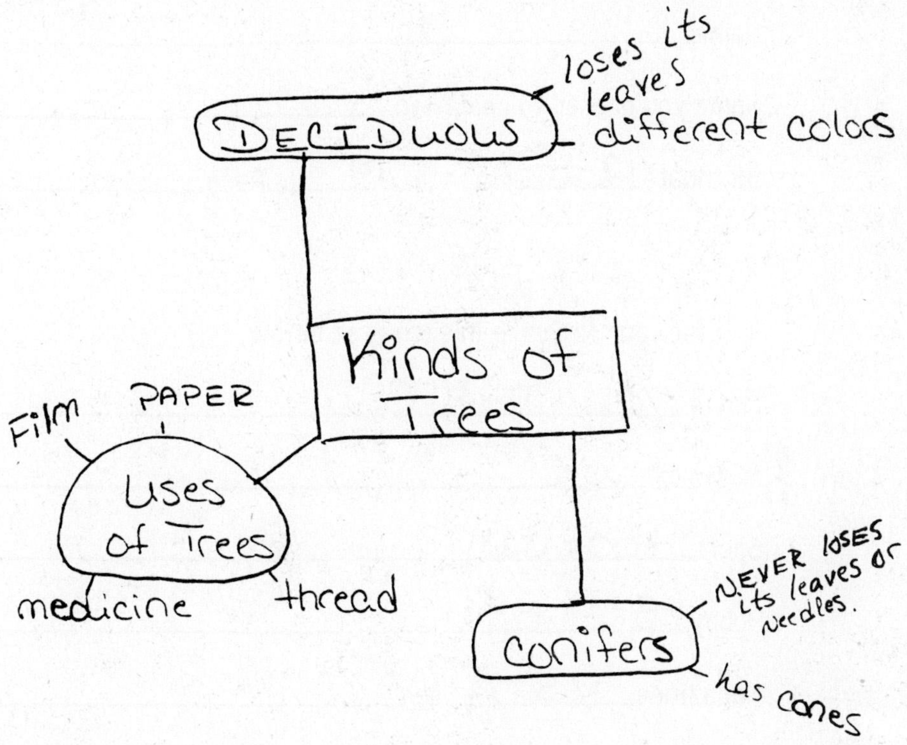

ed the same alternative secondary school as Jayne but was enrolled primarily for the teen parenting program. She was in the same class as Jayne during her first year in the reading program. When Sherita enrolled in reading she was 13 years old and in the eighth grade. Her baby was 4 months old. Unlike other teen moms in the class, Sherita's attendance was relatively good. She was present 150 days out of 180 school days.

Since Sherita was a teen mother, she not only had the normal social pressures of being a teen but also the responsibilities of motherhood. In Sherita's situation, her strong drive to succeed and "make something of herself" became evident immediately when she participated in the class activities. During the first week of school, Sherita completed an interest inventory in which she expressed her desire to become a better reader and writer, and stated her goal to become a lawyer and buy a house. The Personal Preference Inventory (Figure 7.16) gave the teacher a quick first look at Sherita's interest and writing ability.

Figure 7.16

Personal Preference Inventory

Name_____

Name you prefer to be called_____

Birthdate 12-26-76 Age 14   Race B   Sex F

1. List your favorite in each area below.

Movie New Jack City

Music rap

Sport football

Hobby Sewing

Magazines YSb

Books Horror

Subject in school Math

Activity out of school rideing bike

2. List 3 goals you have for yourself in the next 5 years? To finish School to become a lawyer and buy a house

3. What are your goals for this school year? To finish

Figure 7.16 continued

School and make Something of my
self.

4. What happened to get you to Beggs? I had a baby

5. How do you think Beggs can help you? To make some thing out of my self

6. What must you do to attain your goals? Stay in School

7. How do you think a reading class can help you in school and in your life? I will know how to read and write.

Sherita was not formally tested at the beginning of the year since screening was unnecessary for placement into middle school reading. Teacher observations of her reading and writing were used to assess her literacy skills and level of motivation. The teacher observed Sherita during the class time and quickly recorded these observations on paper. Those notes helped the teacher to understand Sherita and realize her strengths and weaknesses as a student.

The reading teacher noted that Sherita had a difficult time settling down during daily sustained silent reading. She observed Sherita talking to her friends before she began to read and sometimes during the reading time. Some days Sherita selected the newspaper to read, but on other days she read short high-interest books written on an elementary reading level. She also selected pamphlets and books about babies, child abuse, and parenting. She was observed on numerous occasions subvocalizing, or reading aloud to herself. Sherita made sweeping motions with her head as she read. These observations were interpreted by the teacher as signs that Sherita had little experience reading silently, had a variety of interests, and had limited attention to the task of reading.

Sherita's comprehension was assessed by examining her written entries in the Reading Response Journal. She would briefly write about the passage but needed encouragement to include details. For instance, after reading the newspaper she wrote in her RRJ:

> I read about mothers and fathers
> Who are getting tired of their Kids
> Because the childern are trying to take
> Over I can see what they are trying
> to Say, I think that the children should
> give their mother and father a little respect.

> Sherita, I agree that children should respect their parents. What did the article say was getting the parents tired of their children? I didn't read the article, please give me some more information.

She was able to give the teacher more details upon request after reread-ing. It should be noted that the entry written by Sherita presented a general summary and stated her opinion. The teacher did not know initially if Sherita failed to include details about the article because she: (a) chose not to include details, (b) didn't know to include details in her entry, (c) didn't read the entire article, or (d) did not comprehend the article well enough to retell the details. Only after the teacher probed and orally discussed this article and other reading passages did she begin to understand Sherita's comprehension skills.

Other entries in her Reading Response Journal indicated that Sherita could express her feelings and opinions in writing. Sherita used her writing journal as another vehicle for expressing her feelings. Her first journal entry follows:

> The worst day I had was when I was in the hosiptil and they would not let me go home And I wanted to go home. They would not let me go home because I had caught a fever and I would not eat and my baby had caught a fever and she was in the intevsive care nursery and they had put a IV in her head and I wanted them to take it out her head.

From this entry in Sherita's journal the teacher discovered important information about Sherita's interests, life experiences, and writing skills. The teacher noticed that the entire paragraph consisted of one very long sentence. Most of her spellings were standard, and her invented spellings were easily deciphered. Since Sherita began writing without hesitation at the onset of writing time, the teacher interpreted that Sherita had no trouble selecting a topic. The teacher also noticed that Sherita wrote quickly but did not reread her writing upon completion.

The observations of Sherita's first weeks of school led the teacher to con-clude that Sherita was a teen mom who was a very social adolescent with a variety of interests. She especially liked to read and write on topics pertaining to babies. While reading, Sherita exhibited behaviors attributed to inexperi-enced readers such as subvocalization and head sweeps. The teacher also noted that Sherita had a limited attention span for silent reading and writing.

She read and wrote quickly but seldom included details in the RRJ entries or reread her other written work. She expressed her feelings easily and did not fear writing. In her writing samples, Sherita did not use standard sentence structure or include details to back up her opinions and conclusions. The following literacy activities served motivational, instructional, and assessment functions for Sherita's remedial instruction within a large group setting. Individual modifications were made when necessary to accommodate her needs.

K-W-L: A Comprehension Strategy

One strategy that was found to help Sherita pay attention to what she read and obtain a better understanding of text was K-W-L (Ogle, 1986). As discussed in Chapter 6, this strategy activates prior knowledge by brainstorming about the topic, relates new information to old, organizes information, and sets a purpose for reading. K-W-L's were especially effective for Sherita because of the social interactions they facilitated. In addition, by using what Sherita already knew about a topic, her own experiences and personal knowledge were validated. She began to recognize that she did know important information. The term *K-W-L* identifies its three principles—recalling what is *known* about the topic, determining *what* the students want to know and what they have subsequently *learned.* The K-W-L is presented in Figure 7.17.

K-W-Ls can be a class, small group, or individual activity. Students will be able to facilitate small group and individual K-W-Ls after the teacher has modeled and explained the K-W-L process to the class a number of times. The teacher should select passages for K-W-Ls so that they represent a variety of topics. K-W-Ls are helpful for understanding content-area text such as social studies and science.

The first step in the K-W-L strategy is to orally brainstorm about the topic. This step may take the longest but is particularly important for the student and the teacher alike. Teachers have an opportunity to discover what the class knows collectively and which students are willing to take risks by adding to the oral discussion. Students learn classroom conduct for oral discussions and have a chance to activate and validate their own knowledge.

The teacher's responsibility is to conduct the orchestra of students and record their input so they can see what is being discussed. The teacher must encourage all students to participate in the discussion, try to focus the discussion on the selected topic, and cue the students for additional information. Therefore, it is particularly important for the teacher to have read the selected passage carefully before presenting it to the class. An example of questions a teacher may use to initiate a discussion follows:

> *Teacher:* Today we will do a K-W-L activity about child abuse. Someone tell the class what a K-W-L is (probe if necessary).

- The title of the pamphlet is _____.
- It was published by _____.
- What do you know about child abuse?

Figure 7.17

A Comprehension Strategy

K-W-L COMPREHENSION STRATEGY PROCEDURE

K-	Know-	What I already know—brainstorming ideas
W-	Want-	What I want to know—predicting
L-	Learn-	What have I learned—summarizing

Step 1	Read the title and look at the pictures.
Step 2	List some information known about the topic. Put this in the *K* column.
Step 3	List questions about the topic. Put these in the *W* column.
Step 4	Read the passage.
Step 5	Confirm or correct what was known.
Step 6	Write down all the information learned and the answers to questions. Put this in the *L* column.
Step 7	Organize the information into categories. (optional)
Step 8	Map the information. (optional)
Step 9	Write a summary using the map. (optional)
Step 10	If questions are unanswered, conduct additional research.

Sources: Eileen Carr and Donna M. Ogle. "K-W-L Plus: A Strategy for Comprehension and Summarization." *Journal of Reading* 30, no. 7 (April 1987): 626–631.

Donna M. Ogle. "K-W-L: A Teaching Model that Develops Active Reading of Expository Text." *The Reading Teacher* 38, no. 6 (Feb. 1986): 564–570.

Samuel R. Mathews, Josephine P. Young, and Nancy D. Giles. *Reading and Writing: Providing Tools for Brighter Futures.* Pensacola, FL: The Educational Research and Development Center, University of West Florida, 1992.

- What do you do if you suspect child abuse?
- What is child abuse?
- What do you think you will find in this pamphlet?

After the discussion period, the teacher may request that the students copy notes from the board. Next, the teacher may ask the students to develop some questions about what they want to know about the topic. The class may come up with questions as a group or may decide to individually write questions down on paper. (A word of caution: Some adolescents in secondary reading classes may not want to know anything about the topic. Teachers must remember to begin the *W* step with careful wording.) The modeling of question statements will help students phrase the questions. For instance, when the teacher asked the class, "What do you think you will find out about child abuse in this pamphlet?" Sherita wrote, "why people beat there children." Figure 7.18 shows Sherita's completed K-W-L on child abuse. The teacher could orally model Sherita's statement into a standard question. "Yes, Sherita, a good question is Why do people beat their children?"

Figure 7.18

KWL
child Abuse

Know
I know that a lot of kids get abused. And that some kids die from child abuse.

what
Why people beat their childern. What makes them beat there kids.

Learn
I learned that children that have been abused don't want to be around other people. And they are scared to tell someone that they are being abused.

At the conclusion of the *W* step, the reading material is distributed and the students are asked to read silently. Teachers may choose to read the passage to the class instead or have the class read it orally. After reading, students are asked to write down under the *L—What we learned* heading, new information, answers to their questions, and/or confirmations of their prior knowledge.

Figure 7.19

Getting to Know You: A K-W-L Interview

KNOW
In the space below write everything you know about the person next to you.

WANT
Write three questions that you will ask this person to help you get to know them better.
1.

2.

3.

LEARNED
Ask the person the questions and then write everything you learned about him/her in the space below.

Source: Samuel R. Mathews, Josephine P. Young, and Nancy D. Giles. *Reading and Writing: Providing Tools for Brighter Futures.* Pensacola, FL: The Educational Research and Development Center, University of West Florida, 1992.

The K-W-L lends itself to a variety of follow-up activities. A natural follow-up is an oral discussion. Such a discussion may stimulate the students by confirming or validating their own knowledge, exchanging new information, and discussing unanswered questions and topics for research. Other times the teacher may wish for the students to develop concept maps using the information acquired or to write a summary of the passage.

Teachers can adapt the K-W-L procedure as an interviewing exercise (Figure 7.19) by asking students to select a partner and write what they think they know, what they want to learn, and following an interview, what they learned about their partner.

Sherita's ability to participate and read for specific purposes improved with time and repeated K-W-Ls. She became a facilitator for whole class and small group K-W-Ls. She would be the first to explain the purpose and procedure to new students. When asked by the teacher about how the K-W-L strategy helped her, Sherita replied, "K-W-Ls show you what you know, and what you have learned. They help you learn stuff you didn't know."

Reading to Adolescent Students

Reading to students like Sherita serves many purposes. One purpose is to expose them to a variety of literature. Another purpose is to build the attitude that reading can provide entertainment. It is also a way to discover different cultures, places, and people, is a stimulus for discussion, and is a means of acquiring knowledge about text structure and vocabulary. Reading aloud to adolescents also provides a vehicle for modeling comprehension, word study strategies, and the art of reading to children.

For the reading aloud activity, the teacher selects a text to read to the class. It might be a poem, a newspaper article, a short story, a chapter or section of a novel or textbook, or a children's book. Since secondary teachers feel the pressure to fulfill course requirements within time constraints, the teacher may select material that could meet a requirement. These readings do not have to be long, and reading aloud does not have to take place each day. The readings may appear to be purely for enjoyment but may serve other purposes at the same time. For example, the teacher may read the children's book *Mufaro's Beautiful Daughters, An African Folk Tale,* by J. Steptoe (1987) to the class. The class will be able to discuss the story structure of folk tales, possibly relating it to other familiar tales. They also may find out about African tradition, different cultures, times and people. This particular book lends itself to a discussion of personality traits. Students could discuss orally or in writing the answer to the question, Which daughter do you most like and why?

An extension activity that was used with *Mufaro's Beautiful Daughters* was a discussion of African word origins and general word-attack skills. For example, the text provides a pronunciation guide for names such as Mufaro (Moo-FAR-oh). As other unfamiliar names and terms were encountered, word attack skills could be continually practiced and reinforced. In addition to word-attack skills, vocabulary activities were incorporated. The name *Mufaro* means "happy man" in the Shona language of Africa. Students could first predict what the name meant and then confirm the actual meaning based on context clues from the text.

Reading aloud to students can fit into most course curricula. When studying biographies an English teacher may choose to read the book, *Flight* (Burleigh, 1991), a children's book about Charles Lindbergh. A history teacher could choose *Flight* to enrich the study of the story of aviation, an art teacher may choose it to discuss book illustrations, and a reading teacher may choose the book to model the K-W-L strategy.

Reading children's books like *Flight* and *Mufaro's Beautiful Daughters* in secondary classrooms exposes teen parents and other adolescents to children's literature that their children may also enjoy. Once adolescents like Sherita began to build confidence in themselves as readers, they can practice their newfound strategies by reading aloud to younger children. This activity was especially helpful for Sherita who had difficulty reading grade-level texts but who needed practice reading. By reading children's books to young children at a neighboring elementary school, she read texts at her independent reading level while at the same time she entertained and instructed younger children. For teen parents like Sherita, this activity provides guided practice and motivation for reading to their own children.

Summary of Sherita

Sherita was unlike Peter in that she did have the basic building blocks of literacy. She simply lacked more sophisticated strategies of comprehension and the guided practice in reading that brings about fluency in silent reading and deeper comprehension. While Jayne required a great deal of effort to gain the motivation to read and write, Sherita stated that her personal goals included becoming a better reader and writer. Capitalizing on her motivation and interests, the teacher was able to provide practice in sustained silent reading by supplying materials on child care, child abuse, and relevant children's literature. Higher level strategies were demonstrated and practiced in whole-class setting through K-W-Ls and concept maps. In order to model fluency in reading, the teacher read aloud to Sherita's class. This also provided an opportunity to model comprehension strategies through think-aloud dialogues and prediction questions.

As Sherita became more confident in her own reading abilities she volunteered to become a reader for a nearby elementary school. Her task was to read children's books aloud to kindergartners. This accomplished three goals. First, her participation made her a legitimate helper for others learning to read. Second, by reading aloud to others, her own reading fluency improved. Third, practice in reading to other young children gave her the confidence to read to her own child. This in itself may contribute to a second generation of readers.

SUMMARY

In this chapter we have addressed many of the needs of adolescent students with reading problems. We presented three different classifications of these students—non-readers, disenchanted readers, and remedial readers. Adolescents with reading problems have many overlapping characteristics which can pose problems for the teacher. In the case studies, we described three adolescents who, for a myriad of reasons, performed poorly on literacy tasks:

- Peter, who lacked many of the very basic elements of literacy;
- Jayne, who had become disenchanted with the system and refused to try; and
- Sherita, who had the competing priorities of teen motherhood and was lacking sufficient literacy skills to perform at grade level.

Our proposed solutions to the problems centered around four guiding principles:

1. establish trust with the students;
2. provide literate role models;
3. reduce the feelings of learned helplessness and passive failure; and
4. legitimize the students' personal knowledge and experiences.

Since adolescents seek to establish their own identities, our approaches had to provide unique and varied opportunities and nonthreatening assessment strategies. One way to achieve this goal was to provide reading materials which reflected a wide variety of interests. These materials included newspapers, magazines, and content-area books.

Another way students exercised choice was in topic selection for writings or dictations. By selecting their own topics and using the writing process, the students acquired a strategy for generating and organizing their thoughts and for writing and revising drafts.

Adolescents were encouraged to write summaries and reactions about what they read using the Reading Response Journal. The teacher's responses were nonevaluative and often were requests for clarification or more details. These responses served several purposes. First, by demonstrating respect for their feelings, a trusting relationship began to develop between the teacher and students. The second purpose served was a demonstration of the importance of supporting one's opinion or generalizations with detailed information. When using the Reading Response Journal, a third purpose was served. The students' written discussions of what they read provided the teacher with a comprehension measure of what they had read.

Through the use of K-W-L's, students realized that they did possess knowledge about a number of topics. This realization increased their confidence and many times helped to overcome learned helplessness. Another strategy which allowed students to use their own ideas was concept mapping. Students were able to brainstorm about a topic and then apply their own ideas to the topic's organization. These strategies served to validate the students' own knowledge and to motivate class participation.

One of the key concerns when attempting to reach adolescent students with reading problems is providing access to literate role models. This access can be accomplished through classroom volunteers, literate peers, and most importantly, the teacher. During sustained silent reading, everyone should read. When writing in the Reading Response Journals, the entire class, including the teacher, should participate. Class activities such as K-W-L and concept mapping provide opportunities for the teacher and peers to model and think aloud strategies for brainstorming and organizing ideas.

When working with adolescents, it is important to remember that they do enjoy having someone read aloud to them. Whether reading aloud to an individual with a DLTA exercise or to a small group or the entire class, reading aloud provides an excellent opportunity for practicing class discussion, prediction, and comprehension strategies through thinking aloud. In addition, reading aloud can be beneficial for teen parents. Whether being read to or reading aloud themselves, they are gaining experiences which can support their efforts to foster literacy in their own children.

Each of the activities provided ongoing, informal assessments of students' prior knowledge and their use of reading and writing strategies. When the teacher discovered a student's strength, that strength was used as a building block for instruction. As areas of weakness were identified, whether skill-based or more strategic, instruction was tailored to meet their needs.

Adolescent students with reading problems come to the classroom with a broad spectrum of concerns. These concerns include the normal teen issues such as dating, peer acceptance, and establishing their independence from their families. In addition, adolescents with reading problems face the social stigma of illiteracy and the reality of falling behind same-aged peers in school. By providing an environment in which trust can be developed, literacy modeled, and choices made within the curriculum, the teacher can help adolescent students return to the status of confident and independent learners.

References

Allen, Roach Van. *Attitudes and the Art of Teaching Reading.* Washington, D.C.: National Education Association, 1965.

Altwerger, Bess, Carole Edelsky, and Barbara M. Flores. "Whole Language: What's New?" *The Reading Teacher* 41, no. 2 (Nov. 1987): 144–154.

Atwell, Nancie. In the Middle: Writing, Reading, and Learning with Adolescents. Portsmouth, NH: Boynton/Cook, 1987.

Atwell, Nancie, ed. *Coming to Know: Writing to Learn in the Intermediate Grades.* Portsmouth, NH: Heinemann Educational Books, 1990.

Bandura, Albert. *Social Foundations of Thought and Action: A Social Cognitive Theory.* Englewood Cliffs, NJ: Prentice Hall, 1986.

Calkins, Lucy McCormick. *The Art of Teaching Writing.* Portsmouth, NH: Heinemann Educational Books, 1986.

Davidson, Judith, and David Koppenhaver. *Adolescent Literacy: What Works and Why.* NY: Garland, 1988.

Erikson, Erik H. *Childhood and Society,* 2d ed. NY: Norton, 1963.

Graves, Donald H. *Writing: Teachers and Children at Work.* Portsmouth, NH: Heinemann Educational Books, 1983.

Hall, MaryAnne. *Teaching Reading as a Language Experience.* Columbus: Merrill, 1981.

Harter, Susan. "The Relationship between Perceived Competence, Affect, and Motivational Orientation within the Classroom: Process and Patterns of Change." In *Achievement and Motivation: A Social-Developmental Perspective*, eds. Ann K. Boggiano and Thane S. Pittman. NY: Cambridge University Press, 1992.

Heimlick, Joan, and Susan Pittelman. *Semantic Mapping: Classroom Applications.* Newark, DE: International Reading Association, 1986.

Johnston, Peter H., and Peter N. Winograd. "Passive Failure in Reading." *Journal of Reading Behavior* 17, no. 4, (1985): 279–301.

Matthews, Samuel R., Josephine Peyton Young, and Nancy Dean Giles. *Reading and Writing: Providing Tools for Brighter Futures.* Pensacola, FL: The Educational Research and Development Center, University of West Florida, 1992.

Novak, Joseph. *Learning to Learn.* NY: Cambridge University Press, 1984.

Stauffer, Russell. *Directing the Reading-Thinking Process.* NY: Harper and Row, 1975.

Stauffer, Russell. *The Language Experience Approach to the Teaching of Reading.* NY: Harper & Row, 1980.

Vacca, JoAnne, Richard Vacca, and Mary Grove. *Reading and Learning to Read.* Boston: Little, Brown, 1987.

Weaver, Constance. *Understanding Whole Language.* Portsmouth, NH: Heinemann Educational Books, 1990.

Reading to Learn in the Content Areas

I n Chapter 7 we addressed the needs of adolescent students with reading problems. However, all readers can experience comprehension problems when faced with content-area texts that are written about unfamiliar topics or in styles that are relatively new to the reader. In this chapter we will present comprehensive strategies for acquainting the reader with new text structures, forming bridges between the reader's knowledge and new knowledge, enhancing the general world knowledge of the reader, and developing vocabulary. Many of the comprehension strategies we discussed in Chapter 7 apply here. Where appropriate we refer to those strategies. The material in this chapter applies not only to adolescent readers who are not disabled readers but also to students in upper-elementary grades who are using subject-area texts and longer fiction materials.

DEVELOPING COMPREHENSION STRATEGIES

Comprehension is the goal of reading, and our most important goal in reading instruction is to help students understand, remember, and use what they read. The importance of good comprehension instruction is not limited to the lower grades, when we typically think of teaching reading. All through the grades, in whatever types of material students are reading, they need systematic help in developing and refining their comprehension skills. They need this help not just from their English or language-arts teachers but from all their teachers in all their subject areas. In the following sections we describe a variety of strategies that are useful in helping students continue to develop their comprehension skills.

Teacher Modeling of Comprehension

We all know that teacher modeling is an important aspect of effective teaching. We do not merely tell readers what they must do; we attempt to show them, modeling how it is to be done. But exactly what to model, and how, has not been clearly pointed out to teachers (Duffy et al., 1988).

Often, modeling focuses on demonstrating how a task is performed. A teacher says, in effect, "Watch me as I do this, and then you try it." When teachers read during free reading time, they demonstrate that adults read for pleasure. When they predict what might happen in a forthcoming part of a story, they model how predictions are phrased; but they often do not model how readers think as they read. To do so, teachers must "think aloud" for students. This helps students see how a strategic reader's thinking proceeds rather than seeing how procedures are carried out.

Modeling "Thinking Aloud"

Modeling mental processes in reading requires that the teacher "think aloud" as he or she reads a passage of connected text with students. Let's listen to Ms. Lacey as she reads with a group.

Before you read a story you get your mind ready to read it by thinking about what you already know. You often use the title and illustrations, especially what is on the cover of a book, to develop some ideas about what the story will be about. I'm going to try to think out loud as I look at this book and read part of it, to show you how my thinking works as I read. The first thing I notice about this book is the big picture on the cover of a huge train engine coming at me out of the dark with snowflakes all around it and snow on top of the bushes. Immediately I think, this story is about trains or a train, about a nighttime journey, about wintertime because of the snow. I think it's about a train journey, not about trains in general, because this picture is of a train moving toward me with its big headlight cutting through the darkness. If it were a book about trains in general I think it would have a clearer picture of a train, not moving, and in daylight so you could see the parts of the engine. This train is shadowy. The shadows and the blurriness give me a sort of mysterious feeling.

The title of the book is *The Polar Express*. I'm not sure at once what the title means. "The" tells me it's about something, about a thing. "Express" can mean something going very fast, like an express bus downtown that doesn't stop at every stop. So I guess that "express" means a kind of train. "Polar" is a little bit confusing, but I think of polar bears; polar bears and the snow in the picture makes me think of cold places, icy places, and the North Pole. All of these thoughts go through my head very quickly as I look at the cover of the book. They help me get ready to begin reading.

(The teacher begins to read:) "On Christmas Eve many years ago, I lay quietly in my bed." Immediately I recall Christmas Eves from my childhood, waiting in bed for Santa to arrive. Listening for a sound that might mean Santa had come, trying not to make any noise myself, trying not to fall asleep. "I did not rustle the sheets. I breathed slowly and silently." I close my eyes and I have a mental picture of myself lying still in bed trying not to make any sound, trying to breathe very, very quietly. "I was listening for a sound—a sound a friend had told me I'd never hear—the ringing bells of Santa's sleigh." I see a picture in my mind of the boy—I know it's a boy because it's a boy in the picture—straining his ears and some friend, I bet he's older, saying in a mean way, "There's no such thing as Santa Claus!" and the boy not wanting to believe it, but not being sure. . . . When I look again at the picture I see that the boy is on his knees on the bed looking out the window, so I immediately think, Well, he's heard something outside the window and maybe he has heard the sleigh! . . .

As we listen to Ms. Lacey explaining her thoughts out loud we see that she is trying to convey that readers make guesses—tentative hypotheses—about words, phrases, and pictures and try to relate what they read to their own experiences. She describes for students the mental pictures she sees as well as the thoughts and words that come into her head. She shows that everything is not known; some ambiguity exists about some words, but she is content to make a tentative guess or association and go on. She shows that the ambiguous parts will be filled in later. She uses a combination of word meanings, associations with her own past experiences, and information from illustrations to form ideas as she goes along.

Modeling in Direct Instruction

Teacher modeling of other comprehension processes has also been shown to be an important part of effective teaching of poor readers (Allington and McGill-Franzen, 1987; Gaskins, 1988). Researchers have found that direct instruction of *how* a comprehension skill was to be accomplished was often a missing ingredient in remedial teaching. Poor readers were often told what they were to do and given exercises to practice it, but rarely did the teacher model how it was to be done.

Gaskins (1988) described how an effective lesson in making inferences from a story proceeded in this way. After introduction of the story to be read and discussion of vocabulary terms, the teacher reviewed what inferences were and explained why making inferences helped readers understand what a writer had not explained directly. Then she modeled the process of making inferences. She discussed what she thought as she read about a person carrying an umbrella on a sunny day. Next she helped prepare students for the exercise by asking them to consider what they already knew about the topic they would read about—Native Americans. After the reading, she guided the students in applying the skill by making inferences about the feelings and motives of Native Americans in the story. Gaskins pointed out that it was the teacher-modeling step that was most often omitted in direct instruction lessons such as this one.

Comprehension Monitoring

Comprehension monitoring refers to a reader's internal monitoring, as the reader goes along, of whether what is being read makes sense. Effective readers continually monitor their own comprehension; they know implicitly that reading is supposed to make sense, and they mentally keep track of whether it does or not as they proceed. When they are understanding satisfactorily according to their purpose for the reading, they proceed; when they are not understanding satisfactorily, they stop and reread. Satisfactory understanding is a relative thing; for example, comprehension when skimming a reading passage for the gist of the information would probably not be adequate for a careful studying of the passage for a quiz. So the *purpose* for reading is an important factor in comprehension monitoring; but the most important aspect of this process is that the readers themselves are responsible for the judgment of adequacy.

This is a departure from typical comprehension teaching, in which the teacher takes responsibility for monitoring and judging the adequacy of readers' comprehension. Typically, teachers ask questions during and after the reading, and use the responses given to decide if a reader's comprehension is adequate. This kind of monitoring serves the teacher's need to know what students are doing, but it does not serve the reader's need to develop independence in reading. Ultimately, it is the reader who must keep track of whether he or she has comprehended what was read and whether that comprehension was adequate for the reading purpose.

What Do Effective Readers Do?

How do effective readers learn to monitor their own understanding? One way they learn is by the *questions* we ask them. Early on in their reading experience we ask good readers to do more than recall information; we ask them to make predictions, form inferences, make judgments, and apply information gained in novel ways. From these questions, they infer that reading requires them to think along with the author and do higher-level thinking as they go. Another important way they learn this is by having extensive practice in sustained, self-regulated reading. They read whole stories and books for enjoyment, to share with others, to act out and illustrate, to talk about and compare. Their sustained reading practice gives them hundreds, thousands of opportunities to practice being effective, self-monitoring readers.

Both factors may be missing in the experience of poor readers. They may be subjected year after year to a steady diet of convergent, literal-level questions, because these are the easiest to ask, answer, and evaluate. Often the hidden assumption is that poor readers cannot, or will not, engage in higher-level thinking about what they read, or that they need more practice in lower-level thinking skills at the expense of more sophisticated thinking skills. We also know that poor readers have much less practice in real reading than better readers; they simply have much less experience actually reading anything than others, so they do not have opportunities to practice self-monitored reading.

Encouraging Comprehension Monitoring

We want to help students develop and practice the ability to ask themselves if what they are reading makes sense as they go along. We teach them to do this by modeling for them and then practicing how to read and monitor their own comprehension. We model by reading aloud successive portions of a text and again "thinking aloud"—describing the mental images and associations we make as we read the words, describing the confusions we feel as we encounter unfamiliar terms or ideas, and describing how we go back and reread as we think. We demonstrate how we summarize information and keep mental track of sequences and cause-effect relationships as we go along. We state aloud what the main idea or main pieces of information are before we proceed to the next paragraph or page. After we model these thought processes, we ask students to do the same thing— read a portion of text, think aloud about the information in it, develop a summary statement, and mentally check that they understand before they proceed to the next portion. We break up reading passages into shorter passages and have students practice in small groups, then with a partner, then individually. Sometimes they respond orally, sometimes in writing such as with a summary sentence at the end of a paragraph or with a predictive question relating to forthcoming parts. We frequently use the reciprocal teaching method described in detail in Chapter 6, where a small group follows the teacher's model of four comprehension steps during reading. Then individuals take turns following those steps, leading the discussion of subsequent portions of the text. Sometimes we ask students to draw rather than write, or to act out or physically demonstrate what they have read as they proceed. We ask them to continually keep in mind the question, Does this make sense so far? And we teach them that if their mental answer is no or I'm not sure, that is a signal for them to go back and reread.

At first, students may have difficulty accepting the responsibility for their own comprehension, mostly because for so long teachers have taken that responsibility on themselves; but we repeatedly explain that the real goal of reading is not to be able to answer the teacher's questions, but to answer your own questions and satisfy yourself. Some readers do not accept this idea readily, but after extensive practice with self-monitoring activities, they slowly begin to adopt this new way of thinking. They begin to ask themselves questions about what they have read, comment on it to themselves, and accept the responsibility for their own reading.

Developing Higher-Level Comprehension Skills

Some students may have had years of experience being asked convergent, literal comprehension questions about what they read but have little experience doing higher-level thinking as they read. For this reason, we avoid the typical "basal lesson" format of reading and answering literal questions about stories and focus our comprehension instruction instead on developing and practicing higher-level skills of prediction, inference, perception of relationships, and application of new knowledge.

For these lessons, we frequently use the K-W-L and directed reading-thinking activity strategies (described in Chapter 6) for fiction and nonfiction texts, where students are asked to recall and organize their prior information about a topic, predict what information a nonfiction text may contain or what might happen in a fiction selection, and read to confirm or disprove their predictions. We also use these procedures for listening activities, as we read to students and stop periodically for them to make predictions about forthcoming parts of a story. As we read and discuss, we focus our questions not only on directly stated information but on sequences of events, causes and effects of events and actions, characters' motives and beliefs, and text structures in nonfiction texts. Such discussions more actively engage students in the act of reading, help them set real purposes for their reading, and give them systematic opportunities to practice effective comprehension.

MAKING THE TRANSITION TO CONTENT-AREA TEXTS

Around the third or fourth grade, students face a shift both in the purposes for much of their reading and in the types of texts they read. Figure 8.1 shows some of the differences between earlier and later reading.

Figure 8.1

Some Differences Between Beginning Reading and Later Reading

	BEGINNING READING (PRIMARY GRADES)	LATER READING (MIDDLE-ELEMENTARY GRADES AND UP)
Focus	Learning to read	Reading to learn
Material	Mostly fiction Short passages, changing topics	Mostly nonfiction Long sections, continuous topics
Purposes	Short term, explicitly set by teacher ("Read this sentence [perhaps aloud] and tell me what it says.")	Long term, generally set by teacher or by student ("Study pages 140–158 for a quiz on Friday.")
Evaluation	Oral reading, comprehension of short, explicit questions	Silent reading, learning of longer material, the ability to use information

Two areas can be problematic for children during this transition. One area is the volume of new information learners may encounter. Topics such as the human circulatory system, the formation of volcanoes, or the effects of the Stamp Act may be entirely new to learners at this stage of their schooling. They may have little prior information on which to base new learning. Another area may be the organization of content-area textbooks. Materials used in primary grades rely heavily on fiction or on fictionalized informational text; but in upper grades, textbooks are organized in ways that are unlike fiction.

Consequently, readers may lack both the prerequisite information to relate new information to prior learning and may have had only limited experience with content-area textbook organization. Helping students develop broad background knowledge and facility with textbook organization becomes important in effective teaching.

Text Structure

Content-area textbooks share several characteristics. In most texts there is a title page, table of contents, a forward or introduction that provides an overview and statement of the author's purpose, and chapters that address the content of the text. Within most chapters there is an introduction that foreshadows the organization and content. Many authors provide an outline of major topics and headings. These topics are usually signaled by bold or underlined text.

When students understand the way an author has organized the text, identifying the major points becomes easier. They are able to take advantage of the organizational structure while reading. One way to teach the textbook organization is by using a textbook overview. Figure 8.2 presents an overview that can be adapted to individual textbooks.

The way the chapters, topics, and sentences are related to each other vary from text to text. These relationships and the organization of information within the topics are referred to as the text structure. If readers can recognize how a text is organized, comprehension proceeds more smoothly than if the reader experiences difficulty identifying the author's organizational plan for the text.

Text structures should be taught through direct instruction and think-alouds, followed by guided practice. Direct instruction should focus on the definition of the structures and identification of signals for those structures. Many examples should be presented by teachers as they think aloud the hints that help them to uncover the various text structures. In the following section we present six common text structures that appear in content-area textbooks and provide instructional strategies for helping readers uncover these structures.

Figure 8.2

Textbook Overview

1. What is the title of the textbook? _____

2. What is the copyright date of the book? _____

3. Why is the date important? _____

4. Name the author(s). _____

5. If there is more than one author, how might more than one author affect the writing

   of the text? _____

   _____

6. Find the table of contents.
   A. How many sections in the book? _____

   B. What is the topic of the first section? _____

   C. How many chapters are in the first section? _____

7. Does the book have an introduction? _____
   If so, what is the purpose of the introduction? _____

   _____

8. On what page does the index begin? _____

9. Does the book have a glossary? _____

10. Open the book to the first chapter.
   A. What has the author done to help you identify the main points? _____

   B. What words appear in boldface type? _____

   C. Why do you think these words appear in boldface type? _____

Source: Adapted from Carol Santa, Maureen Danner, Marylin Nelson, Lynn Havens, Jim Scalf, and Lynn Scalf.
Content Reading in Secondary Schools. School District No. 5, Kallispell, MT, 1985.

Understanding Patterns of Text Organization

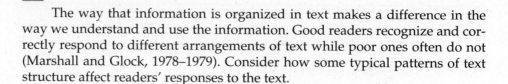

The way that information is organized in text makes a difference in the way we understand and use the information. Good readers recognize and correctly respond to different arrangements of text while poor ones often do not (Marshall and Glock, 1978–1979). Consider how some typical patterns of text structure affect readers' responses to the text.

Taxonomy

What pattern of organization do you perceive in this passage?

THE GUITAR

The guitar is one of the most popular stringed instruments. Because it has a fretboard, and strings stretched across a soundbox that are played by plucking, the guitar is considered a member of the lute family.

For centuries the guitar had a rather small wooden body with soft strings fashioned of animal gut. In the present century, however, several distinct classes of guitars have emerged. The traditional version has lived on as the "classical" guitar, but there are now steel-string guitars and electric guitars as well.

The steel-string guitar has a long, narrow neck and an enlarged body. It makes a louder, more piercing sound than the classical guitar. The electric guitar, an offshoot of the steel-string guitar, has its sounds amplified and its tones modified by electronic devices. It can make sounds loud enough to deafen a rock musician. It can also make a variety of tones, many of which do not sound guitarlike at all.

This piece of text is organized by classifying, by listing and defining the different instruments collected together under the label "guitar," and by showing their relationships to one another. Classifying is a fundamental act of the intellect, and text such as that in the passage is usually the result. This passage can also be outlined by means of a tree diagram, as in Figure 8.3. Classification charts like this are called *taxonomies*.

If readers are to understand this passage, they must perceive the taxonomic structure. If you asked them to recall what the passage said, you would expect them to remember the kinds of guitars discussed, what makes them different from one another, and how they are related within the "family." Taxonomic text structures are frequently encountered in science materials, especially in biology.

The key to creating a tree diagram for a taxonomic outline is identifying the author's most inclusive or most general category. In the *guitar* passage, the clue to the most general category is the statement ". . . the guitar is considered a member of the lute family." This implies that the lute family would include

Figure 8.3

A Taxonomic Outline

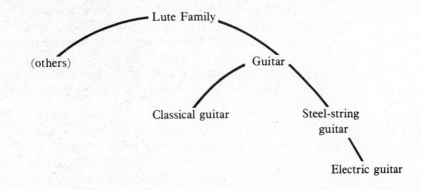

other instruments that have ". . . fretboard and strings. . . ." So, *guitar* is a smaller class of instruments than *lute.* The remainder of the taxonomic outline follows the same logic. Classical and steel-string are two types of guitars, and electric guitar is one type of steel-string.

The ability to classify topics in a hierarchical structure is critical. Class discussion, using the guide to concept mapping in Chapter 7, provides an opportunity to model the development of a taxonomic outline. This time is also a good one to develop the idea of supporting details. For example, the steel-string guitar can be described in more detail using the terms *long, narrow neck,* and *enlarged body.* The taxonomic outline can be expanded to include these details.

Chronology

What pattern of organization do you perceive in this passage?

Burton

The town of Burton, in the Midlands of England, has a history that is typical of trading villages of the region. Nothing of the town existed before the ninth century A.D. The hill overlooking the Avon River where the town now sits was covered with an impenetrable wood.

In about 870 A.D., Northumbrian knights cleared the hillside and erected a rude fortress as an outpost against the South Saxons lurking across the Avon, which then served as the southern frontier of Northumbria. By the time peace was effected some thirty years later, a stone castle had been built, surrounded by about thirty dwellings. Some crops had been grown nearby.

With the peace and political stability of the tenth century, Burton grew in earnest. Pastures were cleared for five miles during the first half of the century, and fine manor houses erected from the wood and the profits of sheep raising. Trails that criss-crossed the settlement grew to well-traveled roads, and by the middle of the eleventh century, Burton served as the chief market center for the surrounding thirty- or forty-mile area. The town grew comparatively wealthy.

But prosperity came to an end when Cromwell and his Roundheads burned the town in the seventeenth century. They marched the residents of Burton off into captivity, and few ever returned.

This account is arranged according to a sequence of events. Its most prominent organizational feature is *chronological.* In order to comprehend the passage successfully, readers have to picture the unfolding of events across the perspective of time. If you asked them to recall this passage you would expect them to remember the events that were described, the time they occurred, and the order in which they occurred. Chronologically organized text can be reduced to a time line, as shown in Figure 8.4. Chronological structures are frequently encountered in historical text.

Since children's stories and chronological texts are organized by the sequence of events in time, the transition into this type of text may be less troublesome than others. The structure of stories is quite predictable. First, there is some event, then a response by the protagonist, followed by some action or series of actions which lead to an outcome. This sequence of events can be used as a transition between the stories of early-childhood books and the accounts of events over time in social studies or history texts. By focusing attention on the similarities, readers are using a schema for stories to understand the time sequence of a chronological text.

Figure 8.4

A Chronological Outline

BEFORE 870 A.D.	AFTER 870 A.D.	TENTH CENTURY	ELEVENTH CENTURY	SEVENTEENTH CENTURY
No town; thick woods	Northumbrian fortress built	Pastures cleared; manor houses built	Roads; market center	Town sacked by Cromwell; town abandoned

Figure 8.5

Time Line: My Life—Past, Present, and Future

1. Look at sample time lines in class.
2. Think about your life since you have been born.
   A. What has happened in the world, in your family, at school, and within your peer group to affect your life?
   B. Think about your future—what will you do this summer? What will you do when you finish high school? What must you do to accomplish these goals? (You may go to the library to use reference materials if needed.)
3. In your journal make notes of these events, one per line. (Include dates or your age when possible.)
   • Read over them, add or delete any events.
   • Number them in the order in which they took place and will take place.
   • Wait a day—talk to your parents and friends about your life.
4. Look over your notes, making adjustments.
5. Construct a first draft of your time line.
6. Conference with a volunteer or teacher. Edit. Redraw on white paper. Illustrate if desired.

A strategy that aids students' comprehension of historical texts, such as *Burton*, is the construction of a time line. In order to acquaint students with the concept of a time line, one teacher asked them to develop time lines of their own lives—autobiographical time lines. This strategy communicates the concept of a sequence of events from an informed perspective—the students' own lives. Figure 8.5 shows a personal time-line activity.

The Pattern Guide

Another kind of study guide is the pattern guide, which is useful in texts where the organization is clear enough to aid the students' access to the information.

Pattern guides take as many forms as there are structures of text. What they have in common is that they all direct the students to construct or fill in some sort of outline that is consistent with the pattern of the text. In order to construct a pattern guide, then, you must (a) decide what pattern of text structure organizes the reading assignment, and (b) create an exercise that requires students to manipulate information according to the structure.

It is best to introduce and discuss the procedure of using pattern guides before assigning one. Then, after the students have completed their guides, it is important to discuss what they did and why, to make sure they see the relationship between the exercise and the pattern of the text. Students are often so inundated with worksheets that they are not in the habit of looking for such significance in them. During the follow-up discussion of the pattern guide, be sure to listen for how aware they became of the pattern of the text and how much they were able to use this pattern to make predictions about and gain information from the passage.

After the students have had experience working with some of your pattern guides, assign them the task of constructing pattern guides of their own. This is an excellent way to call their attention to text structure, though it is not an exercise that every student will find easy to do.

An example of a pattern guide is found in Figure 8.6.

Cause and Effect

The passage about the town of Burton also used cause and effect for organization. How would you outline the following passage in which this pattern is more pronounced?

BLACK ROBES IN THE DESERT

Scientists sometimes question the wisdom of "folk wisdom." The case of the Tuaregs' robes is a case in point. These nomadic people live in the area of the southern Sahara desert, the hottest terrain on earth. For centuries they have worn the same head-to-toe black wool robes. Since black absorbs more heat from the sun than any other

Figure 8.6

A Chronological Pattern Guide for *Burton*

A. Fill in the blanks with an event or events that happened in Burton in each time period:

BEFORE 800 A.D.	AFTER 870 A.D.	TENTH CENTURY	ELEVENTH CENTURY	SEVENTEENTH CENTURY
_____	_____	_____	_____	_____
_____	_____	_____	_____	_____
_____	_____	_____	_____	_____

B. Fill in the blanks with a brief description of what the town of Burton might have looked like in each period.

BEFORE 800 A.D.	AFTER 870 A.D.	TENTH CENTURY	ELEVENTH CENTURY	SEVENTEENTH CENTURY	PRESENT
_____	_____	_____	_____	_____	_____
_____	_____	_____	_____	_____	_____
_____	_____	_____	_____	_____	_____

color, scientists wonder why they've kept them through the years. Some people speculated that they had only black sheep as a source of wool, but an inspection of their herds dispelled that notion. Others speculated that black might have been chosen for its protection against the nightly desert cold, but scientific tests showed that black robes held heat no better than white ones.

Finally, through a series of experiments it was discovered that the black robes are actually cooler than white ones. The explanation is that the sun heats the upper part of the robe, which causes air to rise up through the loose-fitting robe and out through the open neck. In this way a constant draft is maintained through the robes. This draft evaporates perspiration, which cools the wearer.

In order to understand this passage, readers must operate on at least two levels: They must recognize the larger cause-and-effect question, Why do the Tuaregs wear black robes in the desert? and recognize its answer, Because their black robes keep them cool. They must also recognize the more specific set of cause-and-effect relationships that explain the seemingly contradictory statement that black is cooler in the desert.

A cause-and-effect flow chart is shown in Figure 8.7. This chart links the causes and effects and shows how one leads to another.

Cause-effect writing is found in many content subjects, including health, social studies, the sciences, and home economics. Other graphic organizers for cause-and-effect structures are depicted in Figure 8.8.

Written Directions

Some written materials give instructions for carrying out a procedure or performing some action. Simpler materials of this sort communicate a series of tasks that must be performed in some order:

MAKING MICROWAVE POPCORN

Remove the plastic outer wrap from the package. Unfold the bag of popcorn, and place it in the center of the microwave oven with the directions facing **up**. Set your microwave to **full** (100 percent) power. Set the timer for 5 minutes, and listen carefully as the popcorn pops. When popping slows to 2 to 3 seconds between pops, stop. Note how long the popping took this time, and next time set the timer for the same length of time. Remove the bag from the microwave and open it carefully at the top, avoiding the hot steam that will escape.

To understand this passage adequately, readers must attend to the steps described and to the order in which they are given. Readers can demonstrate their understanding by arranging a set of picture cards in the right order, putting the sentences from the passage in correct order, writing the steps in order, acting out making popcorn, or actually making popcorn in a microwave oven.

Figure 8.7

Cause/Effect Flow Chart

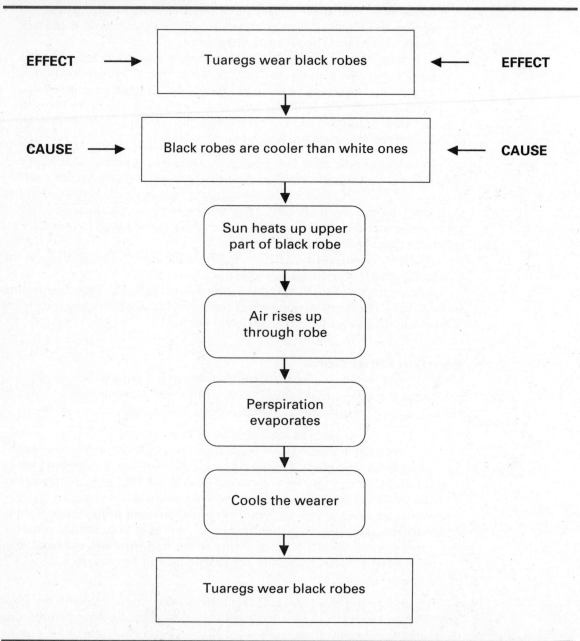

Figure 8.8

Cause/Effect Graphic Organizers

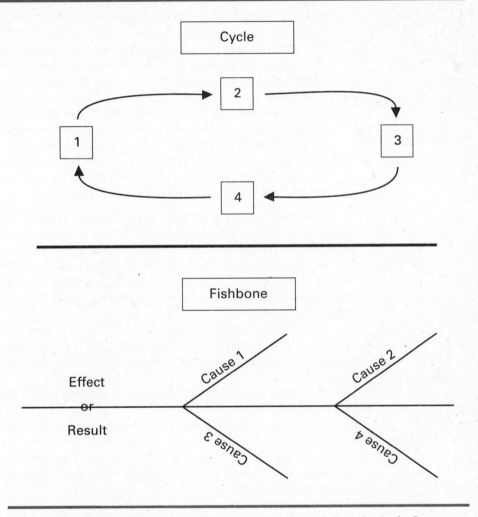

Source: Wisconsin Department of Public Instruction. *Strategic Learning in the Content Area*. Madison, WI, 1989.

WHAT TO DO IN CASE OF FIRE

In the event of a fire in this building, students must immediately and quietly stand beside their desks. The teacher should press his or her hand against the classroom door. If the door feels hot to the touch, the door must *not* be opened. Instead, the teacher is to lower the rope ladder stored in each classroom from the window ledge. The children will then climb down the rope ladder one at a time. As they reach the ground they are to proceed at a walk to the west end of the playground, where they will line up and remain silent.

If the door is not hot to the touch, the teacher may open it and inspect the hall for flames or smoke. If the fire is at the north end of the building, the class will exit by the south stairway. Conversely, if the fire is at the south end of the building, the north stairway will be used. Each class will proceed at a walk to the west end of the playground to line up and remain silent. Each teacher will ascertain whether all the pupils are present at that time.

The understanding of this passage cannot be done by carrying out one sequence of tasks, because no *one* sequence is appropriate for all situations. Readers must recognize not only the tasks and their sequence, but also the situations in which each alternative sequence should be followed. They should be able to role-play the correct procedure for each situation or answer questions such as "What should you do if the fire alarm rings and the teacher tells you the door feels hot?"

The relationship of the ideas in the fire drill passage may be outlined in a flow chart as in Figure 8.9. Material that takes the form of written directions is seen most frequently in math, science, home economics, and vocational education.

The writing-reading connection can also be used effectively to increase comprehension of written directions. Activities such as creating a piñata, making valentines for classmates, or making a model log cabin can serve as stimuli for creating a set of written directions. The process of creating a product, recording the steps for that process, and then exchanging these written directions with others provide students with the means to develop a schema for written instructions.

Comparison and Contrast

In order to understand what something *is,* it is often helpful to know what it is not. Comparison and contrast go beyond simple description by describing two or more things simultaneously and pointing out their likenesses and differences.

WILL THE REAL COWBOY PLEASE STAND UP?

So many people pretend to be cowboys these days that it is getting harder to tell the real cowboys from the dudes. Dudes and cowboys both wear Western hats, wide, tooled leather belts and ornate

Figure 8.9

A Flow Chart of Written Directions Containing Contingency Sequences

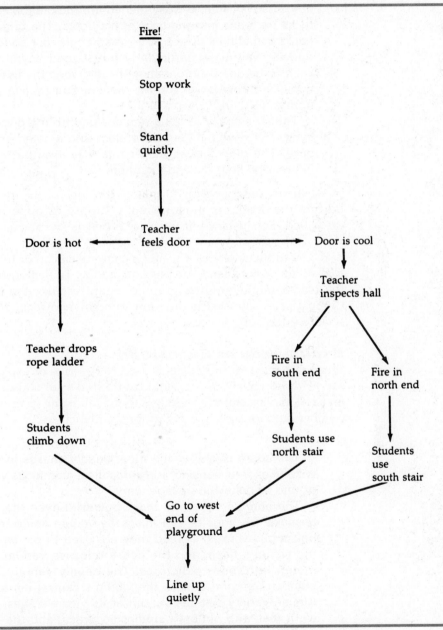

Source: Wisconsin Department of Public Instruction. *Strategic Learning in the Content Area.* Madison, WI, 1989.

buckles, jeans, and boots. The jeans of both dudes and cowboys may be worn or faded, in contrast to their boots. Both dudes and cowboys are likely to wear shiny, expensive-looking boots, but the real cowboy's belt is usually sweat-stained around the top edge, and he often tucks his jeans into the tops of his boots. The brim of the cowboy's hat is sometimes tipped at a rakish angle, but so is the experienced dude's. Neither is particularly bowlegged anymore, although this used to be one way to distinguish between the two. Nowadays both dudes and cowboys are apt to drive pickups or jeeps instead of riding horses.

The surest way to tell a real cowboy from a dude is to look at his eyes. The cowboy's eyes are clear and steady, and he holds your gaze. The dude's eyes flicker this way and that, as if to see what impression he is making on others.

When a description is formulated for one of the things being compared but not the other, we must mentally supply its opposite to the things not described. For instance, if one man's belt is sweat-stained, the other's belt must not be so.

The ultimate test of a reader's comprehension of this passage would be to distinguish between a cowboy and a dude. To demonstrate comprehension, the reader might produce graphic organizers like the ones in Figure 8.10. Comparison-contrast structures are found in many content subjects, especially social studies and science.

Explanation or Exposition

Much text material in schools is used to describe or explain. Since its organization varies widely, it does not lend itself to a cut-and-dried description. The material may be entirely verbal, as in the following example, or it may include numbers and formulas, charts, graphs, and pictures.

THE DEADLY COBRA

The cobra is one of the most deadly snakes in the world. Many wildlife experts consider it *the* deadliest animal. Its venom, its mobility, and its behavior are legendary.

The cobra's venom is more powerful even than that of the rattlesnake. Its fangs do not inject the venom as do the fangs of other poisonous snakes; instead they are used to pierce deep wounds in the victim's flesh, and the cobra releases venom from sacs in its mouth into these punctures. The deadly venom is carried by the bloodstream and attacks the victim's central nervous system. One African variety spits its venom at its victim's eyes; it can spit up to eight feet with almost pinpoint accuracy, and the highly corrosive venom blinds the victim unless it is immediately washed away.

The cobra's mobility is chilling. In spite of its size, it can move with great speed almost soundlessly. It creeps up on its intended victim

Figure 8.10

Graphic Organizers for Comparison/Contrast

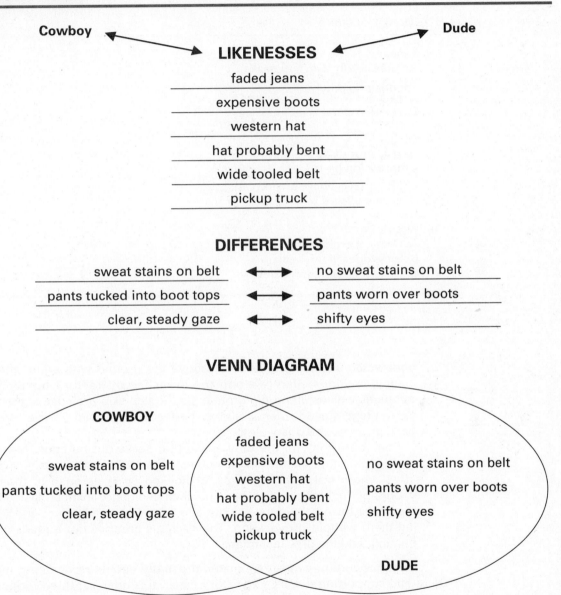

Cowboy   Dude

LIKENESSES

faded jeans

expensive boots

western hat

hat probably bent

wide tooled belt

pickup truck

DIFFERENCES

sweat stains on belt ⬌ no sweat stains on belt

pants tucked into boot tops ⬌ pants worn over boots

clear, steady gaze ⬌ shifty eyes

VENN DIAGRAM

COWBOY

sweat stains on belt

pants tucked into boot tops

clear, steady gaze

faded jeans
expensive boots
western hat
hat probably bent
wide tooled belt
pickup truck

no sweat stains on belt

pants worn over boots

shifty eyes

DUDE

Source: Wisconsin Department of Public Instruction. *Strategic Learning in the Content Area.* Madison, WI, 1989.

Figure 8.11

Expository Outline

THE DEADLY COBRA

I. Venom
   A. More deadly than rattlesnake
   B. Puncture wounds made by fangs
   C. Released from sacs in mouth
   D. Attacks central nervous system

II. Mobility
   A. Has great speed in spite of size
   B. Moves silently
   C. Moves on or above ground easily
   D. Is camouflaged by coloration

III. Behavior
   A. Does not avoid human contact
   B. Seeks out, follows humans
   C. Attacks without provocation

undetected and can move on or above the ground with equal efficiency. It glides silently along the branches of trees or building rafters as well as along the ground. Its mottled skin provides a good camouflage since it blends almost perfectly with dead leaves, tree bark, grasses, and dusty earth.

The cobra may be the only snake that seeks out humans. Most snakes and other animals avoid contact with humans at all costs and attack them only when escape is blocked or in defense of their young, but cobras seem to have no such avoidance instinct. Instead they have been known to seek out and follow humans before attacking them without provocation. Their actions are those of a predator hunting, and the prey is human.

Comprehending expository material usually entails recognizing main ideas and supporting details. Expository material is often captured nicely by the traditional outline format because it explicitly shows the relation among ideas of different levels of importance. Figure 8.11 shows an outline of this expository piece. Figure 8.12 shows another way to graphically represent expository text using a concept map.

Expository writing is encountered in virtually every subject in the curriculum. Whenever information has to be explained, expository prose is the choice.

Figure 8.12

Concept Map

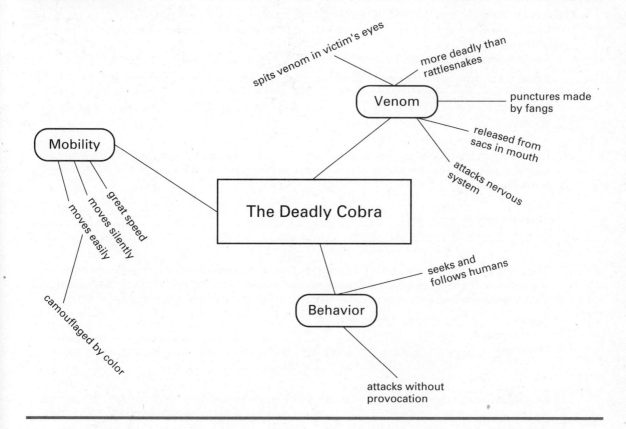

Textbooks from elementary school through college may employ a wide variety of patterns for organizing information. The mental activity involved in comprehending a passage written in one pattern may be somewhat different from that required to comprehend a passage written a different way (Estes and Shibilski, 1980).

These texts often include a variety of structures such as taxonomic, chronological, cause-effect, or compare-contrast. The task in comprehending expository text is to identify how the various topics are related to each other. To accomplish this, it is helpful to understand each structural unit, one at a time. In the cobra text, there are examples of several structures. Figure 8.13 shows a guided practice exercise aimed at helping students identify these text structures.

Figure 8.13

Guided Practice—Expository Text

Directions: Write the signal(s) and the text structure used: taxonomic, comparison-contrast, cause-effect, chronology. Write a one- or two-sentence summary of each paragraph given.

The following questions can be used by the teacher to provide guidance to the students.

"What is this paragraph telling me? Tell the main idea. Is it describing or telling something? If so, tell what. Is it comparing one thing to another? Tell what they are and how they differ or are similar. Is it explaining something? Tell why it happened and/or what happened. Is it telling about a sequence of events?"

1. One African variety spits its venom at its victim's eyes; it can spit up to eight feet with almost pinpoint accuracy, and the highly corrosive venom blinds the victim unless it is immediately washed away.

   Signal   *and*
   Text structure *taxonomic*
   Summary   *The cobra spits venom*

2. The cobra's venom is more powerful even than that of the rattlesnake. Its fangs do not inject the venom as do the fangs of other poisonous snakes; instead they are used to pierce deep wounds in the victims flesh, and the cobra releases venom from sacs in its mouth into these punctures.

   Signal   *more, even, than, instead*
   Text structure *compare-contrast*
   Summary   *Cobra venom is more powerful and is injected*
                   differently than other poisonous snakes

3. Most snakes and other animals avoid contact with humans at all costs and attack them only when escape is blocked or in defense of their young, but cobras seem to have no such avoidance instinct. Instead they have been known to seek out and follow humans before attacking them without provocation. Their actions are those of a predator hunting, and the prey is human.

   Signal   *but, instead*
   Text structure *compare-contrast*
   Summary   *Most snakes avoid human contact but cobras do not*

4. Its mottled skin provides a good camouflage since it blends almost perfectly with dead leaves, tree bark, grasses, and dusty earth.

   Signal   *since*
   Text structure *cause-effect*
   Summary   *The cobra is camouflaged because its mottled skin*
                   blends with its environment

Source: Adapted from Jocelyn Perkins. "Integrating in the Content Areas." Paper presented at the International Reading Association Conference, Atlanta, GA, May 1990.

The ReQuest Procedure and Reciprocal Teaching

Designed by Manzo (1969), the ReQuest procedure gives insights into a child's general sense of text structure. It also provides a vehicle for direct instruction. The ReQuest is an individual procedure, though it can be adapted for a small group. It proceeds as follows:

1. The teacher and student both read the first sentence of a passage to be studied. They read it silently.
2. After they both have read the sentence, the student asks as many questions as he or she can. The teacher answers the questions clearly and completely.
3. Then it is the teacher's turn to ask the questions about the same sentence, and the student answers as fully as possible. By forming questions that call upon the student's grasp of text structures, the teacher models good questioning strategies. This helps the student see how good readers ask themselves questions about text as they read.
4. When the student has finished answering, teacher and student read the next sentence and proceed as before.
5. When the teacher feels that the student has read a sufficient amount of the text in this way to make comprehension of the remainder of the passage possible, he or she should ask the student to read to the end (Manzo, 1969, p. 125).

The ReQuest procedure can be modified in several ways. First, a group of two to five students can team up against the teacher and take turns asking questions. Second, the reading can be increased to cover a paragraph at a time if proceeding sentence by sentence does not generate many questions. Third, teacher and student can work together on interpretive and predictive questions—the latter especially, before the ReQuest is suspended and they read to the end.

This procedure is indirectly diagnostic. By noting the kinds of questions the students ask for each kind of text structure, you can tell whether or not they are on the right track.

An activity that is a significant step beyond the ReQuest procedure is the activity of *reciprocal teaching,* which was previously discussed in Chapter 6. Developed by Brown, Palincsar, and Armbruster (1984), reciprocal teaching is a procedure for teaching comprehension skills systematically. The authors note that while word recognition skills are already taught in a carefully sequenced and managed fashion, comprehension instruction in many classrooms seems designed mainly to practice skills that have not really been taught (Brown et al., 1984; Pearson, 1985). Reciprocal teaching was developed to take students through the steps of reading-with-comprehension, so that after repeated practice, the students come to use, on their own, reading strategies that pay off in high rates of comprehension.

To carry out reciprocal teaching, meet with a group of 5 to 15 students, each of whom has a copy of the same content-area reading material. Begin by modeling four tasks related to a segment of the material.

1. Summarize the segment in a sentence.
2. Ask the students one or two good questions about the segment.
3. Clarify the difficult parts.
4. Predict what the next segment will be about.

The students' responsibilities are to judge whether or not the summary is accurate; to decide whether or not the questions tap what is important about the passage and to answer them; and to help clarify the difficult parts.

After you have modeled the teacher's role five or six times, ask a student to be the teacher. Figures 8.14 and 8.15 are guides we have found that provide support for students as they act out the role of "teacher."

The student then carries out the same steps the teacher did, while you

1. conduct the activity as often as your turn comes up;
2. join the others in judging the accuracy of the summaries and the importance of the questions;
3. support the "teacher" with frequent but appropriate praise;
4. keep the students on task; and
5. challenge the "teacher" to perform slightly above her or his immediately past level of performance (give a more comprehensive summary, ask a "main idea" question following several factual ones, make a more logical prediction of what will follow).

Finally, at the end of each half hour's reciprocal teaching, give the students a passage they have not read before and ask them to make a summary of it or answer a few substantial questions about it (Pearson, 1985).

After performing the outward activity of reciprocal teaching over several weeks, students internalize the strategies of summarizing, questioning, and predicting and use them when reading independently. Palincsar, Brown, and their colleagues have evidence of dramatic gains after reciprocal teaching with junior high school students who were fair in word recognition but poor in comprehension of content-area material (Brown et al., 1984).

Identifying relevant text structures is but one key to reading comprehension. Figure 8.16 lists and summarizes text structures or patterns, and provides questions that may alert the reader to the patterns. Another major component of reading comprehension is the reader's prior knowledge based on life experiences and encounters with media such as books, television, magazines, and newspapers. The development of this knowledge and its activation are addressed in the next section.

Figure 8.14

Reciprocal Teaching

1. Question FORMING GOOD MAIN IDEA QUESTIONS (WHAT IS IMPORTANT IN THE TEXT?)
2. Summarize IDENTIFY THE MAIN IDEA
3. Clarify WHAT IS CONFUSING IN THE TEXT?
4. Predict WHAT WILL BE DISCUSSED NEXT?

Source: Nettie Linton. "Reciprocal Teaching: An Update." Inservice Presentation. The School District of Escambria County, Pensacola, FL, 1989.

Increasing Students' General Knowledge

Many students lack the necessary prior knowledge to be able to comprehend content-area text without difficulty. In addition to life experiences, students can acquire general world knowledge through books, magazines, and newspapers. As they read more, they acquire information about people, places, and things. To facilitate this, classroom library collections should consist of a variety of text genres, text structures, content-area topics, and reading levels. Teachers can also plan a significant portion of every reading period for sustained silent reading.

Figure 8.15

Reciprocal Teaching Guide for Students

Student Name _____

Title of Selection _____

Paragraph 1

    A. Predict: *(I believe this paragraph will be mainly about)* _____

_____

    B. Read

    C. Was prediction correct? (Yes or No) _____ Give reason: _____

_____

    D. Question: _____

_____

    E. Clarify: _____

_____

    F. Summarize: *(This paragraph was mainly about)* _____

_____

Paragraph 2

    A. Predict: *(I believe this paragraph will be about)* _____

_____

    B. Read

    C. Was prediction correct? (Yes or No) _____ Give reason: _____

_____

    D. Question: _____

_____

    E. Clarify: _____

_____

    F. Summarize: *(This paragraph was mainly about)* _____

_____

Replicate worksheet to match number of paragraphs in passage.

Source: Nettie Linton, "Reciprocal Teaching: An Update." Inservice Presentation. The School District of Escambria County, Pensacola, FL, 1989.

Figure 8.16

Information Patterns, Questions, and Signals

ORGANIZATIONAL PATTERN	TYPES OF QUESTIONS	SIGNALS
Taxonomy	What kind of thing is X? What defines it as such? What varieties of X exist?	such as, also in addition, which, and
Chronological	What happened first? What happened next? What did these events lead to?	now, next, before, after, then
Cause-effect	What caused X? What were the effects of X?	since, because, therefore, then consequently
Comparison-contrast	How are X and Y alike? How are they different? How are X and Y related to Z?	instead, unlike, but, as, although same as, however
Direction sequences	What do I do first? How do I do it? What do I do next?	first, second, third, lastly, afterward, next, finally
Expository-explanatory	What is the main idea? What supports that idea?	for example, for instance, most importantly

Reading aloud to students is another important way to help them gain information. It also exposes students to concepts and vocabulary they may not be able to read independently. When reading aloud to students, teachers must remember that good listening is active, not passive. Good listeners make predictions, think along with the reader or speaker, formulate questions and challenges, look for evidence in support of a position, and argue with the speaker mentally. They draw what they are listening to, make lists of steps, create flow charts, and depict causes and effects. They summarize main ideas and sequences, and paraphrase arguments. They predict what might happen in forthcoming portions and listen to confirm or disprove their own or others' predictions. As the teacher reads aloud, students should be given opportunities to answer questions, ask questions, and engage in the other activities mentioned.

Providing opportunities for direct experiences related to particular content areas or themes also enhances world knowledge. Such opportunities include field trips, experiential learning, guest speakers, and videotapes. Strategies such as K-W-Ls can provide a structure in which the benefit of these experiences can be increased.

As we have said through this chapters and others, in order to comprehend text, readers must have prior knowledge that they can relate to the material in the text. Once they possess the necessary background, they must then use strategies to relate the new material in the text to their prior knowledge. In Chapter 7, K-W-Ls and DRTAs were suggested strategies for activating and relating prior knowledge to new material. An anticipation guide (Vacca & Vacca, 1989) is another activity that activates students' prior knowledge and stimulates predictions about the text. An anticipation guide is a set of statements about the text that students respond to and discuss prior to the reading of the text. The teacher's role is to create the anticipation guide, accept a broad range of student responses, and facilitate discussion prior to reading. After reading the text, the teacher should lead students to contrast their own predictions with the author's stated meaning. Vacca and Vacca (1989, p. 145) provide guidelines for constructing and using anticipation guides:

1. Analyze the material to be read. Determine the major ideas—implicit and explicit—with which students will interact.
2. Write those ideas in short, clear, declarative statements. These statements should in some way reflect the world that the students live in or know about. Therefore, avoid abstractions whenever possible.
3. Put these statements into a format that will elicit anticipation and prediction-making.
4. Discuss readers' predictions and anticipations prior to reading the text selection.
5. Assign the text selection. Have students evaluate the statements in light of the author's intent and purpose.
6. Contrast readers' predictions with author's intended meaning.

A sample anticipation guide appears in Figure 8.17.

VOCABULARY

Another critical area of prior knowledge is vocabulary. Vocabulary is an important and troublesome issue in content-area reading. By the time they reach third grade, students must be able to read and understand many words they usually do not use in speech (Chall, 1979). When they are successful at gleaning new words, we rightly conclude that reading has made a major contribution to their education. For those who do not succeed, however, vocabulary constitutes a widespread problem in the middle and upper grades, especially in the content subjects.

Figure 8.17

Anticipation Guide—Mummies in Egypt

Directions: Before you read the article on mummies, mark those statements that you think are true *T* and those statements that you think are not true *NT*. Then discuss your responses with class members. After you read, mark the statements again using the information that you learned.

Before		**After**
1. _____	Egyptians believed everyone had a *ba* and a *ka*.	_____
2. _____	Bodies that were not preserved were said to be mummified.	_____
3. _____	People believed that Pharaohs became gods when they died.	_____
4. _____	To make mummies, embalmers took out the inner organs.	_____
5. _____	The embalmers did not take the brain out through the nose with hooks.	_____
6. _____	Shabtis are magical figures that were tucked into the mummy's wrappings.	_____
7. _____	Everyone who died in ancient Egypt became mummies.	_____

We will deal with two main aspects of vocabulary: (a) background concepts to which vocabulary words can be related and (b) strategies to derive approximate word meanings from surrounding context.

Vocabulary and Background Concepts

Words are labels for concepts. Concepts are stored mental patterns that are derived from experiences. If, for example, we have enough experience with wildflowers, we may begin to recognize different varieties of them. With the help of a guidebook or other information source, we can learn words to associate with the various wildflowers we have come to recognize.

Relating New Words to Personal Experiences

Words are names for concepts. Concepts are categories of experience. Students learn new words when experiences are organized into concepts for the new words to name. When students lack concepts, we must help them organize their experience before teaching the words.

To do this, we must ask students to share in a discussion of what they already know about a new vocabulary term and find out if they have had any personal experiences they can relate to the term. We can straighten out possible confusion about new words' meanings. Moreover, a discussion of this type yields diagnostic insights, because we can find out if the students are able to associate words and ideas with the terms under study. For example, during a prereading discussion in a science class the teacher writes on the board or overhead the vocabulary word *migration*. Students are asked to predict the meaning of the word. To facilitate this discussion the teacher asks questions aimed at activating and retrieving students' prior knowledge about the term *migration*. Questions teachers may use include: What do you think *migration* means? Who or what migrates? How do they migrate? Have you ever seen migration? Describe what you saw. When did you see migration?

If discussion does not uncover many associations, set up an activity to help build associations. In science or social studies, this may involve a field trip, an experiment, a demonstration, or a guest speaker. It may involve role plays: The students can act out *avaricious, hostile, laconic,* and other such words. Role plays will often do as a substitute for real experience, and they have much potential for teaching vocabulary.

Treating Meanings Categorically

Semanticists, specialists in the study of meaning, suggest that it is useful to think of the meaning of one word in relation to the meanings of others. To semanticists, meanings come not by themselves but in family or hierarchical relationships. A duck can be thought of not just as a white or yellow creature with a beak and feathers but as a kind of bird. Moreover, it is useful to know that there are varieties of ducks: mallards, teals, wood ducks, mergansers. Ducks are seen in stages too. A little fuzzy yellow-beaked thing grows up to be a brown-and-green adult duck; ducklings and ducks are stages of the same bird.

One semanticist, Albert Upton (1973), has suggested a set of three questions that people should ask when they are striving for exactness in meaning:

1. What is it a kind of/what are the kinds of it?
2. What is it a part of/what are the parts of it?
3. What is it a stage of/what are the stages of it?

To these we have added a fourth:

> 4. What is it a product or a result of/what are the products or results of it?

These four questions can be adapted to yield much information about any meaning or word under consideration. Depending on whether the item under scrutiny is a *class of things* (that is, ducks in general) or a *particular thing* (that mallard over there with the twisted beak), one side of the questions or the other will be useful but not always both.

Hence for *duck* in general we can say:

> 1. It is a kind of bird; the kinds of ducks are mallards, wood ducks, and so forth.
> 2. (The first part of the question is not relevant.) Its parts are the wings, legs, body, neck, head, feathers, beak, gizzard, and so forth.
> 3. (The first part is not relevant.) Its stages are the egg, the duckling, the young duck, and the mature duck.
> 4. (The first part is not relevant.) Ducks lay eggs that are good to eat, their feathers make soft pillows, the mature birds are thought by some to be tasty eating, good hunting, and so forth.

Concept Ladders

An exercise called the *concept ladder*, which was developed around these four questions, is good for both instruction and assessment. Since it is a paper-and-pencil exercise, a teacher may give a concept ladder to students to complete individually as they do a reading assignment or to a small group of students to be completed together.

In creating a concept ladder, set up columns to correspond to Upton's questions and leave blanks above or below the target word, depending on the information that is needed to understand the term. The students fill in the blanks. Concept ladders are somewhat open-ended, since there may be several correct answers for each blank, but you can limit the choices at first by restricting the answers to a set list from which the student must choose (see Figures 8.18 and 8.19).

It may have occurred to you that the concept ladder pins down the meanings of some words better than others. Many words seem to have a literal meaning that can be fixed in relation to other words as the concept ladder allows us to do; other words, however, seem to have strong meanings that are not so easy to categorize. For example, we may say of an acquaintance:

Sam is a *doctor*.

Figure 8.18

Concept Ladder for *Guitar*

A. Kind of?	B. Part of?	C. Function of? (How is it made?)
Musical instrument	*a band ?*	*out of wood, I guess*
GUITAR	GUITAR	GUITAR
electric, classical, folk	*neck, strings*	*makes good music*
Kinds of it?	Parts of it?	Functions of it?
(name 3)	(name 4)	(what does it do?)

We can say that a doctor is a professional and that there are many subspecialties of a doctor; that being a doctor is the result of long training, and that a doctor produces health care, and so on. However, we can also say:

Sam is a *jerk.*

Now there is strong meaning, but it is not so specific. The thrust of this word is more emotional than scientific. Now we are hearing not so much what Sam is like literally, but how we feel about him. We can invite students to deal with this dimension by appending another question to the concept ladder.

What kinds of feelings does this word give you?

Concept Maps

Another activity that helps students categorize meanings and relate new information to prior knowledge is concept mapping. The guidelines for creating a concept map for a prewriting organizational strategy and as a postreading activity are in Chapter 7. The same directions can be used for developing a map for vocabulary study. This strategy can also be used as a tool for testing students' understanding of the concepts presented. A sample vocabulary concept map is presented in Figure 8.20.

Figure 8.19

Concept Ladder for *Amphibians*

What kinds of amphibians are there?	What is an amphibian a stage of?	What is an amphibian a product of?
_____	_____	_____
_____	_____	_____
AMPHIBIAN	AMPHIBIAN	AMPHIBIAN
What are the kinds of an amphibian?	What are the stages of an amphibian?	What are the products or results of an amphibian?
_____	_____	_____
_____	_____	_____
_____	_____	_____
	_____	_____
		_____

POSSIBLE ANSWERS:

FROG LEGS (SOME PEOPLE EAT THEM)
frogs
eggs in water
salamanders
neophytes in water
turtles

YOUNG AMPHIBIANS ON LAND
waste products
mature amphibians on land
help control mosquito population
more amphibians

Word Sorts

Open and closed sorts were discussed in earlier chapters as a way for emergent readers to compare and classify words by their features. Word sorting lends itself to content vocabulary for older readers. In closed sorts, students know in advance the criteria used to categorize or group the words. Students may be asked to sort a list of vocabulary words or content terms by geographical region, natural resources, or physical characteristics. For instance, a teacher at the conclusion of a unit on animals asked the students to sort the

Figure 8.20

Vocabulary Concept Map

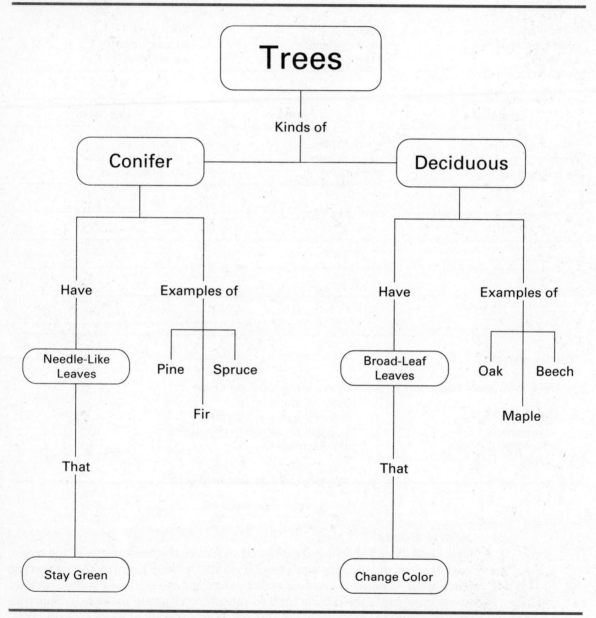

Source: Samuel R. Mathews, Josephine P. Young, and Nancy D. Giles. *Student Literacy Volunteers: Providing Tools for Brighter Futures.* Pensacola, FL: The Educational Research and Development Center, The University of West Florida, 1992.

unit vocabulary words into mammals, birds, fish, and insects.

For open sorting, however, students are asked to sort or group the vocabulary words in logical ways and state the criteria they used for sorting. Sorting is an excellent activity to promote collaborative learning. Students can work in pairs or small groups to complete this task, grouping the list of words in as many ways as possible and stating their criteria for grouping.

Analogies

Analogies, another form of exercise in categorizing word meanings, are suitable for students in late middle grades or beyond. Analogies establish relationships between sets of things or ideas and thus go a bit deeper than synonyms in tapping vocabulary development. You set up analogies by (a) thinking of how the concept represented by your test word relates to another concept and (b) thinking of a familiar pair of concepts that share the same sort of relationship.

There are two approaches to presenting analogies. One approach provides a multiple-choice format.

> Nest: birds :: _____ : beavers.
> (a) dams (b) lodges (c) hives (d) trees

The other provides a fill-in-the-blank format with no stated choices.

> Fill in the blanks with the appropriate word:
>
> 1. Fresh water is to salt water as the desert is to _____ .
>
> 2. Water is to a fish as land is to _____ .
>
> 3. Gills are to tadpoles as _____ are to frogs.
>
> 4. Ammonia is to fish as _____ is to land animals.
>
> 5. Urea is to a grown bird as uric acid is to _____ .
>
> 6. Jelly-like coating is to frogs' eggs as _____ is to chickens' eggs.

Older students are confronted with solving analogies on many standardized tests including college entrance exams. The first step in solving word analogies is identifying the relationship that exists between the given pair. (Figure 8.21 lists some common relationships.) Once this relationship is discovered, it can be used to aid identification of the missing word. This second step can be facilitated using the strategy described in Figure 8.22. The analogy chart (Figure 8.23) can be used as a guide for providing direct instruction, modeling strategy usage, and studying independently.

Figure 8.21

Kinds of Relationships

In analogy questions, the relationship between the first two words may be one of several kinds. Following are relationship possibilities.

1. Degree Relationship

   gale: hurricane::

   A. cyclone: squall
   C. breeze: draft
   E. doldrums: cloudburst

   B. overshadow: eclipse
   D. snowstorm: blizzard

2. Part/Whole Relationship

   earth: solar system::

   A. planet: sun
   C. universe: galaxy
   E. land: continent

   B. moon: rings
   D. tree: forest

3. Cause-and-Effect Relationship

   laser: beam::

   A. Loch Ness: monster
   C. loudspeaker: oration
   E. lightning: flash

   B. limerick: elegy
   D. locomotive: steam

4. Synonym Relationship

   pleasure: ecstasy::

   A. despair: cheerfulness
   C. happiness: bliss
   E. gratification: enjoyment

   B. euphoria: exaltation
   D. rapture: delight

5. Adult to Young Relationship

   bear: cub::

   A. cat: tom
   C. rabbit: doe
   E. sheep: lamb

   B. hog: boar
   D. swan: flock

Figure 8.21 continued

6. Characteristic Relationship

   sheep: mutton::

   A. poultry: duck
   C. meat: stew
   E. bacon: pig

   B. fish: filet
   D. steer: beef

7. Antonym Relationship

   artificial: natural::

   A. warrior: champion
   C. ideal: prototype
   E. eternal: finite

   B. copied: substitute
   D. lithograph: oil painting

8. Purpose Relationship

   colander: draining::

   A. chain: prohibit
   C. mop: sponge
   E. griddle: toaster

   B. weigh: scale
   D. spatula: flipping

9. Common Characteristic

   sniff: nose::

   A. sizzle: steak
   C. smell: odor
   E. crack: nail

   B. smack: lips
   D. shiver: cold

10. Antonym Relationship

    nibble: devour::

    A. creep: streak
    C. chill: thaw
    E. frown: moan

    B. drench: dehydrate
    D. charm: repulse

Source: Dorothy Nolen. "The Current View of Teaching Comprehension." Inservice Presentation. The School District of Escambia County, Pensacola, FL, 1989.

Figure 8.22

Strategies for Teaching Word Analogies

Determine the kind of relationship that exists between the given pair of words. Here, a list of common relationships and an example of each relationship is presented.

A. Make a sentence out of the analogy.

earth: solar system::

  a. planet: sun
  b. moon: rings
  c. breeze: draft
  d. tree: forest
  e. land: continent

Sample Sentence:
1. The earth is part of the solar system just as a tree is part of a forest.
2. The earth is part of the whole solar system just as a tree is part of the whole forest.

B. Be careful not to create too simple an analogy.

helmet: head::

  a. sword: warrior
  b. umbrella: clothing
  c. shoe: stocking
  d. watch: wrist
  e. thimble: finger

Sample Sentence:
Too simple sentence: A helmet is worn on the head.
Better sentence: A helmet is put on the head to protect it.

C. Try reversing the order of the words before constructing your sentence.

sniff: nose::

  a. sizzle: steak
  b. smack: lips
  c. smell: odor
  d. shiver: cold
  e. crack: nail

Sample Sentence:
You use your nose to sniff just like you use your lips to smack.

Source: Dorothy Nolen. "The Current View of Teaching Comprehension." Inservice Presentation. The School District of Escambia County, Pensacola, FL, 1989.

Figure 8.23

Analogy Chart

1. | Gale | is to | hurricane | as | snowstorm | is to | blizzard | degree relationship

Relationship sentence: *A hurricane is a more intense storm than a gale just as a blizzard is more intense than a snowstorm.*

2. | Earth | is to | solar system | as | tree | is to | forest | part to whole relationship

Relationship sentence: *The earth is part of the whole solar system just as the tree is part of the whole forest.*

3. | Laser | is to | beam | as | lightning | is to | flash | cause-and-effect relationship

Relationship sentence: *A laser produces a beam just as lightning causes/produces a flash.*

4. | Pleasure | is to | ecstasy | as | happiness | is to | bliss | synonym-intensity relationship

Relationship sentence: *Ecstasy means nearly the same as pleasure but is a more intense word just as bliss means happiness but is a more intense word.*

5. | Bear | is to | cub | as | sheep | is to | lamb | adult to young relationship

Relationship sentence: *A cub is a young bear just as a lamb is a young sheep.*

FIGURE 8.23 CONTINUED

6. | Sheep | is to | mutton | as | steer | is to | beef | common characteristic relationship

Relationship sentence: *Mutton is the meat of sheep just as beef is the meat of steer.*

7. | Artificial | is to | natural | as | eternal | is to | finite | antonym relationship

Relationship sentence: *Artificial is the opposite of natural just as eternal is the opposite of finite.*

8. | Colander | is to | draining | as | spatula | is to | flipping | purpose relationship

Relationship sentence: *A colander is used for draining just as a spatula is used for flipping.*

9. | Sniff | is to | nose | as | smack | is to | lips | common character relationship

Relationship sentence: *Sniff is the sound the nose makes just as smack is the sound the lips make.*

10. | Nibble | is to | devour | as | creep | is to | streak | antonymous relationship

Relationship sentence: *Devour is the opposite of nibble just as streak is the opposite of creep.*

Source: Dorothy Nolen. "The Current View of Teaching Comprehension." Inservice Presentation. The School District of Escambia County, Pensacola, FL, 1989.

Vocabulary and Surrounding Context

When authors use unfamiliar vocabulary, it is not always possible for readers to determine the meaning directly from context. Hittleman (1978) suggests that the best strategy in such cases is to formulate a hypothesis about what the word might mean and then test that hypothesis against the other occurrences of the word in the text. To do so, readers must be aware of structural devices authors use to signal meaning. According to Deighton (1959) and Hittleman (1978), writers generally use five types of signals:

1. *Definition.* They may use sentence forms like "X is (or "is called") Y." These sentences communicate an explicit definition of the word.

   An iconoclast is a person who deliberately breaks other people's traditions.
   A person who deliberately breaks traditions is called an iconoclast.

2. *Example.* When examples are given of an idea explained by an unknown word, we may be able to figure out the word if we recognize the example. Sentences so constructed often use words or phrases like *for example, such as, like,* and *especially.*

   Venomous snakes, such as the rattlesnake, the copperhead, or the coral snake, are to be avoided.

3. *Modifiers.* Even when a word is not known, the modifiers used to describe it may give an indication of what it is. Modifiers may be relative clauses as well as adjectives or adverbs.

   The minaret that the Moslems built stood tall, slender, and graceful above the other buildings in the town.

4. *Restatement.* Sentences sometimes state the unknown idea a second time using other, more familiar words. One such device is an appositive, a group of words following the word defined and set off by commas or dashes. Restatement is also done by using key words or phrases like *or, that is,* and *in other words.*

   Chauvinism, an aggressive loyalty to one's own group at the expense of others, originally applied to national patriotism only.
   They fired the attendant because of her indolence; in other words, she was lazy.

5. *Inference.* Following are several grammatical patterns writers employ that signal the meaning of unknown words:
   a. *Parallel sentence structure.* When series are used either in the same sentence or in groups of sentences, we can often get an idea of the nature of an unknown word by recognizing a known word in the series.

Each office contained some type of medical specialist. In one was a family practitioner; in another, an obstetrician; in another, a radiologist; and in another, a hematologist.

b. *Repetition of key words.* Sometimes, if an unknown word is of sufficient importance in a passage, the author will repeat it enough times in enough different contexts for its meaning to be figured out.

It is sometimes said that only primitive people have taboos. This is not necessarily so. Even advanced cultures like ours have them. In America, for example, it is taboo to speak directly about death, or about a grown person's age, weight, or income.

c. *Familiar connectives.* Some familiar connectives, especially subordinating or coordinating conjunctions, show us the relationship between ideas and thus allow us to associate an unknown idea with a known one.

John was very excited about the award, but Judith seemed indifferent.

The devices for identifying meanings in context can be taught. If they are clearly introduced, well practiced, and returned to often, they can become a valuable addition to a readers's strategies for dealing with difficult material. Assessing vocabulary in context should include exercises that deliberately test familiarity with and sensitivity to these contextual clues to word meaning.

SUMMARY

In this chapter we presented strategies for enhancing older readers' literacy skills. These strategies are appropriate for students who are faced with texts that contain unfamiliar structures and content. Our strategies cover four areas: monitoring comprehension, understanding text structures, developing and using prior knowledge, and developing vocabulary knowledge.

Regardless of the strategy, in order to increase its effectiveness and the likelihood that students will use the strategy, it should be modeled and taught directly and systematically. Students should have opportunities to practice strategies and receive feedback.

References

Allington, Richard, and Anne McGill-Franzen. *A Study of the Whole-School Day Experience of Chapter I and Mainstreamed LD Students.* Final Report of Grant #G008630480, Office of Special Education Programs. Washington, D.C.: U.S. Department of Education, 1987.

Brown, Ann L., Annemarie Sullivan Palincsar, and Bonnie Armbruster. "Instructing Comprehension-Fostering Activities in Interactive Learning Situations." In *Learning and Comprehension of Text*, ed. Heinz Mandl. Hillsdale, NJ: Lawrence Erlbaum Associates, 1984.

Chall, Jeanne. "The Great Debate: Ten Years Later, with a Modest Proposal for Reading Stages." In *Theory and Practice of Early Reading*, Vol.1. eds. Lauren Resnick and Phyllis Weaver. Hillsdale, NJ: Lawrence Erlbaum Associates, 1979.

Deighton, Lee. *Vocabulary Development in the Classroom*. New York: Teachers College Press, Columbia University, 1959.

Duffy, Gerald G., Laura R. Roehler, and Beth Ann Herrmann. "Modeling Mental Processes Helps Poor Readers Become Strategic Readers." *The Reading Teacher* 41, no. 8 (April 1988): 762–767.

Estes, Thomas H., and Wayne Shibilski. "Comprehension: Of What the Reader Sees of What the Author Says." In *Perspectives on Reading Research and Instruction*, eds. Michael L. Kamil and Alden J. Moe. Washington, D.C.: National Reading Conference, 1980.

Gaskins, Robert W. "The Missing Ingredients: Time on Task, Direct Instruction, and Writing." *The Reading Teacher* 41, no. 8 (April 1988): 750–755.

Hittleman, Daniel R. *Developmental Reading: A Psycholinguistic Perspective*. Chicago: Rand McNally, 1978.

Linton, Nettie. "Reciprocal Teaching: An Update." Inservice Presentation. The School District of Escambia County, Pensacola, FL, 1989.

Marshall, Nancy, and Marvin Glock. "Comprehension of Connected Discourse: A Study into the Relationships Between the Structure of Text and Information Recalled." *Reading Research Quarterly* 14, no. 1 (1978–1979): 10–56.

Mathews, Samuel, Josephine Peyton Young and Nancy Dean Giles. *Student Literacy Volunteers: Providing Tools for Brighter Futures*. Pensacola, FL: The Educational Research and Development Center, The University of West Florida, 1992.

Nolen, Dorothy. "The Current View of Teaching Comprehension." Inservice Presentation. The School District of Escambia County, Pensacola, FL, 1989.

Pearson, P. David. "Changing the Face of Reading Comprehension Instruction." *The Reading Teacher* 38, no. 8 (April 1985): 724–738.

Perkins, Jocelyn. "Integrating in the Content Areas." Paper presented at the International Reading Association Conference, Atlanta, GA, May, 1990.

Rakes, Thomas A. "A Group Instructional Inventory." *Journal of Reading* 18, no. 5 (May 1975): 595-598.

Santa, Carol, Maureen Danner, Marylin Nelson, Lynn Havens, Jim Scalf, and Lynn Scalf. *Content Reading in Secondary Schools*. School District No. 5, Kallispell, MT, 1985.

Upton, Albert. *Design for Thinking: A First Book on Semantics*. Palo Alto: Pacific Press, 1973.

Vacca, Richard, and Joanne Vacca. *Content Area Reading*, 3d ed. Glenview, IL: Scott, Foresman, 1989.

Wisconsin Department of Public Instruction. *Strategic Learning in the Content Area*. Madison, WI, 1989.

Formal Measures of Reading Ability

I n Chapters 4 and 5 we discussed informal assessment of reading. This chapter is devoted to formal measures of reading. Two principal types of formal measures are norm-referenced, standardized tests and criterion-referenced tests. Most students encounter these formal measures in the form of SAT or ACT college entrance examinations, group achievement tests administered during the school year in elementary and secondary grades, and the Graduate Record Examination taken to complete application to graduate school. The results of formal assessments of reading are often used to assess school, district, or state reading programs; identify individual strengths and weaknesses within a curriculum; and compare achievement patterns of schools, districts, and states.

This chapter will provide you with information which will help in determining the appropriateness of formal assessments for particular uses and interpreting their results. Our goal is to help you to make accurate responses to parent questions and determine whether a particular test should be used to assess individual students' scores. In order to use and interpret test scores, teachers must be knowledgeable about characteristics of tests in general and any peculiarities of specific tests. Without this knowledge, interpretations may be difficult at best and inaccurate at worst.

CHARACTERISTICS OF TESTS

When we select a tool to do a job, we typically have an idea about the nature of the job, the level of skill we possess, and the tools we have available. The same is true for selecting a formal measure of reading. When that selection is made, we, or those who do the selection, should know what we want to do with the results, the level of skill or support we have in administering and interpreting the test, and the options available for selecting a test. Most districts have selected one test or a small group of tests which will be purchased and administered to its students.

One way to think about the characteristics of a test is to begin with the idea that the quality of the tool selected to do a certain job is directly related to the quality of the outcome of the job. For reading tests, and tests in general, there are two qualities which are critical to the performance of a test. Those qualities are *reliability* and *validity*.

Reliability

Reliability is a measure of how stable test scores are. It refers to the results obtained from a test, not to the test itself. There are several aspects of reliability to be considered. One is *stability*, or the consistency of test scores across time, from one administration to another with the same group of subjects. Another is *internal consistency*, or the consistency of items within a test. A third is *equivalence*, or consistency across different forms of the same test.

Stability

If a group of students took Test 1 several times, each individual's score would be somewhat different each time. If the scores are consistent, or reliable, the students' *rank order* would remain very similar from one testing to another. Therefore, the student with the highest score the first time would have the highest, or nearly the highest, score the second time; the student with the lowest score would retain very low standing, and the order of students between highest and lowest would remain nearly unchanged. If stability is lacking, a score attained once is unrelated to the score attained another time. Obviously, such scores would have little meaning or usefulness, because they would be heavily affected by random chance.

Stability is estimated using the *test-retest method*. The same test is given twice to the same group of subjects, and the rank order of their scores on each one is compared. If the interval between administrations is fairly short, students will remember a number of items and will be familiar with the format. This method will tend to raise everyone's scores, but the rank order of the scores will remain much the same. The rank order of the scores, not the numerical value of the scores themselves, is what is important here. If the interval between administrations is very long, maturation and the acquiring of new information will affect performance.

Internal Consistency

Internal consistency refers to the degree to which items within a test are related. We can determine internal consistency by comparing a student's performance on an entire test to her or his performance on two halves of the same test administered separately, but since the more difficult items often come toward the end, it would not be a good practice to split a test at the middle. Instead, alternate items should be selected: one-half with all the odd-numbered items, the other half with all the even-numbered items. If the scores on each half are closely related, a measure of good internal consistency has been provided. If performance on the two halves is not closely related, the total test score will not be reliable, and its value is questionable.

Sometimes internal consistency is estimated by the *split-half method* in which students take the two halves of a test as separate tests. The scores on each half are correlated, and an arithmetic formula is applied to relate the correlation to the entire test. Other ways of estimating internal consistency involve giving the whole test once and applying one of several arithmetic formulas to the total score. The computations are beyond the scope of this discussion, but you will find detailed information in almost any text on tests and measurement methods.

Equivalence

When alternate forms of a test are being used, equivalence is important. Many standardized reading tests feature alternative forms that are used for pre- and posttesting, but they must be highly equivalent for the scores to have any usefulness.

The *equivalent forms method* is used to estimate this aspect of reliability. It requires the construction of two different tests, each one an equally good sampling of the content being tested. Each form must also be equivalent in difficulty and length. The two forms are administered to the same students in close succession, and the scores on the two forms are correlated. This method usually yields the most conservative estimate of reliability.

Every standardized reading test being considered for use should have reported reliability estimates, and it should indicate what methods were used to determine such estimates. Reliability can be expressed in numerical terms by a *reliability coefficient*. This coefficient, a decimal number between zero and one, shows how consistent the scores were after using the test-retest, split-halves, or equivalent forms assessments. The closer to 1.0 the reliability coefficient is, the more reliable the scores.

Overall reliability can be profoundly affected, for good or bad, by the consistency of individual subtests. Survey reading tests, generally used for screening large numbers of students, usually have few subtests, and the expressed reliability coefficients refer to the test as a whole. Quite a few reading achievement tests and most standardized reading diagnostic tests, however, have many separate subtests, and the reliability of subtest scores can vary widely. These tests should have reported subtest reliabilities as well as a coefficient for the entire test, and scores on subtests of questionable reliability must be discounted. If a test under consideration has more than one or two subtests of low reliability, another one should be considered.

A final point about judging reliability concerns the *standard error of measurement.* This term does not mean there are mistakes in the test; it refers to the fact that no score is absolutely precise. The standard error of measurement (SE) is a number that indicates how much an individual's score might have varied depending on random chance factors. The standard error shows numerically how accurate any score is likely to be. A small standard error indicates high reliability, because we can be fairly confident that the student's test score and the true score closely approximate each other.

Validity

High reliability is necessary, but not sufficient, for a test to be a good one. A test can yield consistent scores but still not truly measure what was intended to be measured. This quality of actually measuring what was supposed to be measured is referred to as *test validity*. There are several types of validity that are often referred to in test reviews and manuals, and teachers should understand how validity is developed in test evaluation. While reliability is quantitatively estimated, validity involves qualitative judgments as well.

Content Validity

In assessing content validity, we ask if the test is an adequate sample of the content area or process being tested. Content validity is particularly important in achievement tests, which are designed to show subject mastery. An elementary spelling achievement test with only very long, difficult, infrequently used words from college texts would lack content validity because it does not represent what elementary children study in spelling. Content validity is established when test makers study both school curricula and tests and submit their tests to the scrutiny of subject area experts. Some authorities claim, however, that many reading achievement tests lack content validity because they measure only a narrow range of real reading behaviors.

Criterion-Related Validity

Another way of establishing a test's validity is to relate it to other validated measures of the same ability or knowledge. The predetermined *criterion* may be other test scores, grades or subject area performance, or other observable behaviors. A test has criterion-related validity if it calls for responses that relate closely to actual performance. Concurrent and predictive validity are criterion-related.

When a new test is found to be highly correlated to an existing test of established validity, it is said to have *concurrent validity*. Coefficients of concurrent validity are frequently reported by test makers. Just because two tests are closely related is no guarantee that either one is valid, only that they measure the same attribute.

When a score is found to be closely related to later performance on some criterion, the test is said to have *predictive validity*. This aspect is critically important in aptitude tests, since they purport to determine whether someone has the potential to become skilled in a particular field at a later time. If students who do well on a test of mechanical aptitude later excel in school courses like "shop" and drafting and then go on to college engineering and technical schools or seek careers as engineers, architects, and machinists, that test is a good predictor of mechanical aptitude. The Scholastic Aptitude Test (SAT), used to predict the potential of high-school students for college studies, is believed to be high in predictive validity because SAT scores and subsequent college grade-point averages are closely related.

Construct Validity

Human traits or qualities that are not directly observable or measurable, but which are widely inferred from behaviors, are called *constructs*. Running speed or hand width are directly observable or measurable entities. Traits like attitudes, intelligence, or aptitudes are not directly measurable and must be inferred from observable behaviors. Thus intelligence, musical or mechanical aptitude, judgment, problem solving, attitudes, and interests are constructs.

If a test has good construct validity, it allows the students to demonstrate behaviors directly related to the construct. In a test of attitudes toward reading, for example, students should be able to show how positively or negatively they would feel about getting a book for a gift, hearing a book discussed, going to the library or bookstore, or seeing someone vandalizing a book. Construct validity is important in all tests, but it is critical in psychological and personality tests and attitude inventories.

INTERPRETING TEST RESULTS

Once a reliable and valid test is selected and administered, the tests are scored and the results reported to various interested groups (e.g. teachers, administrators, parents, governmental officials, media). There are three types of information which describe test results. These are

1. the distribution of test scores;
2. measures of central tendency; and
3. measures of dispersion.

Distributions of Test Scores

Descriptions of the *distribution* of test scores provide visual representations and other indicators of a group's performance on a given test. There are two dimensions typically used to describe the distribution of test scores. One is the score on the test itself and the other is the number of students obtaining a particular score. Most of us are probably familiar with the *bell-shaped curve* or the *normal distribution* (see Figure 9.1). In this distribution, more students scored in the average range than in either the high or low ranges.

Not all distributions are normal. Instead of most of the scores clustering in the middle, a test may yield a distribution with many very high or very low scores. This is called a *skewed distribution;* it is asymmetrical (see Figure 9.2). If most people get high scores, with few average or low scores, the distribution would be negatively skewed. Likewise, a test yielding many low and few average or high scores is positively skewed. So, the shape of the distribution of scores for a class, school, or district graphically represents the overall performance of a group or groups of students.

Compare the distribution of scores in Figure 9.1 to the distribution of the positively skewed scores in Figure 9.2. At least on the surface, the two sets of scores are distributed differently for different groups of students who completed the test. There are several possible explanations for this difference. One

Figure 9.1

Normal Distribution

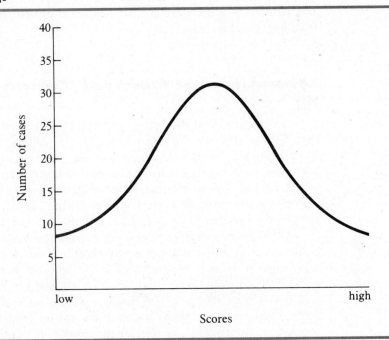

Figure 9.2

Skewed Distributions

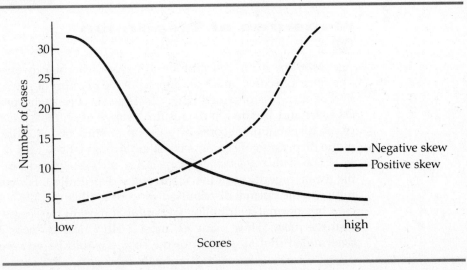

is that for the positively skewed distribution, the test may not have measured the construct which had been the object of instruction. Given the scores, it is likely that the test was too difficult for that particular group of students. Distributions which are highly skewed should be viewed with caution (Kubiszyn and Borich, 1990).

Measures of Central Tendency

Scores are most often thought of in relation to where they lie on some distribution. The most common measure of central tendency is the *mean*, or the arithmetic average. Averages are used, for example, by some teachers in assigning report card grades; a student who got math test scores of 67, 89, 73, 66, 92, and 80 had an average score of 78, which is represented by a grade of, say, C+. A mean score is derived by adding all the scores and dividing the sum by the number of scores added together.

Other measures of central tendency are the *median* and *mode*. The median is the point in a distribution where there are equal numbers of scores above and below it. If four students took a spelling test and got scores of 14, 15, 16, and 17, the median score would be 15.5, since there are two scores below 15.5 and two scores above it. The mode represents the most frequently obtained score. In general, the closer together the mean, median, and mode of a set of scores are, the more symmetrical the distribution will be. If they are widely dissimilar, the distribution will be asymmetrical.

When the media report on test scores or school achievement, they most often refer to "averages" or mean test scores of a school or school district derived from standardized tests or the Scholastic Aptitude Test.

Measures of Dispersion

Measures of dispersion of a set of scores can be expressed in several ways. The *range* of scores on a test represents the breadth of performance by a group of students. It is obtained when the lowest score is subtracted from the highest score and 1 added to the result. A range of scores is only a gross indication of the dispersion of scores by a group of students. A more common measure of the dispersion of scores is the standard deviation (Ebel & Frisbie, 1991).

The *standard deviation* is an index of how spread out scores are around the mean, regardless of the shape of the distribution. For convenience, we will return to the normal distribution concept to illustrate the standard deviation.

In a normal distribution we said that most of the scores would be grouped near the mean. How many is "most"? How near is "near"? Statisticians have determined that 68 percent of the scores would be arrayed around or at the

Figure 9.3

Percentages of Scores within Standard Deviation (SD) Units

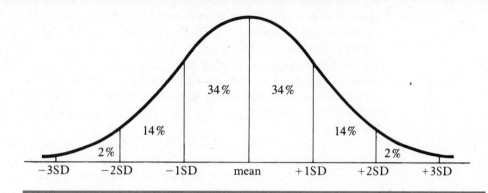

mean, with smaller percentages near the extremes, as in Figure 9.3.

If a student's score was 1SD below the mean, we would know where the score lay on the distribution; we would know that the student did as well or better than 16 percent of the norm group but that 84 percent did better. The range around the mean, from –1SD to +1SD, is considered the average range. A score of –1SD would be at the bottom of the average range.

The concepts of mean and standard deviation are integral to understanding how most scores such as those described below are reported.

Forms of Test Scores

When formal assessment instruments are administered, scored, and returned to the teacher for interpretation, the scores are often reported in several different forms. While each of the forms of test scores are based on an individual student's performance, the final form of the score can vary depending upon the computations performed upon the raw score. The *raw score* shows simply how many items the student got right on the test or on each subtest. Interpreting a raw score directly may be misleading, so raw scores are converted to more easily comparable forms. The most frequently encountered forms of test scores include: *grade equivalents; percentile; stanines; Normal Curve Equivalents; T-scores;* and *z-scores.*

Grade-equivalent scores, often called simply *grade scores,* are frequently used in reporting reading test scores. They represent a level of achievement considered average for a particular grade and month of school within that grade. Grade scores are expressed in two-part numbers; the first number indicates the grade level, and the second number indicates the month within that grade. A grade score of 3.1, for example, stands for the first month, September, of third grade.

Grade scores imply that there is some objective, generally accepted standard of achievement for every month of each school grade. In reality, no such agreement exists on what skills or competencies should be attained by all, or most, readers at any given point. Such expectations are too heavily influenced by local standards, curricular goals, scope and sequences of skills within commercial programs, and learner characteristics for there to be any one standard of achievement. Grade scores are often considered and interpreted to parents, however, as though there *were* such objective standards. Thus, they are often overinterpreted.

Percentiles, another common form of score, are more easily understood than grade scores. Percentiles range from 1 to 99; wherever a score lies within this range indicates relative performance compared with the norm group. A score at the tenth percentile means the student did as well or better than 10 percent but worse than 89 percent of the students in the norm group. A score at the ninety-eighth percentile means that the student did as well or better than 98 percent of the norm group and that only 1 percent attained higher scores. Sometimes percentile scores are misinterpreted by parents who believe the score represents the number of items correctly answered. Such a parent, whose child scored at the fiftieth percentile, would judge that the child had gotten only 50 percent of the items right, instead of correctly viewing the score as average.

Other forms of scores take the distribution of scores of the norm group into account and provide comparable units across the range of scores. These are *standardized* scores which include *stanines, NCEs, T-scores,* and *z-scores* (Thorndike, Cunningham, Thorndike, & Hagen, 1991).

Stanines are similar to percentiles. The term is derived from "standard nines," which means that the distribution of possible scores had been divided into nine parts. Stanine scores range from one to nine, five is the mean, and scores from just below four to just above six are considered average, with one to three below average and seven to nine above average.

Normal Curve Equivalents (NCEs) are derived from the average and standard deviation of a set of scores. They range from 1–99 with a mean of 50. NCEs have become more common since they are used in the evaluation of Chapter I reading and math programs.

T-scores and *z-scores* are fairly common standard scores. Like NCEs and stanine scores, the *T-* and *z*-scores are based on the standard deviation. The *T*-scores range from 20 to 80, with a mean of 50. These values are computed from the standard deviations and indicate how close to the mean of the normal distribution a particular score lies. The *z*-score is based more directly on the standard deviation, with a mean of 0 and a standard deviation of 1. Scores ranging from -1.0 through 1.0 are considered average. The range for *z*-scores is based on the number of standard deviations in the distribution of scores. If

Figure 9.3 represented the distribution of scores on a particular test, the z-score range would be from –3.0 to +3.0.

The decision about the way scores will be reported is often made at the school district level. Most reports include a grade equivalent and percentile, and an increasing number now include one of the standardized scores (stanine, NCE, *T*-score, or *z*-score). As a teacher, the selection of which information to use in conferences with parents will depend on which scores are available to you, your own knowledge of each form of test score, and the type of information you wish to convey. Grade equivalent scores are easy for parents to understand, but percentiles and stanines are probably more accurate and representative if they are properly explained.

During parent conferences, teachers' interpretations of formal measures of reading are critical. Figure 9.4 provides a sample student profile report from the California Achievement Tests. Figure 9.5 is a transcript of a parent-teacher conference in which the test results are discussed. The questions asked by the parent are like those encountered by many teachers. The goal of conferences like this one should be to share information for more valid instructional decisions.

NORM-REFERENCED TESTS

Norm-referenced tests are developed by publishers who administer them to large numbers of students in order to develop *norms.* The norms represent average performances of many students in various age, grade, and demographic groups, and are used to compare the performance of individuals or special groups to the performance of those in the norm group.

Most test makers go to great lengths to include students from various geographic areas, urban and rural communities, racial and ethnic groups, and economic groups. Many tests feature several different sets of norms for local groups that are unlike "national averages"—for example, center-city schools, rural populations, high-achieving gifted populations, highly affluent areas, and the like.

Regardless of the type of test, the form of score, or the quality of the test, formal assessment of reading is but a single indication of a student's performance. Scores on norm-referenced standardized tests must be combined with other, more qualitative information, to make the most valid instructional decision for a given student. Norm-referenced tests serve two general purposes. Many norm-referenced tests are designed to measure achievement or past learnings. These achievement tests vary in the scope of topics covered and the detail with which students' results are reported. Tests that assess specific knowledge and strategies associated with reading provide a range of difficulty which begins at a lower level. These tests, designed to show growth in these areas, are considered to be diagnostic tests.

Figure 9.4

Sample Student Profile

CAT CALIFORNIA ACHIEVEMENT TESTS, FORMS E&F

STUDENT PROFILE REPORT

STUDENT:
BIRTH DATE: 04/09/77

AGE: 13– 0
SPECIAL CODES:

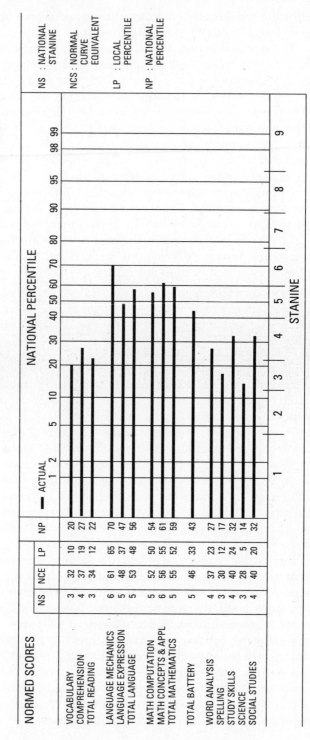

NORMED SCORES	NS	NCE	LP	NP
VOCABULARY	3	32	10	20
COMPREHENSION	4	37	19	27
TOTAL READING	3	34	12	22
LANGUAGE MECHANICS	6	61	65	70
LANGUAGE EXPRESSION	5	48	37	47
TOTAL LANGUAGE	5	53	48	56
MATH COMPUTATION	5	52	50	54
MATH CONCEPTS & APPL	6	56	55	61
TOTAL MATHEMATICS	5	55	52	59
TOTAL BATTERY	5	46	33	43
WORD ANALYSIS	4	37	23	27
SPELLING	3	30	12	17
STUDY SKILLS	4	40	24	32
SCIENCE	3	28	5	14
SOCIAL STUDIES	4	40	20	32

NS : NATIONAL STANINE

NCS : NORMAL CURVE EQUIVALENT

LP : LOCAL PERCENTILE

NP : NATIONAL PERCENTILE

NARRATIVE REPORT

THIS STUDENT'S TEST PERFORMANCE MAY BE COMPARED WITH THAT OF THE NATIONAL NORMS GROUP AT THE SAME GRADE LEVEL BY REFERRING TO THE NATIONAL PERCENTILE SCORES ABOVE. ACHIEVEMENT IN THE BASIC SKILLS IS BEST SUMMARIZED BY THE "TOTAL" SCORES. THE STUDENT'S TOTAL SCORE IS BELOW THE NATIONAL AVERAGE (THE 50TH PERCENTILE). IN TOTAL READING, THE STUDENT'S ACHIEVEMENT IS BETTER THAN APPROXIMATELY 22% OF THE NATIONAL NORM GROUP; IN TOTAL LANGUAGE, BETTER THAN APPROXIMATELY 56%; IN TOTAL MATHEMATICS, BETTER THAN APPROXIMATELY 59%.

SPECIAL SCORES

READING	MATHEMATICS	HIGHER ORDER THINKING SKILLS

N = Not Mastered   P = Partial Knowledge   M = Mastered

SKILLS SCORES

VOCABULARY
24 SYNONYMS
25 ANTONYMS
26 HOMONYMS
27 AFFIXES
28 WORDS IN CONTEXT

COMPREHENSION
32 PASSAGE DETAILS
35 CHARACTER ANALYSIS
36 CENTRAL THOUGHT
37 INTERPRETING EVENTS
38 FORMS OF WRITING
39 WRITING TECHNIQUES

LANGUAGE MECHANICS
43 PRONOUN I, NOUN, ADJECT
44 BEGINNING WORDS, TITLES
45 PERIOD, QUEST, EXCLAM
46 COMMA, COLON, SEMI, QUOT
47 PROOFREADING

LANGUAGE EXPRESSION
48 NOUNS
49 PRONOUNS
50 VERBS
51 ADJECTIVES, ADVERBS
53 SENTENCE PATTERNS
54 SENTENCE RECOGNITION
56 SENTENCE COMBINING
57 TOPIC SENTENCE
58 SENTENCE SEQUENCE

MATH COMPUTATION
61 ADD FRACTIONS
64 SUBTRACT FRACTIONS
65 MULTIPLY WHOLE NUMBERS
66 MULTIPLY DECIMALS
67 MULTIPLY FRACTIONS
68 DIVIDE WHOLE NUMBERS
69 DIVIDE DECIMALS
70 DIVIDE FRACTIONS

MATH CONCEPTS & APPL
73 NUMERATION
74 NUMBER SENTENCES
75 NUMBER THEORY
76 PROBLEM SOLVING
77 MEASUREMENT
78 GEOMETRY

WORD ANALYSIS
09 CONSONANT DIGRAPHS
10 VARIANT CONSONANTS
15 DIPHTH, VARIANT VOWELS
18 ROOT WORDS, AFFIXES

SPELLING
40 VOWEL SOUNDS
41 CONSONANT SOUNDS
42 STRUCTURAL UNITS

STUDY SKILLS
79 BOOK PARTS
80 DICTIONARY SKILLS
81 LIBRARY SKILLS
82 GRAPHIC INFORMATION
83 STUDY TECHNIQUES

SCIENCE
84 BOTANY
85 ZOOLOGY
86 ECOLOGY
87 PHYSICS
88 CHEMISTRY
89 LAND, SEA, SPACE

SOCIAL STUDIES
90 GEOGRAPHY
91 ECONOMICS
92 HISTORY
93 POLITICAL SCIENCE
94 SOCIOLOGY
95 INTERDISCIPLINARY

CLASS:
SCHOOL:
DISTRICT:

CITY/STATE:
FORM/LEVEL:
GRADE:

NORMS FROM:
TEST DATE:
QTR MTH:

RD:
CTBID:

Source: Reproduced by the permission of the publisher, CTB Macmillan/McGraw-Hill, 20 Ryan Ranch Road, Monterey, California 93940–5703.

Copyright © 1992 by Macmillan/McGraw-Hill School Publishing Company. All rights reserved.

Note: Content is accurate per original form. Columns on page 353 only have been changed from four to three to fit the configurations of this text.

Figure 9.5

Parent-Teacher Conference on Test Results

Parent:	I'm worried about the reading scores on the test Dana took last month. They seem so low! What does this mean?
Reading Teacher:	Our district uses these tests for a couple of reasons. First, they are used to determine how our county stacks up when compared to other school districts. The other way we use the results of these tests is to provide a general indication of how individual students are doing when compared to others similar to themselves. There are two sections of the Report. The first section includes *Normed Scores.* They reflect how Dana did when compared to other sixth-grade students. The first two scores, the *National Stanine* and the *Normal Curve Equivalent,* indicate that Dana performed below the average of other sixth-graders. The other two scores, the *Local Percentile* and the *National Percentile,* show within our district and across the nation, how many students performed below Dana on the test. As you can see, Dana performed better than 12 percent of her peers locally, and 22 percent of her peers nationally on the total reading battery.
Parent:	So Dana is really having problems in reading and it looks like she is doing poorly overall. She only got a 10 in vocabulary.
Reading Teacher:	Well, Dana did appear to have difficulty with the test. The score of 10 on vocabulary really means that 10 percent of the sixth graders in our district scored below her on that part of the test. The total reading score matches what I have seen in her classwork. She is in the bottom half of the class in reading. In addition to her classwork, I feel the test is accurate because of her difficulty in other areas such as study skills, science, social studies, word analysis, and spelling.
Parent:	I don't understand how Dana did so poorly on the test. She has passed or mastered more items than she has not mastered.
Reading Teacher:	The skills scores indicate whether Dana *m*astered, *p*assed, or has *n*ot mastered each skill. In this section we must use care when we draw conclusions since each skill is probably only evaluated with a few questions. Remember, the scores in the Normed-Score section are based on a comparison of Dana's performance with that of other sixth-graders'. This means that more of Dana's peers scored above her than below her.
Parent:	So, what do we do now?
Reading Teacher:	I'd suggest a conference with all her teachers. We may be able to identify some strategies for handling many of the areas in question. Her class work could be improved. Let's get together with Dana's other teachers and develop an instructional plan.

Achievement Tests

Achievement tests are designed to measure the current level of learners' performance in a variety of areas. Many achievement tests are actually *batteries* of subtests representing different content or skill areas such as language arts, mathematics, science, and social studies. Tests which provide only a general performance score in each area are often called *survey tests*. Although survey tests can be helpful in pointing to areas in need of additional assessment, very little detailed information can be obtained.

Other achievement tests provide more detailed information within each subject area. These tests can often aid teachers, schools, and school districts in assessing the overall impact of their curricula.

Achievement tests are designed to show the depth of one's knowledge and mastery of subject-area curricula. Because they are designed to assess mastery, or achievement, they are usually administered *after* the appropriate instruction has been given. Tests used for diagnostic purposes are often given *before* a program of instruction, or early on, to reveal strengths and so that instruction can be modified appropriately. Diagnostic and survey tests are usually given "before the fact"; achievement tests "after the fact." Their content is sometimes very similar, but the purpose and timing of the testing differ.

Standardized achievement tests are probably the most common type of formal tests used in schools. Most students take a standardized achievement test of some kind yearly, often a battery covering the major curricular areas. Because subtests are usually given in separate sittings, completion of a battery can take several days or a week. Achievement tests must be given under strictly standard conditions in order for results to be compared across groups, so sometimes a team of school personnel administers all the tests, and sometimes the regular daily schedule is suspended so that all students can be tested simultaneously. The tests are machine-scored by the publishers, and results are sent back to the school.

Almost all achievement tests are group tests and should be used to evaluate groups of students, not individuals. For this reason, they are of very limited diagnostic use. They are useful for evaluating the progress of large groups like whole schools, or all the students from one grade.

Publishers attempt to make the content of their achievement tests represent typical school curricula. A math test, for example, will generally be made up of problems and calculations common to most school math programs for a particular grade. What is "typical" is decided by consulting subject-area experts, by studying textbooks and materials in wide use, and by field-testing experimental test forms. Content validity, or how well a test represents the major aspects of the subject area, is of particular importance, but how closely the curriculum of an individual district, school, or classroom coincides with national trends is difficult to say. Achievement tests in any subject area should be carefully evaluated to see how well their content matches the local programs and materials in use.

Most of the widely used achievement batteries measure reading, language (English), science, math, and social studies. Most have forms for every grade from early elementary through high school, although some school districts do not begin using them until third or fourth grade. Some batteries have reading readiness tests for kindergarten and first grade.

Among the typical wide-ranging achievement batteries are the following: The Metropolitan Achievement Test, with vocabulary, reading, language, spelling, writing, science, math, and social studies subtests and a separate diagnostic battery; the Comprehensive Test of Basic Skills, with readiness, reading, spelling, language, math, social studies, science, and study skills subtests; the Stanford Achievement Test, with reading, language, study skills, math, science, social sciences, listening, using information, and thinking skills subtests; and the California Achievement Test, with reading, spelling, language, math, and study skills subtests and optional science and social studies subtests. All those mentioned, except the Stanford, are designed for kindergarten through grade twelve; the Stanford is for grades one through nine.

There are a few reading achievement tests for individual administration. Two examples are the Peabody Individual Achievement Test–Revised (PIAT–R) and the Wide Range Achievement Test–Revised (WRAT–R). These instruments are hybrids that have characteristics of both group achievement tests and individual survey tests. They are most often used like individual survey or diagnostic tests.

The PIAT–R contains reading recognition, reading comprehension, spelling, math, and general information subtests. Because it includes math as well as various reading skills and general information, the PIAT–R measures mastery of the largest part of typical elementary curricula. The WRAT–R has reading, spelling, and arithmetic subtests. Like the PIAT–R, it covers the areas most heavily concentrated on in elementary school. Both tests are often given as diagnostic screening devices to students experiencing difficulty in either reading or math or to those with generally poor school achievement. Like other achievement tests, the results they yield are solely quantitative, and they have little, if any, diagnostic value.

The PIAT–R, for kindergarten through twelfth grade, has two sections. Reading Recognition includes 16 multiple-choice questions requiring students to identify and match letters and words to the given stimulus. Students are also given 84 words in isolation to pronounce. Figure 9.6 (on page 358) shows items from this subtest. The comprehension subtest requires silent reading of one or several sentences and then matching pictures to the text. Pictures are in a multiple-choice format, and written sentences cannot be referred to by the student. At the upper levels, the comprehension sentences are extremely complex, and words are highly unusual.

The WRAT–R, often used in screening students for special education programs, is designed for ages five through adulthood. The reading portion of the WRAT–R is made up entirely of lists of single words. Pronunciation within 10 seconds is the only criterion. It does not measure comprehension of either text or words, and no reading of connected text is included. Consequently, it does not measure real reading at all. If the test makers do not include comprehension in their view of reading, they should at least acknowledge what the test does *not* do. Far from doing that, the manual states that the test allows for accurate diagnosis of reading disabilities and placement of students in instructional groups, all without reading of words in sentences! We believe that these claims and the content validity of the reading subtest are doubtful.

Advantages

First, like other group tests, group achievement measures offer schools a reliable, uncomplicated way to gather information on large numbers of students. Second, a maximum of data can be gathered in a minimum of time. If the batteries include a number of subjects, many curricular areas and processes can be assessed at one time. Third, if properly administered and scored, they yield potentially informative data on the progress of groups of students, such as the total population of a given grade. When patterns of progress or lack of progress are discerned, curricular changes at the school and district levels can take place. Fourth, these tests are usually extensively field-tested and standardized with great precision. Norming and validating achievement batteries is a big and complex business, and since millions are taken yearly, test manufacturers try to make them as reliable and valid as they can.

Disadvantages

Standardized reading achievement tests are not designed to give diagnostic data, so they cannot be criticized for not doing so, but if used for their proper purposes, they can be effective measures of prior learning. There are some cautions, however, that should be kept in mind.

First, administration procedures must be followed to the letter. Students should take these tests in their regular classrooms rather than in huge groups in the cafeteria or gym, as sometimes happens. Second, as with diagnostic reading tests, subtests are sometimes quite short, and their reliability coefficients may be low because of this and other factors. Third, the time and cost involved sometimes contribute to gross overinterpretation of their scores. Retention of students because of scores on a single achievement battery or public humiliation of school groups and personnel because of score comparisons are clear abuses of test scores, yet such abuses do occur. Fourth, achievement tests tend to call upon recall of factual material rather than higher-level thinking skills. Factual learning and recall are among the easiest processes to measure, but they do not represent all learning or achievement. We must not lose sight of the many additional aspects in reading and other subject areas, such as learning rate, interest, or creative thinking, which achievement tests do not typically measure.

Figure 9.6

PIAT–R Reading Recognition Sample Items

REGULAR MULTIPLE CHOICE ITEMS

DIRECTIONS

Examiner's side:

Point in a sweeping motion across each of the rows from the subject's left to right. Say: **This page has rows of words on it. Read each of the words aloud, going across the rows this way. As you finish each row, go on to the next.**
Point to the subject's starting item.
Say: **Start here and read each word to me. Give me a pronunciation you would expect to find in a dictionary.**

TWO READINESS ITEMS
Point to "GO" in the stimulus area.
Say: **Find one like this down here.**
Point in a sweeping motion to the response area.
Say: **Point to it.**

GO

UP	GS
GO `	BO

Point to the train in the stimulus area.
Say: **This is a picture of a train.**
Point in a sweeping motion to the response area.
Say: **Which of these words begins with the same sound as this picture?**
Point to the word that begins with the same sound.

(train picture)

top	truck
brook `	rain

INTRODUCING THE READING RECOGNITION SUBTEST
• For subjects starting with the Training Exercises, say: **Now I want to see how well you read. First let's practice a little so you will know what I want you to do.**
Turn to the next page and begin with Training Exercise A. (*Note:* Part II of the manual contains instructions on the use of the Training Exercises.)

Gilmore, testing is discontinued when a ceiling number of word recognition errors occur, even if comprehension continues to be adequate.

A number of individual diagnostic tests resemble informal reading inventories, with silent and oral passage reading followed by comprehension questions. They differ from informal reading inventories in that they are norm-referenced. The Durrell Analysis of Reading Difficulty, Third Edition, and the Diagnostic Reading Scales–Revised are examples of these. As in a typical IRI, these tests assess sight vocabulary recognition, word analysis in isolation and in context, and silent and oral comprehension. They include graded word lists, graded story passages with comprehension questions, supplemental tests of phonics and decoding skills, and systems for determining reading levels by counting errors. Assessment of oral fluency includes simple coding of miscues, but these are not analyzed qualitatively. Number of oral reading errors, not types, is what is considered.

The Diagnostic Reading Scales–Revised assess comprehension with a preponderance of questions requiring short answers and literal recall. Some questions are answered by yes or no, as in the question "Is all marble white?" Rate of reading is measured, but does not take into account that good readers vary their rate for different reading purposes. Also, the terms "independent level" and "instructional level" are used differently than is usual. In this test "instructional level" refers to the highest grade level at which the student can read *orally* with adequate word recognition and comprehension, while "independent level" refers to the highest grade level at which the student can read *silently* with adequate comprehension. Thus the "instructional" is the oral reading level, and the "independent" is the silent reading level. Users who are familiar with the more usual meanings of these terms, as discussed in Chapter 4, find the levels indicated by this test confusing. This test also includes 12 supplementary phonics subtests that assess initial and final consonant sounds, blends and digraph sounds, initial consonant substitution, auditory recognition of consonant sounds, long and short vowel sounds and variant vowels, recognition of syllables and phonograms, sound blending and auditory discrimination.

The Durrell Analysis of Reading Difficulty also assesses word recognition and word analysis, oral fluency, and silent and oral comprehension. It includes listening comprehension, identifying meanings of individual words, recognition of sounds of individual letters, blends, digraphs, phonograms and initial and final affixes, spelling, visual memory of words, and "prereading phonics abilities" that include matching spoken with written sentences ("syntax matching") identifying letter names in spoken names (such as *s* in *Esther*), and identifying and writing letters.

The Woodcock Reading Mastery Test–Revised is often used in special education. The Woodcock consists of six subtests: visual-auditory learning, letter identification, word identification, word attack, word comprehension, and passage comprehension. Designed for use in all grades from kindergarten through twelfth, it takes about 30 to 60 minutes to administer.

The letter identification subtest requires the student to identify letters shown in eight styles of type. The word identification subtest consists of 150 words in order of difficulty from preprimer (*the* and *and*) to twelfth grade (*facetious* and *picayune*). They are listed in isolation, and the student pronounces the words in an untimed presentation. The word-attack subtest consists of 50 nonsense words to be decoded and pronounced. Items range in difficulty from *bim* to *wubfambif*. The word comprehension subtest contains 70 items presented as verbal analogies: "bird—fly, fish—___." The subject reads the analogy silently and says a word to complete the set. Figure 9.7 shows items from the word comprehension and word-attack subtests. The passage comprehension subtest consists of 85 modified cloze items; a word is omitted from a sentence, and the subject reads the item silently, then gives a word to complete it. Early items are single sentences with a picture clue; later items contain two or three sentences and have no picture.

The Woodcock yields grade-equivalent scores and age-equivalent scores for each subtest and for Total Reading, which represents the combined subtest scores. Scores can be converted to percentiles, and there are separate norms available for females and males as well as for different socioeconomic groups.

Like other standardized tests, the Woodcock yields entirely numerical data. A grade-equivalent score, or any other form of numerical score, on subtests like Word Identification or Passage Comprehension does not tell the teacher what the student can or cannot do. The examiner still does not know *what* letters the student can identify or what phonics skills have been mastered without detailed item analysis, which is not discussed in the manual.

Advantages

First, as with group survey tests, the most obvious advantage is economy of time. With a *group diagnostic test* like the Stanford, a large group can be tested in less than two hours. Second, some teachers find the information generated by such a test more specific than the results of a general survey test, with its relatively undifferentiated subtests and global scores. Third, group diagnostic tests, like their survey counterparts, are easy to administer without special preparation and are usually easy to score.

An advantage of using a standardized individual diagnostic test lies in the opportunity to closely observe one student's reading. A second advantage is the detailed analysis of discrete skills that many of these tests allow.

Disadvantages

The first disadvantage of using multiple subtests is that they may represent a very limited sample of the desired behavior. They are usually kept very short in order to save time, but subtest length can critically affect reliability. Although there is no general rule of thumb, tests in which individual subtests have few responses should be suspect because they may sacrifice in-depth analysis of specific things for a quick glimpse at many things. Second, tests can be seriously flawed by poor passages and poor questions. The passages

Figure 9.7

Sample Items from the Word Comprehension and Word Attack Subtests of the Woodcock Reading Mastery Test–Revised

WORD COMPREHENSION SAMPLE ITEMS—
DO NOT RECORD ON THE RESPONSE FORM

Point to the first sample item and say: **Listen carefully and finish what I say** (point to each of the three words and the blank space, in turn, while reading the item).

A dog walks; a bird . . . (pause). (*flies*) If the subject gives an incorrect response or does not respond, read the item again, completing it with the correct word.

Continue with the remaining sample items in the same manner (point to each word as the item is read to the subject):

One is to two as three is to . . . (pause). (*four, six*)
He is to she as boy is to . . . (pause). (*girl*)
Grass is to green as snow is to . . . (pause). (*white*)

dog—walks	bird—
one—two	three—
he—she	boy—
grass—green	snow—

WORD ATTACK SAMPLE ITEM—
DO NOT RECORD ON RESPONSE FORM

Say: **I want you to pronounce some words that are not real words. I want you to tell me how they sound.** Point to "tat." **How does this word sound?**

Sample: tat

If the subject incorrectly responds to "tat," point to "tat" and say it clearly. Do not pronounce any other words during the Word Attack Test.

Proceed to the next page and begin the test. Continue testing until the subject has missed five or more consecutive words, or has responded to Item 50.

How do these words sound? Point to each word if necessary. If the subject fails to respond in a few seconds, encourage a response. If the subject still fails to respond, continue the test by pointing to the next word.

1. **ift**	2. **bim**	3. **ut**	4. **rayed**	5. **kak**
(ift)*	(bim)	(ət)	(rād)	(kak)
6. **aft**	7. **nen**	8. **ab**	9. **tash**	10. **wip's**
(aft)	(nen)	(ab)	(tash)	(wips)

*Pronunciation symbols used by permission of the publishers of the Merriam-Webster Dictionaries. See test manual for further explanation.

Source: From Richard W. Woodcock, *Woodcock Reading Mastery Tests, Revised* (Circle Pines, Minn.: American Guidance Service, WRMT–R © 1987). Reprinted by permission.

are usually written to conform to readability formulas, which make them sound stilted. Often they are bland, dull, and sometimes very short. A student's comprehension will be radically affected by interest in and prior knowledge of what is read. Dull passages written poorly do little to promote anyone's reading comprehension. The number of questions following a passage is another important variable. Ten questions of different types will make a fairly good sample, but ten questions all requiring literal recall will not, and asking only four or five questions is usually not enough to really test comprehension. Third, tests that yield an overall reading level but do not assess comprehension are of dubious value. The heart of reading is comprehension, and a reading level that has not included comprehension, even indirectly, is not very useful. Fourth, many of these tests, particularly those that focus on word analysis skills, appear to excessively partition the process of reading into minute parts. It should be kept in mind that word-analysis skills serve to facilitate word recognition, but they do not add up to real reading. Improvement in word attack skills does not guarantee that the student will be able to read effectively with comprehension. So, as with all formal assessments of reading, the results of norm-referenced, standardized diagnostic tests should only be interpreted in light of other formal and informal assessments which reflect real reading tasks.

CRITERION-REFERENCED TESTS

Criterion-referenced tests enable teachers to compare a student's performance to a predetermined goal or outcome, while norm-referenced tests, on the other hand, aid in comparing one student's performance to someone else's. Criterion-referenced tests provide a way of determining whether a student has met instructional goals, or *criteria*.

Characteristics

In individualized reading programs, each student works toward mastery of skills that he or she has not yet learned. Pretests are most often used to determine which skills need improvement. In theory, every student in a classroom might be working on mastering a different skill at any given time. In practice, few teachers can effectively manage such a program, and students are temporarily grouped with others who need work on the same skill or process. Even though the instruction usually takes place in groups, these programs are called individualized because each student works on those particular skills in which she or he is thought to be deficient.

This instructional model requires a measurement method that helps the teacher determine not how students compare to one another but how each student's performance compares with the goals of the program. Criterion-referenced tests compare a student's level of proficiency or mastery of some skill or set of skills to a standard of mastery, or criterion (Kubiszyn and Borich, 1990).

Goals, Objectives, and Testing

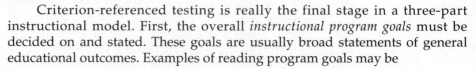

Criterion-referenced testing is really the final stage in a three-part instructional model. First, the overall *instructional program goals* must be decided on and stated. These goals are usually broad statements of general educational outcomes. Examples of reading program goals may be

- to read different kinds of text with adequate comprehension;
- to appreciate different literary genres; and
- to recognize words fluently.

Program goals are often developed at the state level or at the school-division level. Such goals do not specify either how such behaviors or attitudes will be conveyed or what specific levels of competency are required. However, they do serve to define the general directions in which instruction will move.

Program objectives follow from curricular goals. They are still general, but more specific than goals. They define more narrowly the desired outcomes of the instruction, such as the following:

- students will recognize and discriminate among basic speech sounds;
- students will demonstrate effective listening skills;
- students will identify characteristics that distinguish major literary genres.

Program objectives are usually developed at the school division level or at the local school level. They apply to specific educational programs, but still may not specify the level of proficiency desired, nor do they describe how such objectives will be implemented.

Instructional objectives are the specific statements of learner behavior or outcomes that are expected to be exhibited by students after a unit of instruction. (The instructional period may be a five-minute minilesson, a one-week lesson or a month-long unit; in each case the unit of instruction is usually defined.) Instructional objectives define what specific content is taught, as in these examples:

- After completion of the Level 1 reader, students will recognize at sight all the basal words listed at the end of the book.

- After reading this story, students will formulate two inferences about the possible results of the main character's actions.
- By the end of November of kindergarten, students will identify the months of the year in order from memory.

Instructional objectives are often referred to as *behavioral objectives* because they describe the behaviors learners are to demonstrate. Objectives that call for students to "appreciate" or "understand" are common, but they do not describe the behaviors to be shown. Because of this, instructional objectives often do not take into account attitudes or generally "unmeasurable" behaviors, instead focusing on discrete, measurable behaviors. It is this lack of focus that many educators object to about such objectives.

Good instructional objectives identify the *behavior* to be demonstrated, which is the observable learning outcome. They state the *conditions* under which the student will demonstrate the outcome: from memory, by Friday, orally, in writing, given a list of 20 misspelled words, and the like. Sometimes these conditions are referred to as "the givens"; they are contained in such objective statements as "Given a list of 30 basal words from the Level 2 reader, the student will identify 25 words at sight," or "Given 20 two-digit addition problems, the student will compute all answers correctly." They also state the *criterion level* of mastery desired: the number of items correct, a percentage of accuracy, the number of consecutive times performed, the prescribed time limit (where speed of performance is required), or the essential features to be included (as in a composition or essay response).

From instructional objectives come the items that are used on criterion-referenced tests. To achieve its purpose of determining how closely a student has achieved mastery of a skill or objective, each test item must define the criterion or skill being assessed. Criterion-referenced test items are often taken directly from instructional objectives, when such tests are developed locally. When the instructional objectives have been written so that they are sufficiently clear, precise, and measurable, developing such test items is easy. For example, with an instructional objective like "After completing the Level 1 reader, students will recognize all of the basal words at sight," a criterion-referenced test item like "From the list provided, read these words with 90-percent accuracy" may follow.

As with any other kind of test, criterion-referenced test items must fairly and adequately sample the essential skills or knowledge desired. Test items must match the learning outcomes and conditions specified in the instructional objectives; this insures test validity (Kubiszyn and Borich, 1990). If an instructional objective calls for students to discriminate between statements of fact and opinion in newspaper articles, then a test item or items that require them to discriminate between statements of fact and opinion in a letter to the editor is a good match; an item that requires them to state an opinion about the use of letters to the editor is not a good match. Likewise, if an instructional objective requires students to use an illustration to identify 20 bones of the human body, then a test item giving them a picture of a skeleton with 20 bones to be labeled would be a good match; a test item requiring them to name 20 bones from memory would not.

When instructional programs and tests are developed locally, the tests usually match quite well the instructional goals. So, too, do commercial-skills programs that feature their own criterion-referenced tests. It is when tests are purchased separately from programs or when test programs are purchased but instructional programs are developed locally that a mismatch may occur between what is being taught and what, or how, that content is being tested. In some situations, expensive commercial test programs lock teachers into a particular sequence of skills. Since tests should be tailored to meet instructional programs, and not the reverse, this is a case of the tail wagging the dog.

When judging the objectives for a commercial criterion-referenced test or test program, it is important to keep these questions in mind:

1. Do these objectives call for learning outcomes that are appropriate for this subject area? What are the most important outcomes to be desired from instruction? Are they included in this testing program?

2. Do these objectives represent a balance of thinking and learning skills? Is factual knowledge required at the expense of higher-level thinking skills?

3. Are the desired outcomes realistically attainable by our students? What modifications should be made to fit the needs of our students and the realities of our teaching facilities?

4. Do these objectives fit the philosophy of our school(s) and teachers? If not, how can the objectives of the test be modified to better represent our overall goals and philosophy?

Advantages

One of the most important assets of criterion-referenced tests is their diagnostic potential. They can indicate with great clarity and precision what a student can or cannot yet do, and thus appropriate instructional modifications can be made, which is the major goal of any diagnostic procedure. They have much greater diagnostic power than norm-referenced tests because they yield information related to specific goals rather than information relating the performance of children to one another. Second, it is possible for parents and students to see how test scores are related to instructional methods and materials, whereas ordinarily it is difficult for them to see any relationship. This advantage can help to eliminate a misunderstanding between home and school. Third, criterion-referenced tests make it very clear to the public what goals the school has developed and how these goals are to be attained. There is therefore greater public confidence in the accountability of schools. Fourth, they can be made to conform to local standards, teaching conditions, and practices, and thus reflect the actual abilities and achievement of local students more accurately than standardized norm-referenced tests. Fifth, they tend to minimize damaging competition among students, since a student's achievement is not measured in terms of someone else's achievement but rather in terms of a preset criterion. Both parents and students can then concentrate on the goals to be attained rather than on invidious comparisons among individuals or groups. Sixth, they are particularly useful for evaluating the effectiveness of a program innovation or a completely new program.

Disadvantages

First, criterion-referenced tests may be top-heavy with objectives that are easiest to measure, such as factual material. The higher-order learning processes, like evaluation and application of knowledge to novel situations, are naturally harder to assess, and they may be underrepresented in the objectives. Second, the necessity of being clear and precise may encourage partitioning of reading acts into many molecular units. Excessive partitioning leads to a proliferation of objectives, and reading as an integrated process can get lost. Criterion-referenced tests tend to encourage teachers to think of reading as a conglomerate of hundreds of discrete skills instead of a complex thinking and language process. Third, since criteria of quality or accuracy are always arbitrary, they should be considered carefully. There is nothing magical about 80-, 90-, or 100-percent accuracy. If skills are truly hierarchical, as with some math skills, then 100-percent accuracy may be necessary before the student goes on to more difficult skills. If there is no particular sequence of skills in one area, or no generally agreed-upon progression, then all quality criteria are arbitrary, and one may be just as good as another. Teachers using any test with criteria for mastery predetermined should decide for themselves if the criteria seem unnecessarily rigid. Fourth, we must remember that we don't want students to demonstrate mastery only on a one-time basis. We want them to retain what they have learned and be able to apply it to new situations. Important objectives should be tested more than once, and mastery should be shown in more than one way. Fifth, many criterion-referenced tests assess specific skills with very few items per skill. This can reduce reliability. An option is to include a larger number of items for each skill; but the longer the test, the more difficult it is for students to complete.

Perhaps the biggest drawback in criterion-referenced tests is that objectives to be tested have a way of becoming the reading curriculum itself. Some educators maintain that programs that emphasize testing of discrete skills encourage teaching the skills in the same manner. It is difficult, if not impossible, to isolate skills in actual reading because meaningful reading requires the use of many skills and processes simultaneously, and partitioning overlooks this important factor.

Minimum Competency Testing

During the 1970s and 1980s the accountability movement had an impact on education in a number of ways. One major impact has been in the area of *minimum competency testing.* In an effort to provide accountability in schools, some educators, businesspeople, and politicians attempted to determine minimum levels of competence that students should possess prior to being promoted another grade or graduating from high school with a diploma. In order to assess these minimum competencies, *minimum-competency-testing* programs were established in many states (Thorndike et al., 1991). We consider that minimum competency tests are a special kind of criterion-referenced tests since success on these instruments depends upon students achieving certain predetermined levels of mastery on the minimum competencies.

Minimum competency programs differ from state to state and from one school district to another. Most commonly, however, they feature:

- statements of specific skills, often called "performance standards," "basic competencies," or "learning objectives," in reading, writing, and mathematics that schools are responsible for teaching all children and that all students are responsible for mastering;
- tests to determine if students have mastered the required skills;
- requirements that students cannot be promoted to the next grade and/or cannot graduate unless the tests are passed; and
- requirements concerning extra courses, placement in special programs, remediation, and the like to correct deficiencies.

Issues of Minimum Competency Programs

A number of complex issues are involved in this movement. In general, supporters of minimum competency testing believe that it will

- help identify and better serve those students with the greatest educational needs;
- motivate students toward greater achievement in school;
- motivate teachers to teach all students more effectively;
- make high-school diplomas more meaningful (in states that have "diploma sanctions," or regulations requiring mastery on tests before a diploma may be awarded);
- place pressure on schools to provide more instruction in basic skills and to become more accountable for student achievement; and
- create an objective data base regarding school achievement patterns (Lazarus, 1981).

Problems of Minimum Competency Programs

There are, however, a number of concerns expressed by educational measurement and curriculum authorities (Lazarus, 1981; Mizell, 1979; and Thorndike et al., 1991). These include:

1. Minimum competency testing may exclude more children from schools and stigmatize underachievers. When such programs result in denial of promotion or graduation and even implicitly encourage dropping out of school, such programs may be "punitive and exclusionary" (Mizell, 1979, p. 10).

2. Programs may focus on identifying students with basic skill deficiencies without aggressively pursuing effective remediation. Testing is certainly easier than remediating, and effective long-term remediation is both difficult and expensive.

3. Such programs and the rhetoric associated with them may oversimplify the basic competency issues, seeking or creating pat answers to exceedingly complex issues of adult literacy.

4. Such programs may be viewed as a "quick fix" to the problem of the community's loss of confidence in the schools, or as an attempt to restore such confidence while actually having little effect on the complex underlying causes of illiteracy.

5. Students with special educational needs (for example, the handicapped, severely learning disabled, emotionally disturbed, and mentally retarded) may be penalized and further shut out from equal educational opportunity by their failure to meet standard objectives or pass the typical group-administered, paper-and-pencil tests of basic skills. Few states so far have rigorously examined the implications of these programs for exceptional learners.

6. The emphasis such programs place within the school and in the larger community on "minimums" may result in a narrowing of curricular goals, with greater emphasis on so-called "basics" and lesser emphasis on, or omission of, a broad range of school topics and educational experiences for all learners.

7. Although students failing such tests are the ones who ultimately pay the penalty, teachers may be forced by community pressure to restrict the range of topics and methods to those most likely to be tested, so that they can more clearly justify the use of student time and effort. This can result in students' passing the required tests but being poorly prepared in the more global reading, writing, and thinking applications.

8. So much emphasis on "minimums" may create a climate in which the minimum becomes the maximum. Many critics already charge that schools in

general do not fully challenge average or talented pupils, but seek only to assure that everyone has a minimum level of achievement. The motivation of average and above-average students may suffer as a result.

9. When such programs are mandated by the state, local school divisions may wonder who will absorb the cost. The state may finance the actual testing but not the remedial programs that must be a necessary part of the process if it is to serve the students' needs. Localities may balk at subsidizing the necessarily expensive remedial efforts if they are made to feel that the state has usurped local autonomy.

10. Finally, the question of whether students' competence in applying school literacy skills to life experience can be accurately, fairly, and comprehensively tested by means available today must be addressed.

Although there are many problems and concerns with minimum competency testing, the courts have upheld states' rights to establish such testing programs (Thorndike et al., 1991). The pressure for accountability in schools continues; however states are beginning to take a broader view of assessment which includes not only formal assessments, but informal assessments as well.

SOURCES OF TEST INFORMATION

Information on a commercial test or battery can be obtained from a number of sources such as measurement yearbooks, test publishers' catalogs, and technical reports, bulletins, and journals.

Yearbooks and Indexes

These sources are compendia of information and reviews of all current published tests. They can be found in libraries, although many school divisions have a set of their own.

Measurement Yearbooks

The most valuable source, and the first place many teachers turn to with questions about tests, is the series of *Mental Measurement Yearbooks* (MMYs). The first MMY was published in 1938; for many years these were edited by Oscar K. Buros, until his death. The ninth, tenth, and eleventh MMYs were edited by others. The most current is the eleventh MMY, published in 1992.

Each MMY lists tests that have appeared or been revised since publication of the previous volume. Age and grade levels, time needed for administration, subtests included, publishers, and costs are listed for each test. This information is helpful when initially screening a number of tests, and it makes ordering sample sets easy. Most important, these yearbooks contain extensive reviews of many tests written by qualified experts in the field; synopses of reviews appearing in journals and other sources; lists of pertinent books and monographs; and the names of people and journals that review tests.

Measurement Indexes

The MMYs are not cumulative; a test reviewed in a previous MMY may not appear in subsequent volumes. To aid in locating reviews and pertinent information without having to go through each MMY, Buros developed *Tests in Print I* (1961), *Tests in Print II* (1974), and *Tests in Print III* (1983). A more current source of information is *Tests: A Comprehensive Reference for Assessments in Psychology, Education and Business,* 3rd ed., edited by Richard C. Sweetland and Daniel J. Keyser.

Additional Sources

There are several other places where you can get critical information about tests, after you have checked the MMYs and indexes.

Test Publishers' Catalogs

Publishers of commercial tests usually provide informational catalogs and technical manuals without charge to educators. They can provide a wealth of very current information to add to what Buros's reference books provide. The catalogs usually provide descriptions of the tests, subtests included, time limitations, normative information, types of scores yielded, scoring services, costs, and related specific information. Because catalogs are sales devices, they tend to present the tests in the most positive light, so the publisher's claims should be compared with the critical reviews in the eleventh MMY and current journals.

The eleventh MMY lists names and addresses of all test publishers as of 1992. The Educational Testing Service (ETS), Princeton, NJ 08541, publishes the *Test Collection Bulletin,* a quarterly publication listing the most current addresses and services of test publishers.

Technical manuals often accompany specimen sets of tests, which usually must be purchased from the publisher. They provide detailed information about the populations used in standardizing the tests, reliability and validity estimates for individual subtests and the entire test, and other statistical data that are very useful for evaluation purposes.

Bulletins

Free or inexpensive bulletins about tests, publishers, and measurement issues are available from a number of sources. ETS publishes the nominally priced *Tests and Measurement Kit,* which includes guides for developing teacher-made tests and selecting commercial ones. ETS also publishes *TM News* and *TM Reports,* bulletins reporting on measurement trends and issues and summarizing papers presented at national meetings of the American Educational Research Association (AERA). *TM Reports* also includes bibliographies on a wide variety of testing topics, which are extremely helpful to those interested in extended readings. In addition to these bulletins, ETS issues *A Directory of Information on Tests,* which will help in locating other information sources.

The National Council on Measurement in Education (NCME) (1230 17th St. N.W., Washington, DC 20036) publishes quarterly reports (*Journal of Educational Measurement, Measurement in Education,* and *Measurement News*) on a wide variety of topics such as performance contracting, criterion-referenced testing, grading practices, reporting of test scores to parents, and interpreting of national norms.

The Psychological Corporation (555 Academic Court, San Antonio, TX 78204) publishes a number of free or inexpensive bulletins on topics like aptitude testing, test score accuracy, interpretation of reliability coefficients, the costs of tests, and the development of local norms. The Psychological Corporation also provides free single copies of their *Test Service Notebooks,* including reports on such topics as secondary school testing and what parents must know about testing and test selection, as well as their *Focus on Evaluation* monographs, which cover topics like mandated assessment and the political use of test results.

The American Psychological Association, Inc. (APA) (1200 17th St. N.W., Washington, DC 20036) publishes a valuable bulletin entitled *Standards for Educational and Psychological Tests* to guide test developers and test users. It contains information on the proper development and reporting of tests, results and research findings, and the use and interpretation of tests.

Journals

Published several times yearly, professional journals often contain the most current information. Many routinely review new or revised tests in many areas as well as reporting research findings related to testing. In the area of measurement and evaluation are such journals as the *American Psychologist, Journal of Educational Measurement, American Educational Research Journal, Psychological Bulletin,* and *Applied Psychological Measurement.* Reading journals such as *Language Arts, The Reading Teacher, Journal of Reading,* and *Reading Research Quarterly* often include test reviews and critical articles.

SUMMARY

The basic test characteristics that teachers should be familiar with are *reliability* and *validity*. Reliability refers to the consistency of scores a test yields. Aspects of reliability are *stability*, or consistency across repeated administrations; *internal consistency*, or consistency among test items; and *equivalence*, or consistency across alternate test forms. Validity refers to how well a test measures what it was intended to measure. *Content validity* is the quality of adequately sampling the subject area or process being assessed. *Criterion-related validity* is made up of *concurrent validity*, or how closely a test is related to another test of established validity, and *predictive validity*, the degree to which test performance is related to some other established criterion, such as grades in college or job success. *Construct validity* refers to how well the test measures traits, or constructs, that are not directly observable but must be inferred from observable behavior. Intelligence is an example of a construct.

Commonly used descriptive statistics include *distributions, indices of central tendency and dispersion,* and forms of *standard scores.* A distribution is an array of scores from highest to lowest. Many standardized tests assume a *normal distribution,* a symmetrical array with most scores falling near the mean and progressively fewer scores at the extreme high and low ends. Asymmetrical distributions are referred to as *skewed.* Indices of central tendency in distributions include the *mean,* an arithmetic average, and the *median,* the point in a distribution at which there are equal numbers of higher and lower scores. Indices of dispersion in a distribution describe how far apart scores are from one another. They include the *range,* or the span from highest to lowest score, and the *standard deviation,* which shows how far from the mean each score is in standard or equal increments.

Standardized reading tests usually yield several forms of test scores. *Grade scores* are two-part numbers that indicate achievement such as we might expect at a given grade level and a number of months within that grade. These scores are meant to represent the performance of an average student in the grade and month indicated. *Percentiles* are standard scores that show what percentage of the norm population scored higher or lower than the individual tested. *Stanines* are scores in which the distribution has been divided into nine parts; a stanine score indicates which ninth a score fell in. *T-scores* and *z-scores* use the concepts of mean and standard deviation to show where a score lies in relation to the mean of a normal distribution.

Norm-referenced tests are developed by publishers who administer them to large numbers of students in order to develop *norms,* or average performances across grades, ages, and demographic groups. Norms are used to compare the performance of local students and groups to these averages. *Achievement tests* are designed to measure what students have already learned in major curricular areas, and to assess the effectiveness of instructional programs. *Diagnostic tests* are designed to reveal individuals' strengths and weaknesses in particular areas.

Criterion-referenced tests compare a student's performance to a preset goal or criterion, rather than to the performance of other students. Such tests are thought to be effective in showing student mastery of particular skills. *Minimum competency tests* are a kind of criterion-referenced test.

Sources of test information include measurement yearbooks and indexes, test publishers' catalogs and bulletins, and professional journal reviews.

References

Buros, Oscar K. *Tests in Print III.* Highland Park, NJ: Gryphon Press, 1983. (Previous editions: 1974, 1961.)

Ebel, Robert L., and David A. Frisbie. *Essentials of Educational Measurement,* 5th ed. Englewood Cliffs, NJ: Prentice Hall, 1991.

Eleventh Mental Measurement Yearbook. Lincoln, NB: Buros Institute of Mental Measurements of the University of Nebraska-Lincoln, 1992. (Previous edition: *Tenth Mental Measurement Yearbook,* 1989.)

Kubiszyn, Tom, and Gary Borich. *Educational Testing and Measurement: Classroom Application and Practice,* 3d ed. Glenview, IL: Scott, Foresman, 1990.

Lazarus, Mitchell. *Goodbye to Excellence: A Critical Look at Minimum Competency Testing.* Boulder, CO: Westview Press, 1981.

Mizell, M. Hayes. "A Citizen's Introduction to Minimal Competency Testing." In *Minimal Competency Testing,* ed. Peter W. Airasian, George F. Madaus, and Joseph J. Pedulla. Englewood Cliffs, NJ: Educational Technology Publications, 1979.

Ninth Mental Measurement Yearbook. Highland Park, NJ: Gryphon Press, 1985. (Previous editions: 1978, 1972, 1965, 1959, 1949, 1940, 1938.)

Radencich, Marguerite C. "Test Review: Gray Oral Reading Test–Revised and Formal Reading Inventory." *Journal of Reading* 30, no. 2 (Nov. 1986): 136–139.

Sweetland, Richard C., and Daniel J. Keyser, ed. Tests: *A Comprehensive Reference for Assessment in Psychology, Education and Business,* 3d ed. Austin, TX: PRO-ED, 1993.

Thorndike, Robert M., George K. Cunningham, Robert L. Thorndike, and Elizabeth P. Hagen. *Measurement and Evaluation in Psychology and Education,* 5th ed. NY: Macmillan Publishing Company, 1991.

Assessing Factors Related to Reading Problems

I n this chapter we discuss intellectual, physical, and affective factors, topics often thought to be secondary, or contributing, causes of reading problems. It is true that the factors are often considered peripheral to reading, but actually they affect the entire enterprise of learning.

Most classroom teachers are more or less accustomed to testing reading skills within their classrooms. The assessment of intelligence, vision and hearing, emotional and personality development, and special learning problems, however, is usually done outside the regular classroom by the school nurse, school psychologist, counselor, or other specialist.

Oftentimes, teachers are presented with the results of these assessments in forms that are unfamiliar to them. These results are used to determine whether students are qualified for special programs. We will discuss legislation related to special needs; the referral process; ways to assess intellectual and physical special learning problems, and affective factors; how these issues are related to reading; and indicators of higher-than-normal risk for academic failure.

ISSUES INVOLVING SPECIAL-NEEDS STUDENTS

In the past, children with special intellectual, physical, or emotional needs were largely excluded from the regular curriculum. Changes in educational policy for special-needs students are the result of growing public awareness and legislative action (Patton, Kauffman, Blackbourn, & Brown, 1991). By far the most important piece of legislation is Public Law 94–142, enacted in 1975. PL 94–142, the Individuals with Disabilities Act (originally called the Education for All Handicapped Children Act), affects not only special educators but also every teacher at every level. Other legislation has amended and extended its provisions.

Legislation Affecting Special-Needs Students

PL 94–142 mandates a number of far-reaching changes in the education of students with special needs. Following is a list of the law's major provisions, the immediate implications of each provision for the classroom teacher, and a summary of the basic rights of handicapped students under the law.

Provision: Free public education will be provided for all handicapped persons between the ages of 3 and 21 years of age.

Implications: Schools must serve the needs of students both older and younger than those served in the past. The traditional concept of "school-age children" between 5 and 18 has been drastically modified. Since the law provides for grants that create financial incentives for schools to identify handicapped preschoolers and provide special services for them, kindergarten and primary grade teachers are involved in early identification programs.

At the other end of the age scale, teachers in all grades are affected by the mainstreaming of handicapped older students into regular classes (see the information following). This is particularly important in high schools where pupils up to the age of 21 may be included in regular classes. Teachers must be aware of the special needs and interests of handicapped older students and young adults who are placed in classes with younger pupils.

In 1986, PL 94–142 was amended by PL 99–457, which extends the requirements of the original law to children aged three to five even in states that do not provide free public education to children under five. In addition, Part H of PL 99–457 established a federal grant program to provide funds to states to develop and implement statewide, comprehensive, coordinated, and multidisciplinary interagency programs of early identification and intervention for handicapped infants and preschoolers from birth to age 2. This is not a requirement, but the program provides incentives to states to develop such programs.

Public Law 101–476 amended PL 94–142 in 1990. It adds the requirement for transitional services for students (16 years of age and older) with disabilities. These services promote the transition from school to the workplace. Services include postsecondary education, vocational training, rehabilitation services, and referrals for social services.

Provision: Handicapped students will be placed in the least restrictive environment whenever and wherever possible. This often means mainstreaming handicapped children into the regular classroom and curriculum.

Implications: The inclusion of handicapped students in regular classrooms for part or all of the school day affects nearly every teacher. All teachers must clearly understand how the handicaps of students affect their learning, how materials and activities must be adapted appropriately, how their performances are to be evaluated, and how to deal positively with these students' social and interpersonal problems. In addition, regular classroom teachers have to be routinely involved in the assessment of these students' special needs.

Provision: Each handicapped student will be provided with an individualized educational program, called an IEP, which spells out present abilities, short- and long-term goals, and the means by which goals will be achieved. Each student's IEP will be developed jointly by teachers, parents, and the student where possible.

Implications: All teachers working with disabled students have direct responsibility for the planning, implementing, and evaluating of instructional programs. They must expand their understanding of handicapping conditions, management techniques, teaching strategies, and materials in order to develop and use IEPs. In developing and updating IEPs, teachers have to join forces with the parents of handicapped students for greater parental involvement and teacher accountability. In many cases the students can be included in the development of their IEPs, to the extent that they are able to participate.

Provision: All tests and evaluative instruments used will be prepared and administered in order to eliminate racial and cultural discrimination.

Implications: Tests and assessment devices have to be closely scrutinized to eliminate discriminatory aspects. Results of a single test or measure cannot be used to classify students, a practice that has sometimes been followed in the past. In addition, tests must be modified when necessary so that students with disabilities can respond to them in ways that are best for them, for example in Braille or in a sign language. They must be administered in the student's native language, or in sign language or cued speech for hearing-impaired students. These modifications entail widespread changes both in test construction and in the ways tests are administered and interpreted.

The provisions of PL 94–142 also establish certain basic rights for handicapped students:

1. the right to due process, which protects the individual from erroneous classification, capricious labeling, and denial of equal education;
2. protection against discriminatory testing in diagnosis, which ensures against possible bias in intelligence tests (and other tests) used with ethnic and minority children;
3. placement in an educational setting that is the least restrictive environment, which protects the individual from possible detrimental effects of segregated education for the handicapped;
4. individual program plans, which ensure accountability by those responsible for the education of the handicapped.

The law also stipulates that a child receiving special education services must be given a review at least once every three years. The purpose of this review is to determine whether the child is still eligible for special services. The review must include a complete reassessment of learning aptitude, speech and hearing, school achievement, adaptive behavior, and the like.

Mainstreaming and the Regular Education Initiative

The concept of *mainstreaming,* or integrating handicapped students into regular education classes, has been the source of much controversy for many years. PL 94–142 does not require all children with disabilities to be placed in regular classrooms with support services. Neither does it suggest that regular-education teachers should be expected to teach all handicapped students without guidance and assistance from special educators. It does, however, call for the education of students with special needs to be conducted in the least restrictive environment in which the students have probable chances for success (Lewis and Doorlag, 1991).

Better ways of meeting the needs of exceptional learners are being explored today, including helping regular education teachers to use teaching practices that have been found to be effective with exceptional children, using special educators as teacher consultants rather than direct providers of instruction, establishing teams that ensure that only those who truly need special services are so identified, structuring classrooms to promote cooperative learning between students of all ability levels, and using materials and methods to help create more positive student attitudes toward handicapped and exceptional peers.

These procedures have all been advocated by those supporting the *regular education initiative* (REI), the goal of which is to make regular educators more responsible for the education of handicapped children. Although not without controversy, REI seems to be gaining support across the nation (Baum, 1990). To implement REI, extensive inservice and modified preservice training for regular educators is needed. Greater communication, trust, and cooperation between special and regular educators have been called for as the key to implementing REI and restructuring an educational system that better serves the needs of all students in regular, special, remedial, and compensatory programs (Patton, Kauffman, Blackbourn, & Brown, 1991).

Since regular education teachers will continue to have greater responsibility for teaching children identified as having special needs, informal diagnostic methods like those described in this book take on even greater importance and utility.

Identifying Special-Needs Students

Individual school divisions differ in minor ways in the procedures they follow regarding referral and classification, but a sequence of events such as this is typical:

1. A teacher who suspects that a student needs special services requests special screening for the student by notifying the school principal.

2. The principal obtains parental permission for such screening and arranges for it.

Screening must include educational, psychological, medical, and sociological assessments. Teachers are directly involved in the educational assessments. The law requires that a team approach be used, and most schools have a standing screening committee comprised of a special education teacher or assessment specialist, a school psychologist or psychometrist, the referring teacher, the school principal or principal's designee, and, in many cases, the child's parent(s). It may also include a teacher or specialist with training and expertise in the area of the suspected disability, often a reading teacher. Types of tests commonly used in these assessments are discussed in the next section.

3. The principal or other administrator involved arranges a meeting to discuss the screening results with the parents, the evaluation team, the student's teacher(s), and the special education specialists.

4. At this meeting, all relevant assessment and instructional data are detailed. Teachers may present the results of informal diagnostic procedures, which are very useful in developing a picture of the student's abilities and needs and provide a valuable supplement to the formal tests given by the other members of the evaluation team. This group decision-making process is often called "staffing."

After all data have been discussed, the team members individually indicate whether special education placement is warranted. Parental consent *must* be given for such placement.

5. If placement is agreed upon, an individual education plan (IEP) is developed for the student. It must include a statement of the student's present levels of functioning, both short-term and annual goals, projected dates for initiation and duration of special services, specific criteria and evaluation procedures to be used to determine if goals have been achieved, the names of persons responsible for special services and evaluation, descriptions of special services to be provided, and the extent to which the student will participate in regular education programs. Parental approval must again be given for the IEP to be implemented; if they do not approve it, or do not approve any subsequent changes in it, an impartial due process hearing must be held. Special services cannot be provided until after the IEP is developed and approved.

6. The next step is to place the student in the least restrictive educational environment where special services are provided and implementation of the IEP proceeds. Every educator (or agency) involved is required to make good-faith efforts to help the student achieve the goals set forth in the IEP. Parents can request program review and revision if they believe such good-faith efforts have not been made, but if in spite of such efforts the student does not achieve the goals of the IEP, no individual is to be held accountable.

IEPs must be written every year to account for changing goals and abilities. In addition, all special education students must be reassessed triennially to determine whether they still need special services and what changes have taken place during that period.

Assessment Types and Devices

In screening children for special education services, educational devices vary from place to place, but the use of a combination of standardized and informal tests is common, and in some states is required. As you have already learned, formal assessment devices are usually standardized, normative tests. Administration, scoring, and interpretation procedures are clearly set forth. Formal tests yield many different types of scores and are given for many different purposes, but most are given to provide information about a student's standing in relation to other students (see Chapter 9). Informal procedures are usually less structured or are structured differently from standardized tests (see Chapters 4 and 5). Inventories, such as informal reading inventories and spelling inventories, and class work such as arithmetic worksheets fit this category. There is an element of subjectivity in their scoring, it they are scored, and in their interpretation. However, while they lack the kind of normative scores yielded by standardized tests, informal assessments yield results that are directly related to instruction (McLaughlin and Lewis, 1990). Thus, both kinds of assessment provide useful information about students' abilities and achievement.

Screening assessments are often carried out by a team, of which the regular classroom teacher and/or reading teacher is often a part. A team approach to assessment acts as a safeguard against assessment problems such as bias. As you may recall, PL 94–142 contains two provisions to safeguard against test abuses:

1. Testing must be conducted in the language of the student, measures used must be nondiscriminatory and validated for the purpose for which they are used, and no single test score may be used as the sole basis for determining special education placement.
2. In determining mental retardation, concurrent deficits in both intelligence performance and adaptive behavior must be detected.

Assessment instruments have different purposes and assess different aspects of performance and potential. They fall into these general categories:

1. *Learning Aptitude Tests:* Learning aptitude refers to the student's capacity for altering behavior when presented with new information or experiences. These often include intelligence tests, which measure scholastic aptitude, not general aptitude or intelligence, and also indirectly assess achievement in areas such as vocabulary and math computation. Intelligence tests are the primary means used to assess learning aptitude. Learning aptitude is also sometimes referred to as cognitive ability, learning potential, cognitive factors, and similar terms. Some school achievement batteries contain sections that assess learning aptitude, comparing it to present achievement levels.

2. *Achievement Tests:* These are the primary means used to assess students' present levels of scholastic performance. These tests assess what has been learned, not what the child is capable of learning. Achievement test batteries include subtests dealing with reading, spelling, mathematics, written

language, and the like. Tests that assess achievement in single areas only, such as separate reading, spelling, arithmetic, and writing achievement tests, may be used instead of a battery.

3. *Adaptive Behavior Tests:* Adaptive behavior refers to how effectively an individual meets standards of personal independence and social responsibility normally expected of her or his age and cultural group. These measures are used when mental retardation is suspected.

4. *Tests of Specific Learning Abilities:* These test various single learning processes such as auditory discrimination, short-term memory, visual perception, motor abilities, and the like. Some tests assess only one process; others are batteries with subtests assessing different processes. Most intelligence tests also include measures of many of these abilities, such as short-term memory, visual perception, and visual-motor coordination.

5. *Classroom Behavior and Adjustment Tests:* These include evaluation scales and rating scales for behavior, self-concept scales, and interest inventories. These are most often used in the identification of emotionally disturbed students or those with behavior disorders, either as the primary or a secondary problem.

INTELLECTUAL FACTORS

When diagnosing a reading problem, one of the most frequently used instruments is an intelligence test. Why?

Broad trends in the research literature show what seem to be contradictory findings: (a) that good readers tend to be smarter than poor readers, at least in terms of IQ test performance, and (b) that reading problems are not limited to lower-IQ students but are found across the whole range of intellectual abilities. How are these findings to be interpreted?

There has long been some general agreement that intelligence and reading achievement are fairly well correlated, particularly in the upper grades. What this factor means is that better performance on reading tests and intelligence tests tends to occur together; students generally do well on both or poorly on both. It does *not* imply causation; we cannot infer from positive correlations that one factor causes the other, only that they coincide. It may be that above-average intelligence encourages above-average reading achievement. It may be equally true that good reading helps students do better on intelligence tests. Or it may be that *both* reading tests and IQ tests call upon the same kinds of abilities and knowledge. But poor readers may come from all ability levels.

What *do* IQ tests tell us? That depends very much on which test is used.

Not all measure the same skills, and in order to evaluate results, we have to know something about their characteristics.

Tests of Intelligence and Learning Aptitude

Intelligence tests are essentially measures of verbal abilities and skills in dealing with abstract symbols. However, they are not intended to measure innate intelligence or potential but rather to sample behavior already learned in an attempt to predict future learning. The premise of these measures is that present performance is a predictor of future performance (McLaughlin and Lewis, 1990). They are appropriately viewed as predictors of academic success; misinterpretation of their purpose and results leads to misunderstanding and inaccurate judgments about children. The issue of intelligence tests and cultural bias is discussed in a subsequent section.

Group Intelligence Tests

Some tests that yield an IQ or some kind of "ability quotient" are group tests. Group tests usually require students to read and mark answers; they consequently penalize poor readers, who generally score poorly on such a measure. Thus they may underestimate poor readers' potential. Group intelligence tests or tests of learning aptitude are useful only as general screening devices; they should be followed by individual measures if their results indicate a possible problem.

Individual Intelligence Tests

An individually administered test that does not require a student to read or write will give a better estimate of real academic potential than a group test.

The *Wechsler Intelligence Scale for Children*-III (WISC-III) (1991) is the individual test most often used to assess intellectual performance of children between the ages of 6 1/2 and 16 (Sattler, 1992). It is one of a "family" of tests that spans all age levels. The Wechsler Preschool and Primary Scale of Intelligence–Revised (WPPSI-R) (1989) is appropriate for children between four years and six and a half years of age. The Wechsler Adult Intelligence Scale–Revised (WAIS–R) (1981) is used for persons between 16 and 74 years of age. These tests may only be administered by someone specially trained and certified to do so. Modified instructions for administering the WISC–III to deaf children are available (Sattler, 1992).

The WISC-III assesses intellectual functioning by sampling performance on many different types of activities. The test attempts to assess verbal and nonverbal aspects of intelligence separately with 13 subtests—10 required and 3 optional or supplemental. The 13 subtests are organized into 2 scales, with those involving language operations directly in one, the Verbal Scale, and those involving the nonverbal or indirectly verbal operations in the other, the Performance Scale. Each scale yields a separate scale IQ, which can be compared to determine if both aspects of a child's intelligence seem to be equally well developed, and the scale IQs can be converted into a Full Scale IQ.

Raw scores from each subtest are converted to *scaled scores*, standard scores ranging from 1 to 19 with a mean of 10 and a standard deviation of 3. Transforming raw scores into standard units makes it possible to compare results of different subtests.

The Full Scale IQ represents a subject's overall intellectual functioning as measured by performance on the 10 subtests. The Verbal, Performance, and Full Scale IQs all have a mean of 100 and a standard deviation of 15. The test uses the following classification scheme for IQ scores:

130 and above	Very superior
120–129	Superior
110–119	High average
90–109	Average
80–89	Low average
70–79	Borderline
69 and below	Mentally deficient

It is important to avoid overinterpreting IQ scores by keeping in mind that they represent a sample of behavior taken at one point in time and by considering IQ scores only in relation to the range in which they occur, rather than as single, fixed scores. The average standard error of measurement for the Full Scale IQ score is 3.2 IQ points. A Full Scale IQ could thus be expected to vary by plus or minus three or four points because of probable random effects. For this reason it is more accurate to speak of a student's IQ score as "within the high average range," for example, than to say that the student "has an IQ of 117."

Clinicians often look for differences between Verbal and Performance IQs and patterns of scores on individual subtests to recommend further psychological and academic testing (Sattler, 1992).

The *Kaufman Assessment Battery for Children* (K–ABC) (1983) is another popular individual measure, to be administered by a specially trained professional and appropriate for children between 2-1/2 and 12-1/2 years of age. The K–ABC battery contains mental processing and achievement subtests. A Mental Processing Composite, an index of intellectual functioning, is derived from the mental processing subtests. Two other global scores are derived from groups of subtests: Sequential Processing and Simultaneous Processing. Global scores have a mean of 100 and a standard deviation of 15.

A nonverbal scale is available that allows the examiner to conduct several of the subtests in mime with only motor response required. The scale is useful with hearing impaired, emotionally disturbed, speech or language impaired, and non-English-speaking students. The manual gives remedial suggestions for improving students' sequential and simultaneous processing abilities, but these have not been well validated. Also, norms are only available for children up to age 12.6.

The *Stanford-Binet Intelligence Scale* (1986) has recently been radically changed from its old format. Earlier versions of the Stanford-Binet were developed on the premise that as a child grows older, he or she develops knowledge and skills in a fairly steady, sequential way, resulting in a measurable "mental age." For example, if a 7-year-old could correctly respond to items typically correctly answered by 9-year-olds, the student's mental age would be nine years and some months. IQ scores were converted from mental ages. However, the concept of mental age has been convincingly attacked over the years; the development of the Wechsler Scales was a successful attempt to measure intelligence based on a scale other than age. The 1986 version of the Stanford-Binet is not an age scale. Items are arranged in ascending order of difficulty into 15 subsets, which attempt to assess abilities other than strictly verbal. Scaled subtest scores can be combined into several global scores in Verbal Reasoning, Abstract-Visual Reasoning, Quantitative Reasoning, and Short-Term Memory, with an overall score similar to a global IQ score. These changes make the new Stanford-Binet more like the Wechsler Scales.

The *Kaufman Brief Intelligence Test* (K–BIT) (1990) is a brief assessment of verbal and nonverbal intelligence of children and adults from the ages of 4 to 90. It was developed to be used as a screening device, not a substitute for more comprehensive individual IQ tests. The K–BIT has two subtests: Vocabulary and Matrices. Designed to measure verbal and school-related skills, the Vocabulary subtest assesses a person's word knowledge and verbal concept formation. The Matrices subtests measure the ability to solve problems and other nonverbal skills. The K–BIT yields age-based standard scores having the same mean and standard deviation as the Wechsler and Kaufman scales. Scores are generated for each subtest and for an overall K–BIT IQ Composite or IQ standard score (Kaufman & Kaufman, 1990).

The individual intelligence tests we described assess both verbal and nonverbal intellectual abilities. Academic skills such as reading and writing are de-emphasized. Although these tests yield results that can be used to predict academic success, no single test, when used exclusively, can predict or evaluate a child's academic achievement. There are many factors that influence test results. One of these factors is the role of experience.

The Role of Experience

When we consider the concept of intelligence in terms of a student's personality, background, interests, and other related aspects as well as in terms of subtest behaviors and IQ points, we must take into account the role of experience. It is difficult to overestimate the importance of experience, both real and vicarious, in shaping intelligence and IQ test performance.

What kind of experience are we talking about? Essentially, we learn about ourselves and our world in two ways: by real, concrete experience with objects and events, and vicariously, by observing and remembering the experiences of others.

Real experiences in the formative years contribute to what most of us think of as an enriched environment. Enrichment has little to do with economics; it has much more to do with having opportunities to manipulate things, experimenting with causes, effects, and consequences, and being consistently encouraged to extend cognitive horizons and try new things. These characteristics of an intellectually enriching environment know no economic, ethnic, social, or linguistic boundaries. They flourish where adults respect and nurture children's attempts to become competent and where those adults give conscious thought to providing opportunities for children to become independent and capable.

Direct, concrete experience with things and events is one critical aspect; experience with language is another. Verbal intelligence flourishes in the home, and later the school, where children are talked to by adults, where adults really listen to their responses and encourage conversation, where events and behaviors are explained and verbal reasoning is demonstrated, and where adults model language use by expanding and elaborating on what children say. In environments where children are rarely addressed except in commands, where their spontaneous utterances are rarely listened to or responded to, where their requests for explanations are routinely answered by "Because I said so, that's why!" and explanations are rarely given, verbal intelligence is stunted. These children enter the world of language poorly adapted to participate in it fully. Their learning opportunities are restricted by language rather than expanded by it. Whatever their socioeconomic status, they are disadvantaged in school.

The other important aspect of experience is vicarious experience. Fortunately for all of us, we can learn from observing others as well as by experiencing things ourselves. Learning from the experiences of others saves us from having to experience everything personally, and we can derive nearly as much from those experiences as from our own.

Perhaps the greatest benefit of literacy is that through reading we can vicariously experience events, emotions, and ideas completely outside our own environment. We can travel to places we will never go to, including places that exist only in the mind; visit the past and the future with as much ease as the present; meet the most famous people of history and share their innermost thoughts; find the most exciting lovers, battle the most dangerous adversaries, and experience joy, rage, grief, amazement, and every other human emotion by reading. All this makes good reading a lifelong joy and sustenance instead of just a useful skill.

Reading and books, however, are more than a source of pleasure. They remain, in spite of the inroads of TV and films, the largest source of information for many people. Schools still use books and other forms of print as the major vehicles for transmitting information.

This learning, whether vicarious or direct, occurs within a cultural context. The knowledge passed from one generation to another differs among different cultures. The issue of cultural bias in assessment is of major concern when assessing factors associated with reading.

Cultural Bias and Nonbiased Assessment

Since the 1970s, the disproportionate number of minority and/or economically disadvantaged children placed in special education classes has led to controversy regarding the use of traditional intelligence and learning aptitude tests with these children. Attempts to address this inequity by creating alternative assessment devices have lacked sufficient psychometric rigor (Sattler, 1992) or lack the research and developmental efforts to be useful in school settings (Laughon, 1990).

Helms (1992) has presented arguments for examining racial and ethnic differences in performance of intellectual abilities from a cultural perspective. She suggests that when selecting and interpreting assessment instruments, the examiner consider cultural differences in a subject's knowledge and tradition.

PHYSICAL FACTORS

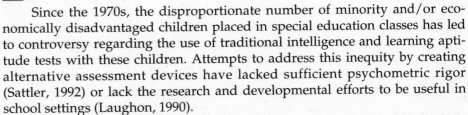

Many physical conditions and processes can be related to reading problems. The factors most commonly considered are visual and auditory. Each of these areas has been extensively studied in relation to reading difficulties, but the research data and the various conditions and processes themselves are complex and sometimes confusing. In this section we will consider vision and hearing.

Vision

Reading is a visual act (for sighted persons), because we cannot read in the dark. It is, of course, much more than just a visual act because more goes on behind the reader's eyes than in front of them, but some visual competence is needed to activate the cognitive processes involved in reading. In order to make sense of print, the reader must be able to gain information from print through vision. For this reason, poor readers are often subjected to vision screening in diagnosis.

Common Vision Problems

Teachers are sometimes the first line of defense against vision problems. They are usually in the best position to spot potential problems and refer children for appropriate screening because they, more than parents, observe children in close contact with reading and writing materials. Also, children with vision problems often don't realize that others see differently, and they don't call adult attention to their difficulty. Therefore, it is important for teachers to understand vision problems and their symptoms. Figure 10.1 summarizes the nature and symptoms of some common visual difficulties.

Astigmatism, hyperopia, and myopia are by far the most common problems. Astigmatism (blurring of part of the image) can occur in conjunction with either near- or farsightedness, but both conditions are corrected simultaneously with lenses. Hyperopia, blurring of the image at the near point, makes reading and writing uncomfortable and tiring, and has long been associated with reading problems (Grisham & Simons, 1986). After more and more close work in the first few years of school, this developmental farsightedness disappears for most children, and many become mildly myopic as they learn to read. Myopia, better acuity (keenness) of vision up close than at a distance, does not interfere with reading. There is some evidence that myopia may be largely developmental and environmentally produced by the demands of close work with print during the school years (Javat, 1990). While nearsightedness does not contribute directly to reading problems, it can give children difficulty in doing board work and can be a cause of inattention during such activities.

These vision problems can be so minor that they have few if any symptoms, and even the reader may be unaware of any problem; or they can be so severe that normal classroom activities are extremely difficult. Usually the teacher is in a position to detect fairly minor problems which, if treated promptly, are easy to correct. All of the aforementioned vision problems are correctable, most with glasses or contact lenses, some with a combination of corrective lenses and muscle exercises.

Although vision problems may be very different, they often have identical symptoms. Teachers can do little more than guess about the precise nature of the problem in many cases, but they should be alert to the continuing presence of these symptoms, which are listed in Figure 10.2. These symptoms are sometimes demonstrated by poor readers whose vision is unimpaired. When any of these signs are displayed frequently, are not common to the rest of the class, and are evidenced even when performing easy tasks, they signal a need for a parent conference and referral to an eye specialist. Referrals should be made through the principal, school nurse, supervisor, or other designated personnel.

Figure 10.1

Vision Problems

TECHNICAL NAME	COMMON NAME	CONDITION	SYMPTOMS
Myopia	Nearsightedness	Clear vision at near point; blurring of distant images	Squinting at the board; holding print close to face; inattention to board work
Hyperopia	Farsightedness	Clear vision at far point; blurring of close objects	Holding print well away from face; disinterest in close work; eye fatigue during reading
Astigmatism		Distortion and/or blurring of part (or all) of visual field, far and near	Eye fatigue; headache; squinting; tilting or turning head; nausea during reading
Amblyopia	Lazy eye	Suppression of vision in one eye; dimming of vision without structural cause	Tilting or turning head to read; eye fatigue on one side; headache
Strabismus	Crossed eyes	Difficulty converging and focusing both eyes on the same object	Squinting; closing or covering one eye to focus; eyes misaligned
Phoria or fusion problems; binocular coordination		Imbalance of ocular muscles; difficulty converging and focusing both eyes equally	Squinting; closing or covering one eye
Aniseikonia		Differences in size or shape of image in each eye	Blurring; squinting; difficulty focusing or fusing image; closing one eye

Figure 10.2

Symptoms of Possible Vision Problems

Appearance	Chronic redness or swelling of eyes or eyelids
	Matter encrusted in or around eyes
	Sores near or on eyelids
	Excessive watering or tearing of eyes
	Eyes appear misaligned
Complaints	Headache in or near eyes
	Burning, itching, or watering eyes
	Nausea or dizziness during visual tasks
	Blurring or "jumping" of print during reading or other visual tasks
Behavior	Excessive blinking during reading or visual tasks
	Squinting, closing or covering one eye
	Tilting or turning head to read or write
	Straining forward to see board
	Holding book or head abnormally far or near

Hearing

The relationship between auditory problems and reading difficulties has long been established. Hearing and language are as intimately related as language and reading. As teachers observe the oral and written language of their students, they can become aware of possible hearing problems.

When children learn to read, they employ their whole experience with oral language. We know that oral language development and learning to read are closely related and that the ability to process and understand *written* language depends in large part on being able to process and understand *oral* language. Hearing problems can interfere with, delay, or even prevent the development of oral language fluency, and it is in this respect that hearing problems can affect reading.

Another factor is the heavy reliance on oral activities and phonics instruction. Across the entire spectrum of approaches, some features of every beginning reading program are standard: learning letter names and sounds, use of simple phonic analysis strategies to decode words, and frequent oral reading. These activities put a premium on clarity of hearing, and the youngster with auditory problems is at a distinct disadvantage.

Thus hearing problems that occur any time in the first eight to ten years of life may affect a child's reading by interfering with language development in the preschool years or with the largely oral reading instruction of the primary grades.

Types of Hearing Problems

Testing of auditory acuity (keenness) involves assessment of the ability to hear speech sounds, music, and noises. In reading, it is the speech sounds that are critical.

Speech sounds are measured in terms of *pitch* and *volume*. Pitch refers to the frequency of a sound; speech sounds are high-tone or low-tone depending on their pitch. Pitch is measured in *hertz*, or cycles per second. High-frequency, or high-tone, sounds have a higher number of cycles per second than low tones. Speech sounds of the normal human voice range from 128 to 4000 cycles per second; consonant sounds are higher in pitch than vowel sounds.

Volume, or loudness, is measured in units called *decibels*. Normal conversation is usually between 20 and 60 decibels.

Hearing losses can affect the perception of pitch or volume or both. If the child can hear some sound frequencies but not others, it can be devastating in learning to read because it means that the child can hear some speech sounds accurately but not others. Hearing loss involving the high-frequency sounds is more common than loss of low-frequency sounds. Children with high-frequency hearing loss can accurately hear vowel sounds and maybe some consonant sounds, but not all of them.

Those with high-tone losses may hear spoken words in a garbled, indistinct fashion, depending on how many consonant sounds are affected. If only vowels can be heard, words are almost totally meaningless because consonant sounds are what make spoken words intelligible. (Read a line of print aloud to someone, pronouncing only the vowel sounds; repeat the line pronouncing only the consonant sounds. Which version could the listener more easily understand?)

Hearing losses are not always as severe as the previous example. Often only a few consonant and blend sounds are affected, but phonics instruction is made very difficult by this loss, and the student may be very poor at word analysis and word recognition. Also, the words that are most often taught in beginning reading frequently vary only in their consonant sounds, as in the "word families" and rhyming word patterns (*cat-hat-pat-mat-sat*). Learning these words can be very difficult for the child with high-tone hearing loss.

Some hearing problems are caused by volume impairment at most or all frequencies. These cases can be helped by hearing aids, which amplify sound at all levels. Since volume loss affects the perception of all types of sounds, it is probably the most obvious and the easiest to spot in the classroom. Loss of only certain sounds is more difficult to spot because the student will hear many sounds normally and problems may be blamed on inattention or carelessness.

Figure 10.3

Symptoms of Possible Hearing Problems

Complaints	Ringing, buzzing or pain in ears
	Ears feel blocked or "stuffy"
Behavior	Frequent requests to have statements repeated
	Confusion of simple oral directions
	Turning or tilting head toward source of sounds
	Cupping ear toward source of sound
	Straining forward during listening
	Unusually loud or monotonous voice
	Frequent pulling or rubbing of ears
	Chronic inattention during listening activities

Symptoms of both types of hearing loss are similar. The main difference is that the child with volume loss will have trouble consistently while the child with selective frequency losses will hear many sounds normally. Common symptoms of hearing losses are shown in Figure 10.3. Screening should be conducted if a student exhibits one or more of these symptoms.

At first glance, some of these signs are similar to those of children with vision problems. Behaviors like inattention, strained posture, scowling, or squinting can be common to children with hearing or vision problems, or to children who are free of physical problems but are simply frustrated in reading.

Another very important factor in the diagnosis of hearing problems is the *duration* of the problem. While volume losses are usually of a more or less chronic nature, many selective frequency losses are temporary. It is very common for children to experience temporary loss of some sounds during and after a heavy cold or upper respiratory infection. These hearing losses can last from a few days to a few months, and while they exist, they can interfere with normal classroom activities.

Children with colds or other upper respiratory infections and respiratory allergies are subject to middle-ear impairment called *conductive hearing losses.* Two types of conductive problems are particularly common in school-age children. One condition is *otitis media,* a collection of fluid in the middle ear. Fluid in the middle ear distends the eardrum outward, inhibiting its ability to vibrate freely and thus reducing the signal transmitted inward. A second common conductive loss occurs when air pressure on either side of the eardrum is unequal. From the middle ear, a tunnel, the *eustachian tube,* runs to the back of the throat at the level of the nose. This tube's function is to equalize pressure on both sides of the eardrum. When heavy upper respiratory congestion is present, the eustachian tube can collapse or become blocked. As a result, the eardrum cannot properly conduct sound. Implantation of plastic tubes in the eustachian tube now corrects the problem.

Children who do not receive the necessary medical treatment for chronic infections may suffer these temporary hearing losses. Those with chronic colds, or those returning to school after a particularly severe upper respiratory infection, should have auditory screening at regular intervals, with particular attention paid to perception of the high-tone sounds.

While middle-ear disorders are more common in children, inner ear disorders called *sensorineural losses,* can also cause hearing impairment. Within the inner ear, the *cochlea,* a bony structure looking like a coiled shell, contains the sensory organs of hearing and the components of the body's balance system. Here the sound waves that have been transmitted by vibration to the inner ear are transformed into mechanical, electrical, and chemical signals and transmitted to the brain (Berg, 1986). The cochlea and its delicate transmission functions can be damaged by excessive noise, certain drugs, and exposure to infections like mumps and rubella (German measles).

Auditory Screening Methods

The most reliable method examines volume in decibels and different frequencies in cycles per second. An instrument called a *pure tone audiometer* is used to produce pure tones generally ranging from 125 to 8000 cycles per second in pitch and from about 10 to 110 decibels in volume.

An audiometer can be used for screening groups of students, but the most accurate screening is done individually. The subject is seated so that the audiometer controls are not visible. Headphones are worn so each ear can be tested separately, and a buzzer or other signaling device is used as a means of responding to the test. The examiner, an audiologist, uses the audiometer to produce each tone at a full range of volume from soft to loud, and the subject signals when the tone is first audible and also indicates its duration. The examiner can occasionally check to see that the subject is not just signaling randomly by using an interrupter switch to cut off the signal momentarily.

If the student fails the initial part of the screening, indicating inadequate perception of any of the pure tones, a *pure tone threshold test* is given. In this procedure, sounds are presented at several different frequencies, and the intensity of the sound is varied to determine the exact decibel level at which the student can detect the sound, called the *threshold level.* Another auditory screening measure is *speech audiometry.* The audiometer is used to determine threshold levels for speech sounds. Speech audiometry is useful in detecting high-frequency hearing losses, where affected students have difficulty perceiving some high-frequency consonant sounds in speech.

A topic related to auditory acuity is *auditory discrimination,* the ability to distinguish between highly similar sounds and to detect whether two (or more) sounds are alike or different. Being able to detect subtle differences in speech sounds helps students to master phonics; those with poor auditory discrimination may have persistent trouble with phonic analysis and may also have speech impairments.

Auditory discrimination can be assessed formally or informally. The student is required to distinguish between pairs of words or syllables that differ minimally (*rat-rap, ome-ote*). Teachers frequently make up and give such exercises themselves. Formal auditory discrimination tests are also common, and some standardized readiness tests include such a subtest.

In beginning reading it is common to combine phonics instruction with auditory discrimination practice. Beginning readers or prereaders who at first seem to have difficulty with auditory discrimination often need only to learn what to listen for and how to respond. In other words, they have no auditory disability but have to learn what the task is. Auditory discrimination skill seems to improve sharply as children progress through the primary grades, which implies that it develops at least partly in response to instruction and experience with the task. It may well be a learned skill as much as an innate perceptual ability.

SPECIAL LEARNING PROBLEMS

Learning disabilities and *dyslexia* are terms used for special learning problems. The issues involved in defining the terms, identifying students with these problems, and discovering methods of remediation have aroused considerable controversy for the past 20 or so years. Disagreement over these issues still abounds, but educators appear to be moving toward a greater understanding of them. In this section, we will attempt to clarify some of these issues.

What Are Learning Disabilities?

A learning disability is a severe problem in learning that qualifies a child for special education services. In 1977 the federal government adopted the following definition of specific learning disability, based on a 1969 definition proposed by the National Advisory Committee on Handicapped Children:

"Specific learning disability" means a disorder in one or more of the basic psychological processes involved in understanding or in using language, spoken or written, which may manifest itself in an imperfect ability to listen, think, speak, read, write, spell, or to do mathematical calculations. The term includes such conditions as perceptual handicaps, brain injury, minimal brain dysfunction, dyslexia, and developmental aphasia. The term does not include children who have learning problems which are primarily the result of visual, hearing, or motor handicaps, or mental retardation, or of environmental, cultural, or economic disadvantage. (*Federal Register,* December 29, 1977, p. 65083)

This definition does not fully explain what learning disabilities are, for it includes conditions such as "dyslexia" and "minimal brain dysfunction," which are themselves poorly defined and understood. It does, however, serve to narrow the term somewhat by excluding children whose learning problem is primarily caused by conditions like visual or hearing impairment, mental retardation, cerebral palsy, or economic deprivation.

While there is widespread disagreement about the specifics of learning disabilities, there is general agreement that learning-disabled students show a discrepancy between expected and actual achievement when provided with appropriate instruction, that they have difficulty doing tasks that others their age can do without difficulty, that their problem centers around some form of language use, and that they are not otherwise handicapped by mental retardation, blindness, deafness, or the like.

In 1990, the National Joint Committee on Learning Disabilities (NJCLD) adopted the following definition of learning disabilities:

Learning disabilities is a general term that refers to a heterogeneous group of disorders manifested by significant difficulties in the acquisition and use of listening, speaking, reading, writing, reasoning, or mathematical abilities. These disorders are intrinsic to the individual, presumed to be due to central nervous system dysfunction, and may occur across the life span. Problems in self-regulatory behaviors, social perception, and social interaction may exist with learning disabilities but do not by themselves constitute a learning disability. Although learning disabilities may occur concomitantly with other handicapping conditions (for example, sensory impairment, mental retardation, serious emotional disturbance), or with extrinsic influences (such as cultural differences, insufficient or inappropriate instruction), they are not the result of those conditions or influences.

Students identified as learning disabled constitute a very heterogeneous group, so much so that some experts have argued against categorizing and labeling them (Algozzine and Ysseldyke, 1986). Although not all children identified as learning disabled have reading problems, poor reading ability is often associated with learning-disabled students (Helveston, 1987; Merrell, 1990; Stanovich, 1988).

Many students identified as learning disabled have basic sight recognition and decoding problems. As we described in Chapter 7 in our discussion of Peter, the adolescent nonreader, poor sight recognition of words and inefficient or inaccurate decoding skills lead to poor comprehension, avoidance of reading and writing, deficits in the amount of reading these students do, and deficits in general knowledge usually acquired by reading. Thus, learning-disabled poor readers tend to share many of the same problems as other poor readers. These students tend to have problems reading right from the start, especially with word attack skills taught in primary grades. It has been suggested that learning-disabled students experience a lag in the development of phonological sensitivity, the awareness and perception of speech sounds in words (Ackerman et al., 1986). Because these students may not learn how letters represent speech sounds in words incidentally, by wide exposure to print as many able learners do, they may need more systematic exposure to letter-sound patterns in words and more practice with decoding than their peers. Many of the remedial techniques we have discussed for helping poor readers develop sight recognition and word attack skills are effective with students identified as learning disabled. Although remedial instruction for these students often focuses on the teaching and practice of reading skills, it should be emphasized that learning-disabled poor readers need the same emphasis on meaningful reading of connected text that other poor readers need. Practicing reading skills without using them in the context of real reading is not effective instruction for any student.

In the long run, LD teachers work with many youngsters who are poor readers, and both regular classroom teachers and reading specialists will find that some of their poor readers may have been identified as learning disabled. Whether or not they have been so identified, poor readers *all* need help in consolidating skills they have mastered, acquiring skills they do not yet have, and closing the gap between their potential as readers and their present performance.

We must all keep firmly in mind that being classified as learning disabled does not mean that a child has a particular set of problems or symptoms that set him or her clearly apart from other poor readers. Nor does it indicate that a particular method of instruction or set of materials is appropriate. Children so classified differ from each other just as much as others do, and no particular method or means has been shown to be more effective than others in remediation. All poor readers, learning disabled or not, require instruction that is tailored to their individual strengths, needs, ages, interests, and prior experiences. All poor readers need to be placed in appropriate materials at their instructional levels, provided instruction that achieves a balance in word identification, comprehension, listening, speaking, and writing, and taught at a pace that is appropriately challenging without frustration.

What Is Dyslexia?

Dyslexia is a medical term for a profound inability to read or to learn to read. Like learning disability, dyslexia is a condition that everyone seems to agree exists, but about which there is little agreement otherwise. No set of symptoms, means of diagnosis or identification, or method of remediation can be identified. No one even seems to know how many children are affected by this profound disability. In spite of these glaring ambiguities, the term is used frequently and widely, yet it is hard to know whether people discussing the condition mean the same thing. Reporters discussing illiteracy and what they call "the crisis in education" may refer to "illiterates" and "dyslexics" as though they were the same group; educators and parents sometimes refer to "dyslexics" when they mean "poor readers," or even "students reading below grade level." Physicians and other medical personnel may use "dyslexic" to describe learning-disabled patients who are poor readers. Perhaps no other term in education has come to mean so many things to so many people. One historical definition which has persisted was proposed by Orton (1937), who described dyslexic children as delayed in reading compared to their peers, suffering from frequent letter and word reversals, and often being able to read only by holding the print up to a mirror. This led to widespread belief that dyslexia was primarily a neurological disorder involving visual perception and memory.

According to Vellutino (1979), *dyslexia* is "commonly used in reference to severe reading disorder in children who are apparently normal in other respects" (p. 321). Vellutino and Denckla (1991) describe dyslexic children as having difficulty establishing a link between the visual and linguistic components of the printed word, thus hindering their efforts at learning to read. They further suggest that these learners are not apparently experiencing other cognitive processing problems such as attention, problem solving, and sequencing.

In spite of years of research and hypothesis about dyslexia, it remains today a baffling problem. No clear consensus exists on its definition, causation, or remediation. The label itself does little to describe what any individual can or cannot do and probably engenders as much fear and confusion as anything else. We can refrain from contributing to the problem by developing a healthy skepticism for others' judgments that someone's reading problem is caused by dyslexia, by avoiding automatic acceptance of diagnostic or treatment procedures that appear to be overly narrow or simplistic, and by exercising extreme caution in our own use of the term to describe a reading problem.

AFFECTIVE FACTORS

Success or lack of success in reading is not just a matter of intellectual functioning and the like. A variety of emotional and motivational factors are also involved.

Interests

One affective factor which affects reading is interest in the activity of reading and interest in topics or materials which students are to read. Teacher-made interest and attitude inventories are very useful devices for learning how students feel about books, reading, school subjects, and common childhood problems.

Figures 10.4, 10.5, and 10.6 are sample classroom interest inventories that you may find helpful. Depending on their reading and writing abilities, the students can complete them in writing or orally, and you will probably want to add other questions. The incomplete sentences in Figure 10.6 are modeled on those developed by Strang (1969, pp. 262–263). Hall et al. (1979, p. 236) give several excellent examples of reading interest inventories and suggestions for their use, and Figures 10.4 and 10.5 are adapted from these. An example of an interest inventory for adolescents is in Chapter 7.

Information obtained by these inventories can be used in several ways:

- to determine if a particular student has very negative attitudes about reading that may affect progress in reading;
- to reveal if a particular student is having serious personal problems that may affect classroom performance and social relationships;
- to discover what specific topics students are interested in reading about as well as what kinds of materials they prefer using;
- to develop appropriate classroom libraries; and
- to develop individualized lesson plans.

Anxiety

Because emotional problems are as varied and individual as the human beings they affect, there are no all-inclusive sets of criteria or symptoms to which we can refer. Our own experience in classrooms and reading clinics has shown us a few characteristic ways in which youngsters react to the anxiety that reading can produce.

Many young children, for example, believe that on the first day of school they will learn to read. They are, by and large, sadly disappointed. Learning to read generally takes a fairly long time, especially if you've been around for

Figure 10.4

Interest Inventory for Primary Grades

(The questions are read aloud to students, and their oral responses are written down by the teacher.)

1. If *you* could decide what you would study in school next week, what would you choose? Why? _____
_____
_____

2. If someone asked you to choose a book or story you'd like to have read to you, what would the book be about? _____
_____
_____

3. If you could magically visit any person from now or from the past, who would it be?
_____
_____

4. If you woke up one day and found you had superhuman powers, what would you do? _____
_____
_____

5. If someone were giving you a book for your birthday, what would you want the book to be about?_____
_____
_____

6. Do you thing a book is a good present? _____
Why or why not? _____
_____
_____

7. If you could magically turn into any kind of animal or bird, real or make-believe, what would you become?_____
_____

What would you do in your new form? _____
_____

8. If you could write a TV show or movie, what would it be about? _____
_____
_____

Figure 10.5

Interest Inventory for Intermediate and Upper Grades

(The questions may be read silently or orally, and the students can answer orally or in writing.)

1. If you had a "surprise day off from school," how would you spend the day? _____
   _____
   _____

2. If someone wanted to give you a magazine subscription for a gift, what magazine would you choose? _____
   _____

3. If you were hired to write a new TV show, what would it be about? Who would star in it? Would *you* be in it? _____
   _____
   _____

4. If you won a contest and your grand prize was to meet and get to know any famous person in the world today, whom would you choose? What would you like to talk about? _____
   _____
   _____

5. If you could transport yourself into any time and place in the past, where would you go? What would you do there? How long would you stay in the past? _____
   _____
   _____

6. If you could somehow become a superathlete overnight, what would your sport be? What would you do as a superathlete? _____
   _____
   _____

7. If you could go into a bookstore and get any three books free, what kinds of books would you choose? _____
   _____
   _____

8. If *you* could choose the books or stories to be used from now on in English (or language arts), what kinds of things would you choose? What would you definitely *not* include? _____
   _____
   _____

Figure 10.6

Attitudes and Interests Survey

(The sentences may be completed orally or in writing.)

1. I think reading _____
2. I wish I could _____
3. Someday I _____
4. I wish my teacher _____
5. My best friend _____
6. I'd rather read than _____
7. At home I _____
8. When I read out loud _____
9. Science books _____
10. When I don't know a word _____
11. I wonder why _____
12. Reading about the past _____
13. On test days I _____
14. Spelling is _____
15. I really love to _____
16. Animal stories _____
17. I don't understand _____
18. I wish I could _____
19. Books about famous people _____
20. When I have to write a paper _____
21. I felt proud when _____
22. My mother _____
23. Sometimes I think I _____
24. Pictures in books _____
25. My father _____

Source: Adapted from Ruth Strang, Constance M. McCullough, and Arthur E. Traxler. *Improvement of Reading,* 4th ed. (New York: McGraw-Hill, 1967). Used with permission of McGraw-Hill Publishing Company.

only six or seven years. Being able to accept this notion, and have the persistence to stick it out, is related to the early development of *competence,* the belief that one is able to succeed.

Children who have developed physical and emotional mastery in their early years, by extended experience with things and people, are *confident* and *error-tolerant.* They are secure in their own ability to succeed even if they fail on the first attempts, and they are able to shrug off and learn from mistakes without becoming unduly discouraged by them. Children who develop a sense of their own competence in their early years approach beginning reading with patience and persistence, confidence that they will probably succeed in the end, and knowledge that occasional failure happens to everybody.

Youngsters who lack these notions are often unable to stick to a task long enough to become good at it. They admit defeat after only a few days or weeks of reading instruction. They seem to be overwhelmed by the whole process and often become inordinately discouraged by mistakes or confusion. When they aren't sure of what to do next, they get depressed or panicky. Activities that involve some element of cognitive risk, like predicting what might happen next in a story, are just too threatening. By avoiding risk, these children sometimes appear to be uncooperative or disinterested, but their apparent disinterest is often a cover for fear (Boggiano et al., 1992; Johnston and Winograd, 1985).

Risk avoiding is a common strategy for children who have not developed the resilience of spirit that we see in a competent child. It is also an aspect of another problem, one related to reading readiness.

Educators, child psychologists, and parents generally agree that children develop at very different rates, each according to an individual timetable. We are rarely seriously concerned if milestones like the first step, first word, or first tooth come earlier or later than those of a sibling or neighbor's child. Likewise we know that children develop the social skills, attention span, self-control, and physical stamina required for school at different ages.

Many children who are happy and secure in kindergarten, however, are unready for the greater demands of first grade. For some children, learning to read is too difficult right from the start, and their anxiety is soon manifested. Children who are developmentally unready for first-grade instruction may share a number of common behaviors attributed to "overplacement." Physically, they are often chronically fatigued, especially in the afternoon, and have much more difficulty than their age-mates in forming letters, following simple directions, and attending to interesting activities. Socially, they often have difficulty making friends and controlling anger, may consistently choose solitary rather than group activities, and may prefer to play with much younger children. Emotionally, they may often feel depressed and anxious, cry easily, and avoid school tasks by daydreaming or procrastinating. They may begin or revert to nail-biting, stammering, bedwetting, or thumb-sucking. They may hesitate to make a guess or prediction, quickly answer "I don't know" when at all uncertain, exhibit excessive neatness in written work, and repeatedly ask for directions to be given again.

Youngsters who chronically exhibit a number of these behaviors are signaling that something is very wrong. Since children cannot be forced or taught how to develop faster, the situation must be modified for them. Too often, we expect the child to change rather than changing the anxiety-producing environment.

Children are not able to change their school situations because they do not control them; adults do. Children who need more time to grow and develop, to experience and to adapt to school, must be given that time, free of stigma. Often, this means an additional year in kindergarten. In some schools, an extra year option has been built into the curriculum. The extra year is a full day of pre–first-grade instruction, often focusing on extended reading readiness, language development, exposure to books, and concrete experiences. It can, in our experience, make all the difference in the world for youngsters not quite ready for a full first-grade experience, because it has no connotations of having failed or not having been promoted. Another year of first-grade instruction is sometimes a good solution. However, the youngster's second trip through first grade should entail different materials and instructional methods, and perhaps a different teacher. It should not mean recycling the child through the same materials and methods that didn't work the first time.

On the other hand, some high-achieving students drive themselves with an intensity that, in an adult, would make friends worry about a heart attack. Such students are often compulsively neat in their written work, scrupulous in attention to detail, and rely on prodigious memory stores. They may take an inordinate amount of time to complete reading or writing assignments because they review and check their work over and over; they may excel at recall of factual information and convergent thinking but have difficulty drawing conclusions, thinking of alternatives, and predicting; they often get deeply discouraged by a critical remark or a less-than-perfect paper. It is unfortunate that these signs of anxiety are often overlooked in the classroom if a student's reading ability is at or near grade level.

As children grow older they become more dependent on what their peers think of them and less dependent on teacher or parental feedback. Added to their growing concern for peer approval, though, is their awareness that reading is extremely important both in and out of school, and failure to master reading can severely affect their self-esteem. Faced with a situation in which they cannot conform to adults' expectations, they may bend every effort to win approval from other students. They may exhibit hostility, defiance, profanity, aggression, and other behaviors that put teachers in an adversary position. These kinds of behaviors and attitudes have been associated with passive failure and learned helplessness (see Chapter 7). In a review of studies of poor readers, Johnson and Winograd (1985) observed the following traits associated with the passive failure of poor readers: aggressiveness, anxiety, withdrawal, negativeness, depression, and feelings of helplessness in academic and problem-solving situations.

Support and Success

Many students who exhibit anxious behaviors and attitudes fall into the category known as "at-risk" or "high-risk." These students are identified as having a higher-than-average risk of failing and dropping out of school and often fall outside the PL 94–142 guidelines. In order to address the needs of these at-risk learners, many school districts have set up alternative education and dropout prevention programs. Placement into these programs is often based on one or more of the following criteria:

- behind in academic skills;
- retained in one or more grades;
- poor school attendance;
- fragile home environment;
- disenchantment with authority and the institution of school;
- learned helplessness/passive failure;
- drug and alcohol abuse;
- teen pregnancy and parenting;
- emotional stress and trauma; and
- juvenile delinquency.

Our discussion in Chapter 7 describes many of these factors associated with high-risk learners. A sample of the criteria used by one district to place students into alternative programs is shown in Figure 10.7. Initial assessment of risk status begins with the same data source as other special factors— teacher observations. Once a teacher suspects a student is at higher-than-average risk for academic failure, the referral process can begin.

Alternative education and dropout prevention programs provide alternative environments for students to become competent readers, writers, and learners. If placement into one of these programs is not an option, regular classroom teachers are faced with the challenge of helping those students whose emotional reactions to school, reading, and academic success have become destructive to the reading and learning process.

What can we do to help those whose emotional reactions to school, reading, and academic success have become destructively involved with their learning to read? We believe it is as important to know what you *cannot* do as what you *can*.

Unless you have special training and expertise in working with disturbed children or in counseling, you will probably not be able to "cure" the severely anxious student singlehandedly. If it consistently takes more than a

Figure 10.7

Dropout Prevention Eligibility Criteria

Instructions: The data below should be collected from school records on each pupil who might benefit from being in the Dropout Prevention Program. Check the name of the component and the criteria that will justify that pupil's placement in that program.

_____ **Youth Services Program** (court mandated)

_____ **Teen Parent Program**
  _____ student with verified pregnancy
  _____ student parent as verified by child's birth certificate or copy of application for birth certificate or hospital records or notarized affidavit of fatherhood signed by both teen parents
  _____ child of student

_____ **Substance Abuse Program**
  _____ student has documented history of substance abuse
  _____ student has significant stress within the family unit in response to and/or related to substance abuse
  _____ student has dysfunctional behavior at home, school, and/or community related to substance abuse as documented by school personnel
  _____ student has inability to be treated in less restrictive environment as documented by student service personnel

_____ **Disciplinary**
  _____ student remanded by the court to community control via social service agencies
  _____ student has repeated record of disciplinary referrals, 10 or more in a semester or has a case for expulsion
  _____ student has committed an offense that warrants suspension as a possible consequence as specified in the District Student Code of Conduct
  _____ student wiill have had a case for suspension of more than four (4) days or possible expulsion
  _____ student has excessive discipline referrals for serious disruptive behavior more than five (5) in a semester

Figure 10.7 (continued)

_____ **Educational Alternatives**

Students participating in one of the Educational Alternative programs for the District must meet one of the eligibility criteria. Enrollment in the program is based on availability, with priority being established by teacher/administrator recommendations.

_____ student has been retained in one or more grades or needs to be retained in the current year

_____ student scored 49% or below on total reading and/or math on the CAT

Reading score _____   Date _____

Math score   _____   Date _____

_____ student is currently failing or has failed two or more academic subjects

_____ student is unsuccessful in school as evidenced by two or more of the following characteristics as documented by school personnel

_____ low self-concept

_____ family member has dropped out of school

_____ demonstrated boredom or lack of motivation by refusing to make an effort to complete academics

_____ student is uninvolved in social clubs, sports or extracurricular activities for reasons other than lack of time

_____ student reports having to work long hours during the school week in order to support family

_____ student has shown lack of interest/motivation through self disclosure/documentation

_____ student has significant family problems

_____ student attends school irregularly averaging 3 absences per grading period or student is absent due to extended illness

_____ student was eligible for and was served by Chapter 1 in their preceding grade

_____ student scored 25% or below on the Grade Ten Assessment Test

_____ student has fallen behind in the number of credits required for normal pupil progression in grades 9–12

_____ student has scored below grade level in math and/or reading (i.e., informal reading/math assessments, CAI labs assessment, etc.)

_____ student has a GPA of 1.5 or less at the end of a semester

Source: Adapted from "Dropout Prevention Data Collection Form," The School District of Escambia County, Pensacola, Florida.

smile and sincere encouragement to get a student to try again, if the student is socially isolated, and if you can observe continued signs of frustration and anxiety, seek help and advice from others. The intensity and duration of anxiety are important factors. Everyone has an occasional bout of depression or feelings of worthlessness, but emotionally troubled children cannot shake it off. We all lose our tempers at ourselves or others and let our anger show in words or gestures. Troubled children have difficulty with degrees of emotion, and annoyance may become rage or withdrawal before they can get control of it. If you at all suspect that a student's moods and reactions are beyond average limits, get some professional advice.

In the area of reading, we can always do something to help. Two key concepts are *support* and *success.* The importance of success in every person's life cannot be overstated. The teacher can orchestrate success by providing activities that students can complete and by providing appropriate recognition of effort and achievement. Extended opportunities to practice newly emerging literacy abilities must also be available. As students become able to do more, self-confidence will begin to reappear. Success begets success.

It will not happen quickly, however. Even with consistent encouragement and support from teachers, family, and peers, and consistent, thoughtful instruction, it can still take years to help a child become a functional reader and writer.

SUMMARY

This chapter dealt with special factors associated with reading. Among these factors are those that qualify learners for special education services under *Public Law 94–142* and subsequent legislation clarifying and extending that law. The factors that fall under this legislation include those *intellectual, physical, emotional,* and *learning disabilities* that prove to be a handicap for learners. Within this legislation are provisions that mandate serving these learners with appropriate educational programs that use the least restrictive environment. The identification of these learners and subsequent placement in special education programs must be conducted with assessment instruments and methods that protect against discrimination, erroneous classification, and undue labeling. One alternative to placement of students qualifying for special education is the *Regular Education Initiative* (REI). This initiative provides for the special education student to remain within his or her regular classroom under the regular education teacher who receives support from special education specialists.

Identification of the special-needs student typically is initiated by the classroom teacher. Before additional assessment and screening can occur, permission must be obtained from the parents and legal guardians of the child.

Once permission is granted, *assessment* and *screening* can take place. This assessment typically includes one or more of the following areas: intellectual; physical; special learning; or affective factors.

Initial assessment of *intellectual factors* typically includes the use of an initial screening instrument such as the Kaufman Brief Intelligence Test (K–BIT). If these initial screening instruments indicate a potential problem, additional testing is conducted using a more comprehensive assessment of intellectual factors such as the Weschler Intelligence Scale for Children, III (WISC III). These tests typically provide scores for subtests, Verbal, Performance, and Full Scale IQ scores. When selecting assessment instruments, care should be taken to select instruments that do not penalize a child with cultural differences.

Vision and *hearing problems* are also associated with reading difficulties. Again, a classroom teacher is often the first to notice potential problems during daily classroom activities. As with intellectual factors, the referral for additional screening begins with parental or guardian permission. Screening in the areas of vision and hearing is typically conducted by professionals or paraprofessionals in the allied-health fields.

The special learning problems we address typically fall within the areas of *learning disabilities* and *dyslexia*. While a universally accepted and detailed definition of these terms has yet to be identified, professionals do agree that they include a wide range of problems related to written and oral language acquisition, comprehension, and production. Children who manifest these problems typically possess average or above-average intelligence.

Affective problems constitute another set of factors that contribute to reading difficulties. Assessing students' *interests* in certain topics or activities can provide information that indicates those topics that may elicit a negative response and guide the teacher to more positive topics. In addition to intellectual ability and interest, the *emotional maturity* of an individual child is critical in determining readiness for particular classroom contexts and tasks. Again, the teacher usually can identify the range of emotional maturity through observing the child's daily classroom interactions. A child's perception of his or her abilities relative to a group of peers also affects emotional well-being.

Children who do not meet the expectations of important adults such as teachers or parents and see themselves as falling behind their peers often develop a sense of *passive failure*. Teachers can provide social and academic support and create opportunities for success for these disenchanted learners by modifying classroom environments. Many school districts have initiated programs that encourage the modification of the classroom environment as part of dropout prevention programs.

Reading is a complex process affected by a student's level of intellectual functioning, experiences, motivation, and physical and emotional well-being. By assessing the impact of these special factors on a student's literacy, appropriate changes in instructional strategies, referrals, and placements are more likely to be made.

References

Ackerman, Peggy T., Jean M. Anhalt, and Roscoe A. Dykman. "Inferential Word-Decoding Weakness in Reading Disabled Children." *Learning Disability Quarterly, 9*, no. 4 (Fall 1986): 315–324.

Algozzine, Bob, and James E. Ysseldyke. "The Future of the LD Field: Screening and Diagnosis." *Journal of Learning Disabilities, 19*, no. 7 (Aug.–Sept. 1986): 394–398.

Baum, D. D. "The Regular Education Initiative: Is It Developing Roots?" *National Forum of Special Education Journal, 2*, no. 4 (1990): 4–11.

Berg, F. S. "Characteristics of the Target Population." In *Educational Audiology for the Hard of Hearing Child,* eds. F. S. Berg, J. C. Blair, S. H. Viehweg, and A. Wilson-Vlotman. Orlando, FL: Greene & Stratton, 1986.

Boggiano, Ann K., Ann Sheilds, Marty Barrett, Teddy Kellam, Erik Thompson, Jeffrey Simon, and Phyllis Katz. "Helplessness Deficits in Students: The Role of Motivational Orientation." *Motivation and Emotion* 16, no. 3 (1992): 271–296.

Grisham, J. David, and Herbert Simons. "Refractive Error and the Reading Process: A Literature Analysis." *Journal of the American Optometric Association, 51*, no. 4 (Jan. 1986): 44–55.

Hall, MaryAnne, Jerilyn K. Ribovich, and Christopher Ramig. *Reading and the Elementary School Child,* 2d ed. New York: Van Nostrand, 1979.

Helms, Janet E. "Why Is There No Study of Cultural Equivalence in Standardized Cognitive Ability Testing?" *American Psychologist, 47*, no. 9 (1992): 1083–1101.

Helveston, Eugene M. "Volume III Module I: Management of Dyslexia and Related Learning Disabilities." *Journal of Learning Disabilities* 20, no. 7 (Aug./Sept. 1987): 415–421.

Javal, E. "Essay on the Psychology of Reading." *Ophthalmic and Physiological Optics, 10*, no. 41 (Oct. 1990): 381–384.

Johnston, Peter, and Peter Winegrad. "Passive Failure in Reading." *Journal of Reading Behavior, 16*, no. 4 (1985): 279–301.

Kaufman, Alan S., and Nadeen L. Kaufman. *Kaufman Brief Intelligence Test Manual.* Circle Pines, MN: American Guidance Services, 1990.

Laughon, Pamela. "The Dynamic Assessment of Intelligence: A Review of Three Approaches." *School Psychology Review, 19*, no. 4 (1990): 459–470.

Lewis, Rena B., and Donald H. Doorlag. *Teaching Special Students in the Mainstream,* 3d ed. New York: Macmillan Publishing Company, 1991.

McLaughlin, James A., and Rena B. Lewis. *Assessing Special Students,* 3d ed. Columbus, OH: Merrill Publishing Company, 1990.

Merrell, Kenneth. "Differentiating Low Achievement Students and Students with Learning Disabilities: An Examination of Performances on the Woodcock-Johnson Psycho-Educational Battery." *Journal of Special Education* 24, no. 31 (Fall 1990): 296–305.

Orton, Samuel. *Reading, Writing, and Speech Problems in Children.* New York: Norton, 1937.

Patton, James, James Kauffman, J. M. Blackburn, and Gweneth Brown. *Exceptional Children in Focus,* 5th ed. New York: Macmillan Publishing Company, 1991.

Sattler, Jerome M. *Assessment of Children,* 3d ed. San Diego, CA: Jerome M. Sattler, Publisher, Inc., 1992.

Stanovich, Keith E. "Explaining the Difference Between the Dyslexic and the Garden-

Variety Poor Reader: The Phonological-Core-Variable-Difference Model." *Journal of Learning Disabilities* 21, no. 10 (Dec. 1988): 590–604, 612.

Strang, Ruth. *Diagnostic Teaching of Reading,* 2nd ed. New York: McGraw-Hill, 1969.

Vellutino, Frank R. *Dyslexia: Theory and Research.* Cambridge, MA: MIT Press, 1979.

Vellutino, Frank R., Martha B. Denckla. "Cognitive and Neuropsychological Foundations of Word Identification in Poor and Normally Developing Readers." In *Handbook of Reading Research,* Vol. 2, ed. Rebecca Barr, Michael L. Kamil, Peter Mosenthal, and P. David Pearson. White Plains, NY: Longman Publishers, 1991.

Index